PRAISE FOR

"Solemates
Lessons on Life, Love & Marriage from the Appalachian Trail"

"....an engaging and inspirational memoir of self-enrichment and enduring love....a joy to read....will leave you planning your own outdoor adventure."
Brooke Kenny - *The Gazette Newspapers*

"....amazing....can teach us all something...comprehensive...has it all...clearly this book can help people; it is a great guide..."
Karen Allyn – *Host of "Forward Motion" on Montgomery Community Television*

"Solemates" is a "must read" for married and committed couples thru-hiking together on the Appalachian Trail.....a remarkable how-to book demonstrating an enjoyable hiking experience, while growing ever closer together. Really a fine book for all to read!"
Gene Espy - 2nd thru-hiker of the Appalachian Trail and Author of *"Trail of My Life, The Gene Espy Story"*

"No one has explored thru-hiking as a couple as thoroughly as have Randy Motz and Georgia Harris...an uniquely engaging account of thru-hiking the trail..."Solemates" is a significant contribution to the A.T. literature."
Larry Luxemberg - Author of *"Walking the Appalachian Trail"*

".....Whether you're planning a long hike or you just enjoy reading about others' hikes and the lessons they learned along the way, this book is for you."
Linda Patton – *Reviewer for "Books for Hikers"*

".....a "must read" book....Their experience embodies the often difficult art of "give-and-take" as they worked through the "downs" and soared into the rapturous realm of the "ups."....has a wealth of information for novice hikers as well."
J.R. "Model T" Tate - *four-time A.T. thru-hiker and author of "Walkin' on the Happy Side of Misery" and "Walkin' with the Ghost Whisperers"*

".....an inspiring page turner.....The fortitude of this thru-hiker couple lovingly embraces every moment spent on the AT. Enjoy! This will kindle your desire to hike!"
Barb Blythe – *20-year member of AMC*

"Delightful", "Irresistible"....a most "Inspirational" must-read book."
Kelleen K. Larsen, *Phoenix, AZ*

"......not the typical hiking book.....It's a great read!"
Terry Kammer – *Damascus, VA*

"Windtalker" and "Mom" have captured the essence of what it means to hike the AT....what it means to be Solemates as well as Soulmates. A great book....instructive....helpful....will generate fond memories especially for those who love; people who love the trail and who love people. 2 hiking poles up!"
Hank "Catskill Eagle" Nicols - *AT Thru Hiker, 2006*

"Solemates" delves into the emotional aspects of a couple who spent six months of their lives and marriage on the Appalachian Trail.......Through their shared experiences we find that love and relationships can become stronger and more meaningful from both trial and mutual support over difficult terrain and circumstances.........Any couple looking to share a difficult but inspiring adventure together, or any person interested in the emotional aspects of conquering the Appalachian Trail, would benefit from reading their story."
Lee Sheaffer – *President, Potomac Appalachian Trail Club*

"I loved it! I had to take a few moments at times and take a deep breath and choke back a few tears as different passages brought back the vivid emotions of the trail! Thank you for sharing your story."
Jeannie "Jellybean" Zortman – *AT Thru Hiker, 2006*

"....I felt like I was reading about my own hike....The chapter about Katahdin moved me to tears...it was so touching to read about everyone's reactions to finally standing on Le Grand K.....what a joy it was to relive my 2006 hike through your beautifully written book."
Jill "Little Wing" Lingard – *AT Thru Hiker, 2006*

"The transformation and other emotional experiences describing the growth of their marriage are vividly and thought-provokingly recounted in their book....Read it. You will thoroughly enjoy it."
Anita Hartigan – *New Concord, KY*

"... short but detailed descriptions... you could almost put yourself there with them as they hiked....a must read for anyone planning or just thinking of hiking the AT or any other trail....Two thumbs up!"
Bryan "Backtrack" Farley – *Long Trail Thru Hiker, 2007*

Solemates

"Lessons on Life, Love and Marriage from the Appalachian Trail"

Randy "Windtalker" Motz
&
Georgia "Mom" Harris

SOLEMATES

"Lessons on Life, Love and Marriage
from the Appalachian Trail"

Cover Design: The Qualtech Resource Group, Inc.
Front and Back Cover Photos: Georgia L. Harris
Trail Photos: Georgia L. Harris

For information, or to order additional copies of this book, contact:

The Qualtech Resource Group, Inc.
18904 Ferry Landing Circle
Germantown, MD 20874
www.QualtechResourceGroup.com

or

www.createspace.com

ISBN: 1440453659
EIN-13: 9781440453656

CONTENTS

ACKNOWLEDGEMENTS

First we want to acknowledge the institution of marriage, without which our hike, and the focus of this book, would have been decidedly different, probably less memorable, and certainly less interesting.

Of course a big THANK YOU goes out to our parents, Vince, Anita, Dottie, and Ralph, for instilling in us the desire to pursue our dreams and the drive to succeed at whatever we set our minds to do. Your encouragement for not only this adventure, but for every other dream we have ever pursued, has been immeasurable. You enrich our lives and we love you.

Thank you to our cheerleaders! Family and friends from all over the country who listened to us rant and rave about this dream for over five years and who cheered us on anyway. You warmed our hearts and we drew on your words of encouragement on the tough days. Through our journals you shared the exhilaration we felt on the mountaintops and in the valleys. Thanks for being a part of our adventure.

To our daughter, Becky, goes our sincere thanks for watching over our house and making sure that our mail did not pile up, that our fish did not starve, and that our plants had plenty of water. Without the skill and dedication of our daughter, Aja, our website, _www.rmghadventures.com_, would not have existed so our supporters could follow our daily journals and leave us messages. Thank you from the bottom of our hearts. To our daughter, Harmony, and son, Travis, who followed our journey from their home in Las Vegas, thank you for your love and words of support. Thanks to all of our children, for joining us on a few of our preparation hikes, for planning to march with us up Mt. Katahdin in Maine, and for your enthusiasm! There were many days we wished you were walking the trail with us and sharing in the adventure. We hope we inspired you to go after your own dreams.

To our best friends, Mike and Diane Mathews, all we can say is, "You guys are the greatest." Thanks for allowing us to turn your basement into a stockpile of food and supplies and for scheduling your hectic lives so that our mail drops arrived just when we needed them. Without your help, our odyssey would not have been possible. We hope some day you can thru-hike the A.T., too, so we can provide you with trail support.

To Jim and Karen Arnold, who made the long drive to Harper's Ferry to transport us home to spend a few days with our kids and who saw to it that we got back to the trail, "Thank You." Your friendship is priceless and your enthusiasm about our adventure was contagious.

Finally, thank you Lord, for planting this dream within us, for giving us the strength and blessings to follow through with it, and for guarding our steps as we did. We valued meeting the people and challenges you put in our path. Lord, thank you for helping us to honor you with all we said and did while on the trail!

We are extremely grateful to the members of our "trail family" who contributed to making this book possible. Their stories and insights helped make it enlightening and entertaining. To Michelle Pugh, Joanna and Daniel Cahill-Carmona, Chris Moore and Elspeth Sharp, Shirley Funderburk, Jill Lingard, Hugh Derby and Pat Flannery, Tim and Nancy VanNest, Jim and Karen Hertlein, Michael Tink and Roseanne Luiz, David Curtis, Jean Zortman, and September Mihaly, go our deepest thanks. Their friendship, both on and off the trail, is a living, breathing testimony to the special type of relationship that is born from sharing the Appalachian Trail together.

Hiking the Appalachian Trail was easy when compared to writing this book. And, as it was on the trail, we could not have completed this book without the unselfish assistance of other hikers and friends. Our warmest thanks go out to people such as J.R. Tate, a.k.a. "Model T," who offered invaluable insight into writing and publishing and who took time from painting his house to edit the first manuscript. Thanks to Vince and Anita, a.k.a. "V&A," who also did extensive editing and who "lovingly" pointed out that "a genteel walk in the woods" is not the same as a "gentile walk in the woods;" to David Miller, a.k.a. "AWOL," who gave so much of his time to counsel us on the ins and outs of publishing companies; and to Lee Sheaffer, president of The Potomac Appalachian Trail Club, who gave up many lunch hours to read over our first draft. And finally, our thanks go to Lynn Sebring who brought her considerable copy editing skills to the table to give this work its professional polish.

Especially from "Mom" to my darling, loving husband: Thank you for your many lists and all of the final, last minute details you took care of while I focused on the work, at work. Thank you also for the many adventures we shared in preparing for the Big One!

To my colleagues at NIST, in the States, and in industry, at NCSLI, and MSC, goes my sincerest gratitude. Thank you for the approved leave, for covering for me while I was out of the office, for helping with shipments, and to some of you whom we saw at various points along the journey. I appreciated getting together with my colleagues for lunch on my last day in the office, and the cake was a wonderful surprise. I knew you would all continue to do a great job in my absence.

Especially from "Windtalker" to my best friend, hiking partner, and inspiration: Thanks for having the dream. There is no one that I would have wanted to do this adventure with more than you and I can only imagine what the future holds for us.

And finally, from us both: To all who live the dream of thru-hiking the Appalachian Trail, past, present and future, we are unequivocally bound together by an experience like no other. For the married couples who challenge the foundations of their relationships by successfully braving the rigors of the trail, we congratulate you. This book is dedicated to all those couples who can, or want to, call themselves "solemates."

DEDICATION

This book is dedicated to Anita and Vince Hartigan (a.k.a. "V&A"), who took six months of their lives to drive their motor home the entire length of the Appalachian Trail, providing us, and many other hikers, with trail support. Their help, encouragement, insight, and anticipation of our needs made our adventure something extremely special and rewarding.

They were our special "trail angels," and we will be forever in their debt. Thank you for sharing this remarkable adventure with us.

INTRODUCTION

"Faith is taking the first step even when you don't see the whole staircase."
Martin Luther King, Jr.

Love, compassion, empathy, understanding, courage, friendship, and compromise are just a few of the fundamental traits locked in the DNA of every human being. Each day, through the simplest of circumstances and the most mundane of human interactions, these characteristics are beckoned to emerge. Though even as ingrained in our biological make-up as these attributes are, we still struggle to get them right. Perfecting and displaying them in the manner for which they were intended becomes a never-ending "work in progress."

The paradox for a married couple is that, while each spouse is undertaking his/her own "work in progress," the couple is expected to simultaneously build a strong and enduring relationship with each other. Accomplishing this, amidst the other marital, social, and financial pressures assailing them each day, becomes a daunting task.

Now add to this relational potpourri a mutual endeavor so outlandish in its scope and so extreme in its consequences it defies rational thinking: an experience where a couple's physical survival, and not simply their marriage, is put to an acid test. Imagine an adventure so different, so massive, so formidable, and so enduring that not only their marriage vows are challenged but their still-developing fundamental human traits are called upon every single day. How would their marriage fare? If they successfully completed their quest, would they become stronger both as individuals and as husband and wife or would this challenge bring to the surface underlying deficiencies in both of them and their relationship that are simply too big to overcome?

The pages of this book contain the story of such an undertaking: our challenge of hiking the entire Appalachian Trail in one continuous hike—all 2,174.6 miles of it. Also included are stories about many of the other hikes we took to prepare ourselves for "THE BIG ONE." The lessons we learned on those preparation hikes barely scratched the surface of what we would learn as we backpacked as a couple from Georgia to Maine in 2006.

"Divorce is not an option." That is what we told the counselor in the early days of our marriage. We had both been married before and in those prior "love is blind" relationships, we wrongly assumed such a pronouncement of marital unity was unnecessary. We both found, through the emotionally trying circumstances unique to divorce, that *"I do!"* and *"Divorce is not an option"* are not synonymous. Having each learned our lesson, we agreed this time that a public, verbal commitment would hold us accountable to each other in a more profound way. This pronouncement of marital solidarity and loyalty saw us through situations where the pronouncement of *"I do"* simply fell short. *"Divorce is not an option"* was a logical and useful adaptation of *"Quitting is not an option,"* a credo instilled in us by our parents. Those five words underscored every individual endeavor we had ever undertaken. This pronouncement of never quitting, and the strength of our relationship, would soon be repeatedly called to task by our amazing adventure.

As we prepared for, and in 2006 thru-hiked the Appalachian Trail, this edict carried us through moments of intense physical pain. It also preserved our relationship through the innumerable instances of psychological and, seemingly overwhelming, emotional challenges of hiking together continuously for six months. Most importantly, it provided us a foundation on which to build a higher level of mutual understanding when physical, mental, and emotional fatigue reared its ugly head and challenged our individual wills to continue. However, as with any proclamation of faith or pursuit of will, simply deciding "quitting was not an option" did not necessarily make it so. Actually applying it to our adventure turned out to be both a blessing as well as a curse.

So why, with all of the other inherent challenges of marriage, would we take on an additional challenge of such magnitude? We still wrestled with the complexities of a blended family even though our four children were scattered around the country. There were now multiple sets of parents and grandparents, not to mention all the aunts, uncles and cousins, also requiring our attention. In addition, we both had sedentary forms of employment which afforded us few opportunities to stay in shape, and we were woefully lacking in backpacking experience. With all the intense physical and mental demands of backpacking and the unpredictability of living in the wilderness, why would we even contemplate such an undertaking? Could it be that this very quiescent lifestyle, our personalities notwithstanding, was the very reason that thru-hiking the Appalachian Trail warranted our undivided attention and got our adventurous "juices" flowing?

The essence of this odyssey was that it was not going to be merely a physical challenge but a test of our relationship as well. It would be a spiritual journey, a chance to reset our philosophical, emotional, and spiritual compasses. As stated by Warren Doyle, who has walked the Appalachian Trail over twelve times, *"Hiking the A.T. is a shared experience with personal results."* It would be a time to get away from the hustle and bustle of urban living long enough to be able to hear the voice of creation without any outside interference. It would be an enormous test of our physical abilities, willpower, and planning strategies and would provide a way for us to express our Type "A" personalities. It would also be wondrously traumatic to spend six months without daily access to email and the Internet.

The one foreboding aspect of this whole undertaking, and the one thing that continuously nagged at our psyches no matter how much we believed in the strength of our marriage, was: "What effect would this 2,175-mile journey have on our relationship?" Would we grow even closer together with an ever-increasing respect and love for each other? Or would we fall victim to the negative relational rigors of being together twenty-four hours a day, seven days a week? Would the cornerstones of our marriage—compromise and compassion—remain the bulwark of our daily endeavors or would we find ourselves sniping at each other over the tiniest of issues? At some point, would we succumb to those pressures and throw in the towel? Only time and our sense of purpose would tell.

Many of the challenges and rewards of hiking together were, and still are, very personal. But as personal as they may be, they are not secrets and we want to share them. We hope to portray what we saw, heard, and felt in such as way that you feel you are there with us. More importantly, we wish to communicate the ebb and flow, the width and breadth, and the height and depth of emotions we experienced. Our goal is to illustrate how, through this unique experience, our love for each other grew in ways no "regular" life experience could have provided.

This is not a chronological journal of our day-to-day adventures on the trail. There are more than enough books available in that style and each one provides useful and, oftentimes, humorous accounts of life on the trail. Instead, we invite you to join us as we backpack together and travel the majestic ridgeline of the Appalachian Mountains as a married couple—a comparative minority on the A.T. We have included numerous tales and anecdotes about the people, places, and things underscoring the relational challenges and rewards we experienced in hiking as a couple. In offering this type of perspective, we want to give couples who intend to hike the A.T., or any other trail, a sense of what lies ahead of them and how we, and others, coped with the ramifications of being together 24/7. For those who read this book and have absolutely no desire to tackle such an endeavor, we hope you will find equally valuable lessons that will be of benefit to you in your relationships. Just like the "blazes" that continuously mark the trail from Georgia to Maine, we hope our experiences serve as "blazes" in your life's journey.

Initially, the whole concept of taking six months off from everything that constituted our very existence and defined who we were, both individually and as a couple, was Georgia's idea. This fact became a source of much surprise and amazed conversation by other married and unmarried hikers. It also altered their perspectives on the role of wives in the marital relationship. More often than not, it resulted in vocalized feelings of jealousy from many a male hiker whose wife viewed his return to the wilderness as nothing more than a vain attempt to reconnect with his machismo. These wives view living in the outdoors as a form of torture and their idea of camping includes, as minimum requirements, a daily hot shower and a source of electricity for their hair dryers. Hike 2,000 miles, or even 10, with their husbands? Not a chance!

Despite our daily reminders to each other that *"Quitting is not an option,"* how we got along on the trail and traveled so many miles "in step" amazed not only others on the trail but amazed us as well. It became a six-month journey into our souls with hours and hours of uninterrupted time in which to reflect on who we were as individuals and as a team. It is our hope this book inspires you to take time to look deep inside yourself and journey through the wilderness of your own being—to arrive at the summit of your own understanding with a renewed sense of purpose and a greater appreciation of your relationships.

It was our good fortune to have hiked with and been a part of a unique "trail family" of thru-hikers—one hundred and fifty by our calculations. Several of them were also married or were in long-term relationships. Their backgrounds and reasons for hiking the A.T. were as varied as their personalities and lifestyles. With so many other wanderers on the trail, ours was obviously not the only story of joy, awakening, and struggle. To illustrate how the evolution of our backpacking experience and hiking the A.T. compared with that of others, we have included quotes and anecdotes from many of those other hikers—both those traveling solo and those hiking as couples. How they dealt with their life on the trail, and with each other, are illuminating, entertaining, and encouraging. In keeping with the tradition of the trail, we will refer to these hikers by their trail names, but so you know who they are in the "real world," they are:

Michelle Pugh & Jeremy Soule: "Brownie & Souleman"
Joanna and Daniel Cahill-Carmona: "Trickster & What?!"
Chris Moore and Elspeth Sharp: "Carbomb & Lichen"
Hugh Derby and Pat Flannery: "Enuff & Too Much"
Tim and Nancy VanNest: "Head-N-Out & Tag-N-Along"
Jim and Karen Hertlein: "Mapman & Robin"
Michael Tink and Roseanne Luiz: "Mike & Zan"
Shirley Funderburk: "Bama"
Jill Lingard: "Little Wing"
David Curtis: "Old Drum"
Jean Zortman: "Jellybean"
September Mihaly: "Brainfreeze"

Throughout this book are numerous terms that are an integral part of the language and life of the trail. *Appendix #1* defines these terms so you can become more a part of the adventure.

ENJOY THE JOURNEY!

CHAPTER ONE

COURTSHIP- The Dream Begins

"The only place where dreams are impossible is in your own mind."
Emalie

We first met at a division meeting of the International Society of Weighing and Measurement in Lancaster, Pennsylvania, where I was chairing the weekend's schedule of lectures, seminars, and discussions regarding issues related to the weighing and measurement industry. Ours was a brief encounter, nothing more than a professional introduction to each other and the shaking of hands. According to Georgia, I held her hand much longer than was professionally appropriate which, to her way of thinking, was some sort of subliminal form of flirtation. I do not recall it being so, and to this day, do not believe I ever have had the skill or *savoir-faire* required to pull such a thing off. However, she was taken by my innocuous gesture. Upon returning home, she immediately scoured the attendee directory given her at the meeting. Her goal: locate my address and phone number in a quest to pursue some type of relationship with me. Being a single dad with three young children at home left me little, if any, free time to do anything more than maintain a household. So the thought of being able to make time to devote to a new relationship was out of the question.

Undaunted by my lack of response to her repeated phone calls, she persisted until she finally reached me at work one day.

"So, do you date?" she inquired.

"Yeah, I suppose," I replied as I simultaneously read over a brochure on the latest advancement in weighing technology.

"Would you like to go out on a date?"

"I suppose we could do that," was my less than enthusiastic retort.

"How about a movie?"

"Okay," I said, having now completed reading the brochure and not entirely sure what we had been discussing.

"I will meet you there," she suggested.

"Not a chance! I will pick you up. Where do you live?" I inquired, now totally focused and displaying what little chivalry I still possessed after several years of being single.

At this point, by her own admission, panic set in because now I would know where she lived; considering she knew little about me other than what she observed at the meeting, for all she knew, I could be some type of stalker. She gave in and the date and time was set for our first extended meeting. I did relinquish a bit of control of the situation and let her choose the movie—the Steven Segal classic, *"Above the Law."* Not the type of flick that you would think a female would choose for a first date. Only later was I to learn the reason for her unorthodox cinema choice.

As they say, the rest is history. We were soon married and over the course of several years of blending families, buying and selling homes large enough to house all of us, dealing with the plethora of situations brought about by divorces, work demands, personal outside activities, and children attempting to walk the emotional fine line between multiple sets of parents and grandparents, our relationship developed.

Time passed and our children grew up and moved on with their own lives. We downsized our living arrangements. I went to school to learn recording engineering and then acquired an entirely new career at a recording studio. We also found ourselves with free time on our hands to pursue dreams and challenges that had been put on hold by our prior family obligations.

"It's time to go after your dream...who knows what tomorrow will bring!"
"Bama" - Georgia to Maine, 2006

In all honesty, continuously hiking 2,175 miles was never something I ever, in my wildest imagination, envisioned doing. In fact, on my extensive "life list" of things to do, it did not even appear as a footnote. Touring with a rock band, winning the Daytona 500, or producing a Grammy award-winning CD was more of what I had in mind as a measure of personal accomplishment. The very thought of these accomplishments got my aging juices flowing. But at age 51, and with the reality of meeting some of my life goals becoming more elusive by the minute, the idea of thru-hiking the Appalachian Trail was still not an alluring replacement for any of them.

However, as any married man can attest, wives can be extremely persuasive when there is something that they REALLY want to do—especially when you are married to one who is very goal-oriented. Therefore, when Georgia suggested, dare I say insisted, that we spend a six-month portion of our fleeting mid-life days hiking the A.T., how was I to resist? Saying, *"No way,"* *"Nadda,"* *"Not a chance in H...,"* was tantamount to relational suicide, and in nine years of marriage I had never slept on the couch. I was not inclined to start now.

Simply agreeing to conquer the Appalachian Trail, when most men my age were dreaming of all the free hours they would soon have to ride around in a golf cart shanking balls into the woods, was the easy part. In my mind there were seemingly insurmountable obstacles to actually doing it. For Georgia, it was simply a matter of employment logistics. Since all of our kids were out of the house and on their own, though not necessarily out of our bank accounts, we were free to do whatever we liked—whenever we liked. I just thought curling up with the latest New York Times best seller or having a video-watching marathon on a rainy Saturday was more of what I could look forward to doing.

My hesitancy in pursuing this grand adventure was not a matter of my being a "softy," though according to my wife, I can be very sensitive. (I often cry during movies with little kids in them or at the conclusion of *"Extreme Makeover, Home Edition"*). What it really came down to was there are things about our 21st-century life, like eating at good restaurants, reading thought-provoking books, or simply getting away for a long, relaxing weekend at a B&B that I, as well as Georgia, truly enjoy. Moreover, technological advancements like DVD players, air conditioning, and computers offer a source of relaxation and comfort we would have to give up after working for so many years to reach the point where we could afford them. Being on the trail would mean we would have to survive without them. Could that even be possible?

Nevertheless, we made the leap of faith and convinced ourselves that living without those things for six months would be a growing experience. In 2001 we decided to go for it and began preparing by regularly backpacking together.

But how did the decision to hike the "granddaddy of all trails" come about for others?

Little Wing:

>   "*I am a university administrator, directing an online degree
> program in Business at the University of Florida. I loved my job
> before the hike and still do....which I've come to find somewhat
> unusual in the thru-hiker community. Many hikers seemed to be in
> more of a life transition than I was—some from college to their first
> job, some preparing to move on to a new career, and some were
> retired. I was, bizarre as it may sound, very content before my hike.*
>
>   *However, I did call this undertaking my "mid-life crisis hike." At
> 40, I was looking for a way to test myself physically and mentally. I
> was in the middle of a career I enjoyed very much, but was looking
> for a break from it that would recharge my batteries. I was also
> fortunate to be working in a setting that supported my decision to take
> off half a year to hike the A.T. I was granted the leave and was
> encouraged along the way with care packages from my colleagues.*"

Old Drum:

>   "*I am a retired Park and Recreation Director and have joined the
> National Story Tellers Network, but I have no need or desire to make
> money from my storytelling aspirations. Ten years before attempting
> the A.T., I set out on a seven-day trip on The Long Trail in Vermont.
> However, I had to quit after only three days because of lots of
> blisters and sore muscles.*
>
>   *Because my wife, who is a pastor at our hometown church, is so
> adventurous, I wanted to do something adventurous as well. I also
> saw this as an opportunity to learn some things about myself.*"

Though still tenuously enthusiastic about our decision to thru-hike the
A.T., we began our preliminary "training" hikes and developed a sense that
six months on the trail was going to be a great opportunity to spend some
quality time with each other. Out in the fresh air, away from all the stresses
of urban living and not having to make a decision that was any more
pressing than, *"Do I want oatmeal or a breakfast bar this morning?"*
seemed like a nice way to escape reality—if only for half a year or so. Each
day we would be an integral part of the magnificent scenery around us—
sights that would be right within our grasp and not separated from us by a
car or plane window. Stress-free months of not having to delete those
offensive emails for penis enlargement pills, low-interest mortgages, or
bogus solicitations from the wife of Mr. Zambazia of Kenya, who was
looking for someone to help launder her dead husband's millions of dollars,

sounded like a wonderful respite. In addition, what great shape we would be in when we reached Maine!

Even though this whole adventure was Georgia's idea and her personality is such that she would probably force herself to stoically endure the mental and physical anguish of hike preparation with contagious enthusiasm, this turned out not to be the case. Through the pain and trials of our preparation, we both suffered miserably and had to keep reminding ourselves of all the wonderful benefits of our impending thru-hike. Each time we climbed on the exercise bikes to train, or when we backpacked together on the C&O Canal Towpath during the genesis of hurricane Isabel, or when our feet and knees hurt from a long mountainous descent, or even when we thought we could never look at GORP (Good Old Raisins and Peanuts) or tuna on pita bread again without retching, we reassured each other that the A.T. was going to be great.

Hiking and camping were nothing new to me. I grew up in New Jersey at a time when it still had plenty of open countryside, so most of my days were spent outdoors riding my bike, fishing, climbing trees, hunting or anything else that would keep me out of my mother's hair. Having some Native American blood in my lineage, I felt that partaking in outdoor adventures, even if it was running from tree to tree in the woods while slinging arrows at imaginary cowboys, was a way of exemplifying my Indian heritage. My adolescent years were spent in the Boy Scouts where my dad was the scoutmaster. I honed my wilderness skills and was one merit badge from becoming an Eagle Scout before high school activities and the rewards of pursuing the girls wrestled away my attention. Summers were spent at Camp Pahaquarra along the Delaware River north of Delaware Water Gap or at the National Boy Scout Jamboree at Valley Forge. I was also initiated into the prestigious Order of the Arrow. Successfully making it through the required three days of silence, walking through the woods in the dark with no means of light, sleeping outside in the rain with no shelter, and having only one match per day to start a fire, put me into this very elite group—sort of a pubescent version of Navy Seal training. Plus, you received this very cool white sash with a red arrow on it that showed everyone that you were tougher than they were. At that time in my life, hiking 2,175 miles from Georgia to Maine would have been a walk-in-the-park or a rite of passage to manhood. Now it seemed like an incredibly daring thing to even think about, much less actually undertake.

Georgia was born with a unique set of genes that have allowed her to excel in virtually everything she has ever undertaken, be it physical or intellectual. These same genes also created in her a distinct aversion to a great many of the things that other women cherish as being uniquely female. She despises crafty things, "dust catchers" as she calls them, idle mundane chit-chat over tea about baby Johnny's first step, and most "chick flicks." Instead, she has set herself apart within many traditional male professional strongholds and has developed a reputation among her peers of being a successful, strong-willed, multi-tasking visionary.

Her drive and will were evident early on in her athletic endeavors. With her family, she would regularly scuba dive and compete in dog-sled races in Minnesota where she won her fair share of competitions. She excelled in martial arts skills and earned a black belt in Tae Kwon Do—thus her choice of a Steven Segal movie for our first date. She was also a high school gymnast and, for a period of time in her life, assisted her family as they navigated the entire length of the Mississippi River in the family's houseboat. She received a Bachelor's Degree in biology from Moorhead State University in Minnesota, where she also minored in chemistry, both of which are typically male-dominated fields. Add to all this a Master's Degree in Technical Management from Johns Hopkins Whiting School of Engineering, and one would have to admit she is not your typical woman.

The decision to thru-hike the Appalachian Trail came out of her resolute desire to sidestep the pursuit of more traditional accomplishments, an innate longing to take on challenges of Herculean proportions, and to accomplish things not typically attributed to females. I am continually inspired by her and admire her immensely for her purposefulness. It is partly because of this, in addition to my own competitiveness, personal drive, and need to repeatedly bolster my self-esteem by successfully completing everything I set out to do, that much like her I work so diligently to accomplish profound goals of my own.

Not once, during all of the hand wringing, training, and the discussions about our impending odyssey did it ever occur to us that hiking the A.T. as a married couple was going to be unusual. For some reason we thought every married person on the trail would be out there with his/her spouse. It was not until we were miles down the trail that we discovered we were in a unique and comparatively small group. Despite the small number of backpacking couples, we still met quite a number of married couples during our time on the trail. What was interesting was that, even though there was a breadth of differences in our ages, backgrounds, hiking experience, how our personal relationships began, and reasons we were pursuing this adventure, we all experienced many of the same challenges. These situations were met with distinctly different approaches, but the outcomes were often extremely similar One example was "Carbomb & Lichen."

Lichen:

"I grew up in Burleson, Texas, and went to college at Texas A&M University where I graduated in December 1998 with a B.S. in Bioenvironmental Science. After graduating from A&M, I obtained a job in Austin, Texas, with an environmental consulting firm and have worked there ever since. I turned thirty during our A.T. hike.

My first experience hiking was in the Great Smoky Mountains National Park during spring break of my junior year of college. Prior to that, my outdoor experiences had been limited to playing in the woods surrounding my parents' house as a kid. In a nutshell, I had not been involved in any formal hiking, and hardly any camping, until 1997. However, as is the case with many children who are exposed to nature and the great outdoors at a young age, my attraction to the A.T. and hiking and camping in general, grew out of the wonderful childhood memories I had of spending so much time in the woods. That first real hiking trip in the Great Smoky Mountains during spring break in 1997 holds another special significance for me. It was during that hike that my relationship with Chris began. Who says you have to frequent bars and clubs to meet the person of your dreams?"

Chris, a.k.a. "Carbomb," was born in Fairbanks, Alaska, and because his dad was in the Air Force, his family moved quite often. In sixth grade he became involved in the Boy Scouts and through his teens became increasingly involved in the Scouting program until it became his primary extracurricular activity. He later attended Texas A&M University and earned a B.S. Degree in Geology and eventually moved to Austin in 1999 where he has been ever since. He has worked for several different firms specializing in geotechnical and environmental consulting. He also turned thirty during their A.T. hike.

Though not sure when he "officially" started hiking, "Carbomb" spent his formative years walking in the woods surrounding his grandparents' house in western South Carolina. He was probably seven or eight. He often followed old roadbeds and game trails with the ultimate goal of making it to the creek that ran along the back of the property. When his family moved to Shreveport, Louisiana, they moved next door to a family with two boys who were involved in a Boy Scout troop. He soon joined Troop 28 and was introduced to formal hiking and backpacking. He ended up going on the "ultimate" scouting backpacking trip three times—a Philmont trek in 1993, 1995, and 1997.

While studying geology in college, he continued his hiking and wandering. Nearly every class included at least one field trip. During breaks he and his friends would plan camping and backpacking trips.

"Carbomb" & "Lichen" had been acquaintances since 1996 when a mutual friend introduced them to each other. Now it was 1997, they were in the Smoky Mountains and their real relationship truly began.

Lichen:

"We sat beside each other in the van on the way from College Station, Texas, to Tennessee. From my perspective, it was just happenstance, but "Carbomb" says it was intentional. We exchanged tapes ("Rent" and Bob Marley) and got to know each other a bit better. Throughout the trip, I noticed that he kept popping up in the same spots I did. Then one night during a storm, the tent that I was sharing with my roommate started to leak. Conveniently, "Carbomb" had been sharing a huge tent with someone else and it had lots of extra room. So we ended up sharing the same tent for a night with several other people, but our sleeping bags were next to each other. Nothing exciting happened other than we would wake up, give each other a pretty blank stare, wondering what the other was thinking, and then go back to sleep. I swear that he put an arm over me that night, but then reconsidered and quickly removed it. "Carbomb" remembers no such thing.

On the last night of the trip, 15 college students had the run of an awesome bed and breakfast in Tennessee. We had been provided way more free beer than we could drink and most of us were acting accordingly. People passed out in odd places, but somehow, I ended up in the best room in the house which was decorated in a "Gone with the Wind" theme. "Carbomb" came to visit and, with some simple hand-holding, intentions were made known. I spent the night alone in the room while Chris spent the night hugging a toilet. But this night was what we consider the beginning of our relationship.

"Carbomb" doesn't remember it, but I first heard of the existence of the Appalachian Trail from him. I was enthralled and very excited at the idea that a trail could be that long. Logistically, how could it possibly go through all those states? How wonderful! I remember being amazed that people would hike the whole thing from end-to-end. It immediately appealed to me. He told me that people thru-hiked the A.T. for different reasons, but the only one I remember, for sure, was him mentioning that some people do it to lose weight. I think he also mentioned that those running from the law would hide out there (although having now actually hiked the trail, I bet those are few and far between). I also vividly remember him saying that it was an

endeavor that a person would have to do <u>alone</u>—it just <u>was not</u> something two people could do together. I know I asked him why that was the case, and I would give anything to remember exactly what his response was.

Now fast forward to 2004. We were living together in our rented Austin, Texas, duplex and feeling very disgruntled with the state of affairs. We were both frustrated with the fast pace of our lives, our jobs, and bemoaned our lack of personal time. During one conversation, as we both vented our frustrations, I blurted out,

"Let's just go hike the Appalachian Trail!"

"Okay, let's go do it," Chris quickly replied.

Soon thereafter he started ordering all the necessary A.T. books and began buying or making our gear.

Before that moment, the A.T. had only come up occasionally in casual conversation between us since first being mentioned in 1997. It was something that was appealing and interesting, something that we would like to do but never seriously considered. We almost conducted our thru-hike in 2005 but decided we wouldn't be prepared enough. Plus "Carbomb" felt he needed to stay at his job for one more year to help his career along. Unfortunately it didn't help but instead made him even more frustrated."

So, why did they really want to hike the A.T.? Obviously it was something that had always appealed to both of them. The aspect of living so simply may have attracted them to it the most, but they were also attracted to the physical challenge of hiking the A.T. The allure of carrying everything they needed on their backs and living out in the wilderness for so long was also a way to get out of the hectic rut their lives had fallen into. Being out there was so completely opposite of their "normal" lives, and now they cannot imagine life without having hiked the A.T. By their own admission, it was unfortunate that it took getting to a point of complete dissatisfaction with their lives that pushed them into making the decision to go.

Although some of their reasons for hiking the A.T. differed from ours, those reasons were just as valid. There were many other motivations for couples to tackle the A.T.—each with its own significance and relevance. Take, for example, the story of "Trickster & What?!"

Trickster:

"I first attempted a thru-hike on the Appalachian Trail in 2003. I was horribly out of shape and really did not have the proper gear or funds. My budget totaled only $1,200 which I had saved from my nanny job. While my friends were staying at hostels in town and eating at restaurants, I was searching for dry places to sleep and eating gas station hot dogs. Numerous times I skipped staying in town altogether and when I did my choice of lodging was rather unique. While in Hot Springs, North Carolina, I spent a rainy night in the school's play yard sleeping in one of those plastic kids' playhouses."

At one point her walking became labored and she slowed to a crawl—the result of having contracted mononucleosis. She was completely exhausted, and her lack of motivation to continue was not helped by the fact that 2003 was the rainiest year in 100 years! She hung in there doing very low mileage for a while but eventually returned home feeling very defeated and depressed that her hike had not been successful.

Right after she got off the trail, she moved to Bingham, Maine, near where the A.T. crosses the Kennebec River. Bingham is a tiny town of only 900 people. She lived there for a year and worked at a home for troubled youth an hour's commute away. Eventually, she moved to Portland, Maine, to attend college and she supported herself by working at a local club and also as a certified nursing assistant on the weekends. Though studying to be a nursing assistant, she continually questioned whether nursing was really the direction she wanted to go with her life.

Her friend Martin invited her to spend a month with him in England where he lived in a small town called Diss in Bressingham. He thought it would provide her with a good chance to sort out what she wanted to do with her life. While there, they hiked the 80-mile Hadrian's Wall and had many philosophical discussions regarding life. It was during that time she made the decision to attempt another thru-hike of the Appalachian Trail beginning March 2005. But, as fate would have it, while dancing at a Christmas party, she sprained her ankle. The devastating blow came when she returned to the States and had her ankle x-rayed. Her doctor told her the sprain was severe and she should not walk on it for more than ten minutes a day. In other words, she would definitely not be thru-hiking. It was during this time of limbo that she decided, if she could not thru-hike, she would at least work in an outdoor-related field.

Trickster:

> *"I wasn't quite sure what I wanted to do, so I began researching my options on the Internet. That is where I discovered [1]Phoenix Outdoor, a new wilderness therapy company opening in North Carolina. The company would be taking "at-risk youth" on therapeutic-based backpacking trips in the North Carolina Mountains. I faxed them my resume and application and after a few weeks, and several telephone interviews, I was offered a job working as a wilderness field instructor. Since I had been using my bike as transportation while living in Portland, I bought a Dodge Caravan and left Maine for North Carolina....into the unknown."*

Dan, known on the trail as "What?!," graduated from Savannah College of Art and Design in 2000 with a degree in Photography. After college he worked in Baltimore, Maryland, for a few years freelancing and working for a publishing company. Dissatisfied with office life and itching to expand his photography portfolio and do more traveling, "What?!" became interested in hiking the Appalachian Trail. He began planning for a thru-hike for March of 2002. He started his hike in Georgia and adopted the trail name *"Gourmet Dan"* because of his extravagant trail cooking. He would prepare fruit-filled pancakes for breakfast; dinner entrées featured fresh meat and vegetables, with exotic chocolate concoctions topped off with a bit of Kahlua. Needless to say, because he was eating this way on the trail and needed to frequently stop in towns to pick up fresh meat and produce, he was not able to move very fast. Also, being a photographer, he was carrying more than twenty-five pounds of photography equipment, including two different cameras (no digital on this trip!), and a large tripod—not one of those nice small ones that works with your trekking poles! Undaunted by the extreme weight he was carrying, "What?!" continued to make his way northward. However, when October rolled around he was still in New Hampshire, facing slippery, frozen rock faces, and blistering winds in the White Mountains. Although he wanted to go on, it was simply not safe to continue and he did not have the right gear for the harsh weather. "What?!," you must understand, was born and raised in Mexico, so being prepared for winter weather was something with which he was totally unfamiliar!

While on the trail in 2002, "What?!" met the hiker "Sasquatch" who persuaded him to move to North Carolina and work at a wilderness therapy program called *"SUWS of the Carolinas."* (The School of Urban and Wilderness Survival) "What?!" was curious so he tried it and ended up working there for over two years and advanced to a master instructor. He acquired numerous wilderness skills and became a bow-drilling master. He can start a fire by friction in less than a minute and, if you have ever tried this, you know how impressive that is! When *"Phoenix Outdoor"* started their wilderness therapy program in 2005, "What?!" was recruited to work there, and that is where he and "Trickster" met.

Trickster:

> *"What?!" and I worked at Phoenix for exactly one year and fell more in love with each passing month. Our relationship advanced so quickly because we literally spent just about all of our time together. We worked together for eight twenty-four hour days and then we played together on our six days off. All that said, he and I knew that we were going to get married after our first date. We were really just perfect for each other and able to be our true dorky selves when we were together. "What?!" proposed to me at The Grove Park Inn and Spa in Asheville on December 20th—the best early Christmas present a girl could ask for! We immediately launched into intensive wedding planning because we wanted to get married before our thru-hike of the Appalachian Trail. We had individually planned to thru-hike the Appalachian Trail that year, even before we met, so making it our honeymoon seemed like an obvious choice.*
>
> *After a lot of hectic wedding planning we were ready. We had our florist, rented space in the Amicalola Lodge near the southern terminus of the A.T., found a musician and procured a caterer. On April 2nd we were married on the lodge's terrace at Amicalola State Park by our great friend Paul in front of fifty guests and witnesses. It was a beautifully perfect day, and a wonderful way to begin our lives together surrounded by our family and friends, many who had traveled far to come to our wedding in the backwoods of Georgia. We began our thru-hike two days after our wedding."*

Another couple, who were closer in age to us and who we often hiked with, was "Enuff & Too Much."

"Enuff" is an African American who was born in New York City, went to college in Washington, D.C., attended medical school in Boston, and then did his residency in North Carolina where he later had a family practice. He eventually moved to Philadelphia, where he worked in the emergency room at an inner-city hospital. He and Pat met in 1984 and in 1986 were married and blended their two families. He loves woodworking and all types of outdoor activities and tends to drive himself to prove to himself that he can do things. He likes to push hard and do things that do not come easy, so that is why he decided to hike the A.T.

As "Enuff" tells it:

> *"I started hiking as a kid in upstate New York and, I mean, a young kid; my parents would carry me on their backs as they hiked. When I was old enough, I joined the Boy Scouts and my love of hiking grew because it was a way for me to get away from the hustle and bustle of the city. It was a source of peace for me."*

"Too Much," on the other hand, comes from an Irish-American family and was born in Philadelphia where she lived all of her life. She became a nurse and was working in the emergency room of a west Philadelphia hospital when she met "Enuff" (her "soulmate").

They started hiking as an extension of their interest in the outdoors and enjoyed the feeling of being more alive there. As a hobby, they did numerous local hikes and then progressed to some short-distance hiking. He and Pat started with car camping and for a long time that was what they equated with the term "camping." However, as time went on, the rugged experience of backpacking and "real" camping became more of an interest for them. They included their kids in what they considered more structured hiking trips but not in its more rugged extension—backpacking.
Enuff:

> *"Our decision to thru-hike the A.T. took place a year or two before the actual hike itself. We had made some other major decisions about our professional future that would require an extensive transitional period in our lives. With these changes on the horizon, we looked for something to do to fill that period before our life together took its new course. Thru-hiking the A.T. was something I saw as a quest, not unlike climbing Mt. Everest. It would be great to do and what a life shift it would be.*
>
> *We began thinking and planning to do it as merely an exciting thing to do—to fulfill a dream by doing something special, big, and unique. Not many people can, or will, do it so that made it even more enticing. Over the years Pat and I ran marathons, our biggest challenge being the Boston Marathon, so we were accustomed to training hard. Because of our competitive backgrounds, we both felt that with the proper planning and training we could do the A.T."*

Too Much:

> *"We had planned on doing some ultra-marathons and then, after we had accomplished that feat, wondered what we would do next. Suddenly, and without warning, I suffered a tear in my meniscus and it was obvious that my running days were over. So, now what? If I could not run, at least I could walk. It had to be something extreme though—something the average person would not or could not accomplish. The Boston Marathon was like the Olympics of marathons so what would be the equivalent of the Olympics in long-distance hiking? The idea of the Appalachian Trail popped up."*

For some, like "Mapman & Robin" and "Head-N-Out & Tag-N-Along" the decision to hike as a couple was remarkably simple.

Mapman:

> *"We always liked to hike and be outdoors. After college, Robin did a National Outdoor Leadership School (NOLS) course in the backcountry from September through December and loved it, though she felt it was too short. At that instant, she knew the A.T. would be great fun.*
>
> *I, on the other hand, had done several camping outings with my son's Boy Scout troop and totally enjoyed them.*
>
> *Twelve years ago, we saw a documentary on the Appalachian Trail, and from then on we dreamed about doing the hike."*

Tag-N-Along:

> *"After forty-four years of marriage and twenty-seven years of truck driving, Tim decided to retire early at age fifty-one and hike the trail. He has always been an adventurous type of guy and I just go along. Therefore, my name is "Tag-N-Along." Wanting to live life to its fullest, Tim, a.k.a. "Head-N-Out," decided that we needed to thru-hike the A.T. This was going to be the hardest thing we had ever done because we had never even climbed mountains before, except for one in Palmer, Arkansas, but that was just a day trip. Bottom line was that we were going to hike the Appalachian Trail on nothing more than a whim."*

Not every relationship began prior to getting on the trail. There are those hikers who began their quest solo, with no thought of finding a mate but, because of fate or the unique circumstances of living in the wilderness, bonds were created that became more than simply a means of survival. Such were "Brownie & Souleman."

The first exposure "Brownie" had to the idea of long-distance hiking came at the Girl Scout camp she attended each summer. There she learned about outdoor cooking, low-impact practices, and "Leave-No-Trace" principles. She went on miniature backpacking trips, where she also learned how to pack a backpack, purify water, and pitch a tent. It was during her first summer at camp that she fell in love with the outdoors. On one trip she met a hiker who claimed to have hiked from Georgia to Maine. She was shocked. Was such a thing even possible? He regaled everyone with stories and anecdotes from his six-month adventure, and that one glimpse at the possibility of spending half a year in the woods was all she needed.

Brownie:

"I was hooked. At twelve, I went home and informed my parents that I was going to thru-hike the Appalachian Trial. Of course, as parents often do when presented with such an outlandish idea by their child, they simply smiled, probably thinking to themselves: 'This too shall pass.' The wild idea remained dormant, brewing somewhere below the surface until my junior year of college. I escaped the rigors of college to backpack as often as possible in the mountains of North and South Carolina. My fondness for backpacking grew and I started making vague plans for a thru-hike on the A.T. I called home one fall and tentatively informed my parents I wanted to graduate early. This would mean attending summer school and overloading two semesters during my junior year at a university where, describing a "normal" course load as "overwhelming," is an understatement. Naturally, they wanted to know why I would inflict this upon myself. I sucked in my breath and explained that I wanted to hike the Appalachian Trail starting March of my senior year. They were once again surprised and probably a little incredulous, but most surprisingly they were supportive. Painstakingly (but successfully), I completed two overloaded trimesters plus summer school. While most seniors were applying for jobs and looking at apartment ads, I was researching tents and water purifiers. I handed in my final term papers, graduated college a semester early (with a degree in philosophy), and was ready for a much-anticipated adventure."

Prior to starting the trail, Jeremy, better known as "Souleman," was living in Middlebury, Vermont, with his parents and was working for the recreation department. He had recently moved back with them after spending over a year in Albuquerque, New Mexico.

When "Brownie" told her parents of her plans to thru-hike, they were supportive, but as dutiful parents, obviously very nervous. Neither liked the idea of their daughter out in the woods alone. To ease her mom's worries, she reassured her she would try to get to know someone to hike with who was starting on the same day. She had already been using *www.Trailplace.com* to do research, but now she began contacting other hikers. When she needed a recommendation for a female pack, another hiker directed her to Katie—a female hiker the same age as her. They began trading emails and eventually talked on the phone. Katie was planning to start on March 15, 2005 with her boyfriend and another guy from her town. Slowly, through communications with other hikers on the website, a group starting on that same date began to develop. The conversations were completely platonic as they discussed gear, hiking, anticipation for the trip, etc.

"Brownie" decided she would start hiking with this group. Her parents now felt better knowing she would be hiking with other people with whom she had at least communicated. In total there were seven people in the group; Katie ("Crazy Katie"), her boyfriend ("Radio"), her friend/coworker ("Bassline"), a guy from Florida ("Rawhide"), a guy from Vermont ("Souleman"), his friend ("Jax"), and then herself..

Brownie:

> *"The entire group planned to meet at Katie's house in Atlanta on March 13th to get acquainted and celebrate her birthday. "Souleman" and I met for the first time at Katie's house that day. He claims that is when he fell in love. The following day the group spent more time together preparing for our quickly approaching hike. But, he and I seemed to be the only ones serious about trying to lighten our pack weight and discuss gear and preparation. On March 15th, "Souleman" and "Jax" rode together to the trailhead."*

There were also couples on the trail who were not married, engaged, or even remotely in the throes of a developing, intimate relationship. A long-time platonic friendship, a mutual love of the outdoors, and an off-handed challenge was all it took for one couple to take on the A.T. Mike and Roseanne from Australia were just two of a rather large contingent of "Aussies" on the trail in 2006. Somehow they were able to complete their entire thru-hike without ever acquiring "official" trail names. Everyone just called them "Mike & Zan."

Zan:

"We both grew up hiking; I was involved in the Girl Guides and Mike was in the Boy Scouts. We met when we were both sixteen and were attending the same high school. All throughout those years, we went on hikes with friends and were active members in the Army Cadets. Hiking is something that both of us have always done, and we have fond memories of doing it. We both share the same love of the outdoors, the desire to challenge ourselves, and to experience life to the fullest.

After high school, we attended the same university where we remained close friends and continued to travel and hike with mutual friends, mostly in New Zealand.

Our journey to the A.T. began during 2005 after we read Bill Bryson's book, "A Walk in the Woods." It was our final year of university and everyone around us was settling in for another year of study and they all had plans for the rest of their lives. We had no idea what we wanted to do after graduation, so taking a year off to travel seemed like a fine idea.

Jokingly one of us said, "You know what would be fun? Let's hike the entire Appalachian Trail."

One thing led to another and the next thing we knew we were booking a plane ticket to the States while people at home were taking bets on whether we would make it or not."

So, here we have seven other couples, all with varying degrees of hiking experience, all with different personal backgrounds, and all with different reasons to take on *"a footpath for those who seek fellowship with the wilderness."* How we would all survive and adapt to the rigors of a six-month journey through the wilderness of the Appalachians remained to be seen. Nevertheless, all of us were excited about the prospect of finding out.

As was the case with all the other hikers, both solo and couples, our dream of thru-hiking the A.T. was now beginning to take on a life of its own. Was thru-hiking the Appalachian Trail a demonstration of reckless abandon or was it the quest to fulfill a burning passion? Would it rid our psyches of the stress brought on by noise, timetables and the crush of civilization? In its place would there be instilled a sense of peace and inner prosperity derived from nothing more than breathing in the wonder of it all? Would we develop a new level of maturity that would give us a new perspective on life? Would we live each precious moment just as it came, with no expectations or laments—moments that would evoke emotions indescribable through mere words? Would we become free enough to allow ourselves to be lost in the breathtaking, natural wonders, which are so unyielding in their power that their impact can only be captured through photos, the words of poems, and melodies of songs?

"Mom's" Tips for Couples:

- You both need to love the outdoors;

- You both need to be motivated by a challenge and be willing to work hard;

- Most importantly, you both need to have the desire and commitment to succeed as a couple.

The first two items are needed by anyone hiking a long-distance trail. However, as a couple, you will need to be able to <u>encourage</u> each other and not be a drain on each other. There will be days when circumstances are not pleasant and when the challenges take you to you to the edge of your personal limits. But knowing that your partner is depending on you for support moves those limits beyond what you ever thought possible. Being able to encourage one another can mean the difference between success and failure. Desiring to start and finish <u>as a couple</u> is something that can be a motivator and sustainer. The commitment to do this together has huge potential for defining and enhancing your relationship.

CHAPTER TWO

PLANNING AND PREPARATION

"To accomplish great things, we must not only act, but also dream; not only plan, but also believe." <u>Anatole France</u>

"What lies behind us and what lies before us are tiny matters compared to what lies within us." Ralph Waldo Emerson

We have never been ones to rest on our laurels and we view each new day as an opportunity to experience and accomplish something unique and significant. In fact, every few years we go on a retreat, just the two of us, to a romantic bed and breakfast. There, in conjunction with the wonderful experience of being pampered by the staff, lounging in a hot tub with a cool glass of white Merlot, and mentally winding down from the chaos of suburban Washington, D.C, we take the opportunity to develop and update a "life plan" for ourselves—both individually and as a couple. This plan is a list of all the dreams and desires we both have for our lives, along with a timetable for living them out and the steps required to make them a reality. These dreams are often as wild and as far-fetched as we can imagine, but they reflect who we are and what type of legacy we want to leave behind for our children and for others. The plans cover the entire gamut of our life experience from financial, educational, recreational, and spiritual to relational, travel, and future employment. Over the last few years, retirement planning has become a priority. This life planning technique, though never purposely designed to do so, has also served to inspire others to adapt the motto of "Dream It.! Plan It! Live It!" and not be content with the *status quo* of their lives.

Periodically we review these plans together to see how we are progressing and it still amazes us how many things on these lists we have been successful in completing. We whole-heartedly recommend everyone have a "life plan." Not only is it an extremely rewarding endeavor, but it puts all of those *"I have always wanted to do that"* items in black and white, which is a first step to making them a reality. If nothing else, developing a "life plan" gives you a great excuse to get away for a romantic weekend. We intended to approach our thru-hike with this same level of forethought and planning.

Why did we decide on such a bold adventure at this time in our lives? We were financially secure and each had a stable and rewarding job. Georgia was expanding on her 16-year career with the federal government, working at a national laboratory, and I was immersed in the music industry through my job at a major D.C.-area recording studio. Every non-working hour of our lives was filled with the pursuit of recreational activities that further enriched our lives. Georgia had her photography and her passion for leading others in the discovery of their unique gifts and talents. She assisted them in using those gifts and talents to positively alter the course of their lives. I had my music composing, playing and singing on our church worship team, and doing live sound for concerts. Putting all of these things aside in order to hike the A.T. was a pretty radical decision. There is a bit of Native American wisdom that says, *"The turtle never goes backwards, and in order to go forward, it must stick its neck out."* I guess we felt like it was time for us to be like the turtle.

Our kids were all out on their own, pursuing their lives and thankfully our parents were not at a stage in their lives where they required our assistance, either financially or physically. In our hearts, we knew there might never be a better time to do what we were planning to do. This was a fleeting window of opportunity and we needed to take advantage of it. We suddenly reached a point where the question was no longer, *"Why hike the Appalachian Trail,"* but instead a resounding, *"Why not?!"* Why not indulge ourselves in an adventure far beyond anything we had ever imagined? And more importantly, why not hike it together? We would later discover, as we hiked with solo spouses on the trail, they all harbored a tinge of regret that their spouse, for whatever reason, would not or could not, share their experience with them. For us, not doing it together seemed strange.

With the decision to thru-hike the A.T. behind us, we now had to do what we do best—*plan*. But how do we begin the long process of planning for such an adventure?

Since we are both "Type A," detail-oriented people and rarely, if ever, run headlong into an endeavor without doing extensive research and evaluation, we of course felt compelled to subscribe to any number of outdoor magazines and periodicals. The total number amounted to more than we could properly read in the limited number of hours we had available each day. But all those hiking and trail magazines covering our coffee table certainly gave the impression that we knew what we were doing and sure looked cool—even if we did not get to digest them all.

Of all the magazines we received, *Backpacker Magazine* was, and still is, the one we most highly recommend to any backpacker be they novice or veteran. As novices, we immediately got sucked into believing that every word we read in the magazine was gospel. Of course, there was relevant and accurate knowledge to be gained from the many articles and exhaustive gear reviews. However, as we acquired, tested, and evaluated the equipment most highly recommended by *Backpacker*, it struck us that our definitions of comfort, warmth, lightweight and "necessary" were quite different than those of the magazine's reviewers. The staff of the magazine, as well it should, is comprised of those who have extensive wilderness experience. Add to that the current trend of backpacking with as little or with the lightest gear available, and the reviews tend to be skewed more toward the "minimalist" side. For us, comfort would need to play a large role in our decisions.

Curiously, in a radical departure from the "roughing it" theme of the publication, occasionally they do tend to glamorize life on the trail. If you were to carry all the things you would need to prepare the gourmet meals they often describe, you would not be able to carry anything else. Somehow, packing bottles of white Zinfandel to have with a dinner of Brie and shrimp cocktail just did not make a whole lot of sense nor did it represent the true experience of trail life. Then again, those culinary delights did appeal to those "day-hikers" who relish that type of thing. Since they are only on the trail for a day, they certainly have room in their packs for the necessary ingredients.

As an illustration of this "suburbanite-oriented wilderness experience," we once did a three-day hike and stayed at the Ed Garvey Shelter, a wonderful two-story shelter in Maryland, which is a relatively short hike from Harper's Ferry, West Virginia—close enough that "weekenders" can readily carry in enough food, booze, and extraneous house wares and electronics to render the shelter uninhabitable by the usual backpackers. We arrived at the shelter to find one such group complete with their espresso machine. God only knows how they powered it but they had enough batteries for all their other electronic devices, so why not the espresso machine? The funny part was they forgot to bring food for their rather large and continuously hungry dog.

We joined the *Appalachian Trail Conservancy* (ATC), the *Appalachian Mountain Club* (AMC), and the *Potomac Appalachian Trail Club* (PATC). Through their newsletters and magazines we were able to keep up to date on trail conditions, hiking tips, trail work opportunities, and other day hikes in our area. All of their publications contain a wealth of valuable information regarding both local and national trail topics. Numerous websites, such as *www.trailjournals.com* and *www.whiteblaze.net*, exist to provide useful information posted by hikers and others in the hiking community.

We spent innumerable hours researching all of the A.T. books we could get our hands on and created an *Excel* spreadsheet that was a compilation of all that information. From an adventure standpoint, we may have been considered anally retentive or even slightly obsessive compulsive. However, we liked knowing there may be snow in Georgia in March, how many miles it was between shelters, and where the post offices were located for mail drops. Knowing where we could get off the trail to restock and take a shower and the fact that when we hit New England our mileage each day would be markedly less than on the rest of the hike were of prime importance to us. Knowing the proper time and location to switch from winter gear to summer gear could be a matter of life and death. Our ages had brought with them a keen awareness of our mortality, so staying alive was an integral part of our planning. For the young or truly adventurous, knowing these things ahead of time are of little consequence. We knew this adventure was going to be tough enough all on its own without us going into it unprepared. We could look at our spreadsheet and confidently ascertain exactly where every shelter, privy, water source, road crossing, B&B, motel, restaurant, laundromat, and waypoint was for every mile of the trail. This spreadsheet was a thing of statistical beauty and was totally invaluable to us—that is, until we were one week into the hike and found ourselves unable to walk the number of miles we anticipated. At that point, the term "flexibility" became a regular part of our vocabulary and lifestyle, and we tossed our beloved spreadsheet into a box for posterity. Despite the fact this document quickly became useless, we still look at it to this day with a sense of pride and accomplishment. Simply doing all the research and placing the data in the spreadsheet provided us with much more detail than any single source. It also gave us a sense of peace because, at least from an information standpoint, we were now totally familiar with the entire trail. Anyone needing a "single source" for all the A.T. information available would find this spreadsheet extremely useful in his or her planning.

As part of our planning and preparation, we went to a seminar at a local trail store to listen to one of its employees talk about his experience at completing the A.T. We thought,

"Wow, we should get some great insight on what to expect from this guy."

However, what we heard was that he did very little training, did no real planning, and made more mistakes along the way than he could even recount. His saving grace was that he was young and had no deadline to meet in completing the trail. He sincerely sounded proud of the fact that he had such a difficult time but still pulled it off. Every year there are any numbers of these "seat of the pants" hikers on the A.T. What amazed us was just how many of them started out from Springer the year we were there.

Since Georgia and I do not have a "whatever" gene in our bodies, the idea of going off on a whim as this young hiker did was a totally foreign concept to us. However, we do periodically experience a tinge of admiration for those who do, but it passes rather quickly.

Most of the information we could glean from our library of backpacking books and magazines pertained to the individual hiker, so we sorely needed some type of guidance on how to plan for a long-distance hike as a couple. Luckily, we were able to locate a seminar at a local outfitter presented by a couple, Al and Allison, who had extensive experience with such a type of endeavor. The seminar was extremely informative, but it became readily apparent right from the outset of their talk that these folks were "ultra-light" hikers who chose to travel with the bare essentials. Could it be that they wrote gear reviews for *Backpacker Magazine*? The thought of surviving for six months sleeping under nothing more than a tarp supported by trekking poles and sharing food cooked and eaten from a single pot was not quite what we had in mind. We decided right then and there that our style of backpacking would be a hybrid. It would be a blending of the elements of ultra-light hiking with the measure of comfort we needed to sustain us through a long walk and that would allow us to maintain some level of sanity. We dubbed our style of hiking as *"comfort-light"* hiking. The foundation of this style of hiking was to carry equipment and clothing that would keep us as comfortable, clean, and as healthy as necessary while still keeping each component as light as possible. It also meant we would not carry anything we would not <u>regularly</u> use.

Having completed our 2,175-mile trek, we are even more adamant about the need to prepare for thru-hiking the A.T. Considering the amount of information available on what it is like to thru-hike the A.T. and what you will need to successfully challenge it, it still amazes us how many people set out to conquer the A.T. with little or no training—or even a cursory understanding of what they are getting into. We heard a tale of three female would-be thru-hikers who, after climbing the 8.8-mile approach trail to the southern terminus of the trail on Springer Mountain, inquired as to whether or not there was a shuttle to take them back into town. It seems those first eight-plus-miles were more than they could handle and they were already giving up their quest to complete the entire trail.

Through our research, we became acutely aware of the fact that the arch nemesis of any hiker is WEIGHT. Therefore, we developed another spreadsheet on which to list all of our gear and clothing. Beside each item we noted each item's corresponding weight, down to the gram, so we could later divide up our total pack weights evenly. Despite all our best intentions and efforts to keep the weights shared evenly, "Mom" always pointed out to me and everyone else that her pack was somehow always larger than mine. I explained it away as simply being a matter of "volume" because the packs always weighed the same. "Mom," being an expert at weighing things, begged to differ—and she still does.

Now we decided, though probably a bit prematurely, that it was time for us to choose trail names—that unique way of communicating with other hikers without ever revealing your true identity. This is a very curious A.T. tradition. You often spend countless hours on the trail without seeing another human being and you long to meet someone with whom you can share the day's experiences. Then, when you finally drag yourself into camp where a host of fellow hikers are bedding down for the night, you all share the most intimate moments of your day's journey, never once using your real name or anyone else's. What is equally odd about this tradition is that in all the time we were on the trail, we never forgot a person's trail name, even if we only met them once. If you think about it, trail names make a lot of sense. Consider the fact that without trail names you may come into a shelter at night to find a dozen other hikers. Now, if one-third of them were named Jim or Mike, chances are extremely good you will not remember who is who. But, with trail names like "Boogeyman," "Bama," "Old Drum," "Little Wing," "Cash," and "Baldylocks," how could you not be able to put a unique name with the corresponding face or personality?

There are some rules that the choice of your trail name should follow. If you wait until you are on the trail to get a name, which is the purist form of this tradition, it is certain someone will give you a name that is less than flattering and will probably represent some oddity in your personality—or some ill-fated event you were party to since being on the trail. For instance, "Oyster" got his name after having been on the trail for only three days, at which time he became deathly ill from eating cans of raw oysters he carried in his pack. If you choose your own trail name, you can make sure that it reflects something positive about your personality or your background.

Being actively involved in our local church, we decided that our names should somehow reflect that spiritual aspect of ourselves. Georgia decided on *"The Prophet"* and I, in an immense lapse of judgment, chose *"The Preacher."* You could find those names in earlier trail logs on the A.T. in

Maryland, southern parts of Pennsylvania, and in Northern Virginia to Harper's Ferry.

After a couple of year's training on the trail I decided, since my preaching skills were not at a level that would justify the *"Preacher"* moniker (I still cannot stretch "God" into a three-syllable word like a Baptist preacher), that I should change my name. So, for a short time in the trail logs, you would find written, *"Spiritwalker,"* formerly *"The Preacher"* until I discovered there had already been a *"Spiritwalker."* Therefore, in November of 2005 I changed my trail name yet again to *"Windtalker"* and that is the one I stuck with. This name communicated the essence of my love for the Native American flute and how its majestic tones become a musical prayer or form of conversation with God and the earth—a rather poetic idea for a trail name if I do say so. I did have a number of people ask me if I served in World War II as part of the Navajo "code talkers." I had to remind them that I was "Windtalker," not "Codetalker."

Georgia also decided to change her name. It seemed that *"The Prophet"* invoked a level of soulful fear in those on the trail who thought they would be subjected to some type of evangelical browbeating if they spent a night in a shelter with her. Therefore, she acquired the trail name *"Mom,"* which is what many of the metrologists she works with call her anyway. As it turned out, she brought a secondary meaning to this name since she became the "mom" to many of the other thru-hikers, giving them advice on taking care of their feet and eating right. With our trail name choices now finally out of the way, it was time to tackle the more crucial aspects of our journey.

There was one formidable obstacle yet to overcome: how to get the time off from work. Had we both just graduated from college with no financial obligation other than a college loan or had we both been between jobs and saved enough money to tide us over until we found new ones, finding six months' worth of free time would be a breeze. However, with both of us approaching middle age and with responsibilities at work coming out of our ears, such was not the case. So, some creativity and fortitude were required in order to keep this small detail from derailing our dream. Suffice it to say, "Mom" had a very cooperative boss who looked forward to vicariously being a part of her adventure. For years in advance of the actual hike, he assisted her with arranging a leave of absence to make her dream a reality. However, she did consider alternative plans in case they were needed. Knowing how difficult it would be to find someone with her skills who was willing to move to the D.C. area, and knowing how long the government hiring process takes, she figured, if worse came to worse, she could quit her job and be rehired in the same length of time it would take to hike the trail.

I, on the other hand, waited until just months before the hike and requested a six-month leave of absence from my position at the studio. I resigned myself to the fact that my request might be denied and I would simply let the chips fall where they may. I had already successfully changed careers numerous times before, so the worst-case scenario would be I would have to do it again. Of course, there was always early retirement, but I was not quite ready for that. As it turned out, my position was going to be held for me and all I had to do was train a replacement to cover for me in my absence.

We began *planning* in 2001 and knew that our initial plan would probably be nothing more than a framework to build upon. Over the ensuing five years we would modify and massage it on a regular basis. However, having a plan meant we were on our way to *"walking the talk."* We had our spreadsheets, data books and magazines. But, we also needed to deal with the formidable physical, emotional, and psychological challenges that would lie ahead. To ready ourselves for these challenges would require extensive training and it was time to get those *preparations* started.

If *planning* our hike was a mind-numbing and time-consuming endeavor, then pushing ourselves through years of *preparation* was even more sobering. Were it not for our mutual commitment to living out this dream and envisioning ourselves standing triumphantly arm-in-arm at the summit of Mt. Katahdin, the effort required to get ourselves physically and mentally ready would have been overwhelming.

We began our physical training five years before our A.T. hike start date. To some, that may sound ridiculous. But, we knew with the demands on our time because of jobs, involvement at church, and our other personal interests, our free weekends to hike and camp would be severely limited. We figured if we started getting ready far enough in advance, we would have enough conditioning under our belts to give us the level of confidence we needed to tackle the A.T. Some people wait until a couple of months before they leave for Springer Mountain, Georgia, to get ready. We would have to say, almost without exception, those who waited until the last minute to prepare regretted it in some measurable way. We were glad we did so much preliminary backpacking because we learned a multitude of things about our gear and our physical and psychological strengths and weaknesses, plus we gained an overall sense of peace about what we could and could not realistically accomplish. There were also added benefits we had never really considered. Through the course of those years of preparation hikes, we came to understand and appreciate not only each other's strengths, but we also came to accept our partner's weaknesses. With that acceptance came the willingness to step up and do whatever needed to be done to assure the success of our partner.

Not every couple used the same approach to planning and preparing for the A.T. as we did. Contrast our method with that of "Mike & Zan."

Zan:

> *"We must admit that we actually did very little preparation for our thru-hike and think we were very fortunate that we had such a successful and blessed hike with very little trouble. Every time we had a problem, it was as if something or someone magically appeared to help us solve it. The trail did indeed look after us. We were truly grateful to have met so many great people, like "Mom's" parents, who enriched our A.T. experience and made us feel like family when we were so far away from our own.*
>
> *Lack of preparation did bring with it some comical and frustrating moments. When we started hiking from Springer Mountain on March 27th, we were totally unfamiliar with the American wilderness. Back home we never had to worry about things like bears and how to protect our food from them. It took us several weeks and considerable amounts of advice from pitying onlookers before we could successfully hang our food in a bear bag."*

If only we were that daring! Had we undertaken this adventure when we were younger, perhaps we would have approached it with the same bold naiveté—though we sincerely doubt it! But with age, innocence is replaced with wisdom and the realization that we needed to make sure we lived to see tomorrow. Age provided us the ability to rationalize our choice of not running off into the wilderness unprepared as a way of preserving our immortality for as long as humanly possible. Life is already too short and it, unfortunately, does not come with "do-overs."

We needed every form of thru-hiking inspiration we could lay our hands on. As a Christmas gift I purchased a large, framed, photograph from the *Appalachian Trail Conservancy* depicting a solitary hiker kneeling at the foot of the holy grail of the A.T.—the northern terminus sign on the summit of Mt. Katahdin. This hiker, shrouded in fog with his head against the weathered surface of the sign, epitomizes the conflicting emotions of triumph, regret, excitement, grief, loss, confusion, and mourning that all thru-hikers experience at the successful conclusion of their journey. This photo, hanging on the wall at the foot of our bed, was a daily inspiration to us. Not a day went by that we did not yearn for the time when we would wrestle with those same colliding emotions.

We continued digesting and analyzing as much backpacking and A.T. information as humanly possible while still leaving enough time to eat and sleep. But now it was time to start purchasing our equipment—a mind-boggling task at best. There were so many choices! However, for us, going to an outfitter invoked the same kind of giddy excitement and potential for impulse buying as going to *Home Depot* or the local music or bookstore. Since we had good-paying jobs and a relatively modest lifestyle that left us disposable income with which to pursue the fun stuff in life, the cost of keeping up with this evolution of hiking technology was of no great concern.

Because we had five years of training and experimentation to pursue, it was not possible for us to wait until the last minute to purchase the equipment we needed. With technology changing so quickly and with newer, lighter, and tougher materials coming onto the market virtually every month, it was an expensive proposition to constantly upgrade our gear.

However, keeping up with gear evolution was one of the highlights of our preparation. Acquiring our equipment so far in advance did have its advantages: the main one being it kept us from enduring the same fate as those who took a more whimsical approach to their thru-hike. Waiting until the last minute to purchase gear had a painful, and expensive, downside. Many of these "wait until the last minute" hikers found themselves overburdened with packs that often weighed in excess of sixty pounds and they ended up shedding a good deal of their equipment at the *Walasi-Yi Outdoor Center*—thirty miles after starting their hike. This outfitter's claim to fame is its tradition of strategically relieving hikers of unnecessary gear from their overweight packs. Many a hiker has been spared days and months of agonizing travel by availing himself/herself of this service. Here the outfitter staff strips down a hiker's pack and lays everything on the floor. Those items deemed nonessential or inappropriate are boxed up and shipped back to the hiker's home at the hiker's expense. Then comes the costly job of replacing heavy packs, stoves, and other accessories with those that considerably lighten the hiker's load—all those things that could have been purchased before getting on the trail. Considering most of the thru-hikers we met were on extremely limited budgets, this "backpack cleansing," I am sure, negatively affected the amount of beer money they had available later on down the trail.

One other huge benefit of hiking as a couple was that our sixty-plus pounds of gear were evenly divided between the two of us—even though "Mom's" pack was larger.

We kept our "comfort-light" credo in mind as we began our quest to acquire the most appropriate and lightest equipment we could find to meet our needs. For instance, knowing we would be tired and sore at the end of each day, regaining our stamina and giving our bodies a chance to recuperate would be paramount. To accomplish this would require us to have the maximum level of sleeping comfort, so we opted to carry *Therm-a-Rest ProLite 3* air pads. While these pads give support and offer real comfort, they are heavier than the "closed cell foam" roll-up pads. We used the "women's version" because it is shorter and, therefore, much lighter than its full-size counterpart. Finally, there was a benefit to being short!

Over the years we purchased several tents and each time downsized to a smaller, lighter design. We finally ended up with an *REI Quarter Dome* three-season, two-person tent which, because neither of us is very tall, served our purposes quite nicely. Yet again, this was one of the few benefits of being short, a plus that would later become a detriment as we struggled to climb some of the more precarious ascents on our journey. The *Quarter Dome* has some other distinct advantages for a couple. It has two doors and two vestibules for storing gear, and we were easily able to divide up the carrying weight between us.

Our initial gear experience was similar to most hikers in that our first packs did nothing more than point out what we should be looking for in our next packs. Because I have a long torso, short legs, and a marginally bad back, it was impossible for me to find a frameless pack that fit me and felt comfortable when filled with trail representative weight. A quick note: Never buy a backpack from a store that is not prepared to fill it with twenty-five to thirty pounds of weight so you can experience what it feels like when full. There is nothing worse than shelling out $195 to $295 on a pack that feels great empty to later find the first time you hit the trail with your gear you are wiped out in the first ten miles. No amount of aspirin will compensate for an ill-fitting pack.

My first pack was a throwback to my old Boy Scout days. It was a rugged, yet comparatively unattractive, external aluminum frame style by *Kelty*. It felt good, had all kinds of cool places to hang stuff on the frame, and had an abundance of pockets that made things more accessible than most of the internal frame packs I had been looking at. I hate having to unpack half my pack to get to that one elusive item I need, so a plethora of pockets and places to hang stuff on the outside seemed the way to go. The only problem was that after two to three hikes the frame developed loud, annoying squeaks at all the flex points. I am sure that is why there was never any wildlife within five miles of us. It also was not large enough for more than two to three days' worth of supplies without having to hang half my other gear on the outside of the pack and on the frame.

"Mom's" first backpack was distinctly different from mine. She chose an *Arc'teryx Bora 95* internal frame pack. It was large enough to hold a month's worth of food and gear. She loved the wonderfully-comfortable hip-belt, but empty it weighed nearly as much as mine did fully-loaded. We sometimes wondered how large a person would need to be to find a pack that weighed in excess of six pounds comfortable.

Obviously, our next packs would be lighter and more functional. As we began our A.T. thru-hike, I was only on my second pack in five years. It was a *ULA P-1* pack that held thirty-five pounds of gear and weighed only two pounds empty. "Mom" decided to try an internal frame pack like mine—although hers was the updated *P-2* model. At the time we had no idea that having identical-looking packs would be indicative of the closeness that developed during our A.T. hike. After doing a number of three to four-day hikes with these packs, we found our backs felt great and we never came close to running out of food or other supplies. Unfortunately, these two model packs are no longer manufactured, having been replaced by a sleeker, more mountaineering-oriented design that did away with many of the features we considered essential and convenient.

Every novice backpacker's greatest fear, aside from being attacked by a bear, is that he/she will not be able to survive unless he/she packs a week's worth of food and toilet paper. Experience eventually taught us we did not need super-large packs because we could simply leave the trail more often to restock. Except for the seventy-two mile stretch through the Smoky Mountains from Fontana Dam to Davenport Gap—and a few extreme wilderness sections of the A.T. in Maine—four days' worth of supplies will always get you near a town where you can restock. And because we shared the load, we were always able to carry plenty of food. In the unlikely event a hiker does run low on food, some other thru-hikers will generally share what they can spare—though it will probably be items they are sick of eating, like *Ramen* noodles. This gesture of goodwill, no doubt, cost you a round or two at the bar in the next town. Thru-hikers are immensely generous, but they are by no means philanthropists when beer is involved.

In selecting gear, we also wanted a lightweight stove that was both easy to use and allowed us to prepare our meals as quickly as possible. When you wake up in the dark or arrive at camp starving after a grueling fifteen-mile day, the last thing you want to do is hassle with a stove. We settled on a *Snow Peak Giga-Power* canister-style stove that required no liquid fuel, repeated pumping, or finesse in lighting. It was purely by accident that we bought the model without the built-in igniter. We simply used a match or lighter. We later discovered the igniters often failed after repeated use, and if it did not work the first time, you wasted valuable fuel as you repeatedly re-clicked it until the fuel lit. We were glad we had the non-igniter version. We knew these canister stoves did not particularly like cold weather, so when it was cold, I put the gas tank in my sleeping bag at night to keep the fuel warm. On the A.T. we purchased a *SnowPeak* wind shield disc that fit over the stove's pot supports and increased the efficiency of the stove considerably. The added efficiency also decreased the use of fuel for the two of us, so a canister often lasted four to five days. We had tried liquid gas stoves, like the *MSR Whisperlite International*, but found it a bit temperamental. We also tried an alcohol stove which, though extremely light, did not work well when cooking for two people because it was slow and controlling the flame was problematic.

For cooking and ease of cleaning, we used a four-piece set of titanium *Teflon* coated pots with the handles removed to eliminate a few ounces of weight. Our eating utensils were disposable *Glad* plastic storage bowls with lids and titanium spoons. Some couples saved weight by using just one pot and no eating dishes. A standard bandana became a washcloth, towel, and head covering to soak up sweat and stave off insects.

Two items we would not compromise on, despite their heavier weight, were a seventy-ounce *Camelback* hydration pack and a high-end water filter. When you are on the trail, hydration can become a matter of life and death. You have two choices: carry an adequate supply of water in a hydration pack or simply carry several plastic water bottles and stay on the lookout for water sources during the day so you can refill them. We walk slowly and did not want to spend precious hiking time refilling bottles, so we chose to use hydration packs. Only twice did we run out of water before we reached camp and both times it was my fault.

When it comes to dealing with drinking water, we filter every drop. On the trail, Giardia is a major concern, and its grisly effects of vomiting and diarrhea can last for days. We are not willing to risk contracting it simply to save a pound of weight. We carry a *First Need* filter, the highest end and fastest pumping filter we have found. The beauty of this filter is that, because it pumps water in both stroke directions, it is amazingly fast. Despite its comparatively heavy weight we never regretted the choice. We also have a smaller *Katadyn* water filter we take along on day hikes or when we are slack-packing.

As for footwear and foot care, that topic could probably make up an entire book in itself. In summary, though, we knew our boots would be the most vital piece of equipment we would have on the trail; so the quest to find ones that would provide us with absolute comfort was an extremely important task. It took me five years of painful experimentation to find a pair of boots that fit me correctly. "Mom," on the other hand, was able to find boots that fit her in almost every outfitter along the trail. She acquired the secondary trail nickname of "Imelda"—an affectionate, though somewhat sarcastic, tribute to the former First Lady of the Philippines, Imelda Marcos, who was the infamous collector of more than one thousand pairs of shoes. The joke on the trail was that "Mom" bought new boots every time her current pair got dirty. Truth was, they repeatedly failed, and by trail's end, she had acquired a grand total of eleven pairs.

(You can see a complete list of our gear in Appendix #2.)

With our inaugural complement of gear in hand, along with lengthy *American Express* statements constantly reminding us of the financial ramifications of this wilderness undertaking, we were finally ready to start training with actual hikes along many of the trails within several hours of our home. These hikes would serve as opportunities to physically train, evaluate our equipment and clothing, and build our confidence. As we were to find out, these were areas of minor consequence compared to the substantial enlightenment we would receive concerning our individual strengths and weaknesses. They would also point out our ability, or inability, to function as a team under the unique situations on the trail. In the final analysis, each hike offered yet another eye-opening experience in how well we would or would not withstand the rigors of our six-month adventure. What affect they would have on our relationship could make or break the pursuit of our dream.

Our passions toward meeting individual goals notwithstanding, we have always worked very well as a team. We counted on this teamwork approach serving us well during our backcountry adventures. We believed we could bring to the table our past successes as a team and merely rely on them in these new situations. Little did we know these preparation hikes would expose many physical, emotional, and relational weaknesses. We would have to overcome these potential obstacles if we were to complete our A.T. hike.

The first obstacle to overcome was of lowering our expectations of what we could reasonably accomplish on any given day. Both of us are extremely driven toward perfection, an attribute brought on by both genetic make-up and family upbringing, so we typically set the bar very high for ourselves. Mediocrity, or accepting *average* as an acceptable level of performance, is simply not part of our personalities. Because of this, we are both very successful at most everything we undertake—a fact we find extremely rewarding but which drives to distraction many of those with whom we work and play. Our preparation hikes would soon provide us with some sobering realizations regarding our personalities and our relationship.

Assateague Island

One of our many preparation adventures was a three-day-weekend of canoeing, hiking, and camping on Assateague Island in Maryland. We did the requisite research, scoured the maps, packed our gear, food and clothing, purchased our camping permit, and, in our minds, we were ready. Despite the fact we had limited experience paddling a canoe in tandem, and at this point had only been out hiking a few times, "Mom's" goal was to have us paddle twelve miles on the bay side of the island to a secluded beach. From there we would hike one-half mile across the island to its ocean side where we would camp. It became quickly evident to me as we struggled into a strong headwind and through turbulent waters, which predicated the small craft warnings that were posted, that we would be lucky if we made our destination by nightfall. Upon my urging, we adjusted our goal so we could reach a small beach just six miles away before it got dark. "Mom" sensed I was correct in my assessment of the situation and begrudgingly capitulated. In a sense, we felt the trip was already a failure because we would not meet our original goal. This feeling of failure was the beginning of a negative emotional undercurrent that haunted us for hours.

Added to our feelings of frustration were the blazing sun, wind-blown seas, and a tide that was quickly going out, leaving us aground on several occasions. The tension between us began to build exponentially. In a misguided attempt to shorten the distance to our goal, and thereby short-circuit the developing rift between us, we left the open waters of the bay and made our way through various channels in closer proximity to the shoreline. We quickly found that the many small islands and inlets we were attempting to navigate had little, if any, similarity to what was on our maps. Even with "Mom's" superior map-reading skills we became somewhat disoriented, which increased our frustration. We needed some time to reassess our position and reinforce our sense of teamwork and compassion towards each other.

We stopped paddling and talked things through, being candid about how we were feeling about our situation and towards each other. It was time to put aside our snipes about who was at fault and focus on the goal of reaching the island as quickly as possible. What we found was that we were equally frustrated about our own lack of experience in the canoe, and because of our lack of endurance, we were beginning to fatigue. Our apparent inability to reach our goal was the cause of our frustration, not any animosity we felt toward each other. It was time to emotionally regroup and put our primary emphasis on the journey, not the goal. From that point on, we were back working as a team, enjoying the journey and each other's company. Before long, and with a few laughs along the way, we reached our destination. We learned a valuable lesson on this trip—open communication and honesty are essential, and willingness not to place blame is critical.

Despite our willpower and lofty intentions, our shortcomings and lack of experience came home loud and clear to us. It was a powerful reality check and a stern lesson in humility—a lesson that would raise its ugly head many times in the future. Yet, all of these initial challenges fortified our resolve and our compassion towards each other. They even allowed us to endure horrendous attacks by mosquitoes and a sandstorm that could have easily ruined our first meal on the beach.

The C&O Canal

Most of our early hikes were three days or less—a far cry from the six months and 2,175 miles we would experience on the A.T. So we decided it was time to undertake a five to seven-day hike in order to get a sense of what it would be like to walk a long way for a long time. However, we were not yet confident enough with our planning regimen to take on a hike of this magnitude in a wilderness area. What if we miscalculated our supply needs and became stranded? Our corpses might not be located until after we were fired from our jobs for not showing up at the end of our scheduled vacation break!

We planned two week-long treks on the C&O Canal Towpath along the Potomac River. This 184-mile trail was formerly the hard-packed dirt path mules used while pulling barges along the canal. It stretches from Washington, D.C., to Cumberland, Maryland. We had already completed several day-hikes on the C&O around the D.C. area, so from September 12 to 17, 2003, we would attempt to hike the towpath from Cumberland south to Brunswick, Maryland. We were confident we could complete the trip in seven days. It would not be a physically strenuous hike from the standpoint of terrain, so we could concentrate on other important aspects of a long hike—things like stepping up our pace, packing adequate equipment and food for five days and then properly rationing it. We learned about all these things and, to our dismay, a whole lot more.

We arrived in the sleepy town of Cumberland at around 8:00 p.m. on September 11th, having left one of our cars in Brunswick. A short hike from the train brought us to the Holiday Inn where we checked in, visited the restaurant for a final good meal, and then turned in for what we thought would probably be our last comfortable night's sleep for a week.

Saturday we awoke early to gray skies and a heavy mist that hung in the air like a wet blanket. We thought this was not a very auspicious start to our first long-distance hike, but the misty grayness added to the consummate beauty of the Potomac River paralleling the towpath. We were both excited about the prospect of attempting to hike in some rainy weather to see how we would deal with it. That experience was part of our "planned" regimen for preparing for the A.T. We quickly established a reasonable pace and took our requisite snack breaks at the appropriate times. We looked forward to making camp at the hiker-biker site some fifteen miles ahead—a wholly attainable goal we thought. It came to pass that we had not learned our lesson about setting lofty goals from our Assateague trip. As the day wore on, we became cognizant of the fact that even though the trail was flat and devoid of any large rocks to abuse our feet, we were developing sore hot spots on several toes. We found this to be very curious and a bit disconcerting, considering all the foot-toughening terrain we had withstood in earlier training. We deduced our foot problems were the result of "repetitive motion." We were stepping on the same exact spots on our feet over and over for hours. Little did we know these hot spots were just the beginning of what was to be our greatest adversary of the trip.

Late in the afternoon, with our feet now unbearably tender, we arrived at our scheduled stop for the day—a very nice hiker-biker site. These hiker-biker sites are strategically placed every four to six miles along the C&O, generally near one of the restored lock houses, and most are complete with a picnic table, a port-o-john, and a water pump. Because we had researched all of the campsite location information prior to setting out on this adventure, we had been quite comfortable with our pace and with how much water we were consuming. We planned on replenishing our hydration packs at the campsite so imagine our horror when we found the handle missing from the water pump. Evidently it had been removed by National Park Service personnel because the water in the cistern was not fit to drink.

Psychologically we had shut down thinking this site was the end of our day. We became quite demoralized realizing we would now need to go another four to six miles at a hurried pace in order to arrive at the next site before nightfall. Even so, we were not sure there would be water there either. Our initial reaction was to point an ill-guided finger at each other for putting us in this situation. After several minutes of apologies back and forth (and more than a few deep breaths), we resigned ourselves to the fact we were in this together and were suffering equally. It is amazing just what level of compassion is derived from a shared experience, be it good or bad. We grumbled, swore a few choice words, and then put our packs back on and headed out onto the trail, now determined to use this negative situation as a growing experience.

The next five miles were the most grueling we had ever done. By the time we reached the next site, both of us were suffering mercilessly with sore feet and aching legs. This was not a situation either of us would have wanted to experience alone. Though being individually strong-willed, the toll of this day required a level of positive spirit neither of us could have summoned up individually. We simply kept reassuring and encouraging each other and shared every step.

The agony we were in harkened back to our first real hike on the A.T. in 2000. On that fateful trip from Ashby Gap to Harper's Ferry in the stifling heat of July, I suffered from knees that hurt so much that walking downhill felt like Tonya Harding had done a 'Nancy Kerrigan' on them. "Mom" sweated so profusely that everything she had on was soaked. That factor, along with an ill-fitting pack hip belt, contributed to a painful rash on her hipbones. We also both suffered from a measurable degree of blisters. That trip, however uncomfortable, taught us several valuable lessons:

1. Never wear cotton clothes, even though they are less expensive than technical hiking clothes;

2. Drink water on a regular basis. I experienced a bout of heat exhaustion that knocked me to the ground and scared the crap out of me;

3. Carry as little weight in your pack as possible; and

4. Add trekking poles to our arsenal of equipment to minimize future knee pain and stress on our backs.

Despite those epiphanies, the level of distress we were now feeling seemed totally new—and we did not like it.

At dusk, we arrived at the next site and here the water pump had a handle. Yet, to add further frustration to an already difficult day, the pump handle was stuck and it took an incredible amount of effort to break it loose. In doing so, I managed to pinch the web of skin between my thumb and forefinger in the pump mechanism, leaving a painful blood blister. To say we were disappointed and extremely unhappy would have been an understatement. This was simply another taste of life's unpredictability on the trail, and we had failed rather miserably in coping with it. Of course, up until the writing of this book we were the only people on earth who knew that!

The lack of water, blistered feet, and numbing fatigue made for short tempers. After a few unprovoked snipes at each other, we decided that completing our daily campsite tasks in silence was a prudent course of action. We set up our tent, filled our hydration packs, and then ate dinner as quickly as our tired and ravaged limbs would allow. It is amazing what a full stomach and few moments of rest can do. There were profuse apologies to each other for our less-than-compassionate outbursts and suddenly we were back on solid relational ground. We called it a day, optimistic we would miraculously recover overnight and be ready to do fifteen miles the next day. Unfortunately, that was not the case. We woke the next morning to beautiful weather which, as it turned out, was the only redeeming virtue of the day. Our feet were a mess. We put aside thoughts of giving up and called upon our mutual resolve of doing whatever needed to be done to succeed. We spent the first hour of the day nursing all of our blisters and protecting the remaining hot spots on our feet so we could make it a few miles further down the trail.

We were able to hike only nine miles on Sunday and even that was a painfully slow process. We decided we needed to rest our blistered feet and aching legs. We knew a nine-mile day would significantly impact our schedule, but decided to leave the trail at Paw Paw, West Virginia, where we could stay at the hostel and nurse our wounds. This was not a decision we came to without much personal soul-searching, because this indicated a level of defeat we were not accustomed to accepting. However, our will to succeed took a back seat to the realization that continuing could very well be the death knell of the entire trip. Our practical and calculating natures held sway over any deep-seeded ambition we had to courageously trudge on and hope for the best. On the up side, our mutual experience with the pain brought with it a new level of understanding that helped to negate our sense of defeat. The last mile into Paw Paw was torturous road walking, requiring us to encourage each other to take each painful step. We eventually made it to town, after spending a good deal of time diving into ditches so we would not be hit by oncoming traffic. When we reached our destination, we tearfully offered each other our sincere and loving gratitude for being there for each other under such awful circumstances. It was a moment of endearment that overrode all the ill-effects of the day. What we learned was that being willing to accept what the trail threw at us was more important than trying to overcome it. The measure of success was in enduring.

Our evening at the Paw Paw hostel was pleasant and restorative in a small West Virginia town kind of way. A night's rest, copious amounts of Vitamin "I," and massaging each other's feet and legs for what seemed like hours did us a world of good. The human body is an incredible marvel of creation, and its ability to heal never ceases to amaze us. When we awoke in the morning, we expected to still be crippled and unable to move. But to our amazement, aside from the tenderness of our feet and some unmistakable stiffness we had grown accustomed to on these hikes, we were in remarkably good shape. We hobbled down the road back to the trail with renewed enthusiasm. By the time we reached the historic Paw Paw Tunnel, we were pretty much back up to our normal walking speed. The lingering pain was a badge of honor we carried with us the remainder of the day and the hike. In preparation for what we felt would be a slow, torturous day, we mentally resigned ourselves to the fact that even if we could only walk one mile per hour, we would still cover ten miles or so and that would be just fine. This was a revelation for two people who believed falling even the slightest bit short of a predetermined goal was a total failure!

We spent the better part of the day having fun—just taking in all the natural beauty around us, and the myriad of wildlife we saw included turtles, deer, muskrat, beavers and birds. As we approached the next hiker-biker site to have lunch, the sky grew ominous and we had a feeling this was going to be another interesting day. Having endured the negative aspects of the day before created a belief in us that we could handle anything this particular day might hand us. It turned out we would need to lean on that belief more than we could imagine.

As we finished our lunch, we heard what sounded like rolling thunder, but "Mom" insisted that it was only a large plane in the distance. Then we heard it again and prepared for the worst. Now we had to make a decision: pitch our tent and ride out the storm or keep going and deal with whatever Mother Nature threw at us. Since the site we were at was on the bank of, and only a few feet above, the Potomac River, we decided this was probably not a good place to ride out a storm of unknown intensity and duration. So, off we went, agreeing that no matter what happened weather-wise we would keep going. Within minutes we were in the middle of the most intense storm we had ever experienced on any trail. Although we had our rain jackets on, we were soaked within minutes. This episode confirmed the fact that the rain gear we had, though lightweight, was simply not adequate for this type of weather. We vowed to purchase better rain gear as soon as this hike was over. What we have found over the years is that rain gear serves to keep you more warm than dry.

Gore-Tex aside, our boots were soon soaked to the point where our feet were sloshing around inside them, which did nothing to help our blisters heal. Our clothes now weighed twice what they did when dry. Not long after the storm started we reached a point on the trail where we walked beneath an abandoned railroad trestle. As we looked ahead we saw a shadowy figure approaching from the other direction. This was a bit disconcerting because we had not seen another human being since leaving the tunnel in Paw Paw. Were our eyes deceiving us because of the intensity of the rain? The figure grew closer and we could see this foreboding silhouette was dressed all in camouflage and was carrying a crossbow and a quiver full of arrows.

Immediately the strains of *"Dueling Banjos"* echoed all around us and we had a sinking feeling we could be doomed to a fate worse than blisters and wet clothes. You see, there is no hunting allowed along the trail. So what was this person really doing here? We anxiously drew near to him, and as we passed in the driving rain he asked in a somewhat sinister tone,

"Are we having fun yet?"

We hurriedly walked by and I fumbled for my miniature penknife to use as a means of defense should we need it.

"Yeah, we are," we responded gleefully, hoping not to invoke any type of aggressive physical response from him.

Our pace immediately quickened and until I felt we were clearly out of crossbow range, I constantly looked over my shoulder to make sure he was still heading away from us. An ironic twist to this unnerving confrontation was that we later found out the section of trail on which all this occurred was called "Devil's Alley." We found that to be amusingly weird!

We used this bizarre chance encounter, which in retrospect was probably not as ominous as we made it out to be, as an opportunity to concoct a tale of hiking intrigue. As the day wore on, we endlessly recounted the story, each time embellishing it with our own anecdotal color. Ever since that fateful encounter in "Devil's Alley," we have been creating stories from the trail as part of our hiking routine. It has provided us with not only a source of free entertainment but has also allowed us to more easily pass the time when the trail is less than inspiring. The fact we often complete each other's thoughts and statements anyway makes development of our "trail tales" a relatively fluid and humorous process.

The rain finally let up, but we were now so wet it really did not make any difference. We resolved ourselves to the fact that the rest of the day was going to be very uncomfortable. We survived our first major weather-related incident and, in the back of our minds, were comforted by the fact that at our next stop we were going to get a good meal at Bob's Place—a restaurant near the Little Orleans Campground. But once again our dreams were dashed, and we were forced to rely on our wherewithal, along with a large dose of good fortune.

Bob's Place had been a very rustic restaurant, complete with a bar, and from what we were told, provided a very good menu. Unfortunately, it burned down several months prior to our arrival. A new and more modern log structure was now erected in its place, and though its reputation for great food was still intact, Bob had developed a more relaxed attitude regarding when it would be open. As we walked in a light rain onto the wrap-around porch, with visions of a hot meal and possibly a cold *Coors Light* dancing in our heads, we were abruptly wrenched back to reality by a sign that read, *"Closed – Gone Fishing."* Are you kidding me? That only happens in Mayberry. But, come to think of it, this area was a lot like Mayberry. No problem: we would go to "Plan B!" "Plan "B" involved calling one of the hostels or bed and breakfasts on the list "Mom" had compiled. They would summarily pick us up and take us back to reality for the night. Evidently, Bob had taken everyone in town fishing with him because no one answered any of the numbers we called. It was looking more and more as if we would have to pitch the tent at the nearby campground and spend a damp and fitful night there.

While we sat on the porch contemplating our dilemma, several trail bikers showed up. They were as wet as we were. But we discovered, as we spoke with them, they had better plans for the evening than we. They had arranged for a person to pick them up and take them to a ranch in Pennsylvania for the night. Wow! We may be off the hook! We could already feel a warm shower and clean sheets. Shortly thereafter, a two-tone Ford F-250, with a crew cab and a special homemade rack in the bed for carrying bicycles, pulled up and out jumped a grizzled farmer with a scruffy red beard. This could quite possibly be our first experience with a "Trail Angel"—those saviors of the trail who, at just the right time, provide various forms of assistance and sustenance to lowly hikers. As he loaded everyone's bike into the back of his truck, we inquired as to whether or not he had room for us at the ranch. He answered that he did, but qualified his answer with what it would cost us for the night. At that point food and dry clothes were a bigger issue than price. We threw our packs in the back, jumped into the cramped crew cab, and off we went.

We drove for what seemed like one-hundred miles into the hills of Pennsylvania, all the while chatting with each other as the truck's defroster struggled to compete with the fog on the windows created by everyone's wet clothes. At one point, our "angel" Leon pointed out that we were passing the "original" Mason-Dixon Line marker. Before we knew it, we arrived at the Buck Valley Ranch. Leon and his wife Nadine had been running this ranch for years and made a respectable living by giving horseback trips through the Pennsylvania mountains, as well as putting up bikers and hikers from the C&O. We were escorted into a huge old farmhouse replete with Nadine's collection of ceramic figurines and the most eclectic array of artwork we had ever seen. We were shown to our rooms, and after a delightful hot shower we changed into some wonderfully dry clothes. Nadine informed us that if we gave her our wet clothes she would take them to their house across the yard and dry them for us. This was amazing seeing she was not expecting us. She nicknamed us, "The Strays." Leon showed us around the house to let us know where the refrigerator full of beer was located and warned us not to stand by the fridge barefoot because we would probably get a shock when we touched the door handle. He then announced dinner would be ready shortly. What came next blew us away!

Besides being a cowboy for many years, Leon had developed quite a knack as a chef. As we sat down for dinner, we were amazed by all the options he presented us. There was salad, fresh tomatoes, chicken, potatoes, corn, rolls, and our choice of beverage—enough food to feed twenty people and we savored every bit of it. While we stuffed in the last bit of chicken, Nadine announced we must leave room for Leon's homemade peach cobbler and ice cream. At this point, returning to the trail the next day did not sound like such an inviting idea. We sat around the living room for hours talking with our new friends. After a few introspective moments sitting on the front porch and looking up at an incredible black and star-filled sky, we headed to our bedroom.

Considering what we had been through the last two days, this oasis from the trials of the C&O truly uplifted our spirits. The warmth of dry clothes, having full stomachs, and being able to sit together under that star-filled sky provided us with a moment to reflect on our good fortune. Our contentment also renewed our desire to reassert our love and devotion for each other no matter what the circumstances. We would discover during our A.T. adventure that this feeling would play a key role in sustaining us through some very difficult days and would heighten the joy we would feel on the good ones. Sharing the emotional wonder of these types of moments strengthened our relationship.

After a stomach-stretching country breakfast the next morning, Leon drove us back to Little Orleans and the trail. We were completely re-energized, so we picked up the pace and just walked, talked, laughed, looked, and wondered. Our sore and blistered feet were still a primary source of aggravation for us. But despite that, it was an unbelievably beautiful day.

One of the wonderful advantages of being on a trail is being almost entirely out of contact with the outside world. With no radio or TV, we concentrate on the immediate world within eyesight and our stress levels tend to go to the negative side of zero. Not being emotionally influenced by world events allows us to wholeheartedly relate to each other without outside interference. However, there is also a downside to this as we were about to find out.

We walked along, thoroughly enjoying ourselves and the beautiful weather and talked about the fact that, despite all the unexpected turns of events so far, we were going to complete the entire one-hundred-thirty miles to Brunswick just as we had planned. But only hours after heading out, we began to notice a flurry of activity along the trail involving employees of the National Park Service. The rumble of pick-up trucks towing flatbed trailers down the trail now constantly interrupted the solitude of our trip. Also disturbing was the fact these trailers were hauling port-o-johns and picnic tables—lots of them.

Since we were deliberately—not to mention—joyfully incommunicado all week, we were not aware a huge hurricane, Isabel, was scheduled to hit the mid-Atlantic sometime over the next few days. As a precaution against losing valuable park property to a potentially flooding Potomac River, the NPS was picking up everything at the hiker-biker sites and taking it all to a more secure location. Even as we watched the campsites being stripped bare, it never occurred to us we would need to cut our trip short. We were just reveling in awe of the beautiful weather, our renewed good fortune, and a growing devotion to each other. We would just have to come up with alternate plans in order to deal with the fact there would no longer be services, like water, available at our remaining overnight stops. We could still get our water from the river, and as for the port-o-johns, they were a nice convenience but not entirely necessary. We had our trusty shovel and plenty of toilet paper. We had survived so much already and we were not going to let something as trivial as a hurricane stop us now. However, developing survival plans was a short-lived endeavor. A park ranger soon approached and informed us we would need to leave the trail by the next day. Because of the storm, no one was going to be allowed to use the trail until the danger of flooding had passed.

We were devastated! Our car was parked another three-day's hike down the trail. If there was one thing we learned on this hike so far, it was that we needed to look at every turn of events, be they good or bad, as an adventure. Each ill-fated turn of events was an obstacle we needed to overcome and still keep our spirits high. Such was this situation and such is life. Within fifteen minutes, we worked out our exit strategy—all the while keeping up our pace as if nothing had changed.

Our plan was now to continue hiking until we reached Hancock, Maryland, where we would leave the trail, hike into town, and find a place to stay. During a snack break, "Mom" pulled out her cell phone (yes, we do admit to the use of technology, especially if it is something that can help us out in an emergency) and called the *Super 8 Motel* in Hancock.

Compared to the previous part of the week, our last evening of the adventure and the ride to Brunswick the following day, were relatively uneventful. We strolled through town, past a captivating, though unusual, array of mom and pop storefronts, off-brand gas stations and the town's culinary hot spot, *Pizza Hut*, until we reached the motel. Having spent all week walking on relatively flat ground, the steep climb up to the motel presented us with a rather unexpected challenge. We were very tired, extremely hot and sore, a tad smelly, and more than a bit frustrated. The realization we were finishing this trip without reaching our goal sapped what little energy we had left. However, this was not the time to wallow in self-pity. We reassured each other we had done our best and agreed that being satisfied with that fact was not simply a rationalization on our part but a reason for celebration. We had grown from this adventure in so many ways, both individually and as a couple. We now possessed a growing belief that by the time 2006 came around, we would be ready to tackle the Appalachian Trail. More importantly, we felt we would be conditioned enough and our relationship strong enough to survive, and possibly even flourish, through such an undertaking as the A.T. Believing this provided a source of joy and excitement.

The air conditioning and hot shower at the motel were welcome amenities. We ordered dinner from a local restaurant and had it delivered to our room. As we ate, we watched the news reports about Isabel, and based on the predictions by the National Weather Service, it was probably good we would not be on the trail for the next few days. Nevertheless, in the back of our minds there was still the nagging feeling we had somehow failed. It was a difficult feeling to share. We had been defeated by the whims of nature and had not been allowed to challenge them to see if we could defeat what was thrown in our path.

We decided that the only way, other than hitchhiking, to get from Hancock to Brunswick, where our car was parked, was to get a cab. We knew this was an expensive proposition but it was our only other option. As it turned out, Hancock only had one cab company so we considered ourselves very blessed by the fact that these folks were willing to put aside all their other customers to take us the thirty-some miles to our car. The next morning we rose early, jumped in the cab, and we were off, weaving our way through the scenic countryside of northern Maryland until we reached Brunswick—and our car.

Months later we realized we had not failed at all. Each horrendous and equally welcome moment of our hike was a source of education, a triumph over self-imposed physical limits and the strengthening of the bond between us—a bond that would be repeatedly challenged as we took on the Appalachian Trail.

Camel's Hump

The final critical element of our thru-hike preparation was nothing we could adequately prepare for anywhere near where we live. We are considered "flatlanders" because we live in a state where an elevation of 1,200 feet constitutes a rolling hillside being designated a mountain. Therefore, it was impossible for us to experience the unique thrill of hiking above tree line. We had to go to the source, Vermont, and take a hike that would expose us to what turned out to be a nerve-wracking experience.

In September of 2005 we made a trip to northern Vermont, near Waterbury, to hike the infamous "Camel's Hump" on the Long Trail. At 4,083 feet, this is the state's third highest peak. To say this weekend trip was a revelation is an understatement! We hit the Monroe Trail near Waterbury, Vermont, early Friday morning and it was an immediate uphill climb not unlike the trek up Weaverton Cliffs north of Harper's Ferry. There was fog, a steady drizzle, and the temperature was in the mid-50s. The trail was not overly difficult but strenuous enough to work up quite a sweat due to the clothes we wore to keep dry. Shortly thereafter we learned another valuable wilderness lesson: Do not let people know you are a "stranger in a strange land" when you are hiking unfamiliar territory. Only later, after reaching the summit, did the similarity to receiving directions in New York City from a native New Yorker aptly come to mind.

Partway up the first ascent, we took a break and met a couple from New Jersey. When we told them this was our maiden trek up "Camel's Hump," they graciously offered us instruction on which series of trails we should take in order to have the most memorable experience. Hey, bring it on! That is what we are here for! Based on their self-proclaimed knowledge of the mountain, our trek would now lead us from the Monroe Trail onto the Dean Trail, then onto The Long Trail and back for what, we were told, would be a most picturesque trip. At first blush, this sharing of information between hikers seemed like a very hospitable thing to do. In actuality, unbeknownst to us, where they directed us was up the most difficult and dangerous route we could have taken—the South approach.

As we passed Beaver Pond and took in the sight of numerous moose tracks in the mud on its banks, we were still shrouded in a dense fog that ebbed and flowed out of the vast landscape like waves endlessly caressing a sandy beach. For awhile, this fog was a blessing in disguise because if we had been able to see the height and immensity of the mountain we were about to traverse, we may have altered our plans considerably. Then, for one brief moment, the fog lifted. As I looked up, I saw what could only be described as a miniature Mt. Rainier towering hundreds of feet over our heads. I immediately pointed out this massive rock outcropping to "Mom."

"I think that is where we are headed," I stammered.

Either out of her innate sense of direction, which is generally better than mine, or simply out of denial, she stated,

"No, I don't think so."

Thus, we trudged on, undaunted.

Just below the summit, we ran into our first real taste of the type of rock scrambling we heard we would encounter all through the New England section of the A.T. What a surprise it was to see blazes prominently painted on the face of boulders as opposed to their normal location on tree trunks. We became increasingly unnerved because we had never experienced this type of trail surface before. And because of the light mist coating the rocks, footing was a bit dicey at times. Distressing hints of doubt and fears of impending disaster began to attack our otherwise unfettered determination to keep going. We made it over the first set of geological hurdles and mistakenly believed the worst was behind us.

Ah, but what was this? A wooden sign indicating there was a way out of climbing to the top of this monstrous mountain. (It was monstrous to us anyway. Remember, we are from Maryland.) The sign stated we only had 0.2 mile to the summit, but it looked more like two miles, with no semblance of a summit visible anywhere. We briefly debated whether we should take this trail to the other side of the mountain and head back down. Then our "Type A" personalities kicked in and we decided there was no way we were not going to finish what we had started. We had come this far and we weren't quitting. The gauntlet had been laid down, so we picked it up and went fearlessly upward.

Before we fully recovered from the next—nearly vertical—section of boulders, we were catapulted out of the lush tree cover into the stark and visually grandiose area above the tree line known as the "alpine area." Adding to the psychological and visual impact of suddenly emerging into this area, the fog had thinned just enough to where we could finally see the top of the mountain. *"Oh shit! We are going up there?"* In addition, we could not see any easy way to get there.

Neither "Mom" nor I have a great fear of heights, but when we proceeded around the edge of a cliff—3,000 feet or so in the air with our butts hanging out in the wild blue yonder while concentrating on locating our next hand- and foothold—we quickly grasped the wisdom of not looking anywhere but straight ahead. It was a bit terrifying and the term "adrenaline rush" took on a completely new meaning. At one juncture, while "Mom" and I gingerly negotiated our way around a large boulder, she decided to stop on a ledge just wide enough for our feet in order to catch a quick glimpse of the surrounding landscape. I realized I was perched in a rather precarious position and shouted, with an obvious tone of fear in my voice,

"Don't stop! Keep moving!"

It was not until later that I discovered I was not alone in being scared as hell with ascending this section of the trail. It was, in a perverted sense, reassuring to know we had both developed a few more gray hairs traversing this area. At the same time, we gained a healthy and adoring respect for the mountain we had climbed.

Obeying the rules of protecting the alpine areas, we gave nature the respect it was certainly due. We stayed off the small areas of vegetation on the trail despite the fact these were the very areas that offered the best footing to the top. We simply stayed bent over, head and shoulders to the wind, hearts in our throats, and with our eyes fixed on those boulders, blazes, and cairns just a few feet in front of us. To the veteran hikers who were sitting at various spots along this section, we probably looked pretty silly while we gingerly made our way up—never once standing upright until we reached the summit.

Silly looking or not, as we came over the crest we presented them with more than just comic relief. When we reached the summit, for the first time that day, the fog blew away and the sun came out. For more than sixty miles in every direction we viewed the most intoxicating views we had ever seen. Those other hikers had huddled in 30 °F to 40 °F temperatures all morning waiting for this moment. But here we were, hiking rookies, and we got to experience it from the very second we arrived. Our decision to endure the difficulty and not take the bypass below the summit was graciously rewarded by the very God that got us this far in the first place.

We completely absorbed the wonder of the endless landscape below us, had a photo session with a local caretaker, and congratulated each other on surviving *"The Hump."* The wealth of emotions that rushed to the surface culminated in an intense appreciation for each other and for the loving bond that carried us to this time and place. No other aspect of "real life" could have produced such strong feelings. It was a moment to cherish.

We were beginning to get hungry so we needed to find a place out of the wind to have lunch. As we headed down the north side of the mountain on The Long Trail, we then realized our "friends" from New Jersey had duped us earlier that morning. It seems most people come <u>UP</u> the north side because it is noticeably easier, requires fewer scrambling skills, and has fewer plunging abysses on either edge of the trail. They had sent us up the most difficult and considerably more dangerous side of the mountain so we basked in the emotional and physical triumph of having done it the hard way.

At the base of the mountain, we turned and gave it one final, adoring look. We had done it and could check off one more training goal in our quest to conquer the A.T. Our confidence was increasing; and because we had conquered both the mountain and our fears together, the emotional bond between us grew ever stronger. We discovered we had more courage than we ever imagined. We were more psyched than we had ever been—about ourselves and about each other! And above all, we had FUN! Bring it on!

Shenandoah National Park

Another notable preparation hike was an ill-fated Thanksgiving holiday adventure on the A.T. through Shenandoah National Park, from Loft Mountain Campground to Front Royal, Virginia. A sudden cold snap brought with it snow that blanketed the ground and temperatures plummeted to 9 °F overnight. We set up our tent inside the Rock Spring Shelter so as to minimize the effects of the wind, but it was only minimally effective; the wind simply gusted and swirled inside the shelter. As we huddled in our wind-blown tent, we became acutely aware of our lack of preparation for cold weather. Despite bringing our water bladders into the tent, overnight they froze solid, which left us no water for cooking the next morning. Our 15 °F sleeping bags were simply not up to the task either. "Mom" put on virtually every piece of clothing she had with her, but I still had to continually rub her legs and arms in order to get her uncontrollable shivering to subside. We spent a restless and fearful night wondering if our lack of preparation would come to a disastrous conclusion.

Morning found the inside of our tent coated in a thin layer of ice crystals. While attempting to prepare oatmeal to warm us both up, I started to become hypothermic and was unable to control my hands. Luckily for us, we had the foresight to have taken a wilderness first aid class and knew how to deal with this potentially dangerous situation. Despite this training, a level of concern, just short of terror, made repeated sinister appearances. We decided we might not be in a position, either physically or emotionally, to successfully challenge the cold. After quickly packing up all our belongings and while still fighting off the numbing cold, we headed toward Skyland Resort—all the while searching for a source of water and attempting to thaw out our hydration bladders. One would think because we were not sweating, we would need minimal amounts of hydration. This was simply not the case. Regular amounts of water are as necessary in the cold as they are in the heat of the summer. After having no success in finding water or defrosting our water bladders, we realized we were in dire straits and had to make a critical and disconcerting choice: we would end our hike at Skyland Resort and evaluate what we needed to do to see that this type of situation never happened again. We were reminded again that we would learn more from our failures than we would ever learn from our successes. For two people who normally plan and prepare so completely so as to ensure success, accepting failure, even if it allowed us to learn something, was still a bitter pill to swallow.

(To read more about our early hiking adventures and, in some instances, misadventures, visit www.rmghadventures.com and www.trailjournals.com.)

The years from 2001 to 2006 were filled with many other preparation hikes—each one with its own set of learning experiences and each with an opportunity for us to understand and appreciate each other's strengths and weaknesses. For example, we learned that for our physical well-being and to minimize the disgruntled gazes from "Mom" that could reduce steel to molten liquid, I was not the person who should be leading our hikes. My stride, though only a half-inch or so longer than "Mom's," was superseded by my innate "need for speed." Especially going uphill, I would continually leave her behind in a state of total frustration and fatigue. When doing ascents, my tendency was to simply put my head down, lengthen my stride, mentally get into a "zone," and keep walking until I reached the top. On the other hand, "Mom" would take her time going up, stop every so often for a break to rest her legs and catch her breath, and then proceed on. In several vain attempts to lead, I attempted adopting her style but continually hiked at my regular uphill pace. When I stopped to rest, I did so only long enough for her to catch up. Then I was off again leaving her behind to take her own rest break. Wrong! The idea was for me to slow down and rest when she did. Despite my best efforts, I was never able to break my "rabbit" style of hiking. Arriving at our destination a few minutes earlier than if she had been leading in no way offset the disgruntled looks and "less-than-loving" tongue-lashing I received by walking so fast. If our marital bliss was not to become a fleeting memory, it would be essential that she lead and I would resolve myself to mirroring her pace.

"Mom," however, could fly going downhill, but my knees just would not allow me to keep pace with her. It was decided I should lead on descents where the inevitable pain in my knees could keep us at the speed of a casual stroll.

Our preparation for thru-hiking the A.T. had a purpose and flavor that reflected our unique personalities. How did other couples prepare for their attack on the granddaddy of all trails?

Carbomb:

> *"By late 2004 we had definite plans to hike the A.T. We had purchased a Data Book and the Appalachian Trail Thu-Hiker Companion, but we wanted to experience the A.T. firsthand. We got our chance while visiting North Carolina for my brother's wedding. We made tentative plans for an overnight hike on the A.T. to be followed by a raft trip down the Nantahala River. We arrived at the Nantahala Outdoor Center (NOC),[a Mecca for both hikers and whitewater kayakers], a little later than we had expected and inquired about the best route to take on this area of the trail. They suggested hiking the Wesser Creek Trail up to the A.T., spending the night at the Wesser Bald Shelter and then following the A.T. back to the NOC. The route seemed simple so we turned down the opportunity to buy a map and drove to the Wesser Creek Trailhead. The creek was swollen from the rains created by Hurricane Frances which had recently pounded the area. We hit the trail around 2:00 p.m. after quickly packing our gear into my old backpack and "Lichen's" smaller daypack. The trail was wet and there were quite a few blowdowns (trees across the trail blown down by strong winds), making the approximate four-mile uphill hike go quite slow; but we were having a great time. We reached the junction with the A.T. about dusk and turned right, thinking the shelter was just down the trail. We didn't have a map and I, ignoring all my Boy Scout training, decided to leave the Data Book in the car at the last minute. So we headed north on the A.T. for about thirty minutes, finally deciding that we must have made a wrong turn.*
>
> *By this time, it was too dark to hike without lights so we stopped to put our headlamps on and I realized I had forgotten my light (Be Prepared?). We turned around and headed back south on the A.T., with me tucked in right behind "Lichen" and her light. After a while we made it back to the trail intersection where we started. There seemed to be a clearing there but no shelter that we could see. Desperate, we continued hiking south on the A.T. hoping to find the shelter and get settled in for the night. Southbound, the trail headed*

uphill to Wesser Bald.I was having a harder and harder time following "Lichen" and her light on the muddy, slick trail. After tromping around for awhile longer, we agreed to camp at a spot on a small side trail we noticed earlier. We managed to get our camp set up with only one light and then thoroughly enjoyed the sub sandwiches we had purchased earlier in the day. Almost immediately after finishing our last pre-sleep chore, "Lichen's" light finally died. Because of the cloud cover there was no moon. It was so dark we could not even see our hands in front of our faces.

The next morning we got up and headed up to the Wesser Bald fire tower. Impressive views! We then started hiking north again, eventually discovering the shelter about 200 yards downhill and slightly off-trail from the intersection of the A.T. and the Wesser Creek Trail. We had been so close the night before! We signed the shelter register and headed back to the NOC. We were hooked!

During our 2006 A.T. hike, it was very exciting to get to the Wesser Bald fire tower and shelter. We had a wonderful time reminiscing about our previous visit and reveling in the fact that we were living out our plans. It was so satisfying to be able to stand at these locations again, but this time after having walked from Springer Mountain."

Enuff:

"Because it is my nature, I did the technical stuff. I researched equipment, tents, and stoves. We went on day hikes and overnights to test out gear and also spent a lot of time dealing with our shoes."

Too Much:

"Following all the instructions and advice from the WhiteBlaze.com website, we walked at least 50 miles in each pair of shoes to test them out and break them in."

Enuff:

"But the A.T. is a different animal. Walking fifty miles in a pair of boots is vastly different from hiking hundreds of miles in them. The shoes fit great for the initial fifty miles, but after four weeks the thrill was gone and they no longer fit well or felt comfortable."

Too Much:

"There was a big difference between wearing a shoe on a mild hike and then wearing that same shoe as you constantly trekked up and down mountains with a heavy pack on your back. I did the planning and logistics. WhiteBlaze.com was my main source of planning information and I absorbed as much of it as I could. We knew that hiking the A.T. would be extremely difficult, so my goal was for us to be as prepared as we could be and cut down on as many surprises as possible. I prepared for the hike much as I had prepared for marathons. For marathons, I memorized everything about the route: the distances, the course and scoured the elevation maps. I planned my training to run a certain number of miles per week, researched what was the best clothing for me and knew what nutrition to bring. Even with all the hike planning, so many things that happened on the trail were out of our control; they were things you did not even think about. You were left with no alternative but to adapt to changing circumstances, which is something I am not very good at. The result was that there were more than a few emotional rough spots for me on the way."

Enuff:

"We read as many books on the A.T. experience as we could lay our hands on. We wanted to familiarize ourselves, thoroughly, with the wilderness experience; right down to how to go to the bathroom on the trail. The reality of the trail is that you still have to deal with things as they come up but reading all those books really helped. We would not have gone out without having read them. We had family support sending us supplies and "Too Much's" sister acted as storage site for the equipment we would need to swap out as the seasons changed."

Too Much:

"At the same time we were making preparations for the hike, we were also engrossed in planning and preparing for the other transitions in our life. Because of that, not all of our time could be devoted to the hike, which made things a bit harder but a lot more exciting. After the hike, we were moving to the Rose Bud Indian Reservation in South Dakota where we would be working in the hospital. We had a house to sell, had to put our belongings in storage, *and had a host of other loose ends to tie up. The trail became just another unknown that we had to deal with."*

Enuff:

"Our physical preparation for the hike was minimal because of our previous marathon conditioning. Most of our preparation centered upon issues of logistics, equipment, and the mental conditioning necessary for such a long odyssey."

Too Much:

"Interestingly enough, we had to educate the general public and our families about what we were going to be doing for the next six months. We had to assure them that we were not crazy and that we had, at least, some idea of what we would be involved in doing.

Our kids initially hiked with us, and we naively thought we would be hiking ten to twelve miles a day in Georgia, which at the time was impossible not only for us but especially for the kids. Though we thought we had prepared for such a thing, the A.T. quickly taught us that we would have to be even more flexible and alter our plans to accommodate the trail conditions and other people—like our friends, who hiked with us in Pennsylvania. Our basic knowledge of the trail, resulting from all of our preparation, allowed us to make those adjustments; though not always without some level of frustration."

Robin:

"Mapman" and I first read several books on the A.T., specifically on lightweight hiking and also read up on how to dehydrate food. Right before our thru-hike, we did a number of long hikes. In the fall, we completed a trek of 450 miles and, in the winter, we did another 350 miles in Hawaii. The purpose of these "training hikes" was to get comfortable with our equipment and, equally as important, to get our feet broken in.

The first week on the A.T., we were able to hike 100 miles, and we kept up an average pace of 16 miles per day throughout the entire trip. Obviously, the preparation-hike miles were worth it."

The Final Details

As the date of our departure for the A.T. grew ever closer, we still had several things we needed to complete. One of the final steps in getting ready for our A.T. adventure was preparing and packaging all of the meals we would need. We had heard horror stories about many of the marginally edible prepackaged backpacker meals and their unusual flavors, so we taste-tested some to see if the rumors were true. What we discovered was that we often had to read the meal description on the package to determine exactly what we were eating. So, we began a quest to come up with our own delicacies.

We purchased a dehydrator, two vacuum sealing machines (we burned up the first one) and numerous books on dehydrated meals for backpacking. Three of the finest books we found on this topic were *"Lipsmackin' Backpackin"* and *"Lipsmackin Vegetarian Backpackin,"* both by Christine & Tim Connors and *"The Appalachian Trail Food Planner"* by Lou Adsmond. We also spent a great deal of time perusing books on nutrition to locate lightweight foods that contained a lot of carbohydrates, calories, and fat. What a pleasure it was to be able to go to the supermarket and deliberately, with total, guiltless abandon, purchase foods that were just loaded with the things rarely a part of our regular diet. At this point, we were quite sure we were going to thoroughly enjoy eating on the trail.

Now, just for clarification, dehydrating and vacuum sealing all our own food was not an inexpensive alternative to prepackaged hiker meals. However, it did open up a completely new world of culinary alternatives and preempted us from living strictly on *Ramen noodles*, peanut butter, and mac 'n cheese. We acquired a bit of a reputation on the A.T. for eating some rather exotic cuisine, even when we prepared it from scratch in camp. All of this was part of our goal to stay healthy. Because "Mom" had worked her way through college as a cook, coming up with nutritious and tasty meals was a challenge she looked forward to.

We found a dry whole milk product, called *NIDO*, at a local international market. It provided us with the fat lacking in non-fat dry milk. "Mom" pre-mixed this milk with high protein *Kashi Go-Lean* cereal, *Go-Lean Crunch* cereal, and orange-flavored *Craisins* and had it for breakfast every day of the hike. I mixed it with *Carnation Instant Breakfast* and protein powder and drank it every other day. We also found we could purchase, online, an entire assortment of nutritional bars by the case at a fraction of what it would have cost us in the store. You just have to love the Internet when it comes to bargain hunting!

(See Appendix #3 for a list of foods we prepared ourselves. We found them to be tasty and they provided the nutrients we needed on the trail.)

We gathered and prepared more and more food and shipping boxes, and our small townhouse became a food preparation and packaging factory—one that would make General Foods jealous. Our dining room and living room quickly became "Food Central," taking on the appearance of the local community food pantry. To the casual guest, it must have looked like we were preparing for Armageddon. With vacuum sealing and organizing all of our meals completed, our living room floor was carpeted with maps, trail guides and food, each packed in *Ziploc* bags, and each labeled with their respective contents. If we had stock in *Ziploc*, we would be millionaires by now just from the increases in sales generated during our preparation!

"Think you have enough toilet paper (TP) there, Windtalker?" Mom asked.

"Well, by my calculations, based on previous hikes, and having the average number of bowel movements per day that we have at home, and barring the contraction of Giardia, a roll should last us three days. With three to four days between mail drops, we should have one roll per box and one backup roll, just in case."

Now it was time to box up everything, label each one to arrive at each of our predetermined mail drops, and then deliver them to our support team, Mike and Diane Mathews. We have been friends with Mike and Diane for years, and since they are both avid campers and love the outdoors, they were more than happy to travel vicariously with us by shipping our mail drops. Little did they know they would need to build a major addition onto their home in order to handle all of our supplies. Without them, our trip would have been a lot less enjoyable and certainly more stressful. And, oh how I looked forward to opening up those boxes and finding "TP!"

Before leaving for Georgia, we needed to do two remaining things—put together the rest of our support team and make sure all of our bills got paid while we were away. We would have more than enough to deal with on the trail without having to concern ourselves with making sure the mortgage was paid and the electricity did not get shut off. Georgia, being our resident financial "wunderkind," took care of seeing that all of our bills were on electronic payment or paid in advance. Further, we paid off both of our cars, which eliminated the need to make car payments while we were gone.

Our support team included my daughter, Rebecca, who took care of our house, fed the fish, and watered our plants—and watered our plants—and watered our plants. By her own admission, her strength is in gerontology not horticulture, a fact we were made acutely aware of when we returned home. We love her just the same. "Mom's" daughter, Aja, became our website guru and designed and maintained www.rmghadventures.com so friends and family could follow our adventure, send us messages, and pray for our safety.

We shipped our summer gear to my parents, Ralph and Dottie, in Goode, Virginia, who would be providing trail support plus a place to take a few "zero days" when we hit Bearwallow Gap on the Blue Ridge Parkway.

In order to get home from Harper's Ferry, West Virginia, the psychological halfway point of the A.T., we would need a ride. This break would give us a few days off during which we could see our family and friends, take care of some personal business, and simply see if our house was still standing. Our friends from church, Jim and Karen Arnold, who were two of the most enthusiastic supporters of our impending adventure, volunteered to pick us up and bring us back to Harper's Ferry after we had suitably recovered.

Last, but in no way least, were "Mom's" parents, Vince and Anita— affectionately known on the A.T. as "V&A." Wanderers at heart, spending more time in their RV than in their home in Kentucky, they volunteered to drive in close proximity to the trail from Springer Mountain, Georgia, to Damascus, Virginia. They would then rejoin us in Great Barrington, Massachusetts, and stay with us until we reached Baxter State Park in Maine. They would provide us with "rolling" trail support; and in our minds, this was going to be an excellent way to eliminate hitchhiking into towns for overnight stays and would save us immeasurable time retrieving our mail drops.

Everything was finally in order and we felt we were ready. But even though on paper the preparations were complete, the unexpected and competing emotions of excitement and trepidation we were dealing with rumbled within us.

As "Mom" wrote, just days before we headed to the airport:

"Today is my last day at work and I am checking things off of my "to do" list right up until the last minute. No one I work with is surprised! The "lasts" really started hitting me last week. The countdown is under seven days. This was our last weekend at home— the last before we leave, and I am still trying to decide which clothes to take! It was our last day at church on Sunday and our photo,

standing triumphantly atop Camel's Hump, was projected on the big screens at the back of the stage. Everyone gave us a final send-off. People will be praying for us, rooting for us, and offering us trail support. Yesterday was my last day driving my Jeep, and tomorrow we fly to Atlanta in anticipation of several months of WALKING!"

The planning was done. The preparations were complete. All the details were covered. On March 23, 2006, we boarded our flight to Atlanta. We were REALLY going to do this—TOGETHER! Any thoughts we had about whether or not we would succeed, and any concerns we harbored about how our marriage would fare, were forced into the background by the excitement of this moment of truth.

"Mom's" Tips for Couples

- Writing down items on your dream list, life list, or "bucket list" is the first step to taking them from a dream to reality;

- Sharing your lists allows you to dream together and help each other accomplish them;

- Sharing those dreams cultivates a mutual commitment to pursuing a course of action;

- Open communication is a big part of planning any big dream;

- Enjoy the planning and preparation as an integral part of any adventure;

- Pay attention to what you can learn from what might appear to be failure. Each day provides lessons and experiences to build upon.

CHAPTER THREE

HIKE YOUR OWN HIKE

"There are only two ways to live your life. One is as though nothing is a miracle. The other is as if everything is." Albert Einstein

"Hike your own hike" is the historic credo of the A.T. thru-hiker. These four words set the parameters and tone for every hiker's journey as changing weather, unfamiliar terrain, physical ailments, and a seemingly unending host of other unseen circumstances come into play—altering the most intricate of plans. The longer you are on the trail, the more you come to realize the trail has a life of its own and you are inexplicably nothing more than a visitor. The trail treats you as if you are the new guy at the office, whose skills and abilities are suspect until you prove yourself worthy and are then welcomed with open arms. Such it is with the trail; you have to prove yourself, follow the rules, and respect and treasure all you see, hear, breathe, and touch. Then you are welcomed and become one with the trail.

But, you can never forget who is in charge. As soon as you get overconfident and start believing you and the trail are equal partners in this endeavor, it will remind you in some unequivocal and uncompromising manner, that you are still a guest in this place. If you allow yourself to be flexible and take each event as it comes, the good and the bad, the trail allows you to let go of the world, and it envelopes you, holding you close to its bosom.

For "Mom" and me, it was both a humble honor and a sincere privilege to hike the Appalachian Trail together. Considering our ages, we counted it a blessing to be able to chase this dream of ours; not a day went by when we did not think of the number of people who cannot, or do not, chase their own particular dreams. We lost count of how many times people along the trail approached us, and upon finding we were thru-hiking the A.T., stated:

"I have always wanted to do that."

"Then do it! It is never too late. Put it on your calendar," was always our reply.

What was especially heartbreaking to us was when some of these folks found out we were doing this adventure as a married couple; they simply shook their heads and lamented that their spouse would never do such a thing with them. If only they knew how rewarding taking on such an endeavor together could be.

As we now travel around the country making presentations about our thru-hike to professional organizations, churches, or groups who are involved in the great outdoors, the underlying theme is always the same: "Dream It! Plan It! Live It!"

Not everyone can live out a dream at the very moment it surfaces. However, if that is what you really want to accomplish, start planning for it. It took us years to reach the stage in our lives when all the pieces necessary to make our dream a reality had suddenly fallen into place like a cosmic puzzle. We were now "empty-nesters" with no enduring obligations to our children and had spent years living conservatively to build a comfortable level of financial security. Despite our sedentary jobs, we were relatively healthy. What better time could there be to pursue our particular dream?

More than just the pursuit of a dream, this adventure ultimately provided a classroom where we learned to make the dramatic paradigm shift from being goal-oriented to focusing more on the journey itself. As we would soon find out, all of our planning and preparation did nothing more than provide a psychological and emotional safety net for the harsh realities we would face in the wilderness. And as strong as we believed our marriage was, this journey would test every element of our relationship. The unique circumstances that define the wilderness experience would present a kaleidoscope of challenges heretofore unavailable in our "routine lives."

Our hike was to incorporate a number of facets that, to the traditional A.T. thru-hiker, would be quite "out of the norm." We would still be hiking all the same body-crucifying miles, just like everyone else—dealing with snow, heat, rain, aching feet and swarms of unrelenting mosquitoes. We were well aware this trip would be difficult enough, just on its own, so minimizing unnecessary suffering would play an important role in successfully completing the entire 2,174.6 miles from Georgia to Maine. In contrast to the multitude of "recent college graduate" hikers we would meet, we had the financial means to take advantage of many of the nicer amenities along the trail, all of which contributed to the fond memories we have of our journey.

For some, "hiking your own hike" means traveling the 2,174.6 miles of the trail as quickly as possible or "speed hiking." For others, it is to leave Springer Mountain in late January or February in order to beat the crowds and be the first one to summit Mt. Katahdin. For still others, it is to take as many blue blaze trails as time will permit in order to view sites not visible from the main trail. Blue blazing also allows hikers to spend as much time in trail towns as possible in order to take in the local flavor and form relationships with the locals that typify the heart and soul of the thru-hike experience. Then there are the "yellow blazers," who spend an inordinate amount of time following the yellow blazes down the roads between towns, as a substitute for miles on the trail.

One type of hiker, an elite group that literally thrives on a minimalist approach to hiking, is the "ultralight hiker." These hikers pare down their pack weights to a mere ten to twelve pounds and in doing so, we believe, choose to substitute safety, comfort, and convenience for the speed and gratification of carrying less weight. Their only clothes are the ones they are wearing; they sleep in a bivy sack or under their poncho, carry no water filter and sometimes no stove, and typically fall into the category of speed hikers.

And finally there is "slack-packing," which in purist hiking circles is a definite "no-no." Hikers stay at a motel or hostel, strip their full-sized packs down to a daypack, leaving their regular packs behind, and get a shuttle to a point twelve miles to twenty miles north, or in the case of "southbounders," south, of where they are currently staying. The idea is to hike back to the same motel or hostel where a soft bed, a restaurant, and a hot shower await them for a second night. Then, the following day, they don their full packs, get another shuttle back to the starting point from the previous day, and continue hiking.

Ultimately, the main reason for hiking the A.T. is that it is all about the journey. To steal a slogan from a political campaign years ago and give it a bit of a trail spin: *"It's about the hike, stupid!"*

No matter which style a hiker chooses, the underlying motivation pushing them forward, aside from the adventure of it all, is the calendar. Baxter State Park, home of Mt. Katahdin and the final summit, closes to overnight stays on October 15th each year. In the back of every northbound hiker's mind is the nagging reality that they need to arrive there in time to successfully complete their journey. To hike all that way and not be able to make the final summit is a gut-wrenching and demoralizing experience— one that is never forgotten and is even more difficult to recover from emotionally.

On our journey, there was one large group we regularly attempted to hike with; and frankly, it was a daily struggle to maintain our own pace and not be sucked into their hiking style. They were what we humorously called "the gazelles"—those mid-twenties, college graduates, or the youthful, deliberately unemployed—whose long legs and overabundance of energy allowed them to hike twenty to twenty-five miles a day. On rare occasions, the distance between shelters forced them to hike fewer miles. Those were the days when they stayed at the same shelters we did. Initially, their speed was an incredible source of frustration to us and it quickly became the bane of our trail existence. Because of their long strides and fast pace, they could sleep until 8:30 a.m. or 9:00 a.m. and be at their designated shelter for the night long before the sun even considered setting. But if for some reason their pace slowed because of a side trip, such as a jaunt to a nearby town for a beer or simply an extended lunch break, it was common for them to arrive well after dark and simply go about their evening rituals as if it were still late afternoon.

"Mom" and I were "the gerbils"—cursed with short legs, equally short strides, and were old enough to be most of these kids' parents. It was demoralizing to leave camp at 6:30 a.m., stay on our strict hiking schedule, and at various points during the day have "the gazelles" fly by and be waiting for us at a shelter at the end of the day. A hiker named "Cash" went rushing by us numerous times and we knew if he kept up his hectic pace we would never see him again. Then low and behold, a day or two later, he would come by us yet again having spent those last few days, as he claimed, "forced to stay in town" partying with some of the other equally speedy hikers. This must have happened at least a dozen times between Georgia and Maine and it actually became quite comical once we accepted the stigma of being the slowest hikers on the trail.

The most distinguishing element of our "hiking our own hike" was that "V&A" provided us with "rolling trail support." Most other hikers were relegated to hitchhiking into towns to restock their supplies or to take a day off ("zero day") in order to rest, take a much-needed shower, and do laundry. We did the same but without the loss of valuable time and the frustration that comes with waiting for a compassionate driver to stop and pick us up. The original plan was that "V&A" would provide us assistance at just the beginning and the end of our hike. For many, having such support may have seemed incompatible with the "wilderness experience," but this was how we chose to "hike our own hike."

Quite unexpectedly, only a month or so into the hike, "V&A" found they were having so much fun providing us and others with trail support and "trail magic," they posed an interesting question to us. Their role as "trail angels" had expanded to talking with the hikers and shuttling many of them into town to have injuries examined or to pick up mail drops. Being excited with these new aspects of their support role, they politely asked if we would mind having them do trail support the entire way. After a rather lengthy discussion, of at least three to four seconds, we offered up our response.

"Duh! Yeah! Are you kidding?"

With their help, our mail drops were picked up before we ever reached a post office; we had a regular shuttle into town for "zero days," where they typically already made our hotel reservations, and they even rescued us from a potential bout with hypothermia. The most convenient aspect of having personal "trail angels" was that we were able to restock our packs with food, water, and dry socks from the trunk of their car. Rarely did we have to carry more than three to four days' worth of supplies. At least once a week, we would spend time with them in their RV so I could enter our trail journals into "A's" laptop and she would post them onto the Internet the next time she had a wireless connection. While I feverishly two-finger typed, "Mom" and her dad would have maps and data books scattered all over as they planned the meeting spots for the next week. Typically, when we met up with them, they had already done reconnaissance in the area. They evaluated which roads were actually passable, a real problem in Georgia and Maine, and also checked out the availability of parking at the road crossings. They became beloved fixtures of the trail as they passed along information to the hikers who stopped by their car for trail magic. At Watauga Lake, Tennessee, they served homemade soup, dumplings, and cold soda to any hiker who had the time and appetite to partake of their goodwill. Because of them, we always knew who was just ahead of us and they were a constant source of encouragement when we were having a bad day.

We spent our fair share of evenings at bed and breakfasts along the trail; and if you are wondering, NO, we never stayed in the RV. We initially received some grief from other hikers about having "rolling trail magic" but only until many of them had benefitted from "V&A's" benevolence themselves. From that point on those critics were apologetically silenced. With such criticisms quieted, we were not about to rekindle their grievances or have them downplay the significance of our thru-hike by staying in the RV. Even when we stayed at campgrounds like Big Meadows in Virginia and Lone Oak Campground in Connecticut, we pitched our tent and braved the elements just like everyone else. We did benefit from having home-cooked meals on a semi-regular basis though. Having "V&A" as our personal trail angels also allowed us to take advantage of one other important benefit. In an attempt to minimize the pounding our backs, legs, and feet were taking each day as we trudged along with heavy packs, they often dropped us off and picked us up at road crossings so we could hike sections of the trail with nothing more than lightweight day packs ("slack-packing"). In Virginia, they camped at Loft Mountain and Big Meadows Campgrounds so they were in close proximity to the entire length of the trail in Shenandoah National Park. Because of this, we were able to "slack-pack" that entire section of the trail.

On one unusually hot and humid day, we emerged from the wilderness to find them sitting in the shade of a highway overpass with cold sodas—a regular treat. They also had ice that we put in our hydration packs to keep our water cold. In Virginia, "V&A" noticed our dramatic weight loss. In no uncertain terms, they convinced us we needed to start adding protein to our diets if we were to succeed in our quest. This was a point well taken and we immediately began adding it to all our meals.

To think they would take six months out of their lives to be a part of what we were undertaking was a humbling feeling; and knowing we could depend on them, should some ill befall us, gave us a sense of security that helped temper many of the unknowns out there. Their contributions to the success of our hike were too many to count and their teamwork was an inspiration to us.

Along the Blue Ridge Parkway, my parents, Ralph and Dottie, took over as our "trail angels" for a few days while "V&A" took several well-deserved "zero days." We stayed at their home in Goode, Virginia, where we switched to the summer gear we had already shipped to them. Then we packed up our winter gear and shipped it home to Mike and Diane. Being with them, we again witnessed what teamwork in a marriage could produce. They have been married for over fifty years and built their house from scratch—even felling the trees that made the lumber their home was built with. They had a huge garden and canned their own food as well as splitting firewood to heat their home. Their dedication to each other inspired us work together to make our dream a reality. In a "real world" sense, they had "hiked their own hike."

They took us out to dinner at the Country Cookin' Restaurant, where we relished the "all you can eat" (AYCE) buffet. We astounded my entire family, brother, sister, and nieces included, with the amount of food we were able to consume in one sitting. Our level of gluttony this early in our adventure was merely a precursor to how much we would be able to eat later on.

Our initial mail drop was to the Georgia Weights and Measures Laboratory. "Mom," in her position with the federal government, works with state metrology labs all over the country. She has developed wonderful relationships with the personnel at these facilities, so shipping our first batch of supplies to the Georgia laboratory kept us from having to go to a post office and allowed the lab's personnel to be part of our adventure. The state lab in Maine became our shipping point when it was time to ship all our gear home. Because it was a bit "dicey" shipping fuel canisters for our stove *via* the mail, "V&A" met us at the Georgia laboratory and then drove us to The Outside World Outfitters in Dawsonville, where we picked up ten canisters I had earlier arranged to be held for us. Then it was off to Dahlonega, Georgia, and the Holiday Inn Express. We checked in and then eagerly opened our mail drop, filled our packs with what we needed, packed up the remainder for "V&A" to put in the RV, and had our last night's sleep in a real bed for what we knew would be quite some time.

Dahlonega, Georgia, is a wonderful place with a rich, if not somewhat sordid, history. Dahlonega was host to the first gold rush in the United States—the Georgia Gold Rush—and was a boomtown with the site of a U.S. mint branch between 1838 and 1861. The facility was then turned over to the Confederate Treasury Department, where operations continued until June 1, 1861. Because of the numerous gold mines scattered throughout the area, in 1838 the Cherokee people were forced to Oklahoma on the abhorrent "Trail of Tears"—a journey resulting in the deaths of an estimated 4,000 men, women and children. The city's name comes from the Cherokee language word "Talonige" or "Dalonige," meaning "yellow money" or "Gold." To this day, the annual Gold Rush Days attracts over 200,000 people for the two-day event.

We awoke on March 24th to a gray, cold, and gloomy day with temperatures just above 30 °F and with snow flurries. We did not begin our trip the traditional way by traveling up the 8.8-mile approach trail to the southern terminus on Springer Mountain. Instead, we chose to start at The Amicalola Lodge. After the requisite stop at the Amicalola Falls State Park Visitors Center to sign in and have our photo taken, we drove to the Lodge Trail where we bid farewell to "V&A" and jumped on the 5.5-mile side trail to the beautiful Len Foote Hike Inn. This was the site of our first "trail magic." At dinner, we celebrated my 56th birthday, complete with a card from all the members of my church worship team back home and a cake baked especially for the occasion by the Hike Inn staff.

In addition to it being a wonderfully comfortable place to stay, The Len Foote Hike Inn, can only be reached on foot and is an outstanding example of ecological synergy and energy-saving innovation. The integration of nature and providing for human needs transcended our longings for the comforts of home. The wilderness would be our home for the next six months and the entire atmosphere of the inn helped to set the tone for our wilderness experience.

(Read more about The Len Foote Hike Inn at http://hike-inn.com*)*

After a wonderful night's sleep and a quick breakfast, we were finally off for the short 7.4 mile walk to the southern terminus of the trail at Springer Mountain—a windblown trip that found us walking through snow flurries much of the time. The adventure was just beginning; and on this day we coined a phrase that, in the many moments of utter disbelief over what we were doing, provided us with a wonderful, and humorous, dose of reality. We simply turned to each other and with a joyful tone, not unlike that of a child opening gifts on Christmas morning, shouted,

"Hey, we're hiking the Appalachian Trail!"

We sensed that what lay ahead of us would be more than just a hike. Little did we know just how life changing it would become.

We had not hiked more than a few days, when much to our dismay, we discovered that all of our training had still not adequately prepared us for this hike. The truth is that the only "real" way to get in shape to thru-hike the A.T. is to just get out there and hike it. We already knew that each state the trail ran through had a personality all its own. Here, in Georgia, it was the innumerable mountains that ascended into fog-laden clouds that seemingly went on forever. For every mountain we climbed there was the corresponding valley or "gap," as they call them in the south, which reduced our knees to nothing more than aching, throbbing slabs of petrified cartilage and muscle. The rule of thumb was to start hiking the trail slowly and keep to a daily goal of eight to ten miles for the first few weeks. In theory that made sense. However, we also had to take into consideration the distance between shelters and campsites, so many days we had to accomplish more— some days less. Those hikers who did not adhere to this "start off slow" rule were the first ones to admit they wished they had. By the time we reached the hostel at Neels Gap, a mere three days into the journey, we witnessed more than our share of feet that looked like they had been stuck in a blender set on puree.

Even though we had gone through extensive training, the first month was grueling and presented physical and emotional challenges for which we were, unexpectedly, ill prepared. It was not until we reached Erwin, Tennessee, that our bodies adapted to the rigors of ten hours of continuous hiking each day—or at the very least, our mental attitude and tolerance for pain had reached a point where we deluded ourselves into believing we were in trail shape. We also felt that our regimen of ingesting copious amounts of ibuprofen, or "Vitamin I" as it is called on the trail, had a lot to do with creating delusions of evolving physical conditioning.

Occasionally, we came upon section hikers who provided us with a bit of physical encouragement; the result of discussing who was experiencing less pain—the thru-hikers or the section hikers. Simple logic would suggest that a section hiker, who was only out on the trail for several weeks, was in much less physical distress during his/her hike than any of us thru-hikers. The section hikers we talked with thoroughly rejected that assumption. The truth was the first week of a section hike is physically brutal—a time of readjusting to long days on your feet slogging up and down mountains with a thirty-pound pack on your back. The second week is a period for ailments to begin healing and a feeling of comfort to return. And by week three, when it is not an ordeal to simply climb out of your sleeping bag and put on your pack, you are finished and it is time to go home. It was reassuring to know our pain might become measurably less after the first few weeks. Pride was almost non-existent—the trail was the great equalizer. There was nothing to be gained by attempting to pridefully hide our pain. Compassion and comfort were the benefits of sharing how we were feeling.

Right from "day one" we discovered that hiking a trail as demanding as the A.T. was going to take more effort than we expected. It became critical that in order to maintain the positive attitude required to overcome the rigors of the trail, we would need to adhere to the hiking routines we established during our many training hikes. So we went about the business of applying those routines to our current circumstances.

Based on past experience and wanting to make sure we did not get separated, "Mom" set the pace and I was content to walk at whatever speed she was comfortable with. What we soon discovered was having her lead had other benefits not apparent before. First, with "Mom" in the lead, she could better see where she was going than if she were behind. I actually enjoyed the freedom of simply following her and being able to look around at the ever-present natural beauty surrounding us. In most cases, having her lead allowed her to circumvent obstacles on the trail that could cause her to trip or fall—something she openly admitted was a great fear. On one occasion, I was uncharacteristically in the lead and the pitfall of me doing so dramatically came to light. We were strolling through a magnificent stand of pines near Tinker Cliffs in Virginia. As we were proceeding down a slight, moss and pine needle-covered incline, I turned around to see how she was doing. At that very instant, both of her trekking poles caught on a root protruding from the ground, causing her to lose her balance and go sprawling, face-first in the dirt. Fortunately, no damage was done other than a bruised ego and dirty knees; but we quickly decided our routine would be altered so she would lead all the time. Never again, except upon her insistence, did I ever lead—not even downhill. This episode reinforced the fact that not only did she want to lead, but for safety's sake, she needed to lead.

There was also one other equally poignant reason why I should not lead. Daylong exercise, combined with a daily diet of food and nutritional supplements, that in all honesty, were largely unfamiliar to my digestive tract, induced a rather non-aromatic result. Bringing up the rear, which generally kept me downwind, was a significant benefit to "Mom."

There were a few occasions when "Mom" hit the trail in the morning with an unusual amount of physical bravado. Merely trying to keep her in sight left me gasping for breath and it would probably have been better for both of us if I had led. But remembering the incident near Tinker Cliffs, and having calculated the direction of the wind, we stuck to our decision and "Mom" stayed out front.

Hiking as a "middle-aged married couple" presented one curious inter-personal idiosyncrasy. This relational dynamic appeared on our second evening on the trail when we stopped at Gooch Mountain Shelter for the evening. By sunset there were over thirty kindred souls in or near the shelter. Even though the group was quite large, it was devoid of any other female hikers and only three of the hikers present had ever met "Mom" before. We were essentially all still strangers and were in the early stages of finding out what made each other tick and where each other's personal boundaries were. What immediately struck us was that all of my male counterparts, those who had already met "Mom" and those who had not, treated her with respect, and they reverted to a wholesome vocabulary that most likely would not have been the norm were the shelter filled with just guys. We did not sense that it crimped their style or limited their topics of conversation. I certainly appreciated it and "Mom" did as well. One might think that any woman with the metal to be a thru-hiker would be considered by her male counterparts as just "one of the boys." What we found to be true was that she, and all the other women on the trail, were treated with the respect they deserved unless their words and actions communicated otherwise. "Mom" was old enough to be a mother to most of them, so there was probably some measure of "motherly" respect that came into play as well.

For some reason, the very thought of not staying together while hiking never entered our minds. Maybe it was just that we wanted to share the same experiences at exactly the same time or that we wanted someone to talk to so we could more easily pass the time. If we were going to hike separately, we may as well have simply hiked solo. But we had both decided this adventure was not a quest for individual accomplishment but was one that was to be a shared adventure. Any individual goals we had were realigned to meet a set of common goals; that was the beauty of it. I guess we also subconsciously needed to guarantee we would stay together, so we divided up our supplies and gear so neither of us could eat nor otherwise adequately function without the other person around.

There were also the issues of safety and encouragement. We could be as careful as is humanly possible, but the A.T. can be a cruel and unyielding taskmaster. The slightest miscue, lapse in judgment, or momentary loss of concentration on our part could have serious and possibly life threatening consequences. Neither of us could imagine walking separately all day wondering if our partner was safe. The fact we experienced numerous falls, some slight and some potentially catastrophic, testified to the rationality of our decision to stay together. It was reassuring, and added to the richness of the journey, to know if some misfortune befell one of us, we had immediate help and comfort.

Hiking the A.T. as a couple was difficult enough as it was; we could not fathom what the emotional ramifications were of hiking it alone. To be hiking solo with no source of encouragement and pressing forward simply through your own will must be incredibly lonely and spirit breaking. Having someone each day with whom you could share—not only the joy of the day but also the pain or discouragement you were feeling—created a reassuring state of mind.

For other couples on the trail there were varied approaches to staying together or hiking separately. For some, "hiking your own hike" meant hiking solo and simply meeting up at the end of the day—an approach which had both benefits and downsides.

Trickster:

"Hmmm, what can I say about hiking together? We definitely learned a lot about our different approaches to time management! "What?!" preferred to take a lot of breaks, sometimes long ones, and had no problem still doing the mileage. I preferred to charge ahead and get all the mileage for the day done as quickly as possible. Breaks made me feel lethargic and just plain lazy. He also liked to sleep in late, but I was up at what he considered the "butt crack" of dawn (6:00 a.m. to 6:30 a.m.), cracking the whip. We worked on this and, as a suitable compromise, decided that he would sometimes

sleep in while I cooked my oatmeal which gave him an extra twenty minutes or so to sleep. After the first half of the trail, we slowed our routine down a bit and our wake up time shifted to an hour or so later.

In one instance, our decision to each "hike our own hike" during the day came back to haunt us. We were in New York when he and I lost each other on the trail because I was hiking ahead and accidentally took an old part of the A.T. I sat on this trail for an hour waiting for him to catch up before I figured out that I had deviated from the "actual" A.T. At this point he was way past the trail intersection where I made the wrong turn and was miles ahead of where I was sitting. Concluding this was probably the case, I felt the pangs of desperation and had no way of telling him where I was. On top of that, it was starting to get dark!

Hiking in the dark really freaked me out but I went on for a few miles into the night. My headlamp started to get dim, so I set up camp for the night figuring that he and I would catch up tomorrow and making camp was the safest thing to do. In hindsight, this was a stupid thing to do, and I should have kept going. Meanwhile "What?!" had hiked an additional eight, rugged miles and was terrified that something awful had happened to me because the trail crossed several big roads leaving me vulnerable to some passing psychotic motorist. As he trudged on, he yelled my name until his throat was sore and finally he ran into some thru-hikers who had been camped out for hours. It was now almost midnight. They said they had not seen me and I definitely had not passed them; so he turned around and hiked back figuring he must have passed me. He admitted that he really did not know what else to do! Needless to say, he was not a very happy hiker when he found my campsite eight miles back on the trail section he had already hiked. In his frantic search to find me, he hiked almost thirty miles that day—up and over Bear Mountain, and across the bridge spanning the Hudson River, twice. He arrived at my campsite at around 3:00 a.m. After that, we agreed we would not hike more than a mile apart and would wait for each other at every trail intersection! It was a difficult lesson to learn to be sure!"

Carbomb:

We were in camp just north of the Hudson River in New York with "Slick B," "Holly Trout," "Bofus," and "Lebowski." We had only been in our sleeping bags for a short time when we heard a man desperately screaming the name, "Joanna!" We listened for a few minutes as the voice came closer and suddenly we saw a headlamp coming toward us. "Slick B" called out that there was no Joanna at the site and asked if she had a trail name. As soon as the voice responded that her trail name was "Trickster," we all knew the voice belonged to "What?!" They had become separated and he was unable to find her. After that night, "Lichen" and I agreed that, to avoid such a fate, we would not hike separately late in the day.

Lichen:

"Our hike taught us to really appreciate our time together. Most of the time we would hike together, but on some occasions, we would hike separately during parts of the day just to change our routine a bit. Overall, we preferred hiking together but did observe that some couples preferred to hike apart. We never grew tired of being with each other."

Brownie:

"One of our constant struggles in hiking together was that "Souleman" is a foot taller and has much longer legs than I. He can comfortably hike much faster, so we normally solved this problem by having me lead. Usually he was comfortable hiking at my pace so we could talk and spend time together. This worked well except for days during which I was exceptionally unmotivated and moving ridiculously slowly.

Another recurring theme for us was disagreement about mileage. "Souleman" always wanted to do longer miles than I did so, if he planned our weekly schedule, he would make every day high mileage with no smaller days to recover. At first, I just went along with this, but it exhausted me and made me irritable. As a compromise, we began planning lower mileage days with the caveat that we would go further if we were feeling good. "Souleman" also decided to have me plan all of our mileage so I would not feel rushed, but I felt awful about planning without him having input. Despite my desire to do shorter days at a slower pace, I always felt I was holding him back. We never really came up with a perfect solution for this dilemma.

Our last recurring hiking partner problem was that we had different ideas of how to space our hiking time throughout the day. "Souleman" liked to rush and get all his miles in early so he could relax at our destination. I, on the other hand, was happier spreading the mileage out over the course of the day and enjoyed taking a lot of little breaks. I also loved to relax in the woods so I would have thoroughly enjoyed having been able to dip my feet in a river or read under a big tree. We never really spent time relaxing like that. Taking breaks energized me and allowed me to keep hiking at a faster pace so we tended to compromise by taking three breaks a day. A typical schedule for us was to hike, take a small break for a snack, hike, take about an hour break for lunch, hike, take another short snack break, hike, have our dinner, and then go to bed. Toward the end in Maine, we began to take breaks more spontaneously and I really enjoyed that."

Enuff:

"We always hiked together and it was very rare when we didn't. Some couples did not find constantly hiking together to be that comfortable. Maybe it was age-related, or the fact that we walked at the same pace, that we didn't think about doing it any other way."

There were also some hikers in our trail family who, for various reasons, were hiking without their "life-partners." However, that did not mean they were apart. "Bama," for example," was in daily contact with her husband, Bill, *via* cell phone. Her penchant for hiking with her phone in her hand, searching for a spot on the trail where she had service, became legendary. It was Bill who transcribed her daily phone calls onto her *trailjournals.com* website; because of this, not only was he able to hike vicariously with her, but she was the only hiker on the trail whose journal was always up to date. This was often an advantage for us because when we were a day or two behind her, "V&A" would read her journals and then update us on what was up ahead, based on her journals. Bill also made frequent trips to meet her at places along the trail and occasionally accompanied her on some day-long slack-pack trips. We met him for the first time at The Lazy Fox B&B in Damascus, Virginia and then again at Hemlock Hollow Farm in North Carolina, where he furnished his bride, "Eel," "Old Grandad," and us with glasses of Merlot. That example of "trail magic" endeared us to him for the duration of our hike.

"Little Wing" had a hiking partner, "Flat Rocks," who left the trail due to an injury, but her "life partner," Scott (later dubbed, "That Guy"), stayed behind to transcribe her trail journals for her. There were times, such as in The Smokies and again in the White Mountains, where he was able to take time off from work to hike with her.

Both Bill and Scott, though not able to be an intimate part of the adventure, supported their partners' quests to complete a thru-hike; so, in essence, they shared in all the ups and downs as well—just not the blisters.

We met and hiked with many different couples, each with different perspectives and approaches to "hiking their own hike." Most of the time, we felt like we were on track with living out this motto; but in all candor, there were times when what other folks were doing and what they were experiencing seemed pretty attractive—even though they sometimes appeared to be creating additional adversity for themselves in doing so. Even though our hike differed in a way others may have seen as desirable, our competitive desire to "have it all" had us falling into the trap of thinking the other hikers' adventures were more memorable than ours. This desire to do what others were doing had not completely given way to us appreciating the uniqueness of our own journey.

Having "rolling trail support" was a wonderful aspect of our trip and we would not have traded it for anything. But because of the tight scheduling it required, our flexibility to, say, stop early at a mountaintop lake, set up camp, and spend a lazy afternoon paddling around in the canoes available there, was never a viable option. Doing so would have made us feel guilty and would have caused undue worry for "V&A" who were waiting at the next road crossing. Even adjusting our schedule or pace because of weather was problematic. One morning in Tennessee, we left the Cherry Gap Shelter area later than normal. We wanted to wait out a passing shower so we did not have to pack up our tent and gear in the rain. "V&A" were waiting at Iron Mountain Gap to re-supply us. When we did not arrive at the scheduled time, they began to worry and anxiously queried every hiker who passed regarding our whereabouts. Each hiker reassured them we were "only fifteen minutes to thirty minutes behind and we should be arriving soon." Needless to say, hikers are no more skilled at correlating speed, distance, and time than your average person, so their calculations of our arrival time were based on their hiking speed and not ours (we are "gerbils," as you recall). Before we totally exited the woods onto the road where "V&A" were parked, we were apologizing profusely about our late arrival—offering up what we considered legitimate excuses. We vowed to maintain a better arrival time record in the future so as not to worry them again. They also sensed a tinge of conflict between us that we were unaware of. They encouraged us to enjoy the hike.

Being on a rather rigid schedule also limited other possibilities that would have further enhanced the joy of our adventure. One was spending more time in trail towns and meeting some of the colorful characters that make the A.T. so memorable. Had we been faster hikers, who could do twenty miles to twenty-five miles in a day if a situation warranted it, we could have spent more time pursuing leisure activities. An extra day in town would have simply required doing two twenty-mile days back to back in order to make up the time and mileage that was lost. Seeing we only were able to cover twenty or more miles on two separate occasions and paid dearly for it, physically, staying on schedule was vitally important. The inescapable truth was we needed to be back to work in no more than six months and keeping to our schedule allowed us to finish within two weeks of our planned date—well before Baxter State Park closed. The park closing trumped any other reason we could come up with as to why we could not do some of the things along the trail that looked like so much fun. Be that as it may, we often lamented not doing our hike the way others did and more fully experiencing the special circumstances that arose on the way.

For us as a couple, *"hiking our own hike"* became a representation of who we were and, quite possibly, who we wished ourselves and our marriage to be by the time our thru-hike was over. It became an extension of our senses of self and purpose—or lack thereof. It exposed the real person hiding within each of us. The simplicity of living outside the complexities of the man-made world led to many new insights. Our encounters with the diverse demands of the trail brought to light the strengths and inadequacies of our relationship. We were not afforded the luxury of putting off dealing with any of these matters—good or bad. To make it through the next hour, day or mile, they needed to be accepted or resolved immediately.

Above all, no matter what the underlying reason for our or any other hiker's choice of style, "hiking your own hike" possessed a common thread: it was the thread of unbridled freedom—the freedom to re-evaluate, re-invent or re-visit yourself. For couples, the added dimension of how they related to each other came into play. We were all able to express our internal journeys through our experiences on the A.T. For "Mom" and me, it was all of this plus the unique opportunity to embrace and deepen every tenet of our marriage.

"Mom's" Tips for Couples

- Individual goals must be set aside in order to meet a set of common goals;

- Hike your own hike; live your own life. Both on the trail and in real life, there are rules that need to be adhered to but within the context of those rules live a life that is truly unique and reflects your personality;

- It is never too late to chase a dream. *"Dream It! Plan It! Live It!"*;

- Plan on taking a "zero day" every 6-7 days; any shorter intervals than that and you add quite a few additional days to the length of your hike. Any more than 7 and your body takes longer to recover. This goes for your day-to-day life as well.

CHAPTER FOUR

WALKING IN STEP

"I'd rather have one walk beside me than merely point the way."
David O. McKay

W hat was the most frequently asked question of us during and after our thru-hike of the Appalachian Trail? No, it was not *"What did you eat,"* *"Where did you sleep,"* or even, *"How many miles did you hike each day?"*

It was oddly enough, *"How did you get along?"* To us this seemed an unusual question; but with so few married couples undertaking the ambitious 2,174.6-mile journey that is the A.T., I suppose it seemed like a logical question for people to ask us.

The magnitude and atypical nature of what we were attempting came home to us dramatically, and somewhat humorously, as we overheard a cell phone conversation between a hiker and his wife. We were relaxing and eating our dinner at the Wilson Valley Lean-To in the 100-Mile Wilderness in Maine as he recounted his experiences of that day. Suddenly and quite loudly, with a voice filled with slightly more aggravation than excited interest, we heard his wife on the other end of the phone.

"Well, I hope you are getting this out of your system!"

It was all we could do not to choke on our mac 'n cheese as we struggled to hold back our snickering. It was just one of the many examples that pointed up how fortunate we were to have a marriage that could stand the test we were putting it through.

So, how did we get along? Being on the trail together for six months, seven days a week, and twenty-four hours a day brought with it numerous unique challenges— challenges we never had to face in "the real world." But perhaps the trail was more like the real world than we ever realized. Being away from the comfort and relative safety of the *status quo* we accepted as meaningful and rewarding brought to the surface what was missing from our urban lives. We suddenly discovered what was really most important to us.

At first, we felt the progress of our relational growth on the trail was painstakingly slow—oftentimes, indiscernible amidst the day-to-day routine of walking and simply surviving. But early on, there were some indications that a metamorphosis was taking place—a convergence of our characters that we were totally unaware of. Concrete proof of this change was brought to light and confirmed in a very interesting and undeniable way. Except for a few rare instances when we made better progress than expected, "A" would always be waiting to take our picture as we emerged from the woods. She also took a photo each time we returned to the trail. Not long after we began our journey, she began noticing a similarity amongst the photos of us she had taken. Upon closer examination, she noticed an interesting and quirky phenomenon. Each time we arrived at a road crossing and each time we re-entered the forest, we were *"walking in step,"* looking like soldiers in a Veterans Day parade. It was quite apparent our relatively short time on the trail was already reaping benefits for us. Not only was it bringing us closer together emotionally, but it had meshed our souls and personas to a point where we were walking in unison. A photo taken in Massachusetts confirmed the further melding of our characters as evidenced by the fact that by then we were even standing the same way while we talked—right hand on right hip.

Oh yes, the answer to the number one question? Well, it was and still is a resounding, *"We got along just great."* Not perfect, mind you. There were those days when the fatigue, the bugs, the heat, the cold, or the fact we had not had a day off to rest for quite some time, finally overtook us. However, paramount to marital survival on the trail, was that we and most every couple on the A.T., quickly learned to identify those environmental, emotional, and physical factors as the culprits of our discord. We then came up with a ways to deal with them. Our moments of discord were defining ones in making our marriage and friendship stronger and in giving us a new appreciation of each other's strengths and weaknesses—which is contrary to most beliefs. Possibly the most overriding factor in making sure our differences were resolved by day's-end was that we were going to be sleeping shoulder-to-shoulder in a tiny tent—and there was no sofa anywhere in sight. As a means of self-preservation, the phrase, *"I love you, BUT..."* was sensibly replaced with, *"I love you, ANYWAY!"*

How does a couple who shares a common goal but who brings to the table varied backgrounds, personality traits, quirks, and expectations survive such an undertaking? To the casual observer it may appear that after the obvious necessity for physical conditioning was addressed, simple compromise and a healthy dose of understanding would be all that was needed. Though these two things were critical before even taking the first step on the trail, believing they are the end-all to dealing with every good and bad experience on the trail could not be further from the truth. The human condition is turned inside-out on a quest such as thru-hiking the A.T.; so above all else, being open and transparent became the critical aspect behind us not only surviving but in growing—both individually and as a couple. We did not want any petty squabbles stifling our enthusiasm.

Because I am extremely competitive, the fact we were repeatedly passed by faster hikers created more than its share of tense moments and emotional outbursts. Quite frankly, on those days when other hikers were continually passing us and I knew our chances of staying in a shelter were growing dimmer by the minute, it was difficult for me to not vocalize my frustration with our pace. My years of experience with successfully racing go-karts and bringing home my share of championship trophies, had instilled in me an unquenchable drive to always finish first. To me, staying ahead of everyone on the A.T. was no different from being on the track. Coming in second was not an acceptable option. Somehow, "Mom" was able to rise above any animosity about being passed and took the situation all in stride. On more than one occasion, I spewed forth a less-than-compassionate evaluation of our hiking speed, but then found myself apologizing for my emotional transgression once I realized "Mom" was totally content with our pace. Being passed was my issue—not hers. This was a fact she repeatedly pointed out to me—and not without a bit of ire in her voice, mind you. Not until very late in our hike did I resolve myself to the fact that our decision to have her lead brought with it this particular consequence. It was a six-month-long lesson in humility that forced me to direct my focus from our goal of finishing and more toward enjoying the journey. What became important was not where we were going but where we were at any given moment. I eventually surrendered my ego and being "average" took on a whole new meaning for me. This change in priorities helped to minimize the chances of me hurting her feelings with my comments about her speed. Things got better and we grew closer.

Periodically however, despite every personal effort and even with the wonders of nature abounding all around us to lift our spirits, we occasionally experienced a day when we simply could not synchronize with each other. The day we hiked endlessly up and down the mountains of Georgia, through rhododendron tunnels pierced by laser-sharp arrows of sunlight, and eventually crossed the North Carolina border near Bly Gap was one such day. Any thru-hiker will agree that crossing this border is a major first milestone and one that warrants a moment of jubilant celebration. The memory of that first border crossing was so dramatic it took on a larger-than-life persona. And the fact that this glorious moment became such a vivid memory was a good thing because the sign marking this border crossing was anything but memorable. The only testament to our first major accomplishment was a small, bedraggled wooden sign, with "GA/NC" etched on it. It was nailed to a tree with a short section of rusty pipe impaled in the tree right below it. So <u>inconspicuous</u> is that marker, that more than one hiker, on a foggy day, had simply walked by it, completely unaware that he/she had reached his first major goal. In fact, we almost missed it too.

As the day wore on, we were not only beginning to get hungry but had to acknowledge that we would not be arriving in camp until sunset. Since we liked having a few hours of daylight in which to make camp and eat dinner before retiring, knowing we were now going to be thrown off our usual routine darkened our mood. To counteract our emotional backslide, we decided to stop at Bly Gap to eat dinner and then move on to our final destination for the day. We initially had the campsite to ourselves and felt the gods were finally smiling upon us for the first time all day. Our joy was short lived when a loud and unruly Boy Scout troop arrived and began to make camp for the night. In our haste to finish our dinner, move on, and rid ourselves of this obnoxious group, "Mom" accidentally dumped our pot of chili over into the vortex of wet coals in the fire pit. So much for dinner! My initial reaction to this situation was less than good-humored primarily because my blood sugar was in the basement and that tends to make me a bit grumpy. The thought of having to settle for a protein bar for dinner, rather than a hot meal, simply added to my malaise. The only thing I could utter was a guttural,

"Oh, way to go! That's just great!"

Immediately sensing "Mom's" own despair and anger at herself for ruining dinner, I made a noble, though feeble, attempt at withdrawing my comment. I then, made an equally lame attempt at consoling her. Was this one of those moments that, in hindsight, would be one of both personal and relational growth? Only time, a full stomach, and a leg massage would tell. Adding insult to injury was the fact we had to clean up our mess and properly dispose of it. We would have preferred leaving our mess where it was and hope that a bear would be drawn to the campsite by the smell. Then we could revel in the havoc wreaked by the bear as it invaded the campsite and scared the hell out of the Boy Scout troop. Even though inflicting payback for spoiling our quiet dinner seemed fair, we decided against leaving our dinner where it laid. We could only imagine the headline on the local news:

"BEAR IS DRAWN TO FOOD LEFT IN CAMPSITE BY
APPALACHIAN TRAIL THRU-HIKERS AND THEN SAVAGELY
ATTACKS BOY SCOUT TROOP CAMPING NEARBY. FILM AT
11:00!"

Feeling that the guilt over the demise of the scout troop would outweigh our satisfaction in getting even, we begrudgingly began to clean up.

"Damn! Now we have to shovel our dinner out of the fire pit, wet ashes and all, put it in a Ziploc, and I have to carry it up this stinking mountain to a place where we can scatter it. That's just great!"

To calm my mood, "Mom" sincerely apologized for dumping our dinner, even though she really had no reason to. She put her feelings aside in order to empathize with mine. It was another example of the growth of our feelings for each other.

Carrying waterlogged ashes and food up the mountainside on an empty stomach was not at all what I wanted to do this late in the afternoon. However, we were able to eat the remaining components of our dinner and that was sufficient, though not wholly adequate, to assuage our hunger for the time being. As we walked the remaining miles to camp, we talked things over in an attempt to ferret out the root causes of our discontent over what just took place. The trail already taught us how important it was not to bury our ill feelings and hope they would simply pass. The trail was way too unpredictable and demanding for anything other than total honesty. The emotional strength it took to hold anger and hurt in would be needed, at any moment, in order to deal with whatever the trail threw at us next. By the time we arrived at camp, we had fully recovered from our belligerent episode and even found quite a bit of humor in the whole incident. We grabbed a bit more to eat and crawled into our tent for a tranquil and guilt-free night's rest.

Were we alone when it came to dealing with the personal and relational struggles brought on by the adversity of the trail? Or were the other couples out there dealing with their own demons too—some similar to ours and some radically different? How did they handle their unique situations in order to *"walk in step?"*

Trickster:

"What?!" and I got into the occasional spat on the trail; I cannot tell you what we argued about, so it must have been just stupid stuff

that came up simply because we never had a break from each other. Our choice of hiking separately when these situations arose, worked out well because, if things did not get resolved, one of us would just hike up ahead and the other would catch up later—when the heat of the moment had subsided."

Brownie:

"Money was one topic we discussed often while hiking. When we got to town, "Souleman" wanted to regale in every single luxury he missed on the trail. He wanted to drink large amounts of soda and buy numerous other beverages each time we were in town. I felt we should sometimes drink water and save some money. While this seemed extremely petty, we often disagreed over how to spend our money in town. Thankfully, we had saved enough money so this issue did not impact our hike negatively."

Carbomb:

On March 26th just thirteen days into our hike, we were unknowingly feeling a little worn out. We don't even remember what triggered it, but "Lichen" said something to me that had me telling her to, "F....k Off!" She was unbelievably shocked because it was so unexpected. No one she cared for had ever said anything like that to her, let alone me! We had never even remotely spoken to each other that way, so it was a pretty big deal. This was a totally unacceptable situation if we were to hike the whole A.T. together. We didn't hike together much more that day and we both came to the realization, that since we had begun the trail, we had not had any "alone time" with each other—away from everyone else. We had not yet had a frank conversation to find out how each of us was really doing. In addition, it had recently snowed on us, we had been cold, and we had not yet had a "zero day," so we were getting a bit mentally fatigued without even realizing it. We had recently been separated from a bunch of other hikers with whom we had grown very close. This was our first hiker family and we were a little downhearted about no longer being with them. So, my snapping at "Lichen" woke us up to the fact that we needed to take a deep breath, get some mental rest, and begin to be candid with each other about how we were feeling.

We ended up going into Franklin, Tennessee, even though we had not planned on it, to have a chance to talk things over. We determined that under the circumstances, my outburst had likely only happened because I was personally frustrated and "Lichen" was the only person nearby to take it out on. We both knew each other very well before the hike and knew that this weird, out-of-the- blue outburst was really triggered by the crazy adventure we were on. It had nothing to do with us as a couple.

It was a big reality check because if this was how the trail was going to affect us, this early into our hike, then what would happen later? We knew we couldn't let things like this happen again and, if we were going to hike the whole trail together, we had to continue to treat each other with compassion and understanding, no matter what was going on. That would be the only way we would make it.

Nothing like that ever happened again on our hike—or since. We're not saying we didn't have disagreements, but after our visit to Franklin, we kept our cool and managed to treat each other respectfully and not take out our personal frustrations on each other."

Too Much:

"As for how we got along on the trail and how we handled the disagreements that did pop up from time to time, it really was not much different than how we interact at home. If there was a disagreement, I would get quiet as I reflected on whether the points brought up in the argument were legitimate. Then, with what I see as a distinctly-female approach, I would decide if there was a legitimate complaint and, if I felt there was, I would take the steps necessary to put into place the changes or improvements that needed to be made. Like I said, our styles were very much like they were at home."

Enuff:

"There was one thing that occurred to me while we were hiking and I saw it as an interesting dynamic. Sometimes Pat would appear to me to be uncomfortable and struggling, and not wanting her to be that way, I would say, 'Maybe we should stop.' Now, my perception was sometimes totally off and the truth was that she wanted to continue. But in an attempt to make her feel better, I would suggest ending the hike. It was a simple matter of communication. Obviously, we worked it out and it did not stop us. These episodes opened our eyes to the fact of how important communication skills are for a couple. Being out on the trail where continuously understanding and supporting

each other is so critical to your very survival, the need for couples to have open lines of communication is even more necessary."

Tag-N-Along:

"We really did not have any disagreements on the trail unless you count the times when there was no blaze to be found and he wanted to go one way and I another."

Resolving marital conflict and getting along is tough enough in the real world; being on the trail certainly does not make it any easier. Yes, the trail does provide an escape from the real-life pressures that negatively impact a relationship. And yes, it does offer a couple unlimited opportunities to focus on each other. However, the trail presents its own set of relational challenges and the tranquility found on the trail is not a salve that will heal a contentious relationship. It is folly to believe that simply prevailing through the shared adversity will bring a couple closer together.

Lichen:

"*One thing that stands out in my mind is that Chris showed an extreme amount of patience during our hike. He was able to hike much faster than I. He was able to cross boulder fields and streams faster, but even so, he was always patient and waited for me as I went at my own pace. He never complained or really asked me to hurry up. I brought this issue up a lot more than he did because it bothered me that we were so often getting to camp really late because of my speed. But he was nice about it, telling me that it didn't really matter to him and that he was just happy walking along behind me. The truth of the matter was, I knew, that it sometimes did drive him crazy—a fact that he confirmed toward the end of the hike.*

But during those times that it did begin to irritate him, he consciously chose to think of something else or to start up a conversation so he wouldn't focus on it. I just think he showed an incredible amount of patience; not only with my slow hiking but with other things, too, such as my aversion to getting up in the mornings.

In the aftermath of our hike, I often remember how thoughtful and patient he was during our hike, and it reminds me how thankful I am for him. We definitely appreciated each other before and the hike simply confirmed it.

After the hike when we got back to Austin and started back to work, we missed being able to spend all day every day together. It's been nine months since we got back, and we still miss each other during the day while we're at work. We don't like that our time together is mostly limited to nights and weekends now."

Contrasting the already-established relationships on the trail were the relationships that literally began on the A.T.—relationships that blossomed and developed into more than a just a shared set of trail experiences and memories. "Brownie & Souleman" met while hiking the A.T. Either out of a need for companionship, security, some mutual physical attraction, or a combination of these things, they became a couple. Whatever the reason, the tale of how they got along, both early on in their relationship and as it grew over time, is quite interesting.

"Brownie & Souleman's" relationship began in 2005 on an ill-fated first attempt to thru-hike the A.T. as solo hikers. The joyful completion of the A.T. in 2006 was their honeymoon. It marked the culmination of a relationship that started on the A.T. and then matured over the following year. "Brownie" even fashioned a *"Just Married"* sign out of white cloth, emblazoned with black lettering, and fastened it to her pack for all to see. "Mom" and I met these newlyweds on the trail after staying at the Eliza Brook Shelter in New Hampshire; and for some reason, though we did not spend much time hiking with them, we developed an "older-couple/younger-couple" bond between us. Even after fourteen years of marriage, we were still discovering new areas of development in our relationship. And here they were, attempting to grapple with understanding, accepting, compromising, and growing in a compressed time span of only months—and with the physical demands of the trail attempting to undermine their success.

Here is how "Brownie" recounts the early development of their relationship in 2005 and the trail's role in the growth of their love for each other.

Brownie:

"The starting group quickly separated, as was expected, but "Souleman," Eddie ("Jax") and I stuck together. For the first three weeks, the three of us hiked together. The guys would hike quickly, wait for me to catch up, saved space between them in the shelter at night, and waited for me to hitch rides. "Jax" was flirting shamelessly with me, and I was equally both flattered and cautious. Apparently, "Souleman" had been trying to flirt with me this whole time, but I was oblivious.

One day, "Souleman" decided to hike with me instead of "Jax." We talked non-stop all morning and we were amazed that we had done ten miles without even thinking. Over the next few days, he hiked with me more and more and then, a week later, on Easter night, the sparks flew for the first time. From that point on, "Jax" decided that he wanted to hike faster than I was able to so he took off up the trail. Jeremy chose to stay and hike with me.

Getting to know another person romantically while in the midst of such an intense physical and psychological endeavor was both thrilling and exhausting. While we ticked off the mileage each day, we had the opportunity to learn more about each other. Our conversations covered everything from family and friends to politics and religion. We learned, explored, argued, and debated. This was a very unnatural dating environment. We were thrown into a twenty-four hours a day, seven days a week dating experience. If dating were a sport, this would qualify as "extreme dating." We came to know each other very well, very quickly, and those who met us were often surprised to learn we had met on the trail. Our emotions ran the gamut between despair and elation, sweat, tears, laughter, pain, and joy. But mostly, we had fun.

While "Souleman" and I share a passion for hiking, our personalities are polar opposites in many ways. This is probably a good thing because the world certainly doesn't need two of me. I am high-strung, high-maintenance, and obsessively organized. I can't sit still; I get worked-up easily, am a stickler for the rules and cannot stand it when things are not "fair." For me, this hike was a break from the "real world" where I measured a day's success by how many things I checked off my to-do list. Here I made a point of not having a list. Instead, I tried to be content with enjoying my surroundings. I breathed in the fresh air perfumed with leaves, mud, sweat, and fire smoke. I enjoyed lazy lunches on rocks warmed by the sun. I listened to raindrops on my tent fly, owls in the trees, and logs crackling on the fire. Rather than seeing how many things I could accomplish, I made it a point to do as little "work" as possible. Instead, I focused on enjoying being in nature and enjoying the company I had so luckily found.

"Souleman," on the other hand, is about as calm as a person can be. He is never stressed, never worked-up, and can lighten any situation. He likes to bend the rules and loves to relax; for him, hiking is merely an extension of his daily life. He has worked outdoors, has lived away from home, has hitchhiked, and has traveled across the country."

There was one characteristic that underscored all of the established marital relationships on the A.T.—and those that developed because of, or in some instances in spite of, the adversities and excitement of being together on the trail. The most important characteristic of the human condition, *empathy*, either came to the surface for the first time or was reinforced by the unique experience of thru-hiking together. Without possessing or developing an intellectual and emotional understanding of each other, we would succumb to the frailties of our own selfish tendencies. Recognizing and accepting our partner's personal weaknesses and needs, those that were challenged by events on the trail, was invigorating. This unbridled acceptance brought forth a sense of liberation that allowed us to be totally human. We became stronger, both personally and as a team, by virtue of accepting not only the shortcomings of our partner but by accepting our own frailties as well. And knowing that being transparent about our weaknesses would not generate a negative reaction from our partner, we were free, perhaps for the first time in a long time, to be ourselves. There was strength to be found in relating to each other this way; strength that opened up the floodgates of all the other emotions that bound us together as husband and wife. Legendary thru-hiker, Warren Doyle, succinctly described the paradigm shift that all thru-hikers deal with when he said,

"The human condition is to be free; to love, to care, to help, to feel, and to grow both physically and emotionally. Our culture-driven conditioning promotes none of these."

For "Mom" and me, this relational dynamic became so important we vowed to continue it in our lives at home.

Trickster:

"I would say that one of the greatest things we learned from our hiking honeymoon together was balance; learning how to balance each other's needs and temperaments so that we were both happy and fulfilled. Our love grew continuously as we learned to, truly, appreciate the support and care that passed between us. We felt like a team that was working towards the same goal. If one of us had a down day, the other one would be there to motivate and encourage. We transferred that into our life off the trail and we continue to cheerlead for each other and push the other to do better....work harder."

One morning, just seven days into our journey, "Mom" and I arose to the typical, early morning clouds that always settled in on top of the mountains in Georgia during this time of year. Overnight, what we called "fog-rain" had blanketed everything in sight, including our tent, with a fine film of dew. This day we also awoke to the incredible realization that by the end of the day we had been on the trail for a week. Though it had only been a short time in the whole scheme of things, a week on the trail signified a significant milestone. What an amazing feeling it was, though we knew we had many, many more weeks to go. We learned to relish every small goal while never letting the major goal of summiting Mt. Katahdin and touching that historic sign leave our minds. Each small goal became a major one within the narrow framework of time we had been hiking. "The Sign"—we were always walking toward "The Sign."

We got a late start and immediately experienced a bit more foot pain than usual. The bruising on the soles of our feet likened itself to what they would feel after walking across a field of golf balls in our bare feet. We just pushed through it. We knew that if the pain we were feeling got the better of us at this early stage, we would eventually be doomed to failure. There was a solace in verbally sharing the physical pain, and because of this openness, we were able to draw on each other's tenacity and resolve in order to tough it out. There were days when only one of us was suffering, but there were no judgmental comments impugning the other's lack of will or ability to accept pain. We both knew that at some point we would most certainly be in the other person's shoes so to speak. If anything, these episodes of physical torment brought us closer together, and our empathy and compassion, not only for each other but for others in general, began to take on a fresh perspective.

Both "Mom" and I are "Baby Boomers," offspring of quite possibly the last generation of parents who understood, appreciated, and promoted the concept of teaching kids to be self-sufficient. Because of this upbringing, we each brought broad skill sets to our marriage. To our parents' way of thinking, seeing that their offspring's self-esteem was kept intact was secondary to them guaranteeing we developed a good work ethic, could cook, clean, iron, sew, handle a variety of tools, maintain a home, and not spend more money than we made. Later in life these attributes kept us from being unemployed, hungry, naked, and allowed us to develop a proper level of self-esteem all on our own. We benefitted from these skills in our lives and found them to be of profound value on the trail.

At home, we share responsibilities, and our gender plays little, if any, role in determining who does what. We find our approach to marriage to be a blend of *"structure and equality, balance and beauty,"* not unlike many of the precepts put forth in the book, *"Rocking the Roles,"* by Robert Lewis and William Hendricks. The key factor for determining which of us does what comes down to "who is better at doing a particular task," "who enjoys performing a particular task more," or "who has the time to do it?" "Mom" loves to cook and worked her way through college as a line chef at a restaurant, and so she can make a delicious meal out of thin air. For her, the supermarket is a wonderland of creative, culinary possibilities so having her do our food shopping becomes a very expensive proposition. Therefore, with a detailed list in hand, I do all the food shopping. Having been a single dad, I also know how to cook relatively well; but because I thrive on cleanliness and order, I am much more at home when it comes to house cleaning and organizing. "Mom" is a "numbers person"—a personality trait made quite evident by the fact that her favorite movie is *"A Beautiful Mind,"* which she has watched six times. From memory, she can recall the birthdays and anniversaries of every person in our family as well those of most of our friends. Because of this passion for numbers, she handles our finances. We each do our own laundry; however, because I like to watch NASCAR races on TV, I tend to gravitate toward ironing which gives me something productive to do while I watch Jeff Gordon and Jimmie Johnson kick everyone's butt on the track. To some couples, this arrangement might seem a bit unorthodox, but we find that dividing up responsibilities aligned with our gifts, talents and passions serves us well. It seems only logical and fair to operate this way since we both have the same level of responsibilities outside the home.

Our roles on the trail became nothing more than an extension of our normal duties at home, distilled down to their most fundamental components: food, water, shelter, clothing, and companionship. There was no clearly defined line between "women's work" and "men's work," and neither of us ever attempted to impose one. For solo hikers, both male and female, the line between gender-specific roles was non-existent. Each was left to his/her own devices as to how best to address the daily responsibilities being faced. Sometimes, in a demonstration of chivalry or if safety was at stake, a man might assist a woman. And, it was not uncommon for the reverse to happen. However, the female hikers were typically considered "one of the guys" and they were generally expected to deal with things accordingly—which most did with great proficiency.

During our hike, "Mom" and I knew what our individual abilities, strengths, and job preferences were and went about undertaking them with a sense of satisfaction and appreciation sometimes lacking in our home setting. The sense of duty underlying the fulfillment of our responsibilities became secondary to the satisfaction of knowing that, because of our efforts, our spouse's needs were being taken care of. This division of duties, under no circumstances, meant there could not, or need not, be changes made as situations arose. We both knew if one of us was excessively fatigued, sick, or injured, the other was willing and prepared to take over and do whatever needed to be done. It was comforting to know that if an unexpected situation did occur, there would be no interruption in the normal scheme of things. It was also reassuring to know that each task would be completed correctly and with an overarching sense of duty and loving commitment.

In some sense, our duties on the trail were typical of what you would expect from pioneer couples braving the new frontier. Upon arriving at camp each night, "Mom" and I would first set up our tent which, even though it was a job either one of us could have done individually, was one we chose to do together out of the need for getting it done quickly. This joint effort occasionally hit a snag when we found ourselves wasting valuable time debating the relative merits of available locations for our tent.

With our shelter erected, I was off to retrieve and filter enough water with which to refill our hydration packs, prepare our dinner and breakfast, wash our dishes, and brush our teeth. Simultaneously, "Mom" emptied our packs and set up the inside of our tent with sleeping bags, clothes, headlamps, journals, and our first aid kit. Having completed this, she set up the stove and got our dinner staged to be cooked. Then, as any good pioneer woman would do, she devotedly awaited the return of her husband, the hunter, from the woods.

As "Mom" cooked, I often acted as a chef's helper, passing utensils and pans to her like a nurse passing implements to a surgeon during an operation. With dinner completed, I washed the pots and dishes as "Mom" dried, or sometimes, *vice versa*. Just as it was getting dark, I hung our food bag so our rations would not become a midnight snack for bears, raccoons and other famished creatures of the night.

It was not surprising to find that other couples' daily "trail roles" were often a mirror image of our own. We did not know if their trail approach was typical of their home lives, but the trail invariably brought out the need for each spouse to step up to the plate.

Mapman:

"Robin usually cooked the meals and I pumped the water. We both carried an equal amount of weight and both worked equally in performing other camp chores and in making decisions. We got along very well and loved hiking together. Robin usually led the way and we were never out of each other's sight. We both appreciated each other's contribution to making the hike a success.

Tag-N-Along:

> *"It was my duty to find a spot to pitch the tent if we were not near a shelter. We would pitch the tent together and then Tim would find the water source while I got things ready in the tent and started supper. I was always in the front because he thought I could spot things better, or so he says. I think it was because I was the faster hiker."*

Once inside our tent for the night, we each had further responsibilities. I jotted down the details of our day in my journal. "Mom" reviewed the photos she took that day, double-checked the map and data book for the next day, and prepared our sock liners for the morning. I will not elaborate, at this juncture, regarding the preparation of our sock liners and another nightly ritual we devoted ourselves to. Instead, I will fully divulge the details of these in a later chapter.

Our daily campsite routine was one that we adhered to every day we were on the trail. Being organized and structured in our approach to things and having a comfortable routine offset all the unknowns we encountered each day. We discovered that other couples had their own roles and routines on the trail—some as defined as ours, and some, less structured.

Enuff:

> *"We did separate certain responsibilities and we fell into a routine rather quickly. I did most of the physical stuff like setting up the tent, cooking and cleaning up. "Too Much" bridged the gap with people and did meal planning. Honestly though, it sometimes irked me that I cooked and washed the dishes but it did become a routine and we accepted our roles."*

Too Much:

> *"Part of the problem contributing to "Enuff's" discontent with doing so much work was that he would not acknowledge the fact that he needed to always stay busy. If there was nothing else to do, he would actually build fires, when we were allowed to. He would make it his job, even though no one told him to, and he would keep it burning as I just sat back and enjoyed the warmth of the fire. At one point, he stopped long enough to say to himself, "Why am I doing this?" and acknowledged that he simply had a need to stay busy; it was just his nature.*

I, on the other hand, was content to just sit back and be as comfortable as I could be. There was simply so much going on each day that emotionally took a toll on me that I did not want to get involved in the evening logistics. I felt I needed to relax, both physically and emotionally, in order to remain psychologically content to continue hiking."

Lichen:

"During our hike, we learned it was best if we divided camp set-up chores, rather than do them together. This became very clear early on at the Blue Mountain shelter in Georgia. Even though there were two of us, it took us a lot longer to set up our tent than everyone else at the shelter. The reason was that we spent the majority of our time wandering around attempting to locate a tent site we could both agree on as suitable for the tent. All the while, we were getting more tired and hungrier by the minute.

"Here's a good spot," "Carbomb" would excitedly point out.

"No, it's too rocky. How about this one instead?" would be my reply.

"That one's too slanted," he would answer with his voice beginning to show the signs of growing frustration.

If that were not enough to have us just throw in the towel and reluctantly plunk our gear down in the nearby shelter, once we did agree on a site, we both had differing opinions on how the angle of the trekking poles should be for our tarp tent. Then it was how the guy lines should be staked, and so on and so on. When this type of situation did come up, as it often did early in our hike, things generally remained quite amicable, but eventually, one of us would get irritable and sometimes feelings would get hurt—not to mention this approach to setting up our tent was very inefficient. We ended up dividing the camp responsibilities as follows: one of us would cook while the other would set up the tent or get water. We also chose to switch those responsibilities every day."

Carbomb:

"I put up our bear bag most every night. From time to time, "Lichen" would give it a shot, but her attempts never seemed to

adequately protect the food bags or we would end up with some of our bear bag gear shredded. Not that I was always perfect! Once, early on, I got our food bags stuck and had to spend an hour trying to free them from a tree.

Neither of us liked to clean the pot after dinner, so our rule of alternating chores each day meant that, if it was your day, you were going to do it whether you liked it or not. There were no exceptions to this rule! For example, even if I had a bad day and it was my night to clean the pot, there was the understanding that "Lichen" was not going to do it for me. It ended up being a comfort to have some systems in place rather than trying to decide who was going to do what on a case-by-case basis.

Our ability to work as a team was not relegated merely to the trail—it also came into play when we were in town taking a "zero day." A "zero," for short, is a time for hikers to leave the adversity of the trail and relax in town, taking advantage of all the unique cultural and social amenities available. It is a time to take a much-needed shower, do laundry and restock packs with supplies from the nearest supermarket, convenience store or outfitter. It is also a time to reconnect with those back home who believe you are a bit crazy and with those who wonder if you are still alive. It is also an opportunity to pick up your mail drop at the post office and to find a place with a computer so you can update your journals on *www.trailjournals.com* or on one of the other online hiker sites. Most of all, it is an opportunity to locate the nearest "all you can eat" (AYCE) buffet where hikers EAT and EAT and EAT! There are tales of AYCE establishments having to put limits on thru-hikers because their insatiable appetites risked the long-term financial survival of the restaurant. If you are incredibly lucky, AYCE restaurants may even serve BEER! (Unfortunately, or fortunately as "Mom" says, beer was never AYCD—"All You Can Drink.")

In order to use our "zero day" time efficiently and be able to retreat to the comfort of our motel room as quickly as possible, we generally divided and conquered. After being together 24/7 for as much as a week, we never felt being apart for a few hours to take care of chores put our relationship in jeopardy. Getting the job done was our top priority. Individual responsibilities changed from town to town, but generally, one of us would do laundry while the other shopped for supplies or ran to a sub-shop and brought dinner back to the laundromat. We functioned in town much as we did at home—approaching the work in such a way as to complete it as correctly and as efficiently as possible so we could have as much "quality time" with each other as possible. What we discovered, even using our methodical approach to "zero days," was that there never seemed to be enough time to actually "rest." We eventually started taking two days off in a row just so we could kick back on the second day. We never did figure out how the solo hikers got everything done and were still able to find time to close the local bar; but based on the aroma of some of them, we were pretty certain the beer took precedence over laundry and a shower.

In their trail support role, "V&A" also had a well-defined division of labor which allowed them to be incredibly efficient and unbelievably reliable. When doing reconnaissance for future meeting places and trailheads, "A" would drive and "V," who is as adept at reading maps as "Mom" is, would navigate and provide pinpoint logistical support. Riding with them on several occasions offered us the opportunity to appreciate how well they worked as a team when on the road. Driving and set-up of the RV at campgrounds was "V's" sole responsibility—one which he relished.

"A" did all of the cooking, except for several weeks when she had to leave the trail to attend to her injured mother. She also assisted with preparing the motor home when it was time to move it to a new location. The importance of this responsibility was humorously brought to light when, during the time she was away, "V" neglected to put down the TV antenna before leaving a campground. He promptly knocked it off the RV's roof when it made contact with a sign at the exit that, ironically, asked, "DID YOU PUT DOWN YOUR TV ANTENNA?" During the course of the entire hike, "A" also baked the most outstanding cookies one could imagine. Lovingly dubbed by "Mom" and me as, "Anita's A.T. Power Cookies," these beauties provided us with virtually all the daily nutrients we needed to get through a long afternoon.

(You will find the recipe for these cookies in Appendix #3)

"V&A" regularly anticipated what perishable items we were running low on, and as a team handled our re-supply needs and also picked up our mail drops. They took turns walking their cat "Meow-Meow," who was trained to walk on a leash. "A," with her camera and computer skills, handled the responsibilities of taking photos of us and made sure our journal entries made it onto our website.

Converting our "home roles" to the trail gave our days their only real semblance of predictability. With all that Mother Nature threw at us, it was reassuring to know that something about each day would be recognizably "normal." And, as much as bringing personal habits to the trail lent a degree of normalcy to the situation, some bad habits, as acceptably routine as they were at home, simply could not stand the test of time on the trail.

"Mom" has always been a "morning person" and that was a real benefit on the trail. I, on the other hand, am a night person so I struggled with getting up each morning. The desire to hold on to my "night owl" tendencies became a losing battle. There is an accepted phenomenon on the trail, brought about by two distinct, yet powerful, factors—both of which severely limited my nocturnal tendencies. First, was the predominant factor that, because we continuously walked for ten to twelve straight hours each day, we were incredibly tired when we arrived at camp. Staying awake until we completed our evening chores was the real battle. In addition, was the fact that, once the sun went down, there was really nothing else to do but sleep. *"Hiker Midnight,"* as it is called on the trail, is the moment when the sun sets. During the winter and early spring, there is often enough darkness for ten to twelve hours of blissful sleep. We never slept more peacefully than we did on the trail (except for the nights when rodents in the shelters scurried across our sleeping bags and kept "Mom" up). Staying up past 8:00 p.m. became impossible!

Even with the extended hours of sleep, it took me quite awhile to become a morning person. Once I did, I found it to be quite a stimulating experience. For instance, I discovered that the sun creates a gorgeous spectacle as it rises in the east. Prior to the hike, I always thought it just appeared in the sky each day a few miles above the horizon. Rising early also allowed us to be the first ones on the trail—often as early as 6:00 a.m. That meant the "gazelles" would not catch us until just before dinner rather than just after lunch. "Mom" was always up before I was, no matter how hard I tried to beat her, so she took down the bear bag and prepared breakfast. The morning routine of breaking camp was a reverse version of the previous evening. The only real difference was that because we each had a particular way to pack our packs, we always re-packed our own. Then we dropped the tent and off we went.

For us, these brief moments of relative normalcy allowed us to maintain the frame of mind necessary to cope with the "anything but normal" occurrences we faced on the trail each day.

Brownie:

"Souleman" is a morning person so he naturally woke up early and wanted to get going. He also requires much less sleep than I do. These two factors made our first thru-hike a real challenge. He would wake up very early and wanted to start hiking, but I needed much more sleep and would be grumpy and tired all day if he woke me to start early. He took my sleepiness as a lack of enthusiasm for hiking and didn't understand how I could stay asleep. Sometimes he would

wake me up and I'd usually plead, "Five more minutes, okay?"
Eventually he gave up waking me and I often awoke to find him sitting
up in the tent restless and ready to go. When we stopped hiking that
first year, we discovered that I was in the late stages of mono; and
according to the doctors, I had it for some time. This is likely why I
was so exhausted and unable to get up early. We didn't have issues
with sleep patterns the second hike because my sleeping rhythm had
changed some and I was better able to get up early and hike."

Trickster:

"In the early morning when we woke up, generally around 5 a.m.,
our routine resembled a great old silent film or, more accurately,
"Night of the Living Dead." Dan and I writhed in our sleeping bags
like zombies about to rise from the dead. We blinked a few times and
then stared blankly at the ceiling of our tent before rising into sitting
positions. We then mindlessly began reaching for things and stuffed
them into our backpacks. Eventually we had to get out of our sleeping
bags and stuff them away too. We usually did not speak to each other
during this entire process. Speech required cognitive thought and it
was much too early for that. Instead we chose to communicate, when
necessary, in a series of grunts. Our bodies were tired and our stiff
joints and muscles complained as we crawled out of the tent to face a
new day. As the minutes ticked by, we each became more animated
and eventually spoke our first words. Another day on the trail had
commenced."

Now be forewarned, all you couples who daydream about how romantic a long distance hike will be—the physical and mental anguish of thru-hiking is anything but romantic. The mental fatigue associated with the tedious concentration of constantly measuring each step, takes its toll. It is an incredible amount of work but is the type of work that will have you feeling more alive than you ever have felt before. It does have its romantic elements; but unlike the enchantment a couple encounters on, say, a sandy Hawaiian beach with a cool breeze blowing through palm trees and azure waves licking the shore, the romance of the trail often has to be sought out. It is found in the majesty of the wilderness that envelops you and in how it touches your soul by caressing your senses.

Not every day was steeped in struggles that tested the bonds of our relationship, making it stronger and more transparent. In fact, most days were filled with memorable moments and fun. We did sometimes experience momentary disenchantment with the trail. But then just a brief glance at a windswept vista or listening to the deafening quiet quickly brought all the fun and romance back. Even on those days that brutalized us with bad weather, incessant bugs, sweltering heat, or bitter cold, there was always something creating a sense of serenity that brought our hearts closer together. Maybe it was a sunrise which turned the mountains blue and the sky pink, or maybe it was an immense waterfall whose rushing waters enveloped the surrounding woods in a soothing, never-ending symphony of sound. Whatever they were, we relished each and every one of those moments.

Learning to find the romance in our new environment allowed us to poetically reinterpret all the absolutely horrid circumstances that had us sometimes wondering, *"Are we having fun yet?"* into tales of unbridled passion for our surroundings—and each other. Moreover, now that the pain in our feet and legs is gone and the mosquito bites have healed, enough *bona fide* romantic moments come to mind to more than offset the less-than-desirable moments. They represented something unique and unforgettable in our lives and each one brought us closer together as we shared in their influence on our lives at that point in time—and forever.

It was March 29th and our plan was to hike to the tent site at Poplar Stamp where we would have a quiet, and hopefully, romantic evening. Being introverts at heart, or more likely because of genetic disposition, we required time alone to recharge our emotional batteries. We did love being around the other hikers, but every so often a break from the maddening crowd was a welcome respite. Although we wanted to spend as much time as possible with other hikers and develop the type of "trail family" bonds synonymous with hiking the A.T., we both expressed the importance of being alone, together. Quiet, sunset drenched evenings sitting under a canopy of tall conifers and discussing, not only our journey, but blissfully talking about our hopes and dreams for the future, were important ingredients of our grand adventure. It was a time to share our inner-most longings and to deepen our relationship. Tonight, we hoped, would be such an occasion.

Being only four days into our journey, our sprits were high and physically we were doing quite well; a few small hot spots had developed on our feet, and we had some cramping, but we were in much better shape than many of the other folks out there. God was everywhere we looked, and the most amazing thing about being on the trail, beside the number of mountains along this path, was the quiet. There were no cars, sirens, boom boxes, and only an occasional plane passing overhead. As we walked, we often would simply stop, breathe as quietly as possible, and listen to just how quiet it was. More than once, the only sound was our heartbeats, and it was the type of quiet where even an atheist could not deny the presence of something greater than himself.

As twilight began to cast its spell over the surrounding hillsides, it suddenly appeared. There, encircled by a stand of pines, whose fallen needles covered the ground in a rich, brown carpet, was the object of our desire—Poplar Stamp Tentsite. It was the romance of the wilderness personified. The air suddenly became still and the sounds of nature cascaded off the trees. This was the type of place we talked about finding, the idyllic place that would accentuate our passion for the trail and bolster our passion for each other.

"Mom" unpacked our packs and prepared to make dinner, and I was off to get water that was not only quite some distance down the trail, but— as I distressingly found out — was less than abundant. I spent an inordinate amount of time digging a pool around the dribbling spring just to get enough water to fill what containers needed to be replenished. In fact, I was gone so long that "Mom" for the first time was worried something had happened to me. However, nothing, not even a struggle to get water, would diminish our longing for this place. It was as if we were preparing for our first date and absolutely nothing was going to stand in the way of it being perfect.

The rest of the evening was a *Hallmark* moment with chirping birds, a gentle breeze, and romantic conversation. All of this was accentuated by a gorgeous sunset that fluidly resolved itself into a wondrous star-filled sky. We felt closer to each other and to our mutual passion of making our thru-hike a reality than we had ever felt. We were experiencing the complete blessing of being able to chase this dream of ours, and anguished over those who do not, or cannot, chase the true desires of their hearts.

Lichen:

> *"It was so odd that, even though we were together almost all the time while hiking and often there weren't people around, we hardly ever felt alone together. We found that it was hard to have those frank personal conversations to see how each other was doing while hiking along the trail or at the shelters. We never knew when we would run across other hikers, and voices have an uncanny way of traveling a long way in the woods anyway. There were always people around the shelters. We learned that we needed to have nights where we were not at a shelter, or to have a night at a hotel, where we could talk frankly to check on how each other was doing. We talked to a couple of other couples, and they felt this way too."*

It was the morning of Good Friday and the thick clouds that enveloped us as we walked the narrow ridgeline toward Clingman's Dome, the highest point on the trail, had us wondering if the spectacular views from there were going to be a dismal washout. We could only see several feet in front of us and the wind was whipping through the trees with unrelenting ferocity. With every step we prayed the sky would clear before we got to our intended destination for the morning so we could take in the sweeping panoramas from the observation platform at "The Dome." We walked to within one and a half miles of the peak, and as if a celestial curtain had been parted, the clouds and fog completely cleared away. Now we could see not only our destination, but also the magnificence of the mountains bathed in the morning sun all around us. As we hiked up one of the steeper grades to the top, the historic significance of this day became indelibly etched in our minds. As we looked up, we saw for a brief moment, a cross formed by two clouds floating overhead in an otherwise cloudless sky. The need to spiritually romanticize that event could not be denied. We stood on the narrow ridge before Clingman's Dome with the clouds now blown miles away and were struck by the immensity of what was below us. How insignificant we felt in relation to the whole landscape at our feet. The aches in our legs were anything but romantic, but we could not shake the realization of how blessed we were to be a part of the creation in which we now stood—we were mesmerized.

Forays at romance were sometimes so hard to come by that the chance to stay in the "Honeymoon Suite" at Mountain Moma's Kuntry Store and Hostel near Davenport Gap, Tennessee was reason for jubilation. It was amazing how our few short weeks of sleeping in a tent or in an antiquated, dusty, mouse-infested shelter altered our perception of luxury. Our romantic get-away was an eight-foot by twelve-foot rustic cabin with a single window and a small, sagging porch out front. Behind the cabin was a delightful stream that danced over and around huge boulders polished smooth by millenniums of rushing water caressing them. In contrast to the idyllic setting out back, out front was a collection of rusty, classic junk cars in various states of restoration. The family dogs wandered in and out of our front yard (at least those who weren't chained to the front bumpers of the cars). The whole thing was rather charming in a "we will take whatever romance we can find" type of way. It was not the Hilton but, after weeks on the trail, it seemed like heaven. Unfortunately, other hiking couples will never experience that unique moment for trail amore', since Mountain Moma's, a legendary institution at the end of the Smokies, has been sold and the "Honeymoon Suite" has been razed.

One of our romantic evenings on the trail, if not the most, was spent at the Pierce Pond Shelter four miles south of Caratunk, Maine. Our memories of this place served as a fitting capstone to all the other heartfelt moments we experienced during our journey. We arrived at the shelter in the middle of the afternoon, and after briefly gazing at the stunning expanse of luminescent water stretching for miles in front of the shelter, we decided this would be the perfect spot to spend the evening. The open side of the shelter faced the water and granted us an unfettered view of the pond and the mountains in the distance. We unpacked and prepared for our stay hoping we would have the shelter to ourselves. This was a place that exemplified "solitude" and "enchantment." I was immediately inspired by the beauty of our location. I grabbed my Native American flute, found a large rock by the shore on which to sit, and began to create music that expressed the passion I felt for this gorgeous setting. The sound of my flute, carried by the wind, echoed off the mirror-smooth surface of the water, and in response, a choir of loons began to serenade us. The windblown aroma of pine enveloped us and an overwhelming sense of peace held us firmly to its bosom. As the day drew to its alluring conclusion, it became apparent we would indeed have the shelter all to ourselves; how fitting it all seemed. We quietly sat at the front edge of the shelter, eating dinner, making sure we did not make any noise that would interrupt the all-encompassing peace surrounding us. We gazed out at an exquisite sunset as it slowly and lovingly turned the sky into a canvas of endless shades of crimson. And as it set, the surface of Pierce Pond became a mirror image of the sky until a blanket of mist washed it all away. It was a sight that would have had Thoreau running to get a pen and paper.

These romantic interludes, as intermittent as they were, left an indelible mark on our hearts. They carried us through the moments of struggle and opened our hearts to the importance of capturing those fleeting moments of beauty whenever, and wherever, they occurred. We wondered if we would be able to sustain our ability to find that level of romance in the day-to-day circumstances of our lives in the real world.

Romanticism "of" the trail and romance "on" the trail were two entirely different concepts. The romance "of" the trail resided in the hikers' perceptions of the wonders that were seen, heard, smelled, and touched as they traveled a road that was excitedly new to them. However, romance "on" the trail, especially the physical kind, was a different animal all together—an animal that most hikers, especially the married couples, rarely participated in.

Enuff:

> *"Physical intimacy? There was no physical intimacy! The physical setting and the stink made it difficult. Maybe if we were twenty-five it might have been different. But, at fifty it gets a little difficult to arrange those intimate moments. The trail made it easier to accept that reality. Because of the lack of solitude, the days without a shower and the ongoing fatigue of the hike, it was okay to simply be together and sleep together each night without any physical, sexual manifestations. That was the level of intimacy that was acceptable."*

Romance on the trail acquired a whole new definition because it was extraordinarily more intimate, yet less sexual. Its essence was rooted in the most seemingly unromantic interactions. *"Are your feet okay?" "Would you like to stop here for a break?"* or even, *"Would you like a Snickers or a Luna Bar?"* became tantamount to foreplay. Chalk it up to age, maturity, or simply the fact we were just too darn tired at the end of the day to even consider any physical alternative; these small, otherwise innocuous, personal interactions were sufficiently intimate.

As for the single hikers we spent time with, God only knows how they spent their zero days in town. Having been their age, in a universe long, long ago, I can only surmise that the most basic human need sometimes overrode the less-than-aphrodisiac aroma of days without a shower. Kids will be kids, you know. Even on the trail.

Romance aside, we found it hard to comprehend how the solo hikers made it through each day without someone with whom to share their daily feelings and experiences. Even with "Mom" and me being introverts, it was difficult for us to put ourselves in their place. Our need to communicate with each other was analogous to our need for food and water. During the first few weeks of endlessly walking and talking—except when going uphill which was impossible for us to do simultaneously—we completely ran the gamut of topics to discuss. We planned our retirement, expanded the websites for my companies, put together a list of all the places we wanted to visit in the world, and discussed our relationships with our parents and children. No topic escaped our scrutiny, except politics, which "Mom" finds distasteful and annoying. But after those first few weeks, much of our communication became non-verbal. Because we are so much alike and were experiencing the same things at the same time, we had no need to constantly communicate what we were seeing or feeling.

Having verbally run every conceivable topic into the ground, it was not unusual for us to wander in silence for hours until something as crucial as deciding when and where to eat lunch, forced us to break the silence. The simple choice of, *"Should we eat here or walk a bit further until we find a more picturesque spot at which to dine?"* more often than not, became an endless repartee that had us passing up suitable spots and inevitably had us eating at a less-than-desirable location. Then began the laundry list of questions regarding what we would have to eat. *"Would you like tuna or peanut butter?"* or *"How about some ice tea?"* and "Mom's" favorite,*" Do we have any more Luna Bars or Snickers Marathon Protein Bars?"* This mundane give-and-take did not do much to expand our collective consciousness but it did break up the hours of quiet.

Brownie:

> *"We were unequivocally happy during our honeymoon hike. We continued our habit of hiking within sight of each other. Often we spoke of the future—where would we live? What jobs would we find? What would we name our children? Our past hike was often a topic as well. We fondly remembered previous locations, situations, as well as the hikers that we met."*

Trickster:

> *"We had been listening to music less and less. The trail provided a music all its own that you can never experience with head phones on. If we ran out of things to talk about, we would make things up, like what kind of house we would live in if we had an unlimited sum of money and land. Our "said" house would include an indoor rollercoaster, heated pool (more of a lagoon really), and, of course, the huge garden/rain forest. There would be a wide variety of wildlife and a giant banyan tree with a tree house resting on its giant, outspread limbs. Hey, we could dream, right? Sometimes the silence was enough to keep us occupied, each of us walking along engrossed in our own private thoughts, passing away the miles beneath our feet."*

In the early days of our hike, because of our single-minded purpose of successfully getting through each day and doing everything possible to ensure our hike's success, what was relationally transpiring between us was not always apparent to us. However, as the days progressed into weeks and then into months, the love and compassion we had for each other blossomed into a bond we sometimes found incomprehensible.

As "V&A" succinctly put it:

"We occasionally saw signs of frustration, but we saw joy and happiness as well. As the hike went on, we saw determination and a deeper feeling emerge between the two of them."

The marital harmony that evolved on the trail —and the lasting positive effects of having depended on each other for every bit of physical, emotional and psychological support twenty-four/seven for six months—is the essence of wilderness adventure novels and behavioral science doctoral theses. *"Walking in Step"* came to mean more than simply putting one foot in front of the other. It became emblematic of everything we discovered about ourselves and each other. We learned to empathize with our partner and to display compassion for the pain he or she was enduring. It reinforced the importance of sharing responsibilities and working as a team. There was the need to continuously adapt to, not only changing situations, but to each other's needs. And there was the absolute necessity to willfully compromise so we could both succeed. Finally, there were brand new definitions for affection and romance birthed from simplicity of our trail existence.

It was simple to describe the obvious moments of marital interplay, those moments where a word of encouragement was all that was needed to reach the next shelter or town. What was harder to define, and even harder to verbalize, were the moments of internal reflection. Those moments when we each realized the person we were married to, and with whom we were sharing this fantastic adventure, was totally committed to "us" as a couple and to what we were undertaking. This wilderness adventure had never crossed our minds when we swore to "honor and obey," "to cherish, for richer or for poorer and in sickness and in health." The more standard twists and turns of a normal marital life were the reasons for those pronouncements. Thru-hiking the Appalachian Trail gave those same vows new meaning and power. However, it would not be until months after completing our journey that the full extent of the relational benefits of living out our dream would surface.

Though there are some disadvantages to backpacking as a couple, they are far outweighed by the many advantages. Yes, as a couple you do have to compromise on your hiking pace and every daily decision has to be discussed. You do have a bit more freedom when hiking single to alter your plans and make forays into the wonderful world of trail town cultures. And, as a single hiker, there is the advantage of being alone—but there is also the risk of becoming lonely. At times, the trail can be a lonely place.

As a couple, you are never alone and you always have someone to talk to and share every moment and feeling with. There is someone there to encourage you, console you, and sympathize with you—no matter where you are. And there is always someone there to help you should you get injured or sick. On the practical side, it takes less time to set up camp because you can divide the responsibilities and your tent is generally warmer at night because of the body heat generated by two people. When you are in town, you can divide the daily chores giving you more time to relax and enjoy yourselves. All in all, hiking together is the best way for a couple to discover, accept, and build upon the individual strengths and shortcomings they both possess. From that process is built the foundation for a strong marriage.

"Mom's" Tips for Couples:

- Discover and accept your mate's strengths and weaknesses. Take these into account when approaching life's situations—divide and conquer;

- Compromise. The end result is more important than your feelings;

- Share your feelings and be transparent. Doing so is a sign of emotional and relational strength, not weakness;

- Always put your mate's feelings before your own. What you get from your mate in return is worth it.

CHAPTER FIVE

....IN SICKNESS AND IN HEALTH

"No Pain, No Rain, No Maine!" Unknown

Putting aside all of the differences in personalities, genders, hometowns and physical conditioning, there were two things all the members of our "thru-hiking family" had in common. First was their insatiable desire to reach Mt. Katahdin, and the second was their fear of having their dream cut short by some hike-ending illness or injury. It was an ever-present concern whose dominance over our thoughts became increasingly menacing as our final destination grew closer. "Burner" vocalized this concern for all of us when, at Gentian Pond Shelter in Maine, he reluctantly but sincerely communicated that, "With Mt. Katahdin so close, we are becoming more aware of the possibility of getting hurt and not being able to finish. Boots are wearing out, bodies are wearing out and people are still trying to do twenty miles a day." Not long after making that introspective statement, he suffered a sprained ankle, right before Chairback Gap, which laid him up in a shelter for a day. Thankfully, he was able to walk it off and successfully completed his thru-hike. Still, the threat of injury was inexorably real to all of us. For middle-aged couples like us, the threat of injury and illness was even more pronounced. Because of our ages, we understood that the healing process would be slower than in our youth. Knowing this, we took more precautions, and staying healthy was a priority rather than an afterthought. Our partner's happiness and desire to complete the journey was at stake, and we did not want injury or sickness to compromise that.

In our everyday lives, the discomfort and aggravation associated with being injured or ill is a simple fact of life. Injury or sickness presents itself as merely an inconvenience and has little, if anything, to do with how we approach each day. You simply suck it up, make adjustments to your day, or you take time off to recover. The trail, however, was a different environment altogether. Every rock, every precipitous climb or descent, every aggressive species of wildlife or flying insect became an issue for concern. The smallest rock or the shortest moss-covered puncheon became an unforgiving adversary, and the slightest miscalculation or misstep became a recipe for disaster. The "gazelles," with their long strides and penchant for speed, seemed to experience more falls in a single day than we did in a month. Whether it was because we are short and have a lower center of gravity or just because we walked too darn slow to fall, we considered ourselves lucky not to be constantly coming into camp at night with bleeding knees and twisted ankles. We were not impervious to falls, but ours were relatively few and benign compared to those of so many others. Had there been no puncheons on the trail, "Mom" would, possibly, have made the entire trip unscathed.

Even worse, despite all precautions, were the injuries that unknowingly crept up on hikers regardless of their physical conditioning and on-trail care. "Little Wing" is from Gainesville, Florida, and had only done one hike—of just under fifty miles—prior to taking on the A.T. Faced with the fact that the highest elevation in Florida was a local landfill, she trained by running up and down the steps with a pack on at the University of Florida football stadium. Even though she was more of a "flatlander" than even we were, as her adventure progressed she developed into one of the strongest hikers with whom we had the good fortune to travel. Despite all this, her journey ended at the base of Mt. Washington after five months and 1,834 miles. A stabbing pain in her hip prompted a trip to the emergency room in North Conway, New Hampshire, where she received the gut-wrenching news that she had developed a stress fracture. She was told, in no uncertain terms, that her hike was over.

"Cash," the amiable personal trainer from Texas with a penchant for creating or simply living through some of the most humorous and entertaining events on the trail, was also an incredibly strong and fast hiker. However, not even his physical conditioning nor regular doses of "Vitamin I" from the quart *Ziploc* bag he always carried in his pocket could prevent the onset of shin splints. The pain became so bad he walked down hills backwards, and eventually he was forced to take several days of rest at the Dutch Haus B&B in Virginia. He healed and completed his thru-hike several weeks ahead of us.

"Oly," a 70-year-old speedster with incredible stamina, was famous for always being the first one to a shelter at the end of the day, and he would eat everyone's leftovers—after completing his own meal. As tough as he was, he had something as innocuous as a broken "stay" in his pack almost take him off the trail. The broken stay dramatically shifted the weight of his pack, affected his hip, and put undue pressure on his sciatic nerve. A few days in Damascus, Virginia, recuperating was all it took for him to get back on the trail. But if "Old Grandad" had not happened by and had not carried "Oly's" pack for him so he could make it to town, the outcome could have been much worse.

Then, of course, there was "Iron Wolf," a burgeoning icon of the trail, who developed a hernia near Damascus. Now, for everyone else that would have been the end of his hike—but not so for this war veteran and amazingly resilient outdoorsman. Only days after his operation, he was back on the trail, oozing surgery scar and all, making his way north to Maine. He was also one of a group of hikers in a shelter in the Smokies who awoke one morning to find that one of their bunkmates, "Phoenix," who was attempting his third thru-hike, had died of a heart attack right next to them. This event, a harsh and sudden illustration of one's own mortality, could have marked the end of a hike for anyone else. For "Iron Wolf" it was a mere fact of life, and his life and hike needed to go on.

"Pi & K'ache," another couple from Maryland, made it all the way to Rutland, Vermont, before debilitating leg pain forced K'ache to visit a doctor. The diagnosis was severe muscle strain and the doctor suggested she stop hiking for a week or two. Since they had previously agreed that if one of them had to leave the trail, the other would continue, "Pi" continued hiking north. In spite of several attempts to hike again, the pain forced "K'ache" off the trail. On August 11th she left Vermont for the plane ride back home. "Pi" continued on and summited without his wife and best friend. They were a great team. They were always there to help one another, each one taking on tasks, and supporting the other when things got dreary. It was hard for "Pi" to hike alone and "K'ache" to recuperate alone because normally they had each other to rely on. For them, doing the big things together with someone they loved really made a difference. It made life wonderful. Now, the dream had unexpectedly ended and "Pi" had no one to share the beautiful moments with.

A hike-ending injury could take place at any time, any place, and as you can see, for any of a million unexpected and bizarre reasons. It was being continually aware of that fact that, we believe, kept us from falling victim to some cruel fate. Or, perhaps it was just luck; we may never know for sure. We just knew we had been doing, and would continue to do, everything we could to keep our dream moving forward. Not getting hurt or sick, trumped every reason to move faster or to take unnecessary risks.

In 2006 the instances of hikers contracting Lyme Disease were almost too numerous to count, and not a day went by when we did not hear of one of our fellow hikers, or a trail caretaker, being brought to a standstill by the chronic fatigue that is the hallmark of this disease. Based on statistics published in the November 2007 edition of the *AMC Outdoors Magazine*, there were 617 reported cases in New Hampshire alone—double that of 2005! Taking into account the northward movement of the deer ticks that spread Lyme disease, which greatly expands the geographic area where they thrive, the chances of contracting this disease grew exponentially. Because of the prevalence of this affliction, every night we made a concerted effort to meticulously check each other for the miniscule ticks that bore this commonplace disease. For me, it was a laborious job because of the liberal number of moles on "Mom" which easily hid their presence. On several occasions we did discover those fiendish rascals lurking in the hair on our legs. Because of our diligence and the fact we each had a partner who was willing to take on this chore, we were spared the agony of having to deal with the disease. Once the symptoms of Lyme were diagnosed, it was not uncommon to see hikers continuing their northward trek with their medication strapped to the outside of their packs.

One of our favorite hikers was "Old Drum," a retired park and recreation director and master storyteller from Missouri. Over the course of his trek, "Old Drum" became the "poster boy" for everything bad that could possibly happen to you on the trail. His bout with Lyme disease almost became trivial when put in the context of everything else he endured. As time went on, his repeated shelter register entry of, *"Old Drum signing in so they can find my body and so my wife can collect the insurance money,"* took on a note of irony. Here is a list of what befell him:

- 38 falls (6 of which drew blood);
- 9 cases of poison ivy;
- 3 bouts with hypothermia;
- 20 blisters on his feet;
- Tendonitis in both ankles;
- Flare up of bursitis in both Achilles bursas;
- 1 concussion;
- 1 hematoma;
- 1 torn tendon (behind left knee);
- 1 mild case of chaffing (right inner thigh);
- 1 severe case of chafing on both shoulders that left scars;
- 1 case of Lyme disease;
- Countless insect and mosquito bites;
- Countless scratches

Even through all of this, or simply because his wife told him he could not leave the trail until he had either summited Mt. Katahdin or was bleeding so profusely he had to be carried off the trail, he successfully completed his thru-hike. His stick-to-itiveness was a true testament to willpower, perseverance, or maybe the lingering effects of his concussion.

The list of maladies that were the trademark of the wilderness existence, such as the bite of the brown recluse spider that left hikers like "Cool Hand" with a rather nasty looking open sore requiring heavy doses of antibiotics, paled in comparison to the one single malady that, though not life-threatening, haunted nearly all of us—blisters!

As if thru-hiking the Appalachian Trail was not difficult enough on its own, hiking it with blistered feet only added to the agony. As counter-productive as having blisters was, we got the impression that many hikers felt having their feet reduced to bloody stumps and on the verge of infection, was a rite of passage or a incontrovertible truth of doing a thru-hike. Hikers often triumphantly displayed their wounds with a perverted sense of pride. More often than not, we were astounded by the fact they were even able to put on their hiking boots—much less walk 15 miles to 20 miles in that condition.

For many, the first blisters appeared on the very first day of their hike and slowly disappeared as their feet toughened from endless miles of walking. For others, they remained a source of pain and discomfort right up until the last day. Solutions to the blister problem came in various forms. Some were prepared with the requisite selection of moleskin, band-aids, and "new skin" patches. The more daring covered their wounds with the hiker's best friend, duct tape. Still others like "Skunk" and "Sherps" (who later changed her name to "Fiddlehead") circumvented the immense discomfort of their blisters by simply walking in their *Crocs*. This, of course, exposed their open sores to unending amounts of dirt which increased the potential for infection.

Many people ask us, *"What was the most important piece of equipment you used on your hike?"* Without hesitation, our answer was, and still is, <u>our feet</u>. They were the one piece of equipment we and every other hiker used every day, all day, for 2,175 miles; if they failed, we would be finished. At the very least, if they were damaged to the point where every step was unrelenting torture, our enjoyment and ability to do the requisite miles each day were severely impacted.

We learned a great deal about blisters during our earlier hike of the C&O Canal near Paw Paw, West Virginia. Recounting the intense pain and the negative impact to our hiking speed associated with those blisters, we vowed to minimize or eliminate their effects on our thru-hike. On one of our later training hikes on the A.T. in Maryland, we were met at Pine Knob

Shelter by "Smilin' Joe," a 2005 thru-hiker who waltzed into the campsite displaying no outward physical signs of having just completed a 25-mile day. A former truck driver and triathlete, he divulged the secret of how he kept from developing blisters during long-distance competitions. It was as simple as using isopropyl alcohol and *Blister Shield*—a micronized wax powder used by marathoners to reduce friction. We were a bit skeptical until he pulled off his socks and displayed feet that showed no ill effects of years of torturous running and hiking one thousand miles to that point. We decided to follow his advice and have used *Blister Shield* ever since—along with sock liners.

"Mom," always one to expand on a good thing, took "Smilin' Joe's" idea a step further and added another vital component to the elixir. Each day before starting out, she would liberally dust our liner socks with a mixture of 50 % *Gold Bond Foot Powder* and 50 % *Blister Shield*. And we made sure to keep our toenails cut short so we did not have to suffer the agony of "black toe," an infirmity that results from toes slamming against the front of hiking boots during steep descents. The result was that during 2,175 miles we did not experience one blister of any significance. There may have also been something about the fact the Johnson family, from our church, prayed every day that we would not get blisters. We believe that played a role in our good fortune as well. We also benefited from the fact that "V&A" met us every three to four days with dry socks and liners; so except on the days when we were suddenly caught in a thunderstorm, we always had dry socks—a critical component in keeping blisters to a minimum.

PAIN! It is a reality of the trail that few, if any, were able to avoid. It began its ominous presence in our bodies right from the very first steps, and our jubilation about being on the trail often surrendered to its agonizing persistence. It never totally subsided but merely migrated to other extremities without notice or reason. The old A.T. adage, *"No Pain! No Rain! No Maine,"* is an apt definition of the A.T. thru-hike experience. No amount of ibuprofen completely conquered the nagging torment of pain's impact on our bodies and our minds. What we all came to find was that mere tenacity and the blind ambition to reach a goal ultimately were often no match for the pain that wracked our every movement. We learned to accept the pain, and, in a twisted rationalization of sorts, welcomed its presence as an assurance we were totally alive and accomplishing something of great value for ourselves. Each time we thought we were finished dealing with the pain, we arose in the morning and were immediately reminded of its insidious presence as we laced up our boots and took our first steps of the day. What we experienced was a hiking anomaly cursedly known as the *"Hiker Shuffle."* The *"Hiker Shuffle"* manifested itself in a measured gait that resembled that of a 100-year-old man attempting to stride with the aid of a walker and 25-pound weights on each foot. This affliction played no favorites and was the great equalizer between us ("the gerbils") and the long-legged "gazelles." This condition stayed with us for months after our hike was completed and still, periodically, resurfaces when we least expect it.

Even though we accepted the pain, we were inclined to give it as much of a run for its money as we could. "Mom" and I had a nightly routine of giving each other foot and leg massages, much to the amusement and bewilderment of those with whom we hiked. It was a ritual we religiously carried out, whether we were in our tent, a shelter, or in town at a hostel or motel. We would lay on our backs, side-by-side, facing in opposite directions, and place the leg nearest to our partner in their lap. To the uninitiated, it appeared we were preparing to do battle in a round of "Indian leg wrestling." We simply rested our legs, one at a time, on the other person's chest and worked the aching muscles until we both were satisfied with the result or one of us cried *"Uncle!"*

As time on the trail passed, we found this nightly routine increasingly envied, especially by those suffering the physical ills of a long day and who were unable to coerce a suitable partner into performing the same procedures. Having seen the despicable condition of some of these hikers' feet, we could readily understand why finding a massage partner was virtually impossible for them. There were several couples though, like "Moe & Ponch," who first saw our practice at The Blackburn Center just south of Harper's Ferry and considered adopting the regimen for themselves. Aside from the obvious physical benefits of this practice, it also became an evolving bonding experience and a point of physical connectivity for us. Hours on the trail, some days covering countless, grueling, miles in relative silence, lent itself to few opportunities for physical interaction. Massaging each other's legs and feet each night was our most valued form of physical intimacy.

Being strong proponents of weekly chiropractic adjustments, and concerned about what effect six months without one would have on our bodies, we made sure we stopped for at least three during our hike. Our first, which only "Mom" took advantage of, was in May in Lynchburg, Virginia, when we were staying with my parents for a few zero days. We both visited our regular chiropractor at Germantown Chiropractic while we were home for a few days after reaching Harper's Ferry in June. The final adjustment was in Rutland, Vermont, at Kirbach Chiropractic in August. An interesting sidebar to our trail adjustments revealed itself after our hike was completed. When we arrived home, our backs, despite the punishment they had taken over the last six months, felt incredibly good. So good in fact, that at each appointment we complimented our doctor on how effective his adjustments had been. It was not until we had been home for about a month that we began to experience symptoms we had not had for quite some time. Perplexed and confused as to what was the culprit, we made it known to our doctor during idle conversation that we religiously popped "Vitamin I" the entire time we were on the trail. The obvious, and rather comical, diagnosis of our current discomfort was that the residual effects of the ibuprofen had finally worn off and our spines were back to the condition they had been in before the hike.

Regular massages not only played a vital role in relieving the multitude of aches and pains we experienced, but it forced us to take a rest, though brief, from our in-town routines on zero days. In Hot Springs, North Carolina, we visited the famed Hot Springs Resort and Spa for a pampering massage, and had another one at a campground in Shartlesville, Pennsylvania, where the masseur stated he had never worked on anyone with such developed ankle muscles. We also treated ourselves to a massage in Connecticut. There were three other episodes of physical euphoria before our adventure was complete: in Rutland, Vermont, Lincoln, New Hampshire, and in Monson, Maine. On two separate occasions we soothed our aching muscles in the hot tub at the Royalty Inn, in Gorham, New Hampshire—being careful not to let our toughened feet get soft.

We also made sure that before we took our first steps on the trail each day, we spent ten minutes or so stretching the muscles in our legs and backs. Initially, I was more than a bit skeptical about the need to stretch muscles that were going to be stretched naturally while we walked. A leg cramp which nearly brought me to my knees partway up a steep climb, not long after leaving camp, quickly made me a convert.

We readily admit these chiropractic adjustments, along with regular massage therapy, and our nightly ritual of massaging each other's legs and feet made all the difference in the world and helped make it possible for us to make it the entire way. Then again, the steady diet of ibuprofen could make these claims a bit suspect.

What was most important was that the trail made us more aware of what our bodies were doing and feeling. We were forced to impose a level of physical care and understanding we passed off as bothersome and inconsequential in our normal lives. Considering how great we felt, despite the pounding our bodies took, we vowed that once we were home our approach to maintaining our bodies would dramatically change.

In the harsh wilderness domain that was in large part foreign to us, the chances of encountering a situation that would bring our sojourn to an abrupt end were immense. In an attempt to minimize any undue adversity, we took every precaution humanly possible to assure our memories of this hike were ones of beauty, self-awareness, and enjoyment—not pain and suffering. We were certain that having only memories of pain and suffering would do little to enhance the life we vowed to spend together after the hike. It is bad enough getting sick in the relative comfort of home, but becoming ill on the trail takes on an entirely new dimension. For us, taking a Wilderness First Aid class, something we strongly urge everyone to take, hiker and non-hiker alike, prepared us for the major calamities we might encounter. It also provided us with a level of confidence that we could handle most anything the A.T. might throw at us. However, one of us becoming deathly ill on the trail, where a doctor or pharmacy could be a three-day walk away and where carrying a large assortment of antibiotics and other medicines were weight-prohibitive, gave us reason to pause. Our goal was to make sure a debilitating illness did not strike us down. Always in the back of our minds was the nagging thought, *"I hope neither of us gets sick today."* That thought made being together unquestionably important. Caring for someone who is ill can be an emotionally draining experience. You want so much to ease the suffering but often cannot. Because of that, his/her suffering becomes your own, and as much as you help, you feel helpless. Out on the trail, this feeling is magnified by the sheer isolation of the environment.

As a hedge against getting sick, we routinely took vitamins and added to our drinks a powder called *Emergen-C* which contained the vital nutrients and minerals our bodies burned up each day. "Mom" also had her acupuncturist send her herbs to counteract the "hot flashes" that made determining her actual body temperature a challenge. We washed our pots, utensils, and bowls after every meal, much to the amusement of people like "Shattered," an A.T. ridgerunner who spent the night with us at Icewater Spring Shelter in the Smokies. It was routine for some hikers, especially those hiking solo and who cooked and ate out of the same pot, to simply scrape the inside of their pot after a meal. A more thorough cleaning was done in town on a zero day. We may have used a bit more water and fuel than everyone else, but allowing dirty pots to serve as Petri dishes for potentially debilitating bacteria just did not make good sense to us.

The most important step we took was to filter every drop of water we used—be it for drinking or for cooking. With a daily intake of three-plus liters of water, waterborne diseases, most notably Giardia, were a constant threat to our health and well-being. Giardiasis is a diarrheal illness caused by a one-celled, microscopic parasite, *Giardia Intestinalis* (also known as *Giardia Lamblia*). Once an animal, or person, is infected with *Giardia Intestinalis*, the parasite lives in the intestine and is passed in the stool. Because an outer shell protects the parasite, it can survive outside the body and in the environment for long periods of time. *Giardia* infection can cause a variety of intestinal symptoms, which include diarrhea, gas, or flatulence, greasy stools that tend to float, stomach cramps, upset stomach, or nausea. These symptoms may lead to weight loss and dehydration. Trying to deal with this on the trail was an extremely unpleasant and uncomfortable endeavor.

The "purist" hikers rarely filtered their water. Whether it was due to years of experience, whereby they built up a tolerance to this intestinal pest, or simply because they were lucky, they did not seem to get sick. We knew we did not fall into either category, so common sense took priority over being tough—or lucky. The end result of filtering all our water and our healthcare regimen was that we never got sick—not even as much as a cough, sneeze, or runny nose. We never felt healthier than we did on the trail.

Even if we did everything possible to keep ourselves from becoming ill, sleeping in a shelter or hostel with someone who was sick became problematic. More than one unfortunate hiker contracted the flu by staying in cramped hostel quarters. One of our early hiking companions, "Old Grandad," contracted some type of virus and by the time "V&A" rescued him and dropped him off at a motel in Bland, Virginia, to fight it off, he was so ill he had to leave the trail and never was able to return. As a rule, we only stayed in hostels where there were few people or where it was obvious no one was sick. Shelters, on the other hand, were a different story altogether. If there was rain in the forecast, we slept in a shelter rather than in our tent. Whether or not anyone in the shelter was sick became irrelevant. Not having to pack up a wet tent in the morning seemed an acceptable trade-off for the potential health risk involved.

One memorable and unpleasant occurrence at Trimpi Shelter in Virginia reinforced our determination to choose our sleeping arrangements as judiciously as possible. It looked like we would have the Trimpi Shelter nearly to ourselves, along with "Bama" and "Little Wing," though we did notice a backpack in the shelter when we arrived. Since the shelter slept at least eight, we had plenty of room to spread out, and we all looked forward to a quiet and comfortable night. Luckily, the section hikers who arrived later decided to stay in their tents, thereby preserving our spacious accommodations. We put out our sleeping bags on one side of the shelter with "Bama" and "Little Wing" on the other. Soon, up from the water source, clad all in black and seemingly dressed for cold weather, came "Marco Solo" with his full water bladder. He introduced himself, packed up his things and bid us a fond farewell. Fantastic! We would be living in the lap of luxury tonight—just the four of us with plenty of room to spread out—and a fireplace, no less!

Not five minutes later, "Marco Solo" was back, mumbling something about trying to make it to the next shelter not being a very good idea. He went into the shelter, put out his sleeping bag on one of the lower four-person bunks, and quickly got in. Rather odd we thought, considering how warm it was. It was not long before we understood what he meant with his mumblings as he ran out of the shelter and promptly vomited all over the ground. He was very apologetic for his behavior and believed it was something he ate in Troutdale earlier in the day. He crawled back into his sleeping bag where he shivered and moaned and did not reappear until the next morning. When he mentioned his gastrointestinal problem might be a reoccurrence of the malaria he had endured three times before, "Mom" and I moved our bags over to the four-person bunk on other side of the shelter with "Bama" and "Little Wing." Right before nightfall, two other hikers arrived and set up their bags in the two, single-person upper births. What was going to be a relaxing evening inside our neat little hideaway turned out to be a crowded and sleepless one. It was good we were all friends.

Trickster:

>"I guess you can never know exactly how a day is going to turn out. You can plan, of course, estimate mileage, predict the weather or terrain... but in the end, sometimes it's just not up to you! At around midnight, "What?!" woke me up because his stomach was bothering him. I listened helplessly, as he moaned beside me. Less than twenty minutes later, he was sitting up groaning and then scrambling to reach an empty Ziploc, into which he soon began emptying the contents of his stomach. I didn't know what to do other than to rub his back. The process of sitting up and reaching for empty Ziplocs continued into the early morning until one of them sprung a tiny leak in the corner. "What?!" didn't realize this fact and he set the bag down beside his Therm-a-Rest mattress. Moments later he began cursing when he realized that puke had seeped out and was now all over the bottom of the tent. He and I frantically pulled out our bandanas and tried desperately to clean up the smelly mess. Merely the thought of us both having to sleep in it, almost made me feel like throwing up. He finally managed to get a little sleep, but in the morning, we were both, totally, exhausted. "What?!" was now extremely dehydrated from all the vomiting, combined with also having diarrhea.

As a loving and caring wife should do, I left to get us both water, thinking the water was close by. I soon learned the water was not exactly what one might consider "close." Following the trail to the water took me down, down, down, and then down further until I finally reached the water source. It felt like I had walked a mile and the process ended up taking a very long time. But the fact I was doing this to help someone I cared so deeply for, made the long trek tolerable. When I got back, Dan let me know that, because I had been gone for so long, he had been worrying something had happened to me. He was worried about me? Love is an amazing thing. We both lay inside the tent until after 11 a.m. and then started packing up our things.

After some long, slow miles of hiking, brought on by the fact that "What?!" had been unable to keep down any food that would provide him with the calories he needed to keep up his energy, we climbed Roan Mountain and, eventually, arrived at Carvers Gap. It was there we decided to hitchhike into town. A bottle of ginger ale, gulps of Pepto-Bismol purchased at a small convenience store, and an attempt to put down a burger and fries did little to quell his upset stomach. Miraculously, though, after a winding ride back to the trail in the bed of a pick-up truck and one final load of puke over the railing of a fence immediately after exiting the pick-up, he was fine. Go figure!"

If being injured became the greatest fear of thru-hikers, their greatest joy and most frequent topic of conversation was FOOD. At virtually any moment of the day, you might overhear thru-hikers talking about what they ate, where they ate, when they would eat again, what they planned to eat, and how much they ate or planned to eat. Considering the average thru-hiker burns 4,000 to 6,000 calories a day, the need for food becomes an outright obsession. It is not the type of gluttonous obsession born of habit or the boredom that plagues many Americans; it is one that is the direct result of running on a constant calorie deficit after so many weeks on the trail. We were no different; but because we were hiking as a couple and had trail support, we approached some aspects of food a bit differently than other hikers.

As "Jellybean," a female truck driver and amazingly powerful thru-hiker, so aptly put it when asked why she was hiking the A.T.,

"I liked the idea that I could live in the woods for days at a time and walk a different trail every day! I also thought it would be a better weight management plan than walking on a treadmill."

It was seldom we purchased a dehydrated backpacker meal. These are the ones which simply required pouring a cup or two of hot water into the pouch, giving it a quick stir, and then waiting, while the contents turn into a mixture with the consistency of wallpaper paste. Eating these meals required a liberal understanding that what you would taste very often would not resemble the meal described on the front of the package. We dehydrated our own meals so we knew what we were getting and had a much wider variety of culinary options. In fact *Ramen noodles*, that staple of almost every hiker's diet because it is cheap and lightweight though providing very little in the way of nutrition, was seldom on our menu. We did use it sparingly when preparing spaghetti and meat sauce or as a filler with chicken broth.

Because we could re-supply from the trunk of "V&A's" car, we were able to prepare three to four days' worth of lunches each time we met up with them. This kept us from having to carry a heavy jar of peanut butter or food that would spoil before we saw them next. Our lunches consisted mainly of peanut butter and jelly (or honey) on square, whole-wheat bagels, tuna rolled up in tortillas or stuffed in small pita breads, pepperoni slices with cheese, *Luna* bars or *Pria* bars, lemonade, or powdered ice tea. "Mom's" favorite was *Gatorade* mixed with *Tang*, which she drank the entire length of the trail.

Dinners were the highlight of the day, not only because we knew we were done walking until the next morning, but because they consisted of delicacies exhibiting a vague resemblance to what we were used to eating at home. There was spaghetti and soy crumbles sauce, vegetarian chili, garlic toast, tuna fillets, salmon fillets and, my favorite, quasi-*KFC* bowls. These gourmet beauties consisted of mashed potatoes, gravy, and corn with diced chicken breast, tuna, or salmon sprinkled on top. And to top off our meal virtually every night during the last several months of our hike, we split a one-half pound *Hershey's* dark chocolate bar and washed it down with ice tea or *Gatorade*. This was generally enough food to carry us until morning when we would rise and be absolutely famished—again.

In an effort to illustrate the diet of the average thru-hiker, I designed a non-USDA- approved food pyramid while walking one of the long, quiet, mindless sections of the trail. This graphic amounts to a nutritionist's worst nightmare and, if reviewed by Jenny Craig, would probably have her immediately go into cardiac arrest.

Thru-Hiker Approved Nutritional Food Pyramid

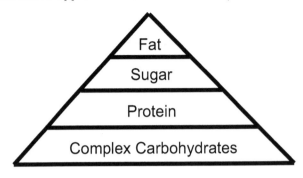

The food categories on this chart typically consisted of the following wholesome and delicious foods:

- Pizza, with every topping known to man (and a few that are not)
- *Pop-Tarts*, a snack and breakfast staple
- Beer, never the light kind but generally some rich, full-bodied ale from Ireland
- Cheeseburgers, with the works and a large side order of fries
- Soda, not that weenie diet or de-caffeinated stuff
- *Snickers* bars, a staple at every meal and snack break
- Mashed potatoes, always with lots of gravy
- Peanut butter, either on bread or right out of the jar with a spoon
- Ice cream, (*Ben & Jerry's* is the perennial favorite) though care had to be taken on very hot hiking days so as not to over-indulge and end up depositing it onto the ground a few miles up the trail
- Trail mix (GORP), that age-old favorite consisting of "Good Old Raisins and Peanuts"
- Margarine; though generally used to keep food from sticking to pans, it is not uncommon for hikers to ingest it straight from the squeeze bottle as a fat-filled, semi-liquid snack.

To this day, with the completion of the A.T. behind us, talking about food is still at the top of our list of subjects when we recount our six months in the wilderness.

Even if we wanted to entertain some level of restraint when it came to over-indulging ourselves with the local cuisine in town, most places where we stopped to eat made it rather difficult, if not impossible, to do so. Miss Ginny, owner of the Lazy Fox Bed and Breakfast in Damascus, Virginia, is a cooking legend. The folks who came up with the term, "bed and breakfast" had Ms. Ginny in mind when they added the word "breakfast" to their description. We knew we were in for a treat of astounding proportions when we saw her starting to prepare breakfast the night before. The morning we stayed with her, we arose to the aroma of one of her legendary breakfast extravaganzas. The dining room table was almost eight feet long and she covered every inch of it with platters of food. In what seemed like an endless array of choices, that made *Denny's "Grand Slam Breakfast"* look like a snack, she brought out heaping plates of bacon, sausage, eggs, pancakes, various fruits, apple crepes, grits, hash browns, biscuits, gravy and just about any other breakfast food we could name (though not a *Pop-Tart* was to be seen anywhere). She actually scolded us for not cleaning off all the platters, but the array of hikers at the table that particular morning was a more "mature" lot and our ability to eat that much food was nothing more than a distant memory.

Our largest meal took place at a motel in Front Royal, Virginia. So memorable was it in its diversity and quantity that it has taken a permanent place on our list of memorable meals and moments on the trail. We arrived at the *Quality Inn* at about 1:00 p.m., took care of journal entries and photo downloads and then, unable to fend off any longer the nagging pangs of hunger and months of operating with a calorie deficit, began our culinary adventure. We called the local *Domino's* and ordered a large pizza and a dozen *Chicken Kickers*. Knowing that our order would be at least thirty minutes in arriving, we headed down the street to pick up some appetizers, dessert, and drinks. By the time we returned to our room, we had accumulated a large bag of chips, a jar of salsa, two bottles of soda, two pints of *Ben and Jerry's Cherry Garcia* ice cream and a 20-oz can of *Budweiser* with Dale Earnhardt, Jr. emblazoned across the front. Our dinner arrived, and less than an hour later, we had polished off every bit of food in sight. Not long after that, we looked at each other and, in unison, posed the question,

"Are you still hungry? I am."

We promptly shared a half-pound *Hershey* dark chocolate bar for a snack and then turned in for the night. We knew, at that moment, that we were going to miss being able to eat like that after the hike.

Putting all kidding aside, eating enough food to maintain the level of strength necessary to carry us through each day was not a laughing matter. Losing large amounts of weight—though a foregone conclusion with a hike of this magnitude—was not something to be taken lightly. In the first six weeks, I lost fifteen pounds; and on a frame that started at only 160 pounds, losing upwards of 10 % of my bodyweight was a bit disconcerting. "Mom" also lost a great deal of weight in the first two months, but oddly, she did not lose nor gain any appreciable weight again until the last two months when her weight took another nose dive—totaling 30 lbs at hike's end.

There is a well known, though somewhat, overused illustration to demonstrate the negative effects of an action over time; it is the analogy of the frog in the pot of water. If you put a frog in a pot of boiling water, it immediately tries to jump out of the pot to save itself. However, if you put that same frog in a pan of cold water and then apply heat, the warming, and then boiling of the water, is so gradual the frog does not realize what is happening to it. Losing weight on the trail was much the same thing. Our loss of weight was gradual and constant, and because there was seldom a scale around on which to monitor ourselves, we did not realize how much we had lost. The only real indicator was our clothes were becoming too big and we needed to pull in our belts another notch. We naively thought this was due to "toning up." However, there were those who took note of our rapidly emaciating bodies and called it to our attention.

At Blackhorse Gap in Virginia "V&A" met us at the trailhead and, in no-uncertain terms, let us know we needed to halt our rapid decline in body weight by eating more protein. I had pretty much burned up all the body fat I started out with and my body was now using up muscle to fill the energy void. I guess you could say I had hit "critical mass." "Mom," though physically not at the same point as I was, agreed that adding protein would be a wise decision. From that point on, protein became a staple of every meal. We regularly devoured the most protein-enriched snack bars we could find and added protein powder to anything that would easily blend with it. Had it not been for this major addition to our diet, it is highly likely our bodies would have given up long before our wills. Instead, we became "lean, mean, hiking machines!"

Having sedentary jobs has its drawbacks—the major one being it is next to impossible not to gain weight even if you work out every day. Prior to the hike, in an effort to maintain weights applicable to our heights and ages, we resigned ourselves to living on *The South Beach Diet*, which frankly, worked well for us. What a change in mindset we experienced once we were on the trail. There, burning so many calories a day required that we open up a whole, new wonderful kingdom of epicurean choices. Not only was it the infinite choices before us, but the fact there was virtually no limit to how much of these choices we could take advantage of. We still look back on the biggest meal we ever ate with amazement and pride and only wish now that we are off the trail that we could continue to eat the same way.

Some experts claim that if thru-hikers, upon completion of their hike, continue to eat the way they did on the trail, they can gain as much as a pound per day. We cannot dispute such a claim but what we do know is that, now that we are off the trail, eating *Ben and Jerry's* as a steady diet will have us back on *South Beach* before we can say, "strawberry cheesecake."

As we came down off the summit of Mt. Katahdin on that sunny day in September of 2006, not only did the significance of what we accomplished set in, but the level of physical exertion we expended took hold—and we were totally, and utterly, exhausted. No longer could our minds, realizing the odyssey was over and that their jobs were complete, overcome what our bodies were experiencing. When we were in New Hampshire, and when day hikers discovered we were thru-hikers, they commented that we must be in great shape. I mean, we had walked all the way from Georgia, how could we not be? The truth of the matter was we were probably in our best shape somewhere in Connecticut or Massachusetts. From that point on, the wear and tear of the journey caught up with us and our bodies began breaking down rather quickly.

For all of us, as we got closer and closer to what "Mom" called, "Le Gran K," sheer willpower and adrenaline took over. All the memories of the struggles of the last five-plus months—the rain, the cold, the heat, the mosquitoes, the falls, the Lyme disease, the Giardia, the twisted ankles, and bloody knees—were now locked away in our psyches. At some point in the future, as the realization of our accomplishment set in, those memories would be released and relived. We had survived, in sickness and in health, and were all the better for it. It only remained to be seen if overcoming so much adversity and conquering the multitude of unique personal battles we all brought with us would carry us through the remainder of our lives. Only time, or perhaps another long-distance hike, would tell. We did make a conscious decision, though, to stay healthy as we aged together.

"Mom's" Tips for Couples:

- For older couples, regular medical care along the trail should be a necessity, not an afterthought.

- Because of the intense physical stress brought on by walking ten to twelve hours a day, it is important to take better care of yourself on the trail than you ever would at home.

- If a solo hiker gets injured or sick and has to leave the trail, the only one impacted is the solo hiker. If one member of a couple has to leave the trail, his/her partner is affected as well, and your shared adventure is ruined.

- Plan and budget for regular medical care along the trail, i.e., massages, chiropractic adjustments, spas, etc. They not only help keep you healthy but are enjoyable and add a unique and refreshing dimension to your adventure.

CHAPTER SIX

FAMILY

"We are not human beings on a spiritual journey. We are spiritual beings on a human journey." Stephen Covey

Little Wing:

> *"Try this: Go somewhere, anywhere, like the beach or the mall, and pick out six random people of all ages, sizes, genders, and backgrounds. Now all of you go sleep side by side like sardines in an 8-foot by 10-foot tin-roofed box, with one side of the box missing, while it pours down rain all night. That was my night last night and I had it good. Poor "Flat Rocks" was the odd man out and had to sleep on the shelter floor with rain and wind whipping his face all night. The people I bunked with could not have been more delightful. It just amuses me that just a couple days ago we were all strangers to each other and now we're perfectly accepting of lining up our sleeping bags practically on top of each other."*

They came from all over the world and from every conceivable background. They were young, they were old, and they were every age in between. They were male and female, short and tall. They were a rag-tag collection of passionate wanderers, each of whom looked upon this adventure with equal doses of excitement and apprehension.

There were as many diverse reasons these people thru-hiked the Appalachian Trail as there were personalities. The "twenty-somethings," like "Team Fourward" who were longtime friends from Michigan, were fresh out of college and gravitated to the trail in order to prolong the inescapable reality of finally having to stare their futures in the face. Being on the trail meant they could postpone for another six months getting a real job, an apartment, and acquisition of the inevitable mountain of debt that comes with pursuing one's future. There were those who relished their time on the trail as a type of therapy to sort out the emotional and psychological blowback of a failed relationship or a painful divorce. Then there were the "Baby Boomers" like us, who were close to bidding a fond *adieu* to their years of toiling in corporate America. With a newfound sense of self and a boatload of free time on their hands, we viewed a thru-hike as the next logical step on the road to retirement. For us and those like us, it was an opportunity to accomplish something of lasting value simply for ourselves— not as part of some larger corporate mission statement. Most importantly, it was a chance for the married couples to share an incredible moment in their lives together—to push their understanding and compassion for each other to new limits. While pursuing this shared goal, they also hoped to set an example for younger couples to emulate.

Brownie:

> "Along the trail we met many phenomenal couples who influenced us greatly. We loved meeting other couples who served as role models. "Hazy-Sonic" and "Firefly," "Mom" and "Windtalker," "Montreal" and "Kutsa," and "Carbomb" and "Lichen" were among the most influential couples with whom we spent time. Learning about their relationships and goals these couples set for themselves encouraged us to think about our future and our plans."

The explanation for what drove all of us forward, day after day, week after week, and month after month was something that the casual observer would never be able to comprehend. The fact was, after months on the trail and with the obvious reasons becoming somewhat mundane, we sometimes wrestled with an adequate explanation ourselves—but only for a fleeting moment, before putting it aside and trudging forward to the pinnacle of our quest. The goal of the journey was always Katahdin and the trail was the long road to it. But what became more important to us than reaching Katahdin was that "the people were the trail." The trail indeed had a character all its own, but the people were what gave the journey its character and distinctive flavor and the people were what kept us all going.

With the exception of the couples and longstanding friends who had already spent years getting to know each other, we all started out on Springer Mountain as strangers. Prior to physically meeting on the trail, we did meet some fellow wanderers by means of the Internet. We exchanged emails containing well wishes and expressed our sincere desire to meet somewhere along the A.T. We would, at last, be out of the virtual world and hiking in the real one, and we were excited about putting a face and a personality with the hiker who shared our dream. But how would we all get along? How open would we be in exposing our true colors and personal tendencies? Would this new social environment we were all a part of be totally different from the "real world" from which we all had escaped? What roles would we all play in each other's lives? Would the fact we did not know anything about each other, aside from sharing the same adventure, open up a new world of possibilities to better understand others as well as to better understand ourselves?

On the first morning of our quest, we left the Hike Inn in snow flurries at 7:00 a.m., heading to the southern terminus of the A.T. at Springer Mountain—a mere 4.4 miles away. At the summit we were met by a ruthlessly cold wind that turned out to be a harbinger of what was to come. We were also met by Roger, the nearby shelter caretaker, and by Jamie, who had us fill out an official form he needed for a thesis he was writing on hikers. Over the years, we have become aware of one incontrovertible truth and it is that, as we get older, the world seems to get increasingly smaller. The concept of our lives, and those of others, being linked by a mere "six degrees of separation" now appeared to be more than just a theory. We found out while talking to Jamie that he was student at the University of Maryland, Baltimore County, which is not far from our home. Here we were miles away from anywhere and already on our very first day we were reminded of home. After having our "traditional" Springer Mountain photo taken, we were off to tackle the 7.6 miles to Hawk Mountain Shelter and enjoy our first "official" night on the trail.

The day would be one of many other "firsts." We would be meeting our first thru-hiking companions. It would also be our first occasion to hang our food bag from a bear cable, and perhaps even catch our first glimpse of a black bear. All that excited anticipation overshadowed any apprehensions we may have had about completing this adventure and gave us the impetus to complete twelve miles our first day out. We were happier and, oddly, more content than we ever remembered being. When we arrived at Hawk Mountain Shelter, we had a full house. Because it was so cold and windy, with temperatures just above 20 °F, only "Oly" stayed in the shelter. The rest of us retired to the relative warmth of our tents. As we all gathered at the shelter for a quick dinner, we began the bonding process that was an inescapable and ongoing function of the trail. The typical uneasiness that comes from meeting and conversing with strangers for the first time was noticeably absent. We immediately began introducing ourselves to each other and quickly raced through the normal conversational formalities. Most notable in the group was Peter, from the United Kingdom, who was later dubbed "Peter Rabbit," because of his hiking speed. He lumbered into camp under the weight of a pack hovering around sixty-eight pounds. We were already straining to move with our thirty-eight pound packs, so we could barely imagine what Peter was experiencing with a pack nearly twice as heavy. Even though we barely knew him, our feelings for his predicament oscillated between being compassionate and being judgmental about him being so unaware of basic long-distance hiking requirements. As he emptied his pack to prepare dinner, it was easy to see why it was so heavy; for out came a bottle of olive oil, cans of assorted delicacies and other less-than-trail-worthy containers. He was in such agony because of his heavy load, our compassion won out and we prayed he would make it to Neels Gap where he could trim down his weight at the outfitter and purchase lighter gear that would make his trip more enjoyable. Only one day on the trail and we already cared deeply for someone we barely knew.

Mountain Crossings at Walasi-Yi Center at Neels Gap, Georgia, is the first major gathering point for north bounders on the Appalachian Trail. With its hostel and well-stocked outfitter, it is the first place all of us got a chance to meet the people we would be hiking with for the next six months. It was also our first experience with life in a hostel—complete with its raucous atmosphere of unbridled excitement and burgeoning camaraderie. There was no denying the fact we wanted to get to know as many of these vagabonds as possible, and we even hoped to meet some of the icons of the A.T. who, almost annually, made the trail their home. Names like "Baltimore Jack" and "Model T" were known to all and to meet them would be like meeting royalty. In some way, spending time with them would make our trip even more exciting. But, even though the entire facility was buzzing with hiker activity, the shear magnitude of strangers in our midst had us feeling a bit uncomfortable, lonesome, and out of place. It seemed we were the only married couple in there and our introverted personalities only added to our feeling of melancholy. As the frivolity in the hostel reached a fevered pitch, it became apparent to us that for the "twenty-somethings" socializing, both on and off the trail, was going to be as much a part of their hike as was reaching Katahdin—maybe more so. "Mom" and I were content to simply share this magnificent adventure with each other and having the urge to socialize with everyone on the trail was just not part of our personalities. Not that we did not want to meet and get to know them; it was simply not as big a priority as was chasing our dream. Little did we know, whether we consciously pursued it or not, we would soon become integral and unique members of a family unlike any we had ever known before.

While we were in the process of signing in, getting our bunk assignments and chatting with the few hikers we already knew, we heard a female voice, with a distinct southern accent, wafting across the gift shop area next to us. Not typically being a "people-person" and generally not at all comfortable in approaching a new face, I summoned up all the courage and self-confidence I had developed over my whole three days as a thru-hiker and called out,

"Are you Bama?"

"I sure am! "Windtalker, is that you?"

"It sure is!"

"Bama" hailed from Alabama and was one of the first people to leave us a message on *www.trailjournals.com*. This website is where many thru-hikers post their daily journals and photos, and it is where folks who are following their progress can leave them messages. When she wrote us to say she was starting her hike about the same time as us, we immediately felt a kinship with her—even though we had never met. "Bama" started the day after we did and became one of our regular hiking companions for most of the trip. She retired from BellSouth in 2002 after twenty-nine years of service. I thought that anyone who could stay at the same job for that long definitely had what it took to stick it out from Georgia to Maine. After her first backpacking trip on the A.T. fifteen years before, she decided she would thru-hike after she retired; and she wanted to do it before she turned sixty. Because of the closeness of our ages, we related well with her but lamented the fact that her husband, Bill, was not hiking with her. Early in our journey we desperately wanted to align ourselves with as many married hikers as possible so we did not feel so out of place among all "the kids." Even though Bill was not with her, we had our life experiences as husbands and wives in common and spent as much time as possible with her—when we could keep up with her. We eventually got to meet Bill and we still stay in contact with each other. Since she had business to take care of, we said we would see her on the trail and headed into the hostel where we located our bunks, unpacked what gear and clothing we needed for the night, and got ready for the highlight of our day—a hot shower.

For us, being open with relative strangers was new and at times quite uncomfortable. But as time went on, we grew more accustomed to it and eventually looked forward to those personal interactions. With this also came a growing comfort level for "Mom" and me with respect to being open with each other. We discovered our sense of "not fitting in" with the single hikers because we were married was our problem, not theirs. Being part of a family is wonderful that way. Because we are married and raised a family of our own, I suppose our perspective on "the kids" hiking with us, many of whom were the same age as our own children, was a bit different than their perspective of each other. Our inherent desire to nurture them initially got in the way of us developing an intimate relationship with any of them. It also had us instinctively, though often regrettably, judging some of their actions and decisions. It took us some time to accept the fact they were adults and they were simply being themselves. Once we acknowledged that fact, our relationship with many of them grew and we are still friends with many of them to this day.

We were amazed at how quickly our relationships with other hikers developed if for no other reason than we were all in the throes of experiencing the same things at the same time and everyone's goals were the same. That was the common ground we all shared and the walls quickly came down because of it. There were no pretenses, no egos getting in the way, and all semblances of false fronts seemed to evaporate into the crisp mountain air. Any reluctance to being open with total strangers quickly gave way to the overarching need to share what you saw, heard, and felt. Through these shared moments, genuine personalities exposed themselves and a sense of kinship emerged. We would become a family and the trail was our new home—the canopy of trees, stars and clouds, our roof. It was a home with endless rooms, each decorated with the wonders of creation.

We all began our journey with a similar goal in mind; whether or not we were aware of it, our lives would become inexplicably woven together because of that goal. This would be a new type of life for all of us, and we would do it together. We would share the same experiences, both good and bad, yet come away from them with different perspectives of both the experience itself and how it impacted who we were. As a couple, those perspectives also impacted our relationship and enabled us to express feelings for each other and the life we shared in ways that amazed us. As a group, our interactions with each other became a microcosm of human dynamics—a world of constant awakening to the need we all harbored to be a part of a family. The shared goal to succeed quickly brought with it the instinctive desire to look out for each other, to take care of each other, and to form everlasting relationships; even the solitary, solo hiker could not escape the emerging camaraderie of our extended "trail family." In many ways we were a "tribe." Because of our mutual experiences, the bonds that developed on the trail became so broad and so deep they began to overshadow relationships we had with other people we had known for years—not just six months. There was a hard-to-describe togetherness—born from sharing a cramped shelter while rain pelted the thin, tin roof overhead—that only a thru-hiker can experience. We were sharing it with people we hardly knew but that we instinctively cared deeply about. We were sharing this new life together like a family and it was extraordinary.

Bama:

> *"My thru-hiking experience reinforced how good people are: the fellow hikers, the trail angels, the towns' people, and even the people who trusted us enough to pick us up hitchhiking to town. I witnessed so many unselfish acts among a group of people that had only met maybe days before. There was the loaning of gear, giving someone food when they ran out, or helping someone who was injured. The trail family was always there when you most needed them."*

Our own opportunity to help a fellow hiker came at Hogback Ridge Shelter when we stopped for an early dinner. Among the other hikers to arrive, while we savored our tuna fillets and couscous, was "Bluebird." She informed us she was shortening the number of miles she would hike each day in order to conserve her energy. By her calculations, she could hike fewer miles and still make it to Baxter State Park before it closed for the season. Unfortunately, what she did not include in her calculations was that by hiking fewer miles it would take her extra days to reach the next re-supply point. She soon realized she did not have enough food to get her to Erwin, Tennessee, where she planned on getting more supplies. Over her insistence that she would pay us for it, we gave her several days' worth of food we felt we would not need. We probably would have given her our food even if it meant we would have come up short. It was the least we could do and it felt right. In America the concept of people living, working and playing together in "community" is becoming a thing of the past. Because they can purchase everything they need, people feel they simply do not need each other any more. On the trail it is entirely different. To survive, we all needed each other. No action, no giving of care or encouragement, no sharing of what we had, no "Thank You," and no "I'm sorry" was ever taken for granted.

Helping "Bluebird" gave us a sense of satisfaction we had not felt for some time and it was simply because we were helping someone in our community—no questions asked. The impact of this offering of help to a fellow wanderer was not lost on us as a couple because it brought back memories of the years we selflessly gave to our own families and we found we missed that. The fact we agreed to do it without even giving it a second thought and without even discussing it drew "Mom" and me closer together. Through the act of sacrificing our own comfort and safety to see that

"Bluebird" was not going to go hungry, "Mom" and I had learned something important about each other.

Much like in the military, on the trail there is also an unspoken, yet universally held, code of the wilderness stating no one will be left behind on the field of battle. We all felt an unceasing, fraternal obligation to see that everyone made it to the end so we could all feel the excitement of having made it together. With this passion to see your comrades succeed also came the pain and anguish over those who, for one reason or another, could not see their dream fulfilled. When "Little Wing," "K'ache," and "Banjoman" had to leave the trail at various times due to injuries, a profound sense of loss came over all of us knowing we had lost one of our own. We all realized it could have just as easily have been us; and even while we were still moving forward each day, we felt we had somehow failed because one of us was not going to make it to the end of the trail. For the single hikers, a fellow hiker leaving the trail meant the loss of an old, or maybe, brand new friend. It meant the loss of whatever that person brought to the table with respect to the group dynamic. Maybe it was the hiker's sense of humor, sense of direction, or ability to keep up with them, glass for glass, at a local bar. For the couples, especially the married ones with children, the loss of a fellow hiker conjured up different feelings because the sense of family was more emotionally intimate and less socially driven. It was as if a member of their "blood family" was off the trail and it saddened us for many months.

But no matter what the relational circumstances, single or married, physically caring for another hiker knew no bounds in this family of the trail. No other event epitomized the "comrade-in-arms" ethic and the developing family bond indicative of the trail more than that of the potentially catastrophic fall and heroic rescue of "Old Drum" in the White Mountains. Here is his version of what took place told in his own inimitable way.

"AS THE TRAIL TURNS"

I offer the following "soap opera" script to illustrate what could happen on the trail. Some of the names have been changed to protect the hiker's identity. A fictional story (?) for your reading pleasure:

This is radio station KWAT. And now, the continuing saga, **"AS THE TRAIL TURNS"**

ANNOUNCER: *"When we last left 'Old Dumb,' he was entering the White Mountains of New Hampshire. He had* *successfully completed the long climb up Mt. Moosilauke. The trail was good. His descent from the mountain was successful but left him shaken from the steep and dangerous descent. We pick up the story the next day when "Old Dumb" has just completed the most difficult climb of the journey over the steep, rocky ascent up South Kinsman Mountain—so precarious that 'Old Dumb' had to pull himself up hand over hand. Now 'Old Dumb' is walking the relatively easy (at least he can walk upright) ridge to North Kinsman."*

OLD DUMB: (He looks up to enjoy the view, trips, and proceeds to fall face first into the stony mountain). *"Ooph." Then, "Sh___! %#%$*^!!!* (Censored by the FCC).

ANNOUNCER: *"'Old Dumb' is lying on the stony mountain face down. He cannot get up. Blood is running down his face and spreading all over his hands and arms. He is seeing more stars than are in the sky in Yellowstone Park on a clear August night. He unbuckles his pack and stumbles to his feet. 'Old Dumb' is alone. He picks up his pack, puts it back on, finds his trekking poles and valiantly limps on. It is a half mile later when he reaches the peak of North Kinsman and there sits three fellow thru-hikers he knows. Two young girls in their early twenties, 'Pill Box' and 'Juke Box,' are quietly smoking "roll your own" cigarettes, noting that, ironically, their brand of tobacco is 'Old Drum.' Hmmmm.... The other hiker is a forty-six year old fellow who has done the trail before. His name is '#2.'"*

#2: *"'Old Dumb,' what happened?"*

OLD DUMB: *"I just had a little fall a ways back on the trail. I'm okay."*

JUKE BOX: *"You are not. You are a bloody mess. Get that pack off now."*

OLD DUMB: *"I'm okay."*

#2: *"You are not hiking with that pack on any more today. You can barely walk. The Kinsman pond campsite is just six-tenths of a mile down the trail. We'll carry your pack."*

OLD DUMB: *"That is a steep down. You can't carry another pack while wearing yours. I'll carry my own. Just let me clean up the blood."*

ANNOUNCER: *"'Old Dumb' takes out his baby wipes and cleans off cuts on his scalp, his forehead (where he discovers a large knot), his nose, both hands, his left knee, and major cuts to his right knee and his right arm from the wrist to the elbow."*

#2: *"You are lucky we are still here. We were trying to beat the storm that was coming in, but it broke up and we suddenly had a great view so we stopped. Otherwise you would be on your own."*

PILL BOX: *"EEEEEK!"*

THE OTHER HIKERS IN UNISON: *"What is the matter?"*

PILL BOX: *"Look at his knee cap. It is sticking out the side of 'Old Dumb's' knee!"*

OLD DUMB: *"It looks like it is growing. I don't feel any pain and I hiked a half mile on this knee."*

ANNOUNCER: *"'Old Dumb' is now quietly worried that he has finally done something that will end his hike.*

#2: *"That settles it. 'Juke Box,' you take one end of his pack. I'll take the other. 'Pill Box,' you go first and make sure he takes the safest way down."*

ANNOUNCER: *"A while later they arrive at the campsite where caretaker, 'Leaf,' a 2004 thru-hiker gets out his only instant ice pack which 'Old Dumb' puts on his knee. Just then, three more thru-hikers walk into the campsite, 'Sleepy the Arab,' 'Too Much' and 'Enuff.' 'Too Much' is an emergency room nurse, and 'Enuff' just happens to be a physician. 'Trail Magic is real. I am saved,' thought 'Old Dumb!'"*

TOO MUCH: *"'Old Dumb'" what happened to you?"*

OLD DUMB: *"Oh, I had a little fall between the Kinsmans."*

TOO MUCH: *"What do you think 'Enuff'? That certainly looks like a hematoma on the knee. Tell us where you hurt and show us all your injuries."*

ANNOUNCER: *"'Old Dumb' points out all the wounds. 'Enuff' pays extra special attention to them."*

ENUFF: *"What medications are you now taking?"*

OLD DUMB: *"Toprol for hypertension, a half aspirin to prevent a heart attack, Omega 3, calcium pill, multivitamins and, of course, I eat ibuprofen like it was candy."*

ENUFF: *"No ibuprofen tonight. No aspirin for ten days. The rest is okay. What is that on the cuts?"*

OLD DUMB: *"Betadine that the caretaker gave me."*

ENUFF: *"Do you have any Neosporin?"*

OLD DUMB: *"Yes."*

ENUFF: *"Clean the Betadyne off and put Neosporin on all the cuts. 'Too Much,' you go to the pond and fill Ziploc bags with cold water to put on all the bumps."*

ANNOUNCER: *"'Old Dumb' chooses to not put up his tent in this condition. He stays in the shelter with 'Sleepy the Arab.' 'Sleepy' always causes 'Old Dumb' to smile when he sees this veteran thru-hiker.*

After a night filled with a pounding head and a very sore, tender knee, 'Old Dumb' hikes on the next morning to the first of the AMC huts where he rests for a day. He had a little help from his friends. 'Too Much,' Enuff,' 'Pill Box,' 'Juke Box' and '#2' divided up his gear among them and carried it for him so he was able to hike with an empty pack to the next hut. 'Old Dumb's' left eye was now swollen completely shut and two days later both eyes turned black. Of course, since there were no mirrors available, he didn't know how bad he looked until someone took a picture and showed him. The swelling in the left eye eventually went down allowing him to open it.

Remember, this was just a story of what might happen to a hiker in this rugged area. I am glad that it was about 'Old Dumb' and not me. Or was it? Stay tuned for the next exciting episode of 'As the Trail Turns.' Now a word from our sponsor."

The seemingly endless array of characters we hiked with over the course of our adventure was, doubtless, no different than that of anyone else who ever had the good fortune to walk, climb, stumble and crawl along the A.T.'s vast and ever-changing terrain. Above everything else, this journey turned out to be about "the people" and the indelible impression each made on our memories and lives. Some of the married members of our new family you have heard about already, but there were so many more hikers, over one-hundred-fifty to be exact, who for many miles and some for only a few days, made our journey an even more special event. "Mom" and I would often sit and talk about how thankful we were, not only to be hiking the A.T., but about the opportunity our adventure was providing us to associate with so many diverse and interesting people.

"Oly" was a 70-year-old hiking machine who left at the crack of dawn each day and power-walked himself so quickly ahead of everyone that we rarely saw him except at night at camp. The fact he did not carry a tent was the impetus for his lively pace for he needed to be the first one at camp each night to assure himself a spot in the shelter. Though he was not planning to thru-hike to Katahdin this time out, he needed to be at Harper's Ferry by a precise date so he could accompany his family on a trip to Disney World—a trip, by the way, he was paying for, and thus felt he should be a part of. His iron will, friendly disposition, and his age were inspirational to us despite the fact it annoyed the heck out of us that we could not keep up with him.

There were "Tattoo & Pigeon" from Colorado, one of the first couples we met on the trail. We pitched our tent next to theirs at Betty's Creek Gap Campsite where a late evening thunderstorm, complete with an incredible amount of lightning, had us all cowering in our windblown abodes. The next morning, as we all rose to discover the large pools of muddy water surrounding our tents, "Pigeon," with a level of excitement reserved for children who find themselves at the entrance to Disney World for the first time, described how awesome the celestial display had been. To our amazement, she informed us she had never seen lightning before. Her childlike enthusiasm was contagious and it made us think about our own kids. She and "Tattoo" were also notorious "late risers" so, for a bit of fun, as we passed their tent at Locust Grove Gap early one morning a few days later, we called out,

"Rise and shine campers! It's another beautiful day in North Carolina."

"Baldylocks," you guessed it, a bald solo hiker, became notable on the trail by virtue of the fact that very early on in his hike he lost his treasured *Nalgene* bottle with an Ani DiFranco decal on it. For months in the shelter registers along the way, he left frantic inquiries about whether anyone had seen it and had possibly picked it up. The bottle itself was nothing special but the decal was a collector's item and held great sentimental value to him. He offered a reward to anyone returning his beloved bottle to him. We, one day, spent a precious hour with him eating lunch at a shelter while he passionately told us of his family and his life. His sincerity and openness created a fondness for him that we carried with us the entire length of the trail. It set an example of intimacy we admired and longed to foster between us.

Then there was "Cash." We knew, from the first time we met this gregarious and incredibly likeable fellow from Texas, that he would be one of the personalities that would forever stick in our minds as representative of the unique individuals who call the A.T. their home.

When we first met "Cash", we had just completed a tumultuous 16.7-mile day hiking from Brown Gap, North Carolina, up and over the famous and incredibly beautiful Max Patch Bald. As the sunlight quickly began to fade, we came upon an abandoned forest service road that crossed the trail just north of Garenflo Gap. It was wide, level and grassy—a perfect spot to pitch our tent. But as we soon discovered, all that wondrous grass shrouded an evil secret. Underneath was the hard-packed gravel which once made up the surface of the road, and putting in tent stakes to hold out the wings of our tent fly became an act of frustrating futility. We finally got the stakes in but they had taken a beating—in more than one sense. As we were finishing up and hanging our bear bag, we were joined for the first time, but as it turned out not the last, by a young couple from Australia, "Mike & Zan." We availed them of our experience putting in tent stakes, and as they ate their dinner, we talked about Australia, a place we planned to visit some day. They, in turn, attempted to have us sample that traditional Aussie delicacy, *Vegemite*. Fortunately, its reputation had preceded it and we opted not to oblige our hospitable hosts. It was now quite dark and time to turn in. We later found out they were not a "couple" at all but merely two longtime friends who shared a love of adventure. As time went on and we were able to interact with them more, we were inspired by the depth of their relationship and the level of care and understanding they displayed toward each other. The strength of the bond between them, though platonic, was captivating. Through them we rediscovered how important friendship is within a marriage.

It had only been a half hour, scarcely enough time for "Mom" and me to finish our nightly leg massage ritual and take a few "Vitamin I," when up on the mountain overlooking our campsite, we all heard this eerie, blood-curdling sound. It seemed to be heading right toward us. We could not make out what it was—possibly a coyote, a bear or a wild boar? Anyone in his right mind would have grabbed the nearest available pointed object as a weapon, grasped it tightly and then would have buried himself as far down in his sleeping bag as humanly possible. This defensive posture would be similar to when you were young and you swore there was a monster under your bed. To keep it away, you hid under the covers as if they were some type of "anti-monster force field."

But hey, we were in the wilderness, and I had begun to take on the appearance, and in my own mind, the fearless persona, of a mountain man. As the "man of the tent," I had a responsibility to investigate this intruder and protect my fair maiden. So as the sound got ever closer I grabbed my knife, not even giving a second thought to the fact that for it to be even marginally effective, I would have to go "toe-to-toe" with this unknown foe—a situation that could be my demise. I unzipped the tent fly to face our aggressor head on with "Mom's" "damsel in distress" cries ringing in my ears!

"Are you nuts? Get back in here!" (This would not be the last time we kept each other in check.)

What I saw was the glow of a tiny headlamp bouncing quickly down the narrow, rocky trail and I realized the howling sound was coming from a hiker who was obviously in a breakneck run toward us. Relieved, though somewhat disappointed the intruder was not more ominous than it was, I retired back into the tent just as the hiker came to the intersection of the trail and road and came to a less than graceful sliding stop in the damp grass. The next sound was that of the frustrated pounding of rock on tent stake as our new campmate brutally coaxed his stakes into the unforgiving roadbed.

In the dark of early morning, we awoke to the gentle patter of rain on our tent. I retrieved our bear bag from the nearby tree and brought it into our tent as Mom brought in our gear to keep it dry for our walk into Hot Springs. As the sky lightened, so did the rain. All of us made a hasty exit from our tents, packed up, and got ready to roll. Our new hiking partner also awoke from his now wet and sagging tent and introduced himself as "Cash." He told us his amusing story of running down the steep trail because he believed some type of wild animal was coming after him. In a vain effort to keep the beast at bay, he began making loud "whoooing" sounds while running as fast as he could—despite the fact that he had only a small mini-headlamp attached to the brim of his hat and it only lit the trail a few feet in front of him. Satisfied he had outrun his furry adversary, he slid into our campsite and quickly set up his tent as a final refuge. The thought of this tall, muscular, late twenties, personal trainer, high-tailing it down a treacherous trail to evade what was probably nothing more than an owl caroling through the darkness, had us in stitches. His self-deriding style of recounting his ordeal made it even more comical, and we immediately developed a fondness for him. We sensed this would probably not be the last outrageous story we would hear from him. Mom lovingly nicknamed him *"He Who Howls in the Night,"* and this episode would become only one of a laundry list of his legendary 2006 thru-hike adventures. His comic demeanor and carefree spirit struck a chord with us, and we found our approach to each day taking on a more happy-go-lucky nature. If you are not careful, backpacking as a couple can become serious business, but "Cash" showed us how amazingly funny it can sometimes be. He never seemed to mind hiking with a couple of "older married folk," and it felt good caring about him like a son.

We can never forget "Kutsa," from Israel, complete with her long, braided pigtails and everything she owned stuffed into her backpack. Though she was married, she was making her fifth solo attempt at completing a thru-hike. Trail lore has it that on her first attempt she had damaged her feet so badly that when she arrived at the Woody Gap road crossing, only 19.9 miles into her hike, she literally had to crawl to the road to flag down a car to take her to town for medical assistance. The couple who picked her up and nursed her back to health was the same couple who, years before, picked up Bill Bryson, the author of *"A Walk in the Woods"* and took him to town. It was also said that on one of her prior attempts she made it as far as Mt. Katahdin; but because of a fear of heights, she was unable to do the summit. It was just not in her nature to pick up where she had left off and just hike that last 5.2 miles. Each year she started from Springer Mountain because her goal was not to just complete the A.T., but to complete it as a thru-hike. We were amazed by not only her fortitude but by the fact she carried no stove and ate only cold food. Her outgoing personality and jovial demeanor continually lifted our spirits, and what we took from her friendship was the desire to pass that benevolence and support on to others. Hearing the stories of her past hikes also made us more aware of the enormity of our undertaking and we became increasingly thankful we were doing it together. Kutsa's husband, a Canadian movie producer whom she met on the trail during one of her previous A.T. attempts, joined her in

New England. From there they hiked together for several weeks. Unfortunately, she did not make it to Katahdin this time either, and we never got to meet her husband.

In the latter stages of our hike we had the good fortune to travel with a legend of the A.T., "Model T," and his hiking partner, "Ranger Dawg." This was "Model T's" fourth, and he claimed last, thru-hike because at the age of 69 his body was having some ongoing arguments with his mind over whether or not his legs could go where his brain wanted to go. This particular hike was a fund-raising mission to raise funds for the building of a homeless shelter by the Salvation Army in his hometown. He has written two books about the A.T., *"Walking on the Happy Side of Misery"* and *"Walking with the Ghost Whisperers."* We first became aware of this A.T. icon when "Mom" saw his book, *"Walking on the Happy Side of Misery"* at The Lazy Fox B&B in Damascus. Because of the humorous, though ominous, tone of the title, coupled with the physical angst of our hike, she decided it was far better for her to wait until we completed our hike to read it. (We both read it soon after arriving back home.) These two gentlemen radiated "grandfatherly" wisdom—no doubt the result of the rugged individualism honed by their military backgrounds. They treated us as equals but, to us, they were much more than fellow hikers. To us they were an inspiration and "Model T," especially, epitomized the manner with which we wanted to interact with other hikers. It was also nice to finally hike with someone older than I. Though his wife did not hike with him, she supported his wanderings and we hoped that some day we could meet her and tell her how much we appreciated and admired her husband. We wanted our life on the trail, and how we related to each other, to be an inspiration to others as well.

And what would a community be without music—the universal language that brings us all together? Even on the trail, there was always some type of music breaking down the relational barriers and creating a common ground where we could all gather as one.

There was "Slick B," who carried a mandolin—and sometimes also a travel guitar—the entire length of the trail. Many a night he and his back-up vocalist, "Mule," serenaded us with the strains of classic tunes by the likes of Neil Young.

When he arrived at a shelter with "Slick B," "Treehouse" would accompany him on his Djembe (a skin covered hand drum, shaped like a large goblet, and meant to be played with bare hands) or he would solo on his Native American flute. We always knew when "Treehouse" was at a shelter because we could hear that drum a mile away. He also used his flute skills as "work for stay" at the AMC huts where he played for the guests. At Madison Hut in the White Mountains, he and I played duets on our flutes—much to the enjoyment of everyone there.

For me the Native American flute I carried was a tool of personal expression—when I played, those listening got a sense of what was in my soul. We walked for months through the forest and <u>saw</u> the trees—some mighty, some ravaged by time and the elements, and some mere babes, struggling to establish their position in the tapestry of sights, sounds, and smells that made up the world in which we traipsed. But, though we <u>saw</u> them, we never heard them speaking to us. Oh yes, we heard the wind as it rustled through their withering leaves, and we would even hear them creak as they struggled to hold their rigid posture against the onslaught of an approaching storm. But when I played my flute, the tree whose wood made up the instrument I held in my hand hauntingly spoke to me and to all who heard its cry. It told beautiful stories of its rich life and begged the question, *"Why did you not listen so you could hear my story when I stood proud in the forest? No matter, I have your attention now and my stories float on the sounds I give to you."*

"Banjoman," who worked at a radio station in Maine, would nightly entertain everyone as they sat in a shelter or huddled around a fire. Not long after starting his hike, he decided his banjo was just too heavy so he opted to replace it with a lightweight, backpacking guitar. However, he did not change his trail name. I suppose "Lightweight Backpacking Guitar Man" just did not have the same ring to it. He often wore a tee shirt that read, *"Hike Faster – I Hear Banjo Music."* We could never figure out if it meant when you heard banjo music, you should hike faster so you could get to it, or as might be the case in Georgia and Tennessee, you should get away from it as quickly as possible. Does the movie *"Deliverance"* ring a bell?

Music brought to light the personalities of the musicians and opened the door to their souls, letting out what made each so unique. Each time the strains of classic rock and folk music filled the air there was something other than the trail bringing us together. Music broke through the thin barrier dividing the generations and the singles and couples. Once they knew I was also a musician, it no longer mattered that I was married; a new ground for relating to each other emerged.

Too Much:

"I have ten brothers and sisters, so part of the trail experience reminded me of just how large a family can become. Like my real family, my trail family was always looking out for each other, keeping track of where everyone was, or wondering where you were. It really

was a "family feeling." I liked this dynamic but it also had its drawbacks, because, just as it did living at home with so many people, there was very little time alone. I sometimes found the constant existence of a crowd to be oppressive."

As much fun as it was being part of a large and enthusiastic group of hikers, nearly all of us approached our thru-hike with the burning desire to find some measure of solitude. We all wanted to dispose of the internal clatter of life pervading our every waking moment and wanted to replace it with a sense of peace and an awareness of the wonder that was all around us. With so many hikers on the trail, this solitude was often hard to come by. But the upside to the lack of solitude was the level of security and safety provided by that endless wave of foot-stomping humanity. The effects of extreme weather or the trepidation of scaling rocky, vertical terrain became a bit less overwhelming when shared with others. The personal connections that came from making it through those dangerous situations strengthened not only our friendships but our determination as well.

In Pennsylvania it seemed at times that the rain was never going to end. During those moments of soggy discontent, we simply thought back to 2003 and the hardy group of thru-hikers who hiked for seven straight weeks in rain. Their clothes never got dry and their shoes literally rotted off their feet. In comparison, we had it made, and our constant whining about the inclement weather was a bit embarrassing. That being said, we would have waterlogged tales of our own to tell by the time our week in Pennsylvania was mercifully over.

As I recall from our journal, it poured all day as we made our way toward Duncannon, Pennsylvania, home of the historic Doyle Hotel:

"Despite intermittent showers, interspersed with blinding downpours, we did the 17.6 miles to town in only 7.5 hours. We took a lunch break at Darlington Shelter and a second lunch break at the Cove Mountain Shelter. This happened to be the home of a group of porcupines that arrived at the shelter each night to lick the salt off hiker's faces, their boots, or from any surface where a hiker had been sitting. "Sacrificial" plywood had been installed at the front edge of the shelter, where the hikers typically sat, and it was obvious the porcupines had been noshing on it for quite some time. There were also numerous rocks scattered on the shelter floor which had been put there to throw at the porcupines in order to stave off their nightly invasions.

The skies opened up yet again as we hooked up with "FDR," coming down the long descent into Duncannon. By the time we sloshed our way into the entrance of "The Doyle" at 3:30 p.m., we were a sorry looking bunch. Soon "Mule," "Feng Shui," "Burner," "River Weasel," "Dick Tracy," "Bare Bear," Jellybean," and "Mike & Zan" joined the waterlogged and increasingly boisterous crowd, and we all swapped tales of our day—each attempting to outdo the other with his/her description of how wondrously awful it had been. While water from our clothes dripped on the floor and we wolfed down cheeseburgers, mountains of fries, and endless bottles of cold beer, we found ourselves drawn to a table near the far end of the bar. There, "Angel Mary," who had been at the flooded Clark's Creek, a day's hike from town, was showing a video she had made of the creek's flooded conditions. The video showed hikers attempting to negotiate the current by using a rope she and "Baltimore Jack" had stretched across the swollen creek so the hikers would not be swept away into the stream."

Seventeen long miles north of Duncannon, the A.T. crosses Clark's Creek on a makeshift road, running from Rte. 325 into the forest on the other side of the creek. The road itself sits atop four or five metal culverts which allow the creek to pass under the road. The days of heavy rains had swollen the creek to a point where its volume now exceeded the culverts' ability to handle it all. The result was the water exiting from the downstream end of the culverts had created massive "hydraulics" and the remaining water, flowing over top of the road, was a two-foot deep set of raging rapids. It was not so much the depth of the water, but its unyielding velocity, that made crossing so treacherous. When attempts at crossing the culverts by means of the rope eventually failed, members of a forestry crew transported the hikers across the stream on the blade of their front-end loader. However, with the creek still rising, even this mode of transportation had to be abandoned when the front-end loader began to float off the road.

We all hovered around the camera's tiny screen attempting to catch a glimpse of what we could expect the following day. It was a sobering, yet exhilarating, scene. Somehow our spirit of adventure and the adverse circumstances we had already been exposed to equipped us with a monumental sense of daring-do that overrode our common sense.

Reports persisted that the floodwaters of the Susquehanna were rising near Duncannon and the hotel's owner informed us he needed help putting sandbags around the hotel the next afternoon. We decided, as much fun as helping out might be and as much as we enjoyed the unique "ambience" of

The Doyle, we wanted to "get the hell out of Dodge" before we were trapped there for who knows how long.

FLOOD WARNINGS! The next morning we threw on our packs and headed down the street with fond, but bizarre, memories of The Doyle in our heads. According to the hotel's proprietor, our room had just been renovated but, glancing at the grimy window propped open with a stick at a cockeyed angle, the single light bulb dangling from the ceiling and the fan that served as our only source of air conditioning, we could not imagine what our room was like prior to being "renovated." The bathroom was a shared arrangement, so being discreetly attired was prudent when you ran from the shower back to your room on the musty, "vintage" carpet. We appreciated the laundry room, though we had some reservations about the safety of having the dryer vent hanging out the window. All of these less-than-luxurious accommodations were made tolerable by the fact that we were, at least, inside where it was dry and because The Doyle served the most astoundingly tasty hamburgers we had ever eaten. Prior to The Doyle, our most romantic nights had been spent in B&Bs around the United States. But somehow, the archaically austere accommodations at The Doyle struck an adventurous chord in us. Our time there now ranks right at the top of our "Most Memorable Hotels" list.

As we headed out of town, we passed a large "sinkhole" next to the sidewalk. We heard later that it almost swallowed up a young boy. The hole, created by rushing floodwaters under the street, appeared to be, at least to a four-year-old, a huge puddle. Being a kid, he jumped into it; and when he did, he immediately went in over his head. Luckily, his mom was watching and pulled him out before he was sucked under the street through a drainpipe. The north end of Duncannon was closed to traffic because the street was submerged under two feet of water and mud. However, "Jellybean," "Bare Bear," and we were able to get by on the sidewalk that remained just above the water line.

It was finally a sunny day with no rain in the forecast, but it was still impossible to stay dry because the rain had been replaced with unbelievable heat and humidity—the kind of humidity that sucks the breath right out of you through your skin. Thankfully, we were hiking with just our daypacks, which made things a bit more bearable. "Jellybean" and "Bare Bear" left us in their dust, but we met "Mike & Zan" as we crossed over the swollen Susquehanna River on a walkway which was part of the mammoth bridge taking traffic across the river. Even the wind from the passing 18-wheelers did nothing to cool us off. The weight of the humid air could have easily replaced gravity as a means of holding us tight to the earth; it was so unbearably oppressive. After tiptoeing across a set of railroad tracks on the far side of the bridge, we began a long, hard climb out of Duncannon that had us re-thinking the wisdom of not staying in town one more day. The gruesome climb, however, was rewarded with astounding views of the flooding river, and it was quite obvious Duncannon was, indeed, in great danger of being flooded by day's end.

Our delightful walk with daypacks was short-lived as we met "V&A" at Rte. 225 for some trail magic and switched to our full packs containing three days' worth of food. The plan for those next three days was now in a state of flux because of all the flooding. We would have to take each day and each situation as it came. We found ourselves unexpectedly excited by this and looked forward to the uncertainty of it all. We finished the day by pitching our tent near Rte. 325 and Clark's Creek with "Mike & Zan," "Homeward," "Stinky," and "Orangutan." The group gathered at the swollen creek to survey the situation "up close and personal," and for what seemed like hours, we sat there amazed by the power of the raging water in front of us. There, tied to the limb of a nearby tree, was the flimsy length of clothesline which had been strung across the creek the day before as a makeshift lifeline for those foolhardy enough to try to walk across. Now it lay lifeless, half submerged in the creek, having succumbed to the violent rush of water holding it under. We sat with "Mike & Zan" and stared at the scene as if, by some type of mind control, we could force the waters to recede. But Mother Nature was in control, and it was abundantly clear to us there was not a darn thing we could do about it. The best we could hope for was to come up with a solution that would get us where we needed to go the next morning without drowning any of us. We were a "trail family" and families help each other and look out for each other. The river crossing would be a test of the strength of that family bond and it was reassuring to know we were not alone in taking it on. We agreed not to let something like a flooded creek stand in our way and vowed we would help each other get across—no matter what. Since we were the "elder couple" in the group, we felt a tinge of parental responsibility in seeing that everyone got across safely.

We arose the next morning to the sound of heavy equipment being fired up. The workers who had been there several days ago had returned to try to cross the creek so they could continue their work in the state forest on the other side. Our dilemma now had a solution! "Mom," who as usual was the first one up and dressed, ran across the road to ask if we could hitch a ride across the creek on their tractor. The driver, a trail angel whether he knew it or not, sympathized with our plight and admired our "chutzpa" in wanting to cross under such conditions. We quickly broke camp and headed to the banks of the creek. He then proceeded to take "Mike & Zan" and us across, two at a time, on the blade of his enormous tractor while the others opted to sleep in an cross later. It was so cool! "V&A" later accused us of "yellow blazing," because we got a ride through this twenty-five foot section of trail on a yellow front-end loader. Once safely on the other side, we all sat and ate breakfast and reveled in our good fortune in making it across. We felt a bit of a parental responsibility in seeing to it that "Mike & Zan," two of our kids, got across safely. In doing so, their success also became our success and that made us feel good. The feeling of family was beginning to truly blossom.

On the trail north of Vernon, New Jersey, we had a day like no other—bar none. To say it was eventful would be a gross understatement. It was a day of both "good news" and "bad news"—the "good" being there were not as many mosquitoes and the "bad" being it rained most of the day. As "Mom" so aptly put it,

> *"100 % rain is more effective than 100 % DEET at keeping away the mosquitoes, but neither is 100 % effective."*

It was another horrendously humid morning accented by a long, steep, rocky ascent. Fortunately, this ascent was not as difficult as we were led to believe, so the effects of the humidity were only horrendous—not unbearable. We were about two hours into the hike when the humidity reached full maturity—torrential rain! Since it was warm, we covered just our packs and let the rain wash our clothes as we walked. Though not wanting to stop and spend any more time in the downpour than necessary, we did reach a point where we were hungry and simply had to take a break. As fate would have it, the rain let up just long enough for us to wolf down a PB&J bagel and a *Kudos* bar.

Off we went, and before long we met up with "Bama," "Little Wing" and "Old Drum" who were just finishing their lunch at a boulder they nicknamed "The Flat Rock Café." We continued on ahead of them and the next wave of thunderstorms hit as we were climbing a section encircled by large boulders and massive rock façades. At first it seemed we were trapped with no way to protect ourselves from the torrent of rain and the danger of the incessant lightning. Then suddenly, there they were: two large overhanging rock slabs large enough to get five people under and still keep everyone relatively safe and dry. We took our places, had a quick snack, and waited for the others to arrive. "Bama," "Little Wing" and "Old Drum" appeared just in time because the lightning was getting ominously closer and decidedly more frequent. From the worried looks on their faces, it was apparent they were in desperate need of a refuge as well. Through the cacophony of constant thunder, pounding rain, and the crackling of lightning, we shouted out to them to join us in our "hideaway." Making his way through the veil of torrential rain, we saw "Mulligan" and urged him to join us; but after a brief moment of indecision, he decided to move on. We all huddled beneath those rocks chatting about our good fortune in finding such a sanctuary at such an opportune time and found comfort in the fact we were sharing the distress of the moment with friends.

After what seemed like hours, the storm reached its final crescendo. It moved out on a stiff breeze, leaving behind nothing more than a dripping mess and a growing sense of togetherness among the five of us. We emerged from under our respective rocks and were immediately faced with a tall, somewhat rickety, wooden ladder leaning against the face of an enormous, vertical rock face. Even on a warm dry day, this ascent would be somewhat perilous; but now, with the ladder and lichen-covered rocks soaking wet, it was going to be downright scary. We climbed the ladder and one by one handed our hiking sticks up to the person ahead. Very cautiously, at one point crawling on our hands and knees, we each inched our way up and over another 20-foot high boulder above the ladder. We all made it safely and congratulated each other on our feat. As it turned out, this was just the beginning of many similar hurdles to come.

"Mom" and I took off ahead, trying to make time and to see what lay ahead. The white blazes abruptly made a right-hand turn and disappeared over the edge of a huge rock face—one that required us to slide down with our bellies flat on its near vertical face. We stretched for handholds and footholds with the weight of our packs threatening to send us plummeting to the ground far below. It was a difficult and nerve-wracking descent and the concern we felt for each other's safety totally consumed us. As "Mom" proceeded down, she was unable to see exactly where to put her feet and hands because her body was pressed so tightly against the face of the rock face. I had to direct her every move from my vantage point above. As I came down, she did the same for me from the safety of the trail far below. Without each other's assistance and words of encouragement and comfort, traversing this section could have been disastrous. We knew that it would be equally perilous for the others and we vowed to stay to help them down. By the time they caught up to us, I had located an alternate and somewhat less difficult way down. Coming down that route would require they take off their packs and hand them to me before starting down. Our biggest fear was for "Old Drum," whose boots were so completely worn out they had no tread left on their soles. Each time he took a step on the wet boulders, even on flat ground, he slipped. It was slow and deliberate going but everyone made it. The success of having done so was just another piece of the journey that endeared us to each other. The rest of the day was much of the same deliberate walking, and it took forever to cover our planned fifteen miles.

We triumphantly passed another milestone and crossed the New Jersey/New York state line, indicated by "NJ/NY" in white paint on a large flat rock. Considering the day we had all experienced, it was a time for "high fives" all around, requisite photos of the accomplishment, and a shared moment of jubilation.

Crossing into New York was an exciting moment for "Mom" and me, even if we had done it alone; but sharing it with the others made it even sweeter. By the time we all reached NY 17A, where we took a break at the Bellvale Creamery Ice Cream Shoppe, it was nearing the end of the day; and everyone decided to hold up at the Warwick Motel in nearby Warwick (which has since burned down). "Bama," "Little Wing" and "Old Drum" caught a bus that regularly stopped at The Creamery, and we caught a ride with "V&A" whom we had contacted earlier to let them know we were okay. As it turned out, our earlier decision to ride out the storm under those rocks was a fortuitous one. Later that evening we discovered several tornados had touched down in Westchester County on the Hudson River, just a few miles from where we were hiking. Television news reports of the tornadoes had reached the entire country so a few phone calls were required to vanquish the fears of family and friends who feared we had been swept away like Dorothy and Toto. There is something about facing danger and overcoming the fear that accompanies it which uniquely bonds people together. Sidestepping impending disaster and conquering our fear that day brought "Mom" and me even closer together. We now better understood the depth of our devotion to one another, and as a couple and a team, that devotion extended to those around us. It is an uplifting and regenerative feeling—one that only those who have survived a perilous situation as part of a close-knit team can relate to.

It had been a wonderful though long, grueling, mosquito-infested walk from the New Jersey/New York border to the green mountains of Vermont. Each day had been imprinted on our minds by a special moment, situation or personal interaction. The further north we traveled, the larger and more diverse our trail family grew and the more "Mom" and I felt at home with our fellow adventurers. Our focus was still primarily on each other but there was no evading the fact we had an obligation, or more correctly a desire, to care about those with whom we came in daily contact. There was something about being a couple on the trail that brought out the parental instincts in us. We were not sure if that feeling was communicated to the others around us but that is how we saw it.

One of the things we looked forward to all day as we wandered along the muddy and root-strewn trail in Vermont was a stop at the Cloudland Farm; there we had lunch and purchased some of the farm's organic ice cream and root beer soda. Man, they tasted good and helped to lift our spirits for the rest of the day! While sitting at a picnic table in the shade of a large oak tree savoring our delicacies, we could not help but notice the sense of peace pervading the countryside. We had been at the mercy of the wilderness for a long time and the demands of our adventure opened us up to the expression of emotions that had been dieing to surface for a long time. As we held hands, the peace of that sun-drenched countryside embraced us and the sense of togetherness we felt nearly brought us to tears. It was a moment that renewed our affection for each other. Because storm clouds were beginning to gather, we left the farm much sooner than we would have liked and by 3:00 p.m. we reached Thistle Hill Shelter. We set up our tent in the shelter to ward of the ever-present mosquitoes and crawled in to take a nap. Our naps were short-lived as we tossed and turned with thoughts of the impending storm and all we needed to accomplish before being relegated to the dry confines of the shelter. We decided the sunshine was at a premium so we headed out to the local water source to get water and wash up in the wonderful waterfall there. The water spilling over the rock ledge above us was freezing cold but felt refreshing and was a welcome distraction from the travails of the day. Now clean and with our water bladders full, we walked back to the shelter and found three section hikers we had met the night before unpacking their gear. No sooner did we say "Hello" and jump into the shelter, than the skies opened up. Until that moment, we had been feeling somewhat guilty about taking such a short day. With the rain now pounding on the roof, we were glad we stopped short. As the evening progressed and the rain continued, things got a bit crazy. Suspecting we were probably going to have a full house, we took down our tent and claimed our little section of real estate at one end of the shelter. And arrive they did—one hiker right after another, all looking for a place to get out of the rain. The last to roll in were two SoBo's (southbounders), "Coppertop" and "Drew."

Up until this point, we had never observed anything less than complete and unadulterated regard for a hiker's safety and comfort by other hikers. And we could never remember a time when other hikers needed to reprimand another for behavior unfitting a thru-hiker. As a family who cared about each other and who put others first, there was never any need to— compassion just happened on its own. Tonight would be different. "Coppertop" had been with his sister whom we later found out was hiking for the first time. Since her pace was not up to his, a veteran hiker, he went on ahead leaving her to her own devices. At 8:45 p.m. she finally arrived, thoroughly soaked, cold, hungry, and so tired she was barely able to muster the strength to climb into the shelter to sit. From "Coppertop's" perspective the shelter was full so he suggested she set up her tent. Knowing her situation could have very well been our own and sympathizing with her plight, we all told her we would make room, no matter what. Everyone repositioned themselves and their gear, and with the little strength she had left, she emptied her pack and crawled into her sleeping bag. No one verbally confronted "Coppertop" about his lack of concern for his sister, but the air of disapproval and disbelief could be cut with a knife. At that point, he realized he should probably join the rest of us in seeing that his sister was taken care of and avoid the a verbal tongue lashing from the rest of us for being less than a chivalrous and loving brother. He made her some dinner while she lay shivering in her sleeping bag. Evidently he was unaware of the "hiker's code," or maybe it is just a set of guidelines like the "pirates code" from *"Pirates of the Caribbean,"* which states that during a storm there is always room for one more in a shelter. Even though we had just met her, she was family and we were responsible for her well-being. We hoped "Coppertop" learned a valuable lesson on trail etiquette and family interaction from his evening with us and would carry it with him on the rest of his southbound trek. We also had to believe his sister felt more of a feeling of family with us than with him at that point. Each occurrence of empathetic inter-personal interaction caused us to search within our selves to see how we measured up; as a couple, measuring up equated to a deepening love for each other.

The family dynamic that developed on the trail could readily serve as a textbook example of the essence of what a family should be. The endless acts of love, empathy, compassion, and kinship displayed on a day-to-day basis would make even the most tightly knit suburban family appear dysfunctional. Every feeling and moment, no matter how benign, was to be shared. The real joy of the moment came from the sharing of it, not necessarily from the moment itself.

In four previous thru-hike attempts, over thousands of miles," Kutsa" had never seen a bear. However, a mile from the entrance to the Shenandoah Mountains, that all changed during a brief encounter that was mixed with excitement, fear, and jubilation. We were only minutes behind on a very steep trail when we came upon her, standing like a statue in the middle of the trail with the grandest smile. Her face was illuminated with a giddiness we had not seen in an adult in a very long time, and she was so excited she could hardly control herself. Before we even heard the first word of her tale, we were drawn into the force field of excitement surrounding her like steel to a magnet. You see, there had been a bear on her right, only 20 feet from her on a rocky ledge just above her head. As she told the story, they just looked at each other, both wondering who would run away first. Had it been anyone else other than "Kutsa," they probably would have screamed and run away—but not her! This was a moment she had been dreaming of for years. Everyone in the group was so happy for her and her childlike excitement touched all of us in a profound way. It was as if we had seen the bear ourselves. The sharing of that moment was one we would not have wanted to miss for all the money in the world, and the joy of being part of her trail family was incredible.

We were now a little over fifty miles into New Hampshire and what a day it had been! We took on Mt. Mousilauke, "back-slacking" from north to south—the first real physical test in the long-anticipated White Mountains, and we kicked its butt! WOW! We got our shuttle to the base of the mountain and immediately started up the northern slope; 3,500 feet up in 3.5 miles. We tiptoed up slippery rock and wood steps, holding onto re-bar inserted into the face of rocks as handholds, and clutched onto roots along the trail's edge for safety. All the while, a magnificent waterfall cascaded down the mountain just to our right. As we were going up, we met "Bama" and "Snickers" on their way down from the Beaver Brook Shelter where they stayed the night before and where we would subsequently stop for a morning snack.

By 9:30 a.m. we cleared the tree line and walked through the "alpine area" toward the summit on a rocky trail lined with cairns. The fog and clouds rolled in and out on the back of a strong wind and the temperature plummeted dramatically. In the distance, as we approached the huge pile of rocks that marked the summit, we could see shadowy figures climbing on the rocks. Drawing closer, we found "FDR," "Baldylocks," "Slick-B," "Bruiser," and "River Weasel" all relishing the moment and taking photos of each other. We stayed there for quite some time, just languishing in the exhilaration of the moment and the astonishing, fog-bathed views from this place. Everyone was so pumped, we could feel the adrenaline rushing through each other's veins. The excitement was infectious. As "Baldylocks" put it,

"We were like kids on Christmas Eve last night knowing that we would finally begin The Whites today, and we just couldn't sleep because of the excitement."

Not content simply to experience that remarkable milestone by themselves, the entire group sat there on the summit for hours, in the bitter cold, so they could share that moment with every other thru-hiker who came by. They sacrificed their own comfort and their need to make it to the bottom of the mountain by nightfall in order to be part of their friends' moment at the summit. On our way down, over a much longer but less steep trail, we ran into virtually everyone we had been hiking with over the last several months, and they all had that look of excited anticipation in their eyes as they headed to the top. Little did they know their joy at reaching the peak would be shared with other members of their "trail family," some of whom they already knew and some they would come to call family from that point forward.

Not only did we have our "trail family" looking out for us, we also had our real family, "V&A," who always seemed to know when to show up, and sometimes did it when we least expected.

On June 25th near Carlisle, Pennsylvania, we celebrated our fourteenth anniversary by again walking in the rain all day. I convinced "Mom" that a couple's fourteenth wedding anniversary is their "Water" anniversary, so the wet weather was a fitting compliment to the day. It must have been, because everything that happened that day had something to do with water. First, during breakfast, "Mom" took a drink from her water bottle before realizing there was a huge slug right on the mouthpiece. Disgusting! That was one segment of wildlife she would have preferred not seeing so "up close and personal." Needless to say, she had an upset stomach the remainder of the day just thinking about it. Then, ten minutes into the hike, her water bladder sprang a leak and the two-gallon *Ziploc* bag she had it in, for safety should her bladder erupt, also had a hole in it. The water was now running out of the bottom of her pack, down her back and legs. For the rest of the day we had to share water from my water bag.

Worst of all, it rained all day—AND HARD. In fact, Harrisburg, Pennsylvania, not far from where we were hiking, recorded over four inches of rain in a twenty-four hour period. Other than scaling a bunch of boulders in the woods early in the day, we spent most of the day walking through open, flooded corn, soybean, and hay fields. That had us more than a bit concerned because of the amount of thunder and lightning enveloping us. As we slogged our way through the fields, we thought back to our wilderness first aid training and what we learned about how extremely dangerous it is to be fully exposed to this particular wrath of nature—and with hiking sticks in each hand serving as lightning rods, no less! The thought crossed our minds more than once.

"What would we do if one of us was struck by lightning?"

It was a sobering notion—losing your best friend to such a thing. But we both tucked away that fear in the recesses of our minds, allowing it to be overshadowed by the sense of adventure we felt in facing such a potential disaster and eluding it. The heightened sense of impending doom washed away the relative monotony of just walking, and it was as if deliberately exposing ourselves to the potential of being injured or killed was a way for us to become closer. Within the context of our mutual fear and concern for each other, we became one person.

Near day's end we crossed the footbridge above Rte. 11 near Carlisle—our destination for the day. We shuffled along the highway's narrow shoulder, with tractor-trailers rumbling endlessly past us and, in their wake, a steady, cold wind blew, which only added to our misery. We knew "V&A" were most likely concerned about us because of all the rain and lightning, and we joked about the fact they were probably out on the road attempting to locate us. We had not walked fifty yards before we heard a car horn behind us. Thinking after all we had survived this day we would meet our "Maker" by being hit by a car, we prepared to dive into the nearest ditch. But first, one last look to see what or who was going to hit us was in order—we wanted our executioner to see the whites of our eyes. We quickly and nervously, turned around, and lo and behold, there were "V&A" right behind us. What were the chances they would find us at exactly the time and place where we came off the trail and onto the road?

They gave us a ride to the nearby *Holiday Inn* where we spent the night drying our clothes and trying to get warm. To celebrate our wedding anniversary, not to mention our good fortune, we had a wonderful dinner—and I finally had the lasagna I had been craving for weeks. As we sat at the table and relived the events of the day, the equipment malfunctions, the rain, the lightning, and our good fortune, a renewed sense of inner strength welled up inside both of us. It was a feeling that bound us even closer. This shared emotion could never have manifested itself in our marriage had it not been for the love and compassion we felt for each other because of the travails we had overcome together. "V&A" could have just as easily have stayed in the warmth of their RV and left us to our own devices. And we would have made it to Carlisle and the comfort of the hotel by ourselves. But, their single-minded purpose, born of years of pursuing goals and adventures together, along with their concern for members of their family, brought them to our aid.

Little Wing:

"One thing I never anticipated was how important PEOPLE would become to me. Before actually hiking the A.T., I thought of it as being mostly a solo, introspective journey. I consider the community of fellow thru-hikers I met during the 2006 season to be like family members and hope to remain in touch with them for years."

Enuff:

> *"I am looking forward to going to "Trail Days" next year to see our hiking family and to recapture that unique feeling of "the group" again. I miss some of the people we hiked with and I know I will probably not see most of them again. I do miss listening to flute music at night, the fishing, and the banjo music. It was a very "together" feeling with everyone pulling in the same direction and it reminded me a lot of the western migration."*

We embarked on this six-month exploit to challenge each other, and ourselves, and to add yet another major chapter to our book of personal accomplishments. It was to be a search for things buried deep inside of us that would make us stronger individuals. Being introverts and attaining our sense of inner peace and resourcefulness from moments of isolation away from the masses that emotionally and physically drained us, our search for solitude was of paramount importance. But what we found was entirely different and more meaningful. Our burning ambition to conquer the trail suddenly took a back seat to a growing desire for friendship, compassion, and empathy—not only with each other, but also with those around us. Buttressed by our new circle of "family," the relationship between "Mom" and me also blossomed more than we could have ever imagined. We developed an intimate awareness of each other's emotions. A higher level of mutual understanding pervaded our thoughts and actions our "normal" lives never could have nurtured. In the end, it became "about the people," and that included us. Our lives and marriage would never be the same.

"Mom's" Tips for Couples:

- The trail is all about the people. Simply because you and your partner have each other, do not miss out on opportunities to meet all the interesting people on the trail and become part of "the family." There is a place in that family for everyone. Your real life should be no different;

- Look for opportunities to experience the wonderful feeling of helping others along the way. The lifelong benefit of being there for someone, especially a stranger, brings rewards for you—both individually and as a couple;

- Find time for solitude away from the crowd. Give yourself time to reflect on your journey and how it is impacting your relationship—on the trail and as you live your life together.

CHAPTER SEVEN

ANGELS, HEROES, AND INSPIRATION

"The true measure of a man is how he treats someone who can do him absolutely no good." Samuel Johnson

Prior to our hike we read more online trail journals than we could count, so we were aware our journey across the Appalachian Mountains would be dramatically life changing. What none of those journals adequately communicated was how our encounters with those on, and along, the trail would equally change our lives. As we interacted with our burgeoning "trail family," both hikers and those who supported the hikers as they passed, our preconceptions, distorted by years of living in the narcissistic crush of D.C. suburbia, were torn apart. How we now related to those familiar to us and with those who we might never see again, influenced how "Mom" and I related to each other. After six months of trail education in human dynamics, in an environment stripped of all pretenses, we more fully appreciated and accepted not only who we were, but who others were as well. The impact of these revelations manifested themselves over and over again as we made our way toward Maine.

Anyone who completes the entire length of the Appalachian Trail, be it a section hiker—who completes the trail over many years, hiking a section at a time—or as a thru-hiker—who completes it all in one season—is welcomed into this wilderness fraternity. Thru-hikers, be it because of their dogged fortitude or simple lack of common sense, are considered a somewhat elite group, though not in a "snobbish" or exclusive way. Yes, we were all a family but that family grew far beyond merely those who wandered the muddy, rock, and root-strewn path we call the A.T. It also included those on and along the trail who supported us, who provided "trail magic," and who maintained the trail so we could chase our dream. They were the angels, heroes, and source of inspiration that kept us going when we most needed it. Admittedly, it was rather nice to be treated like celebrities, or conquering heroes, by these folks when they discovered we were thru-hikers. Typically, our "trail aromas" gave us away long before we ever mentioned we were on our way to Maine. And if our sense of worth or accomplishment ever waned, it was the people along the trail who brought us back to the astonishing reality of our undertaking. Without them, the trail and our journey would have been quite different.

For example, there was the day we clawed our way up the twin peaks called "The Kinsmans" and discovered that not only were these mountains just a glimpse of the romantically agonizing hike that was to come, but that strangers on the trail could so impact our lives. Although it was only an 8.8-mile day, the hike was physically arduous and took us a full eight hours to complete. First, we had to climb Mt. Kinsman's south slope (4,358 feet) — two hours of technical climbing up boulder faces while clutching onto roots and trees lining the trail so as to make any amount of vertical headway and keep from sliding back down the slope. We took a snack break on a rock ledge overlooking the expansive valley below. As we munched on our protein bars, washing them down with cups of powdered ice tea, a hawk swooped down. Our lofty position allowed him to soar so close we felt as if we could reach out and touch him. This closeness to nature took hold of us and filled us with a sense of pure gratitude—for each other and for the life we were living together. What was profound was how something as huge and far reaching as the view below us could provide us with such introspective focus.

When we finally pulled our way to the top, MY GOD, what a sight stretched out before us! We could see all the upcoming mountains we would be hiking over the next hours and days, and below was a large pond we passed just yesterday. The surrounding vistas lying at our feet were so mesmerizing we did not want to head down right away. We wanted to savor the moment, so we took a snack break and said hello to "Carbomb & Lichen" as they went by. With our snack break over and the vastness of the valleys below etched indelibly in our minds, we descended into a conifer-laden valley and up Mt. Kinsman's northern slope (4,293 feet). As awe-inspiring as the views around us were, the most emotional moment of the day for us came as we scaled a very long, narrow, steep, and difficult section.

Halfway up, we encountered a large group of day-hikers on their way down. They inquired as to whether or not we were thru-hikers and when we confirmed we were, they stepped aside to let us pass—and applauded us until we were out of sight. It was at that moment we became fully aware of what we were in the midst of accomplishing and how inspirational our adventure was for other people. Little did these day-hikers know how much their appreciation of what we were doing bolstered our spirits and positively impacted the level of dedication "Mom" and I felt for each other. At that moment, we also sensed that doing this odyssey <u>together</u> was as important as whether or not we succeeded in completing it. The individual sense of joy we felt was superseded by our shared joy in living that defining moment.

Brownie:

> *"The trail demonstrated to me the true goodness of people. I never imagined so many strangers would help me in so many ways. I have a renewed dedication to helping other people in even the most unexpected circumstances. I will never forget the amazing feeling of being surrounded by people who shared a common goal."*

Our expanding circle of family not only included those whose lives, if for only a brief moment, intersected ours as we walked the trail, but more importantly, it included those who dedicate their lives to serving the hikers who annually journey through their towns. Woven into the fabric of our unique sojourn was a trailside culture that exuded a sense of community sorely lacking in urban America. In today's self-absorbed, transient society, people hardly get to know their neighbors. They pass each other on the sidewalk without even saying "hello." Heinous crimes are committed in plain view of apathetic witnesses and rarely does any personal intervention occur. Out on the A.T. and in the towns through which it passed, it was so different and wonderful. Everyone was sincerely glad to see us and took an interest in who we were and what we were feeling. They wanted us to succeed, to be safe, and to enjoy the adventure. We were welcomed into homes, hostels, and restaurants as if we were prodigal sons. Moreover our appearances, which in most areas of the country would be cause for a moment of fearful concern or a salvo of snide remarks, were viewed by the A.T. townspeople as a badge of honor and strength. Because of the outpouring of trust and caring exhibited by the townspeople we encountered, our lives were transformed and we became more trusting and open with each other—and with those around us. Nurturing that feeling oftentimes became infinitely more important than the trip itself.

It was April 16th and by the time we reached Davenport Gap in Tennessee we were "toast," so seeing "V&A" sitting at the road crossing was a welcome sight. Amazingly, we had officially completed the Smokies without a single day of bad weather which, in the annals of thru-hiking, is a rare occurrence. We were conspicuously sunburned as we approached the road crossing, hand-in-hand, like two star-crossed lovers. As we frantically searched through our packs, it became evident we had not brought the next page of our *"Thru-Hiker's Companion"* book. As detail-oriented as we are, forgetting something so important was pretty uncharacteristic. Had we not left it behind, we would have known the Standing Bear Hostel, our intended stop for the night, was <u>not</u> at Davenport Gap at all but was 2.4 miles further down the trail. Our enthusiasm took a sudden nose-dive as we pondered our situation. Hey, we had wheels, so we had options!

We loaded our packs into the car and drove to the hostel, fully intending to stay there and then pick up where we left off the day before. This seemed like an acceptable alternative to trying to make the remaining miles before nightfall—which was highly unlikely. When we arrived, it was evident the hostel was full because the lawn was crammed full of tents. Therefore, despite the negative reports we heard from some hikers on the trail, we went to the legendary "Mountain Moma's" hostel—home of the "Huge Cheeseburger." As it turned out, the reports were ill-founded and we were treated like part of the family. Since everyone else was at Standing Bear, we had the entire facility to ourselves, including the showers (which felt great after collecting a healthy layer of grime over the last six days) and uninterrupted use of the laundry room. Our arrival had been way past the restaurant's normal closing time but "Moma," being the gracious southern hostess she was and having a reputation for looking after hikers as if they were her own children, kept the grill open so we could savor her famous cheeseburgers. And, in celebration of Easter, which we had totally forgotten in the passion of our trek that day, she even provided us with Easter candy for dessert.

Then there was the sultry July day in Massachusetts when we hiked around Goose Pond and came across an old chimney and a tombstone with no name on it. This pond was just one of the many ponds and marshes we would pass this day. It was astounding just how many marsh areas there are at the tops of these mountains. Anywhere else in the country, you would only find them in the low areas between the mountains or near beaches. Here they seemed to flourish at higher elevations and the sense of peace we experienced by nothing more than sitting on their shores refreshed our souls and inspired us to pursue a slower, and ultimately, more satisfying pace of life when we returned home.

In the afternoon, we took a slight detour to visit one of the icons of the A.T., *"The Cookie Lady."* Just off the trail a short distance down a paved road sits a blueberry farm operated by Marilyn Wiley and her husband, Roy, who for twenty years have been welcoming hikers to their home for free blueberry cookies and water. Though we did not get to meet Marilyn, we did sit in their front yard and visited with Roy for quite some time. As "Mom" relaxed in a nearby lounge chair and I sat on a picnic bench, we nibbled Marilyn's famous blueberry cookies while Roy entertained us with his "down home" wit and charm. When I asked about the large building at the far end of his property, he told us he was a pilot and he had his plane housed in the hangar in his backyard. Across the entire back edge of his property, stretching for some one thousand feet was his grass runway. It was obvious he was quite proud of his newly completed hangar, and even at his age, which I would guess was somewhere in the late 60's (though I never thought to ask), he was still a capable and avid pilot. He was so captivating and so forthcoming with his stories that we found it very difficult to return to the trail. We walked away discussing how different the people were in "this part of the world" and how unhurried and how happy they seemed to be. Could we ever live a life of such relaxed happiness? We vowed to try and were thankful it would be some time before we had to return to lives so counter to those of Roy and Marilyn's. For some their home was just a place to rest, get cold water, and eat remarkably tasty cookies. To us, it was more than that. What struck us was the dedication of Marilyn and Roy to looking after thru-hikers. They took valuable time from operating their blueberry farm and small store in order to share the goodness of the life they spent together. It was a labor of love—a love that overflowed into the lives of the hikers who came their way.

Little Wing:

> "My faith in humanity was restored by the generous kindness of strangers in small towns along the way who offered unsolicited trail magic. We don't see this kind of stuff on the six o'clock news. More than once, I was moved to tears and the entire experience has opened me up emotionally. To quote "Brainfreeze:" "It's like being on the trail dilates your heart a little bit, and you're more open to the effects of experiences." I couldn't say it better myself."

Some towns and their citizens are so in tune to the A.T. hiking experience they readily devote town resources, facilities, and supplies to the smelly vagabonds who annually drag themselves into town for some R&R. All the A.T. information books go to great lengths to highlight those towns "friendly to hikers." Such a town is Palmerton, Pennsylvania.

July 5th was quite a day—not very long, but very memorable! We woke up to drenching rain and a long descent into Lehigh Gap. We heard the morning rain would end but there were predictions of additional late afternoon thunderstorms (wow, what a surprise), so we modified our plans a bit. At 10:30 a.m., the heavy rains let up so we headed out though still hiking in showers on and off most of the morning. After a brief brunch and still uncertain of how our afternoon would play out, we ran into "Ridgerunner Roger," who strongly advised against trying to do the ascent out of Lehigh Gap in the afternoon with thunderstorms in the weather forecast.

> *"That ascent is EXTREMELY steep and difficult, and once you get to the top you still have miles of totally exposed mountaintop to walk across with absolutely no place to hide from lightning."*

Upon hearing this, we made our decision to rendezvous with "V&A" outside of Palmerton, The sun finally came out as we headed down the steep descent to Lehigh Gap, eating large handfuls of blueberries along the way and drinking *Coke*s "Ridgerunner Roger" left in one of the springs we passed. Personally wanting to experience as many of the "historic elements" of the trail as possible, I decided we should stay the night at the old Palmerton jail; so we had "V&A" drive us into this quaint and very hiker-friendly town for the night.

When the town built its new police station and jail, the old one was converted into town offices and a community activities center. The townspeople decided to turn the basement, which previously housed the jail, into a hostel for hikers. It also serves as a meeting place for local scout troops. The facility is large with showers, bunk beds, tables, benches, towels, a hiker box, and a furnace room where you can hang your wet gear to dry. And, if you still have the energy after a day's worth of hiking, there is an indoor basketball court just off the shower room. When we first arrived and signed in, we were presented with "goodie bags" prepared by one of the local Girl Scout troops. It contained toothpaste, a toothbrush, a small roll of toilet paper and a card letting us know who put together our "goodie bags." All of this was provided absolutely "free of charge" and was indicative of how we were treated by everyone we met in town—from the waitress at Bert's Steakhouse, where we had dinner, to the folks at the *IGA* supermarket where we went to pick up a few things. Everyone seemed friendly. They waved at us and took a genuine interest in what we were attempting to accomplish. They were sincerely glad to see us and that was comforting. Their hospitality was so different from what we were accustomed to at home. We began to utterly detest the unfriendly atmosphere of D.C. suburbia and looked forward to being away from it as long as possible. We also wished we could have been there the day before because this was the type of town that we just knew had a splendid Fourth of July celebration—complete with a parade and fireworks.

After our home-style dinner, we sat on the steps in front of the jail in the cool evening air, waiting for the evening cleaning crew to arrive and unlock the front door so we could get back in. As we sat watching the sporadic parade of traffic on Main Street, where pedestrians actually received the right of way, a gentleman strolled up and stopped right in front of us.

"Hi, my name's Kevin. Do you folks need a ride back to the trail in the morning?"

"Thanks! That would be great. My name is 'Windtalker' and this is 'Mom.'

Since most people in Palmerton did not generally walk around town in *Crocs*, the fact we had ours on was Kevin's first clue we were from out of town—and the far-away look in our eyes confirmed we were thru-hikers. Kevin, a.k.a. "Billygoat," and his wife, a.k.a. "Granola," are trail angels and regularly provide shuttles and trail magic to hikers. We informed him we were hiking as a married couple, but he never asked us how we were getting along. I guess only married guys whose spouses are not hikers asked us that question. "Billygoat," having a hiking wife, already knew the answer to that question, I suppose. Meeting other backpacking couples, especially those who provided "trail magic," was inspirational to us. Our brief encounters with them left us with a burning desire to do the same and, hopefully, comfort and inspire other hiking couples. It was good to know that the number of couples who share their lives together backpacking was a far larger number than we thought.

Among the throng of memorable people we met along the trail, we had the good fortune to come in contact with many other wonderful couples who, as a team, were living their dream of serving hikers by providing food and lodging. Most certainly, they were trying to make a decent living, but we never sensed the income they derived from running a hostel, a motel, or a restaurant was what motivated them. It was always about "the hikers" and what the hikers needed. Their unique personalities, how they interacted with each other, and their ceaseless adherence to pursuing a "simple life" gave us hope. They exuded a zest for the peaceful life we hoped would rub off on us. If it did, after our hike was over, we could retreat back into society with that new perspective on life firmly intact and with their inspiration as a roadmap.

It was the last day of March and our night on Tray Mountain at 3,580 feet had been awesome! At first, it had been so clear we could see the lights of the homes in the gaps miles below and a new moon pierced the pitch-black sky. Then it all suddenly changed! The wind built to an ear-piercing crescendo until it sounded like a 747 coming up from the valley, over our tent, and then retreating into the gap on the other side. It was wonderful; it was scary; it was a lullaby that lulled us into a deep and restful sleep.

As they had on so many other mornings, clouds settled in on top of the mountain covering everything in sight with a sloppy layer of dew. We got a late start, 7:45 a.m., and soon realized we were experiencing quite a bit more foot pain than usual. There were lots of long climbs, as well as the requisite descents, that only exacerbated the pain, but there was no way it was going to stop us. The sun finally came out, beginning as mere "sun dogs" piercing the clouds and giving us hope that the day was going to be another memorable one. As the sun broke into full view, it evaporated the mist from the surrounding hillsides and the day began to get quite warm. We stopped at Deep Gap at 3,550 feet for lunch and a much-needed "boots-off/pack-off" break before starting the 1,175 feet, 2.2-mile descent to our destination for the day. As we neared the final gap for the day, gasping for breath and repeatedly wiping sweat from our foreheads, there it was—"trail magic"! "Hike-Ku" had left cans of *Mountain Dew* in a stream near the trail along with packages of my all-time favorite, *Nutty-Buddy* bars. He left a hand-written sign in the middle of the trail letting everyone know where these delights were located. The note also advised us that we needed to pack out our trash when done. It was a portent of what was to come.

We arrived at Dick's Creek Gap late afternoon, and "V&A" gave us a ride to the Blue Berry Patch Hostel, our stop for the night. But first, there was more "magic!" "V&A" brought us fried chicken, coleslaw, biscuits, peach cobbler, and orange sodas for dinner. We were so starved that just the smells emanating from those red and white bags, with Colonel Sanders' cartoon portrait printed on the front, had us drooling before we ever got out of the car at the hostel.

For years, Gary and Lennie Poteat have been welcoming hikers into their quaint hostel, a large converted garage next to their home. Gary is very familiar with life on the trail, being a 1991 thru-hiker himself. Complete with several picnic tables placed end to end, comfortable bunks, a hot plate, and a refrigerator full of cold sodas this place was like heaven on earth to us—perhaps that is what is it was designed to convey. Being devout Christians, Gary and Lennie have never shied away from proclaiming their faith and every thru-hiker guide notes that fact. Operating this hostel is a ministry for them and they are proud of it. Their love and caring for hikers is a visible manifestation of their faith.

Out back—overlooking their large garden where they harvest their own vegetables and blueberries, and guarded by a small herd of pet donkeys, and a short walk from the hostel—was the shower house. Being able to wash away the stink and grime we accumulated over the last few days was a luxurious treat. We felt like human beings again—and we again smelled like ones too. While we showered, Lennie did our laundry for us so it was finished when we returned. We polished off our *KFC* dinner with the help of

"Dave," our hostel mate for the evening, and hit the sack. I was anxious to partake of one of their acclaimed breakfasts the next morning. The gargantuan breakfasts we ate along the trail helped to hasten my conversion to being a morning person.

"Mom" battled leg cramps most of the night but awoke, as I did, totally refreshed and ready for breakfast the next morning. We shuffled into Gary and Lennie's comfortable sunroom, sat down at a huge oak table near their antique wood cook stove, and joined both of them in prayer. Communal praying was something we had been sorely missing while on the trail though we did silently pray each day that we would make it safely to Katahdin. Then it was time to dig in. Living primarily off the land, the Poteats serve natural, home cooked treats such as eggs, pancakes with their homemade blueberry syrup, biscuits, sausage, orange juice, and coffee.

In everything they said and did, it was obvious to us they were devoted not only to God and hikers, but to each other as well. There was much to be learned simply by watching and listening to them, and because of their love for us, our faith in not only people, but in God, was strengthened. It seemed that more and more couples were being unexpectedly put in our path as inspiration for our relationship.

August 1st was bathed in the same heat and humidity that plagued us for the last few days. We headed up the venerable Stratton Mountain, an imposing 3,936-foot behemoth that took us the better part of the afternoon to scale. We became a bit despondent as we walked and walked and walked, but never arrived at the gravel road indicated in our guidebook. This road was a visible indication we were nearing the top, so locating it was important for our morale. We were wondering,

"Are we walking that slowly? It has been hours and we have still have not seen the road."

Quite unexpectedly, we came upon Bob and Debbie, father-and-daughter section hikers, taking a break. They informed us we were only about 0.6 mile from the top. Apparently, we had missed the road because it was not as visible as we anticipated it would be. Rejuvenated by the fact we were further up the mountain than we thought, we continued to the summit. There, in a large clearing, hemmed in by mammoth pines and spruce, and guarded by a soaring fire tower, stood a small, white one-room cottage, the home of the mountain's caretakers, Jean and Hugh Joudrey. We located a large rock to sit on, took off our packs, and were warmly greeted by Jean. For an hour she told us of their life on the mountain.

For six months each year, they live in their mountaintop hideaway, and, as members of the Green Mountain Hiking Club, provide trail maintenance and watch over the hikers who wander through their front lawn. We learned from Jean, who spends her quiet hours on the mountain painting, that the dragonflies flying around us were not only beautiful but play an important role in the "circle of life" in this region. The dragonflies are a good thing since they eat the black flies that continually torment hikers to a point where many of them leave the trail. When we told her about seeing a porcupine, her eyes twinkled and she told us we were very lucky to have seen one and told us how destructive they can be in their quest to eat salt. She told us she and Hugh regularly leave their car at the bottom of the mountain, and when they need more supplies, they simply hike down the mountain and drive to the nearest town to shop. However, on one occasion when they attempted to take their car into town, they were suddenly confronted by the frightening fact they had no brakes. Evidently, porcupines, in an attempt to remove the road salt from their car, had chewed through the brake lines. It is not unusual for them to also eat the chrome off bumpers.

As she was finishing her porcupine story, her husband arrived from the trail where he was doing maintenance. We asked her about their solitary life on the mountain and found they were quite content living there. They spent their days enjoying each other's company, doing trail maintenance, and pursuing their personal interests—all this while being surrounded by the majesty of the Vermont woods. After listening to her impassioned description of their life together, "Mom" and I discussed how wonderful such a life would be, miles away from the confines and demands of modern living that oftentimes suffocated our ability to relax and experience the natural world around us. The obvious joy permeating Jean and Hugh's lives made us envious and even more determined to break free of the "rat race" when we finished our hike.

It was now September 16th and we had about 6.2 miles left to go to reach the highway where we would meet "V&A" and head into Monson, Maine. Unfortunately, the sugar rush we experienced after our breakfast of soda and donuts disappeared halfway up Buck Hill. By this time in our hike, we had become so intrinsically bonded to each other we even "pooped out" at the same instant So, without either of us even uttering a word, we simultaneously stopped for a protein bar break. We jokingly shared our frustration over the fact it always seemed to take longer than it should when we wanted to get to a place quickly. Even this far into our hike, we had not entirely grasped the concept that it was about the journey—not the destination.

Finally, we arrived at ME15, our designated meeting place, threw our packs into "V&A's" car, and they drove us to Monson. We made a quick stop at Shaw's Hostel to pick up some new tips for "Mom's" trekking poles and there, sitting on the lawn, were "Lebowski," "Bofus," "Treehouse," "Identity Crisis," and "Slick-B," who had taken the "blue blaze trail" (short cut) to Shaw's. A short drive down Monson's quaint main street brought us to The Lakeshore House where we checked in and met our wonderful hosts, Rebekah and Jeff Santagata. We heard how friendly the folks were in Monson and how they catered to the hundreds of hikers who came through each year, but we were simply blown away by the hospitality of Rebekah and Jeff. Here was a couple who was living out their dream of leaving the "rat race" and operating a small, rural, lodge. To do so, they recently transplanted themselves in Monson to make that dream happen. Their gregarious and cordial manner only helped to bolster our conviction that these small New England villages had a way of stripping away the hardened norms of urban living. In its place was a sense of contentment which permeated their relationship and touched all whom they met. It was a contentment that was infectious, and we longed for it in our lives. In their teamwork approach to running their lodge and in the way they lovingly interacted with each other, we saw a lot of ourselves, and it made us feel good about our relationship.

As was our practice throughout the hike, if we possibly could, we would get a massage during a zero day. Since we were spending an extra day in Monson to rest before entering the "100-Mile Wilderness," we queried Rebekah about massage therapists in town. Astonishingly, one of her best friends had a massage therapy business that she had recently moved from the center of town to a location about seven miles away. Before we could ask for a local phone book to make a call for appointments, Rebekah handed us one of her friend's business cards AND the hotel's private phone. We scheduled appointments with Lindy at *Trail Magic Massage Therapy* for the following afternoon.

"How did you make out with getting in touch with Lindy," Rebekah asked, as she fluttered between the kitchen, the bar, and the hotel's restaurant.

"Fantastic," said "Mom." *"Are there any shuttles in town we can call to take us there tomorrow?"*

"Shuttle? You won't need a shuttle. I have to be here in the restaurant all afternoon tomorrow anyway, you can just take my car."

"Are you kidding? That would be wonderful. Thank you so much,"
we both stuttered.

We walked away in utter amazement at her offer and we could not imagine anyone doing such a thing in Maryland. Hell, we do not even leave our car unattended for two minutes to unload groceries into our house without locking the doors, and here was a person willing to lend her car to nearly total strangers who just walked in from the trail, who smelled awful, and who, unbeknownst to her, could be full-time car thieves.

As promised, at 12:30 p.m. the next day, she graciously handed us her car keys and off we went to see Lindy at *Trail Magic Massage Therapy*. This would be our final tune-up before the "100-Mile Wilderness." Linda McLaughlin's home stands beside a wandering, tranquil river and the view from her backyard is of two alpine mountain peaks. It is the perfect setting to relax your mind before she relaxes your body. She did a wonderful job getting rid of all of the aches and pains and relaxing us for our run to "Le Gran K." Three hours later, we returned Rebekah's car to her. She was somewhat taken back when we told her we filled her gas tank, but we emphatically convinced her it was the least we could do in response to her grand and trusting gesture. All along the trail, especially in the South and in New England, this desire to offer assistance, coupled with an unbelievable level of trust offered to strangers who had just walked in from the wilderness, was something we longed for at home.

They are called "trail angels," the unsung heroes of the Appalachian Trail who, for nothing more than their love of the trail and hikers, provide food, transportation, encouragement, and frequent ego boosts to all the hikers fortunate enough to pass their way. Many "trail angels" are former thru-hikers so they have a profound understanding of the difficulty of what we were attempting to do. This understanding gave birth to a love for every thru-hiker chasing his/her own dream, and it fueled their desire to help in any way they could to make that dream a reality. They know what it feels like to make it to the top of Katahdin, and they want as many other people as possible to feel that sensation. They give unselfishly of themselves as a way to say,

"We are with you all the way. Keep walking. You can do it!"

Their love of the trail and level of compassion for their fellow hikers is a testament to the profound effect that hiking the A.T. has on a person. It is their way of giving back to the trail some of what the trail has given to them. Their level of generosity is a rare commodity in our current society. As we benefitted more and more from their passion, we decided when we completed our thru-hike we would "pay it forward," so to speak, and keep the trail angel tradition alive for future hiking generations. Interacting with these angels of the trail renewed our belief that people are inherently good and caring. The fact they had lived out such a life-altering event and now had the opportunity to serve others, became the compelling reason for them to rise to the occasion and help other hikers. We remember each and every one of them with great fondness.

"V&A" were not only our personal trail angels, but they assisted other thru-hikers in a multitude of ways. For instance, they gave "Comfortably Numb" a ride into Damascus after he spent a very cold and wet night near Mt. Rogers and was in desperate need of a place to dry and thaw out. There were numerous injured hikers, such as "Wounded Knee," who benefited from their ride to a local hospital for treatment. And, when hikers least expected it, "V&A" could be found at a road crossing with *Snickers* bars, chicken and dumplings, drinks, fruit, trail updates and ready smiles for every hiker passing through. But, they were not the only ones making the journey more memorable.

Many of these angels were couples who brought their mutual love of the trail and for each other to the trailheads along the way. There were Bruce and Myrtle at Hog Pen Gap in Georgia, the very first angels we encountered, and we met "Jeopardy" & "Java," a former thru-hiking couple, who set up an extensive "hiker feed" next to Nahmakanta Lake in the "100-Mile Wilderness" of Maine. After trudging so many miles, their hot dogs, fruit and sodas were a welcome treat. What were equally welcome were their outgoing demeanors and hospitable natures. They were the last angels we ran into before the end of the trail.

We will never forget two other former thru-hikers, Richard Boisvert (a.k.a. "Potato Man") and Ray Ronan (a.k.a. "Walkin' Home") who set up two large tents in a parking area in Maine. For almost a week, they provided three squares a day and a place to crash for the night to every hiker who had the good fortune to pass their way. They paid for everything out of their own pockets and they positively would not accept donations from any hiker. Angels were even with us as we strolled into Katahdin Stream Campground after our triumphant summit of Mt. Katahdin. "Dirt Diva" and "Compass Rose's" parents welcomed us with snacks and sodas—a fitting end to an incredible day.

Our encounters with trail angels were as numerous as they were unexpected; and "trail magic," the "manna" of the thru-hiker, always seemed to appear unexpectedly. It was that unexpectedness that made it "magic." We never expected "magic," nor did we feel entitled to any; so when it suddenly appeared, say, as a cooler of cold soda at a road crossing on a hot July day, it was amazing. Sometimes trail magic was jugs of fresh water on a section of trail where the springs had gone dry; it even came in the form of a passing motorist who, upon finding you were a thru-hiker, invited you to his/her house for dinner, to take a shower, and to do laundry. For us, it was meeting "Batty" on the long downhill trek into Pearisburg, Virginia, where he stopped us, opened his pack, and there, encased in what looked to be ten pounds of ice, was our choice of beer or soda. For us, trail magic was the way our faith in our fellow man was continually reinforced. Here are but a few more of the moments of magic we experienced and hope their influence on us, and how we now view our responsibility to those we come in contact with, will also serve to influence you in the same way.

On one particular day in North Carolina, we were determined to knock off as many miles as possible so we left early without eating breakfast. We were to soon experience one of the most incredible days so far on our long journey. First, we encountered trail magic in the form of a cooler filled with cold soda left by two former thru-hikers, "Shades of Blue" and "Mary." According to the note left with the cooler, they put out this magic <u>on their wedding day</u> and asked each person who took a soda to sign the journal tucked away inside. We took one, left them a note, and headed up to the marvelously picturesque top of Max Patch Bald (4,629 feet), where I savored it as if it were fine wine. The enjoyment of that soda was made richer by the fact these two people transferred the love they had for each other on their wedding day to those on the trail they also loved and cared about.

We left the Daleville, Virginia a bit earlier than usual, at 6:30 a.m., and slack-packed the 13.6 miles to Blackhorse Gap where we met "V&A." There we grabbed our full packs and spent a relaxing afternoon hiking the last few miles to the shelter. We stopped at all the overlooks on the Blue Ridge Parkway and took an extended break at Harvey's Knob Overlook where we snacked while "Mom" called her daughter. We chatted with "Backwards Bob," "Mountain Girl," and a young man who did not have a trail name yet. By mid-afternoon, we were already at Boblett's Gap Shelter where we spent the rest of the day with "Identity Crisis," "Kutsa," "Chill," two section hikers from Colorado, and a free-lance photographer from Roanoke, Virginia by the name of Brendan Bush. Brendan had an old black and white, 4-inch by 6-inch format camera, a cherished possession of his father's, and he proceeded to take portraits of all of us. In addition, he also provided all of us with cold *Ice House* beer. *(Brendan later sent us copies of the photos he took and they proudly hang on the wall next to the photo of us at the summit of Mt. Katahdin—yet another example of trail magic.)*

In Connecticut as we came down the mountain to US 7/CT 112, we were extremely hot and dangerously low on water. "Mom" stated she would like a soda and we could get both water and a soda at the gas station near the road intersection at the base of the mountain. With our oasis in view, we scrambled down the mountain to discover this particular gas station was no longer in operation and was completely locked up. Learning to overcome the harsh realities of being on the trail, such as this particular situation, was an ongoing and oftentimes brutal education. On the trail, having hopes dashed and expectations unfulfilled were regular occurrences. It was those types of moments which forced us to find a deeper resolve and a broader acceptance of things out of our control. We also developed a growing desire and a profound capacity to empathize with each other and give each other strength. Parched and exhausted, we hiked the next 1.25 miles through open cornfields, in the blazing sun, and wishing all the while we had filled up with water at the last spring before leaving the mountaintop. But then, just when we thought we could go no further, we arrived at the Housatonic Regional High School. There on the lawn, under the shade of a huge tree, sat "Holly T" and a friend. They were providing trail magic in the form of soda, *Snapple* fruit drinks, and watermelon. We first met "Holly T" at the Ensign Cowell Shelter in Maryland, and she was now off the trail because she had to get back to college. Despite the fact her dream of thru-hiking the A.T. had been derailed due to a lack of time, her love of the trail and devotion to those still hiking benefitted us and others.

In Massachusetts we once again endured another slow, grueling, treacherous descent to arrive at the Guilder Pond picnic area. There on a picnic table were two coolers full of soda and sandwiches—trail magic left for thru-hikers by the Cerny Family and "Box of Fun," a thru-hiker from 2005. We ate our lunch and enjoyed a couple of sodas that were welcome treats on such a hot and humid day. We have said it many times before, but thank God for all the trail angels and what they brought to all of the hikers—all out of the pure goodness of their hearts and their desire to serve people they probably have never met before—and possibly never may meet.

It was also in Massachusetts that we became trail angels. After four solitary days, we ran into a northbound thru-hiker at the Tom Leonard Shelter where we stopped to replenish our dwindling water supply. There, also getting water was our old hiking companion, "Sherps," who had now changed her trail name to "Fiddlehead." We had not seen her since Unicoi

Gap many months before. She originally hiked with "Cosmic Punchline," but he was attempting to reach Maine in ninety-nine days and she could not keep up with his fast pace. At one point, she also got off the trail to attend a wedding. She told us she had been behind us for weeks and was happy to have finally caught up to us. After refilling our water supplies, we went our separate ways but caught up with her again when met "V&A" at our pick-up point. Since we had quite an array of extra supplies, we made up a couple of "hiker boxes" that we left in the trunk of "V&A's" car for other hikers to pick through. She took advantage of them and grabbed a number of items she needed to get her to her next supply point. Once we reached Vermont, we also left supplies behind at The Inn at the Long Trail and several other places. The love and compassion exhibited to us by trail angels had not been for naught, and providing magic now gave us as much pleasure as being on the trail. What an epiphany!

We heard there was a couple who for days had positioned themselves along the trail and were providing hikers with hot meals like eggs, bacon, hamburgers, hotdogs and drinks. Because we left camp so early in the morning, we arrived at Benedict Pond in Massachusetts, where they had set up their magic long before they had even arrived. However, there sat their gas grill, four chairs, a cooler, and a note from "Mr. & Mrs. Tunes." Here were two people who, we had heard, sat by this pond for a week and cooked food for every thru-hiker coming past their location. Their note apologized to us for not being there at 7:30 a.m. to take care of us! We should have apologized for stopping by so early. Anticipating that some hikers, like ourselves, may come through at an early hour, their note directed us to help ourselves to the drinks and food hidden under the lid of the grill. Now 7:30 a.m. was a bit early for soda, but "Mom" and I split a *Sierra Mist*. Their concern for us inspired us to leave a roll of toilet paper behind for some other hiker who may need it. Leaving the "TP" was like "paying it forward."

On a "zero day" in Vermont, it was time to do laundry, make journal entries, and locate a massage therapist. We intended to take the local bus from The Inn at the Long Trail into Rutland to also visit a chiropractor for a long-overdue tune-up. As we stood by the road in front of the inn, we turned around to see "Baldylocks" and "Knock-Knock" coming out of the inn with a third person, whom we did not recognize. All three headed to a pickup truck parked in the lot. We shouted our greetings to each other, and the third gentleman who was obviously the owner of the truck asked if we needed a ride. We replied we did and hopped into the truck with the other hikers and our driver, who turned out to be a Green Mountain Club member and 2004 thru-hiker, "Mad Hatter." It was not until the following year at the Long

Trail Festival that we were to meet his wife and hiking partner, Kathy, a.k.a. "MaBudda."

We had great chiropractic treatments and then started walking out to the road to wait for the local bus back to the inn. We did not stand there but ten minutes before a patient came out of the doctor's office, asked if we needed a ride, and said the chiropractor suggested he give us a ride back to the inn. We were not sure if the good doctor insisted we be given a ride because he wanted to help some thru-hikers or if he felt our backs were in such bad shape that any walking we could avoid would be a benefit to us. Our driver was very gracious and we chatted about hiking and biking all the way back. It was truly a day of trail magic of dramatic proportions. Total strangers going out of their way to help other total strangers; it was a concept firmly taking root in us and gave us a new perspective on what was important in life.

Have you ever been lost in an unfamiliar town or city? The very thought of approaching a total stranger for directions can bring even the brawniest man to his knees in pure frustration and terror. So imagine what a surprise it was for us to receive unsolicited directions simply because we looked lost. Such was the case for us on a winding road in Vermont! As usual, we were the first ones in camp to get up and on the trail and were met with unseasonably cool weather; so we began our hike in long pants and long-sleeved shirts. When we arrived several hours later at Quechee-West Hartford Road, we were pleasantly surprised by "V" who was waiting with our daypacks, juice, and muffins. The temperature had now reached a balmy 55 °F so we switched to shorts and sleeveless shirts. We would now enjoy slack-packing our way into Hanover, New Hampshire — trail magic at its unpredictable best! We finished our morning snack, threw on our packs and began the long morning of road walking—beginning with the quaint little town of West Hartford.

Our trail data book warned us there was minimal blazing along the main road out of town and we needed to be careful not to miss the turn onto Tigertown Road. To minimize our confusion, "V" gave us some directions. However, despite those instructions, our attention became focused on the nearby river and other rustic scenery along the way, and we forgot to keep an eye out for the blazes. We were now lost. It was like mentally dozing off while driving your car and then frantically wondering in a panic, *"How did I get here?"* That is how we felt. Did we miss the turn or had we not yet gone far enough? Whichever it was, the fact we had packs on—a sure sign we suffered from diminished mental capacities already and the bewildered looks on our faces—caused two women driving by in a convertible to stop.

"Are you looking for the trail?" they asked.

"We sure are. Did we miss the turn onto Tigertown Road?" conspicuously revealing our embarrassment over now being lost on a road after having walked a dirt path from Georgia without as much as making a wrong turn.

"It is right down there," they replied, pointing to the next side road in view.

"Thanks very much. We appreciate it. We're on our way to Maine from Georgia," I added, in an attempt to mitigate any perception that we had no real idea where the heck we were going.

"Good Luck," they called out as they drove away.

With so much trail magic coming our way, we had to wonder how much luck we would actually need.

We eventually found ourselves walking through the "New England picture postcard" town of Norwich, Vermont, with its revolutionary war era homes, surrounded by white picket fences and manicured lawns. The town truly is beautiful—at least the part we walked through. From there we faced the hot and foot-torturing road walk along Highway 5 into the nearby village of Hanover, New Hampshire. Halfway to town, with our feet now on fire from the hot pavement, we remembered something "Baldylocks" once said when faced with a decision to follow the trail down a road.

"If I wanted to walk on streets," he said, *"I would have stayed in New York City."*

Getting off the hot pavement and riding in an air-conditioned car the rest of the way was a captivating idea, but we fought the urge and steadfastly marched on. The final leg of our walk took us across the bridge spanning the Connecticut River, which separates Vermont and New Hampshire. We stopped halfway across to take our obligatory photos at the VT/NH state line etched into a pillar on the center of the bridge. We continued into town, walking past Dartmouth College—or as they pronounce it there, "Dat-mith"—and onto main street where we ran into "Baldylocks" having coffee at a sidewalk café. "Mom" became extremely jealous, because it had been quite a while since she had savored a latte.

Now, "trail magic" comes in all shapes and sizes and always when you least expect it. As we crossed Main Street to head out of town to meet "V," there in the crosswalk was a $10 bill. As soon as the "Walk" light came on, I dashed out to get it and ended up chasing it down the street as a breeze kept grabbing it and moving it just out of my reach. Undaunted, I dodged oncoming traffic and, to anyone in close proximity of my pedestrian ballet, I must have looked like some hopeless derelict scrounging for his next Jim Beam money. I finally retrieved it, nonchalantly shoved it into my pocket, and completed my trip across the street without making any eye contact with the multitude of onlookers who probably thought I was crazy. Most of them had no idea I was a thru-hiker, which had they known, would have explained everything.

By the time September 15th passed, it would have been almost two weeks without a zero day and we had hiked just under 119 miles in twelve days. The beginning of our two-day rest before heading into Maine's "100-Mile Wilderness" was only a few hours away. We approached the East Branch of the Piscataquis River fully expecting to ford it in our *Crocs* but were able to simply "rock-hop" across. As we scrambled up the embankment on the far side, we spied a cooler that, much to our delight, was loaded with "trail magic" from "Strider," a thru-hiker from 2003. We viewed "Strider" as one of the "elite of the elite" because 2003 tormented that year's thru-hikers with forty-nine days of rain; everyone who finished that year was in a category all by himself. We gorged ourselves on chocolate chip cookies and *Coke*—not a typical breakfast mind you, but still part of the "thru-hiker's four basic food groups"—and hiked the last quarter mile to Shirley-Blanchard Road where, surprise, "V&A" met us. We grabbed our daypacks, and as if we had not had enough sugar already, loaded up on the donuts they brought with them. "Bruiser" and "Lightweight" had spent the night near the road, so when they woke up "V&A" offered them donuts as well. As we approached we saw them sitting by the side of the road lounging in "donut ecstasy." What was truly ironic was that just the day before they had both been agonizing over not having had any baked goods for some time. It was a mildly surreal moment when, out of nowhere, "V&A" arrived with a family-size assortment of freshly made donuts from Abbot Village Bakery. It was a moment that would have made Rod Serling envious.

We could not help but be touched and influenced by all the "trail angels" who, through their selfless acts, demonstrated their desire to stay in contact with the A.T. and their extended family in a meaningful way. As husband and wife and as parents, we also discovered within these acts of kindness the need to reach out to our own families, both parents and children, if nothing more than to contact them by phone more often. As we ruminated on the many acts of kindness and giving we experienced on the trail, we saw a spiritual aspect in these acts—the giving of one's self to others you do not even know so their lives could be enriched or made a bit easier. Is that not what life is supposed to be about? Would not the world be a better place if everyone followed the example of these trail angels? Meeting the angels was like experiencing a living sermon.

Perhaps, because "Mom" and I come from the sprawling metropolis of Washington, D.C., an area that now stretches as far north as Baltimore and as far south as Richmond, Virginia, we approached the cultures along the trail with a sense of wonder, amusement, and surprise. Washington, D.C., and its surrounding communities, is steeped in partisan politics and struggles to balance the effects of cultural diversity. It suffers from a transient population that moves about bumper-to-bumper in BMWs, Mercedes, and limousines, and it is protected by an invisible, economic force that buffers it from nearly every negative economic downturn plaguing the rest of the country. To the world, it might appear to be a "utopia"—the ultimate place to live. As we traveled the A.T., we found that nothing could be further from the truth. It was refreshing and heartwarming to spend six months in communities that, by and large, represent "the real America"—the simple and unhurried America that still holds fast to the timeless ideals of trust, honor, hard work, friendship, family, and God—the America that has little, if anything, in common with the culture in and around Washington. The most enduring virtue of these communities was the love of life and the simplicity with which they pursued it.

Our individual lives, and the way in which we would pursue our married life in the future, were deeply impacted by these peaceful and unhurried oases from the "post-modern" world in which we currently lived. When the time was right, "Mom" and I would permanently leave all our suburban madness behind in search of a life more like that of the people along the trail who housed us, fed us, drove us around, trusted us, inspired us and, beneath it all, loved us. The folly of the lives we were currently living was continually brought home each time we compared the human interaction in D.C. to that of the people in the towns we encountered on our journey.

Stretching from Washington, D.C., to Cumberland, Maryland is the C&O Canal Towpath—the location for several of our infamous training hikes. It is a national historic park that on any given day sees hundreds, and on weekends, thousands, of walkers, hikers, and bikers. We spent many a day hiking sections of this trail; and since our first step on it, we were amazed at the lack of courtesy, respect, and friendliness displayed by the people who travel it. As people approached each other, there was a pronounced effort by both parties to deliberately look away so as to avoid making visual or vocal contact with each other. *"Hello," "How are you?"* and *"Nice day, isn't it?"* are all phrases that have been covertly discarded from societal interaction in Washington, D.C. (Having visited many other large, metropolitan areas, this phenomenon is not restricted to just D.C.) In stark contrast, all along the trail we met "folksy" people from small-town America who greeted us as if they had known us all our lives.

As an example, we started our day slack-packing out of Damascus, Virginia, to VA Rte. 859. From there we strolled for a short, but memorable, distance on the Virginia Creeper Bike Trail. This converted railroad bed is a mecca for bikers and hikers alike and winds it way for miles alongside a beautiful river. As we made our way along the trail, the day's crop of bike riders was already out in full force, and almost without exception, as each one approached us, they waved and gave us a sincere *"Hi"* or *"Good Morning."* At first, we were so dumbstruck by these overt displays of friendliness we did not know how to react. Eventually though, the core elements of human contact laying dormant in our personalities took hold. Despite years of social "deprogramming" we had experienced in our culture back home, we began to answer back. *"Hi. How are you?" "Beautiful day, isn't it?"* It just seemed much more natural to act this way. We definitely preferred this type of social interaction to the type we were forced to accept as "normal" at home. This genuine warmth began to permeate our interactions with each other. We felt a sense of marital camaraderie that had been missing from our lives. We had survived for so long in a culture practically devoid of meaningful and unfettered day-to-day social contact that we had trouble understanding how such simple displays of human connectivity could have such a profound effect on us?

Sadly, the vibrancy and warmth of many of these wonderful small towns are quickly becoming but a memory of a more peaceful and less hurried time. Places such as the Stratton Diner in Stratton, Maine, which has been in the same family for over thirty years and has been serving home-style meals to citizens and hikers alike for all that time, was up for sale when we visited and may very well close forever. As we sat and ate our dinner there one night, we read all the newspaper articles hanging on the wall. Yellowed with age, they documented the history of the diner, the town, and the surrounding area. It saddened us to think that this family had poured their hearts and souls into this restaurant and into their community; and now because of economic factors out of their control, a dynasty, and a landmark, was coming to an end.

Theirs is an inspiring, yet heart-rending, story being played out in small town after small town we visited. The wheels of progress—interstate highways, fast food chains, shopping malls, and youth heading to the cities where the opportunities were supposedly better—were all taking a toll on the health of those communities. The legacies built from years of hard work and caring for their communities were beginning to fade. In its place were empty, boarded up buildings lining empty streets. Families who had thrived for generations were now wondering what the future would hold. Fortunately, the cordiality and sense of community of the people in these towns lives on.

They remain places where value is placed on who you are and how you treat people, rather than on what you own and how important you think you are. They are places where children still play in front yards and in back woods without the constant threat of being accosted. There are church pancake breakfasts where neighbors, who have known each other since childhood, still gather to eat and swap stories. Saturday afternoons are filled with community picnics in town parks where the local fire company offers up plates of barbeque and potato salad while the local bluegrass band fiddles way. If there are any societal problems in those towns, brought on by the incursion of the moral breakdown of larger, surrounding cities, it certainly does not pervade the town's atmosphere. Living in those towns are people who doggedly endure, and we, as thru-hikers, reaped the benefits of their unwavering faith in God, their sense of humor, their love and compassion for their fellow man, and their remarkable, down home, hospitality. They are places we would long to retreat to for solace and peace in order to regain a sense of self. They are places that typify the enduring bond of family and community we were experiencing with our thru-hiking brethren and they are places we would always fondly remember.

Our months on the trail offered us more moments of personal inspiration than we can possibly recount. Many were distinguishable by virtue of how we immediately reacted to them. Some would only surface later as we fought to regain some type of balanced foothold on our lives. Sometimes it was standing on a mountaintop with the clouds at our feet that inspired us to look deeper within ourselves to discover what is meaningful in life. Sometimes it was lying in a shelter late at night, gazing at a universe above us that was immeasurably more beautiful than any photograph "Mom" could take or any piece of music I could compose. These moments made us aware of how blessed our lives were. Then there were the people who inspired us—people, who until this adventure, would have been unknown to us and whose lives would never have impacted ours in the surprisingly meaningful ways that they did.

Of all the people we met on the trail, one stood out as the epitome of what a life filled with purpose and wonder should be. Her name is Cicely Ward, a.k.a. "Wise Owl," and her "never-too-late" mindset dramatically presented itself to us a few months into our hike. Being a small part of this woman's journey of fulfillment put "Mom" and me in a new frame of mind—one which would carry us through the long days ahead on the trail—and would nurture our desire to live our life together in a more compelling way.

It was June 2nd and we began our day at the Dutch Haus B&B, in Montebello, Virginia, with our host, Lois Arnold, serving us a magnificent breakfast of eggs, sausage, pancakes, etc. With our stomachs contently bloated, we took a shuttle to the Tye River to "back-slack" the monster mountain, "The Priest," which would bring us back to Montebello for a second night. As we sat on a rock outcropping taking in the valley below, along came "Old Drum;" as is always the case when in his company, we chatted for a very long time. As we continued our hike, we ran into "Wild Bill," "Old School," "B-Rad," "Expo," and "Recess." It was a great day, but unfortunately, we tended to rush and passed up several other overlooks where we could have taken in the lush views below. We arrived back at the B&B in the early afternoon where we met up with "V&A," prepared our gear for the next few days, and transferred our gear to their car for the run through the Shenandoah Mountains. The rest of the day we relaxed and chastised ourselves for not being more intentional about slowing down to smell the roses. Right then and there, we decided that, starting tomorrow, we would slow down our daily speed. We would also shorten the number of miles each day so we could take side trips to overviews and chat more with our fellow hikers. As much as "Mom" and I enjoyed each other's company, not spending more time with people we cared about, and with those whom we may not ever see again after the hike, was having a profoundly negative effect on us.

Our second night at the B&B put us in contact with some new and old friends from the trail. At dinner that evening, we met "Baro" and "Jangles" for the first time, and there as well were our old friends "Baldylocks," "Goldfish," and "Stumbles." The guest of honor at dinner that evening was "Wise Owl," an 84-year-old woman from Indiana, whose dream had always been to hike part of the A.T. Through a non-profit organization called *www.nevertoolate.org*, she teamed up with a guide from *www.webehiking.com*, who planned out and guided her through a five-day, forty-mile section of the trail. Her arrival for dinner hailed the completion of her dream. She entertained us with her ageless wisdom, subtle wit, and offbeat jokes, which were indicative of her feisty demeanor. She was then presented with a certificate and an Appalachian Trial T-shirt for the completion of her dream. Through the raucous applause of all of us who were inspired by her accomplishment, tears welled up in "Mom's" and my eyes as we marveled at what the realization of her dream meant not only to her, but also to us. It was as if she had summitted Katahdin with us, and it was all the more special because of her age. For years, we had been telling ourselves and others, *"If you have a dream, never let not chasing it become a regret. Go after it with every ounce of your being, no matter what your age. Leave a legacy of being a "dream chaser."* Being there for her award dinner reinforced our desire to continue doing just that.

When we began planning our escape from reality into the mountains and valleys that would take us from Georgia to Maine, never did we imagine it would be anything other than a six-month respite from our tumultuous lives—an opportunity to see if we could withstand the mind-boggling ordeal of walking that far. In retrospect, that was of minor significance when compared to how our marriage and we as individuals matured through our interactions with people on and off the A.T. Not a day passed where we did not find ourselves doling out or receiving streams of encouragement, compassion, and friendship. Sometimes it was just saying, *"Hang in there. You can do it. Just put one foot in front of the other,"* to a hiker who was considering getting off the trail. Many times the tables were turned, and it was we who were the recipients of compassion from someone we had never met before, be it a hiker or just someone along the trail.

Whether on the trail or in a town through which it passed, it was continually made evident that we as human beings are all connected. We all need one another and every one of us benefits from knowing the other. This realization brought out feelings in "Mom" and me that long-ago became buried beneath mountains of emotional and cultural trash. The desire to emotionally connect with others and a new understanding of our humanity made us feel alive in a way we had long since forgotten. The result of this metamorphosis was that as a couple we were now bound even closer together and we were confident our love for each other would stand the test of time—and life. The strength of the relationships we observed from the legion of married couples along the trail who fed us, housed us, and provided us with magic had a deeply-felt effect on us. Our hope was that our relationship on the trail—how we trusted, loved, and cared for each other—was visible to the other trail couples and was a source of inspiration for them, as well.

Our journey into the unknown was filled with unexpected surprises, some wonderful and some not so much so. But no day, no matter how boring or tiring, was considered a wasted day. Each one brought with it moments that had us taking pause, re-evaluating our lives and our marriage, and growing ever closer to each other. We were far away from the familiar and mundane and in a world where everything was new and excitedly different. It was a clean slate on which our relationship could evolve. The angels, heroes, and inspiring people we met along the way fueled our excitement and opened doors to our personalities and relationship we never knew existed. Perhaps those hiking without a life partner felt many of the same things we did. We may never know. What we do know is we had each other to share each indelible moment and each intimate personal awakening, and with that sharing came intense intimacy.

"Mom's" Tips for Couples:

- There is much to be learned about life and relationships by merely observing those who pass through your life;

- Never give up pursuing your dreams—it is never too late;

- You never know when a total stranger will influence the way you look at life—and each other.

The Journey Begins – At the southern terminus of the A.T. atop Springer Mountain in Georgia

Walking in Step

Our Ever-Present Trail Angels – Vince and Anita, a.k.a. "V&A"

*Carbomb
& Lichen*

*Enuff &
Too Much*

"Romantic Luxury" – The Honeymoon Sweet at Mountain Moma's Kuntry Store

Not So Romantic Luxury – Trimpi Shelter privy still got a rating of "Two Cheeks Up"

Welcome Friends – Bama & Little Wing with Mom
Unwelcome Friend – Norman the cow stays for the night at Elk River.

*Negotiating
Dragon Tooth's
treacherous
descent.*

*Puncheons –
Mom's nemesis.*

Mike and Zan "yellow blaze" Clark's Creek during the floods.

Mom braves the winds after leading the climb to Webster Cliffs.

Some days we stood above the clouds....

.......and some days we traveled through them.

The peacefulness of the trail helped us to find enjoyment in the simplest things – Our toy bear good luck charm.

And oftentimes, the peacefulness provided solitude and musical inspiration.

Inspiration also came from those we met – 84-year old "Wise Owl" after she fulfilled her dream of hiking a section of the A.T.

The goal is within reach – Standing at Rainbow Lake with Mt. Katahdin in the background.

CHAPTER EIGHT

LAUGHING TOGETHER & Simple Pleasures

Happiness does not consist in things themselves but in the relish we have of them." Francois, duc de La Rochefoucauld

The most important thing we discovered, or rediscovered, on the trail was that it was imperative we live each day as if it were our last. This realization did not come as some "smack me in the forehead" epiphany, for it was not a new concept to either of us. Individually, "Mom" and I attempted to live this way most of our lives and now that we were married, it only meant we would now pursue this personal mission together. However, while we had been checking things off of our never-ending lists of dreams and accomplishments, we failed to realize that those tiny, unassuming, and fleeting moments between the planned major events held as much significance, enjoyment, and wonder as the major ones—possibly even more. Nothing on the trail was trivial. Everything had meaning and importance in the forest's circle of life. And now, everything also had importance in the scheme of our lives. It was so easy to get swept away in the tidal wave of a busy life that what also was swept away was the ability to see things through the lens of humor and the joy of simple pleasures. Now, with no responsibilities other than sleeping, eating, and walking every day, we were totally free to have life cast its refreshing spell over us.

Famed pianist and comedian, Victor Borge, once said that laughter is "the shortest distance between two people." This statement was never truer than it was for us as we trudged, sometimes begrudgingly, toward Maine. The ability to laugh at both the profoundly silly and seemingly trivial not only shortened the distance between us, but it oftentimes helped to shorten the miles we walked each day.

The trail spoke to us with a maternal primal eloquence that opened our eyes, as well as our hearts, so we could sense, understand, and rejoice in each moment of each day. We discovered entertainment, joy, and humor in places and situations we never noticed before—or at the very least we would have deemed them inconsequential. Now each moment, place, and thing became impetus for soulful celebration and brought with it a renewed appreciation for all that life was offering us. Moreover, having a friend, or in our case a spouse, to share those moments with drew us closer together than we ever dreamed possible.

Now, That's Low!

We stopped at Low Gap for lunch and spoke with a man from Bristol, Tennessee, who was filling a station wagon full of gallon jugs with water from a pipe coming out of the side of the hill. In between spouting accolades for the purity of the water trickling from that rusty pipe, we heard all about the great hunting and fishing in the area, and despite reports to the contrary, we needed to be concerned with bears in this area. He urged us to be cautious. "Mom" and I vowed to do just that. We knew we were certainly more cautious about bears than he was about his source for drinking water.

For weeks we had been traversing the titanic mountains that support the A.T. on their backs. Of course, for every up there had to be a down, so we spent an equal number of days tiptoeing down these mountains' steep slopes to the valleys below. In the south, the valleys are called "gaps" which is a bit more creative than simply calling them valleys. However, that is where the creativity comes to an abrupt end. It seemed as if every "gap" we wandered into was named "Low Gap." As we munched on our lunch of peanut butter and jelly on bagels and washed it down with "good ole" *Gatorade*, we derided ourselves for not being more playful in our approach to the trail. So now, desperate for some type of lighthearted diversion, we systematically began to rename all the "Low Gaps" listed in our data book. We decided the new names should express our creative sides as well as our senses of humor. First, in keeping with tradition, there was "Low Gap" but following that one we named the next "Lower Gap" and concluded with "Lowest Gap." Randomly interspersed throughout the rest of the trail were "Not So Low Gap," "How Low Can You Go Gap," and our personal favorite, "You Call That Low Gap?" We hoped this idea would catch on with the Appalachian Trail Conservancy and they would rename these gaps on their maps. Considering how many gaps there are and how leg numbing they are to descend, that little bit of levity might make the trip more enjoyable for future hikers.

Thanks for the Memories

Too Much:

"One of the things I distinctly remember about being on the trail as a couple was the time we arrived at a hostel in Tennessee. A very nice couple had converted the back of their home into a place for hikers, complete with wonderful showers, and they even drove hikers into town to eat. After so many days on the trail, we were really looking forward to sleeping together in a bed without having our sleeping bags between us. When we arrived, there were already a number of hikers there, but knowing we were coming, they displayed the type of kindness and consideration that is a hallmark of thru-hikers, and they saved a room for us—the only room designated for couples. They felt we would want time together and have our own space, so that particular room was waiting for us.

We thought it was so sweet that they saved it for us until we realized the room was filthy and the carpet was saturated with cat urine that reactivated itself as the day wore on. We never lost sight of the fact that they were being so kind and so sweet in saving us the room but, considering its condition, I think we would have preferred not to have had the room. In retrospect, the whole situation became quite humorous."

Enuff:

"And, to add insult to injury, this was also the day that we mixed up some of our medications and accidentally took a diuretic which kept us up peeing half the night. It felt like we had bladder infections and every five minutes we had to go to the bathroom."

Too Much:

"We thought that we were taking something to help us sleep but that medication got mixed up with a water pill which, obviously, had quite the opposite effect. We had to trudge repeatedly across that dirty carpet in order to go outside to a community bathroom. At the time, I was hoping that things would have been a little bit more accommodating for us and that we would have been able to have some of that intimate time that was so rare on the trail. As I look back now, it was one of those sweet memories from the trail that makes me smile."

Beauty and the Beasts

April 29th was a day of contrasts, surprise encounters, and even a bit of entertainment. The contrasts were in the terrain and weather. The encounters—well, they made for great storytelling and could easily become staples of A.T. trail lore. We woke up to 40 degree temperatures and thirty-five to forty mile per hour winds that threatened to blow in rain late in the day. Since the preceding week had been so warm, I left my gloves behind and now had to wear a pair of socks on my hands to keep them from freezing. We climbed Little Hump Bald (5,459 feet), down into Bradley Gap (4,480 feet), and then onto Big Hump Mountain (5,587 feet)—all of this in less than four miles. The entire area before us, the Roan Highlands, provided views so beautiful and winds so strong, both nearly blew us away.

The first encounter was with two stray dogs that joined us on the way down one of the balds. We first saw one in hot pursuit of a deer in the thicket to our left and then they both ran across the trail in front of us. Seemingly out of nowhere, the second dog just appeared on the trail not far from the gap between the balds. Both dogs looked half starved but both had collars with the name of their owner and a phone number. During one of our breaks, we gave them what tuna we could spare and they inhaled it within seconds. In a display of "karmic intervention," we later came upon a pile of dried dog food right on the trail which someone had obviously dropped there by accident. Our furry friends wolfed that down, as well. Even the dogs got "trail magic" on the A.T.! During the eight miles our furry friends hiked with us, we attempted calling their owners several times (when we had cell service), but to no avail. The dogs stayed with us all the way to the Rte. 19E intersection—at the Tennessee/North Carolina border—where we had to leave them. The older of the two dogs headed down the road toward town, and we tied the younger one to a guardrail in hopes of someone picking him up. We met "V&A" and persuaded them that we needed some town food before heading back onto the trail. We drove to a local restaurant for lunch, and while there, we asked the proprietors of the restaurant if they knew the dogs' owners. Sadly, they did not. They did allow us to use their phone to try to contact the owners one last time. By the time we returned to the road crossing, the dog was gone—adopted by two other thru-hikers.

Late in the day, we arrived at the Elk River campground—a wide-open area, blanketed with lush grass nestled at the base of a large mountain. This is where our next encounter took place—one that could easily go down in the annals of A.T. lore. The Elk River flowed nearby and this place easily could have graced the front cover of any issue of *Backpacker Magazine*. As we set up our tents, we looked across the river and there, running through the woods toward the river and us, was a COW! It forded the river, which came up to its back, got onto the trail on our side of the river and proceeded to walk right toward our campsite. Great, we made it all the way through the Smokies without a bear attacking us but now a COW was going to kill us! We did not even have "cow bags" to hang our food in.

"Mom" has a sordid history with cows, so just the appearance of this bovine sent shivers down her spine. As the story goes, she was out driving "one dark and stormy night" in her very first car, an old Ford LTD—with one headlight out. With the sense of confidence that comes with youth, she was driving along while eagerly talking with other drivers on her CB radio. Suddenly, from out of nowhere at the crest of a hill, stood a cow! KABLAM!!! She hit it broadside—killing it instantly! The LTD faired much better and she drove it from the scene with nothing more than a smashed-in grille that now looked like the toothless mouth of an old man. Her dad nicknamed her, "The Cow Killer."

There was also the "Mississippi River Incident." While navigating their Egg Harbor boat up the Mississippi River from the Gulf of Mexico to Minnesota, "Mom" repeatedly attempted to convince her dad into letting her pilot the boat for awhile. He eventually succumbed to her persistence and gave her the wheel; but only minutes later, while traveling through a narrow channel, her earlier foray with a cow came back to haunt her. As she looked down toward the bow, she saw a cow swimming across the channel! Oh, not again! With a timely evasive move, she averted another cattle homicide.

So, you can now understand her concern when our intruder made its sudden and unwelcome appearance. However, it was not only "Mom" who was driven to the brink of panic by its visit.

"Old Drum" had set up his tent in a valley near the river's edge and had then gone inside to rest. He did not see the cow come across near his site and he was also not aware we were camped right above him. Suddenly, we all turned in the direction of "Old Drum's" tent when we heard loud, panic-ridden cries of *"Away, you beast!"* accompanied by the clanging of pots. We all burst out laughing, knowing he was in no real danger and he would be so embarrassed when he realized what "wild beast" had been stalking him.

Despite our repeated urgings to leave, the cow stayed in our campsite the entire night, grazing, tripping over firewood in the fire pit in the middle of the night, and curiously checking out our cat holes after their use. We surmised, judging by this last unusual behavior, that there may have been some canine in this cow's lineage. We nicknamed him "Norman" after Billy Crystal's cow in the movie "City Slickers." Our Norman evidently suffered from insomnia because no matter what time of night I got up to relieve myself, there he stood, only feet from our tent, his eyes glowing in the beam of my headlamp. "Old Drum" later informed us that "Norman" was a girl, so unless "Norman" was suffering from some gender issues, we would have to change his name to "Norma." Our greatest fear was that, like the dogs, this cow would follow us up the trail. (That did not happen, thank God!)

Big Pack – Little Pack

As soon as "V&A" decided to provide trail support the entire length of our hike, plans were put into motion to "slack-pack" large sections of the trail so as to save our backs and feet. To do that, we needed our daypacks from home. Before reaching Damascus, Virginia, I called our daughter, Rebecca, but as was usually the case with my upwardly mobile and amazingly busy offspring, I was unable to reach her. I simply left a very detailed message as to which packs we needed her to ship to us. I also left instructions as to where they could be located, what colors they were, and finally, how to meet with Mike Mathews in order to get them shipped to us ASAP. Then I called Mike, and not reaching him either, left him a message listing the same instructions I had given our daughter. Mission accomplished—or so I thought!

Several days later when taking our "zero" in Damascus, "V&A" drove us to Troutdale, to retrieve a mail drop we had previously arranged for Mike and Diane to ship there. With great anticipation, we also looked forward to picking up our daypacks so we could begin slack-packing. Now Troutdale is not really a town but simply a collection of residences and farms scattered for miles along a rambling maze of narrow asphalt and dirt roads nestled among the rolling hills of Virginia. Had it not been for the post office building and the Troutdale Trading Post, one would be hard-pressed to find a semblance of a town at all. Our first stop was the Trading Post. It was there we planned to pick up our mail drop and we also expected to find our daypacks waiting for us. Alas, we found only our mail drop sitting on the floor amongst mountains of other boxes which appeared to be filled with items for an upcoming yard sale. No reason to worry, just yet; perhaps our packs had been sent to the post office instead. That seemed logical.

If there was one thing we came to appreciate about the small towns in the south and later in New England, it was their "down home" hospitality. Troutdale was a prime example. The matronly woman behind the counter at the post office greeted me with a southern charm typically reserved for socials and afternoon tea parties. Her demeanor swept away my annoyance in finding out she did not have our packs either. I exited the post office still with a sense of hope in my gait because there were still a few places we could look. One was the local hostel, a long shot at best, and the pastor overseeing this hostel let us know he had not seen our package. Our final visit was to the Fox Hill B&B where we had originally planned to stay while passing through. It was also one of the places we had included on our list of potential "ship-to" points. We went up a long dirt driveway with gravel scattering in every direction. With each passing minute, the driveway became increasingly narrow until we began to wonder if "V&A's" car was going to make it to the top without plunging into the ravine below. With "A's" knuckles now white and with our hearts in our throats, we made it to the parking lot in front of what appeared to be nothing more than your standard, though extremely large, southern-style brick plantation home.

I walked up to the front door and knocked a few times before I noticed a sign telling me to go to the cottage out back where the owners could be located. I followed instructions, went around the back, and after pounding on the door for quite some time, I was confronted by the female owner. I say "confronted" because it was a less-than-pleasant experience compared to the hospitality I had just experienced at the post office. What I was able to glean from her curt response to my tale about our package was that it was still at the post office. She believed this to be true because she had been notified there was a package for her to pick up. Upon arriving and seeing how big the box was, she decided she was not going to attempt carrying it back to her house. She insisted it would not even fit in her car. I returned to our car, empty-handed yet again—I had to keep reminding myself, *"This is all part of the adventure, stupid!"* I had to wonder though, if indeed it was our box, why was it so large? We headed down the "driveway from hell" and back to the post office.

At this point, we were still not accustomed to the fact that life in small, southern towns is a bit "laid back"—the level of customer service being grossly understated when compared to what we were accustomed to in the "big city." When we got back to the post office, there was a sign on the door that read, *"Closed for Lunch."* Clinging to what little bit of patience I had left, I shuffled back to the car mumbling something about the lady behind the counter probably being the town's only mail carrier, judge, and school bus driver, as well. We bided our time and eventually she returned. I went back inside and recounted the conversation I just had with the proprietor of the B&B.

> *"Oh my, I know what it is. I should have remembered this when you were in here before, sweetheart. It came Priority Mail, right? We don't get much of that here. I usually remember everyone who gets that kind of mail."*

My hopes were now soaring.

"Here it is over here. I pushed it out of the way because it was so big."

Looking at the size of the box, I realized I needed a knife to cut it open because it was too large to fit into "V&A's" trunk, too. Out to the car I went to get my trusty knife and was met by curious gazes and probing questions from "Mom" and "V&A" as to why I needed it.

Successfully sidestepping their questions, I returned to the post office lobby with weapon in hand. Like a child on Christmas morning, I excitedly cut open the box and rifled through the packing material. Then, accompanied by a string of expletives reserved for truck drivers, rappers, and Howard Stern, I removed the packs from the box and headed to the car. Grasping one pack in each hand, I angrily displayed what was in the box. In my hands were our two largest, oldest, and heaviest packs! By no stretch of the imagination did they meet any of the criteria I had left in either of my phone messages. The whole situation was so bizarre, that for a brief moment, it was if I was in suspended animation, unable to comprehend the gravity of the situation. I also did not immediately see the humor in this circumstance and I angrily stomped to the car and threw them in the trunk. I had no idea what look was on my face when I approached the car, but it must have been memorable because "Mom" was fighting to hold back laughing out loud. As we drove away, "Mom" spun our "Mayberry moment" into what could be a great television ad.

"Cost of shipping packs priority mail so we could have them right away and not have to buy new daypacks in Damascus: $35.00."

"Cost of driving around Troutdale, Virginia, trying to locate a package shipped to us with our daypacks in it: $50.00."

"Look on "Windtalker's" face when he opened the box and saw two full-sized, heavy, backpacks: PRICELESS!"

"Mastercard—For fixing all the screw-ups in life."

We then drove right back to Damascus where we went directly to Mt. Rogers Outfitters and purchased two, new lightweight daypacks!

Two Cheeks Up

After being in the wilderness for so long, it was astounding how each new experience, no matter how mundane, filled us with a sense of childlike wonder and delight. Even a quick stop with "Cash" one morning at Hog Camp Gap to play on the swing hanging from a large oak tree served as a welcome diversion and brought back fond childhood memories. Our imaginations, which remained dormant during our protracted marches toward maturity, were reborn and I was again able to punctuate run-of-the-mill moments with a renewed, though twisted, sense of humor lost somewhere during high school. ("Mom" would probably beg to differ, saying my sense of humor has always been on the aberrant side.)

Early on in our hike, I decided it would be my mission to photograph and evaluate as many privies on the trail as possible. This would be my personal form of entertainment and a way to differentiate one shelter site from another. Much like Ebert and Roeper, who are highly respected for their movie reviews, I vowed to rate all the privies using a system of "Two Cheeks Up" as the highest rating, "One Cheek Up" as simply average and "Go Dig a Cat Hole" for those not even worthy of use.

The Trimpi Shelter hosted the most austere privy we had ever seen. This sanctuary for gastrointestinal relief was nothing more than a metal throne sitting atop an open platform—with no sides and no roof. The design obviously had the need for copious ventilation and a minimal use of building materials taking precedence over the need for privacy. There was a modest level of privacy provided by a 4-foot by 8-foot sheet of plywood nailed to two posts between the privy and the shelter. In order not to inadvertently surprise another hiker who was making use of this facility, one needed to only bend over and look underneath the edge of the plywood to see if there was a set of feet on the platform.

The designer of this privy also had an even more twisted sense of reality than I for he positioned this platform in the middle of an old logging service road. As you settled in to "take care of business," your greatest fear now was that an ATV would come roaring up the service road and catch you with your pants down. The view from the platform, however, was long and wide and the quiet of the morning presented one with the unique opportunity to watch the forest come alive from its deep sleep. It was from this very "throne" that one morning, as the woods awoke, I summoned the subjects of *"The Land of A.T.,"* including the court jester, who by all appearances was a bit "squirrelly," and I proclaimed,

"This will be a good and beautiful day; free from rain and wind; a delightful day to wander through "The Land of A.T."

And, thus it was!

As I sat there, mulling over the perversely comical position I was in—comical position, get it?—off in the distance I heard the duet of what I dubbed the *"Deliverance Woodpeckers."* On two different-sized trees that provided distinctively unique tones, they hammered out what sounded very much like the dueling banjos theme from the movie *"Deliverance."* I found it quite disconcerting so I hurried back to the shelter, looking over my shoulder the entire way so as not to be mysteriously and mortally wounded by a woodpecker beak driven into the center of my back.

My rating for this privy: "10" for the <u>view</u>, "10" for <u>ventilation</u>, "1" for <u>privacy</u>, and a "9" for <u>the conservative use of building materials</u>. This led me to give this privy an overall rating of "Two Cheeks Up."

In Maine, the trail clubs construct some of the most unique privies on the trail and many of them are even given name—at the Piazza Rock Lean-To stood one of my-all-time favorite privies. This lavishly appointed latrine hosted not one, but two, holes side-by-side and between them was fastened a cribbage board. It was obvious this unit was designed for the hiking couple with free time on their hands, no self-consciousness, and a twisted sense of humor. The name of this privy was *"Your Move"* and the irony of the name was not lost on us. I gave this privy a "10" for <u>design and construction</u>, a "10" for <u>cleanliness</u>, and a "10-plus" for <u>originality</u>. Overall, it received a "Two Cheeks Up!"

Zoned Out

The section after Vandeventer Shelter in Tennessee was reported to be "relatively" flat so we figured that it should be a quick, easy run into Damascus, Virginia—at least we all hoped so. We began the day with a road walk over the Watauga Lake Dam and spent the rest of the morning traversing the ridgelines overlooking the huge lake formed behind it. As was our routine, "Mom" and I stopped for a morning snack; and as we sat right along the edge of the trail, along came "Piper" and "Miss Fortune." Up the hill they marched in lockstep, their arms pumping, and glazed-over eyes peering straight down at the ground. It was quite obvious they were "in the zone." As "Piper" got within two feet of us, I began to say *"Good Morning"* but barely got the *"G"* out, when she stopped dead in her tracks—quite startled by the fact she had not seen us. Even more startled was "Miss Fortune" who ran smack dab into the back of "Piper." She nearly jumped out of her boots, threw her trekking poles into the air, clutched her chest, and then spewed out several obscenities about having several bodily fluids scared out of her. We all burst out laughing with the absurdity of the moment and just how focused some of the speedier hikers can be when they are trying to complete major miles in one day.

Holy Moley!

Even some of our run-ins with the native wildlife offered up a source of amusement. The hilarity of some instances did not become apparent until the next day when the surprise and terror of the moment had faded into obscurity.

IMPORTANT NOTE! *"When choosing a tent site, be certain there is no evidence of mole activity in the immediate area where you wish to pitch your tent."*

Unfortunately, we were not able to heed this advice because we were party to the very event that provided the reason for the aforementioned warning. During what should have been a restful night's sleep on soft ground beside a picturesque, babbling brook, I was suddenly awakened from a vivid dream by a headlamp shining directly in my eyes. Accompanying the light show was the sound of "Mom" pounding on the floor of the tent next to me. My immediate reaction to what I was seeing was she appeared to be playing that carnival game where you try to hit gophers in the head with a mallet as they pop out of their holes. She loudly exclaimed,

"There are moles tunneling under our tent! I cannot only feel them burrowing under me, but I can also hear them chewing through roots! Help me!

Being less than sympathetic to her plight, I was laughing before I even had a chance to completely wake up.

Her pounding grew more intense and continued for about thirty minutes. During her rampage, my fear was that her aggressive behavior would escalate to the use of a knife or trekking pole as a weapon, and we would end up with a tent floor full of holes. Eventually, the moles decided common sense was the better part of valor and they ceased their underground excavation for the night. Unfortunately, the chance of continuing a wonderful night's sleep had evaporated. I laid there chuckling to myself about the whole event because the moles had only been on her side of the tent. It was not until morning that "Mom" admitted the whole incident was "pretty hilarious."

As our journey to "the promised land" meandered through the changing seasons, we found that lightheartedness and searching for the humor in innocuous situations bound us together as strongly as any emotion. It made no sense to anguish over situations for which we had no control. It was also frivolous to waste the energy we needed to hike by being angry at the weather, the bugs or circumstances that would be nothing more than a memory by day's end. Through laughing our relationship reached a point where there was, most times, an overriding sense of calm. This calm allowed us to communicate and connect with each other in ways we had never experienced before. We reached a point where it became quite evident laughing was also good medicine—laughing reenergized us both physically and emotionally. We decided that if something happened we knew we would be able to laugh about the next day, why not just laugh about it when it happened?

Brownie:

> *"We learned to laugh at situations on the trail and that seemed to make us bond. The first week on the trail, it rained non-stop. Much of Pennsylvania was flooded– including the part through which we were hiking. The water on the trail was often above my knees and occasionally up to my waist. We trudged through the water as it continued to rain and tried to find the humor in the situation. When we got really stressed we would make a game of the situation and start running through the water screaming as loud as possible or making ridiculous water-related jokes."*

Road Kill

Perhaps it was the months of walking or the effects of prolonged calorie deficit. Maybe it was the heat or maybe it was simply the need for us to occupy our minds with something other than putting one foot in front of the other. Whatever the reason, we had been noticing something very unusual. It may have been pure coincidence, but we had observed that every day since we started our hike, there had been large feathered beasts hovering overhead. Did they know something we had yet to fathom? Why were they circling endlessly over every mile of the trail? Were these creatures subsisting on the carcasses of previous fallen comrades—the ones whose names had suddenly disappeared from the shelter registers and their bodies from the trail? It was a bit unnerving to look up each time we stopped for a snack to see these "feathered beasts of prey" swooping ever closer in anticipation of our demise. It was certainly an incentive to keep moving— and quickly. What was additionally disturbing was that these winged scavengers only seemed to be over the heads of the married couples. Was their presence a harbinger of what was to become of our relationships, or was it just that they knew we were eating better than the single hikers and picking our bones clean would be a more nutritious dining experience?

Thankfully, we never had to find out. Once we pointed these buzzards out, "V&A" claimed to be able to tell when we were approaching a road crossing based on the buzzards' flying patterns.

We later discovered our delusions about birds were not unique to us or the other married couples. Even some of the single hikers were suffering a somewhat similar fate. One morning at breakfast, "E-Rock" had us in stitches with his observation that the whippoorwills he heard each night outside his tent were calling him to *"Wake up now! Wake up now!"*

The Cowboy of Grayson Highlands

We arrived at the Wapiti Shelter in Virginia at 5:30 p.m. to find friends, old and new. "E-Rock," "Mister Blister," "Stumbles," "Enuff," "Too Much," and "Kegger" were already setting up camp. Arriving a little later was "Lush," "Baldylocks," and "42." We heard in graphic detail how "42" had almost been struck by lightning during the storm earlier in the day. We asked "Kegger" how he got his name and, though he assured us that he did not carry kegs of beer in his pack, he did start out on his journey carry six-packs. As we spoke he was drinking a 24-oz Foster's Ale he received from a trail angel earlier in the day.

"Kegger" was from Texas, and because he was a Texan, he had BIG stories. For example, he was sure he could ride one of the famous feral ponies gracing the slopes of Grayson Highlands from where we all had just walked. Never mind the numerous warnings we received to not even feed the ponies, "Kegger" decided not to heed the warnings and even went a step further.

"Hey, they are just ponies and I am from Texas. This will be a piece of cake."

As stealthily as possible, he approached one of the ponies, grabbed its mane, and quickly hoisted himself aboard. As he told the story, he had us laughing until our sides hurt. He continued to recount his exciting, yet remarkably brief ride.

"Those ponies are really fast," he explained as he told about going only twelve feet before being, unceremoniously, thrown to the ground.

"Kegger" explained that as he looked up from his prone position in the highland's tall grass, a group of people—who had been passing by and had watched his attempt at immortality—had captured it all on film and were now doubled-up in laughter. He rose to his feet, dusted himself off, checked for minor injuries, and then having not yet resigned himself to accepting the error of his ways, proclaimed,

"I know why I got thrown off so easily. You can't ride those ponies with your pack on."

You guessed it! He took off his pack, corralled another victim, and tried one more time. And yes, he was thrown off just as quickly the second time. It would appear that everything is bigger in Texas—well, maybe not common sense.

Grin and Bear It

Our primary goal was to thru-hike to Maine. However, we had a secondary goal of equal importance, and if we accomplished it, our journey would be even more memorable. We wanted to experience the blood-curdling, gut-wrenching, and awe-inspiring thrill of coming face to face with both a bear and a moose. In my mind, any day we saw wildlife was a successful day, so seeing these two denizens of the wilderness would be nirvana for me.

We spent months on the trail and saw nothing more than just "scat," that telltale sign of bear activity, and we began wondering if our quest to see a bear would fall victim to the same fate as our attempt to see a moose in the wilds of Alaska in 2000. As more and more hikers reported seeing their first bear, our anxiety over not seeing one grew to dynamic proportions. This anxiety was not lost on "V&A," and unbeknownst to us, they had something in mind to remedy the situation.

One morning at Big Meadow Campground in Shenandoah National Park, we finished a hearty breakfast of some of "A's" scrambled eggs, bacon, and toast. "Mom" then went out to the tent to prepare her pack for the day. Suddenly, there was a muffled scream and she breathlessly came to the RV door and insisted I look in the tent right away. Suspecting there was some wild animal inside devouring the contents of our packs, I slowly approached the rain fly and pulled it back. What I saw caught me totally by surprise. There, sitting on our sleeping bags was a black bear! No, not a real one but a stuffed toy "A" had picked up for us to carry in our packs for good luck. I turned and saw "Mom" at the RV door with the warmest smile on her face and "V&A" were inside laughing hysterically.

Over the next several days, this stuffed bear became a constant hiking companion. We hoped it would bring us luck in finally seeing a real one. We often stopped along the trail and strategically placed our bear in the crook of a tree limb or on a rock outcropping. There "Mom" would photograph it. Had it not been for the red ribbon around its neck, we could have easily passed those photos off as the real thing. It was idle and somewhat juvenile entertainment but it made for some memorable and pleasantly entertaining moments for us. If all else failed and we did not see a bear, we could simply *Photoshop* the ribbon off the bear's neck and convince everyone we had finally seen a bear—not once, but numerous times. Only the careful observer would be able to tell it was the exact same bear in every picture. Surprisingly enough, just a few days after receiving our "play bear," it brought us the luck it was intended to provide.

We were slack-packing from Thornton Gap, one of the entrances to Shenandoah National Park. We came down from "Mary's Rock" where we had taken a break, did some rock climbing and photographed "Baby Bear" sitting on a rock looking out over the valley below. As we wound our way through a deep thicket of mountain laurel, there was a rush in the underbrush to our left. Then, like a toy rocket launched by some young future NASA engineer, a bear cub shot up a tree not twenty yards from where we stood. It was so sudden and the bear scaled the tree so quickly, it took us a moment or two to compose ourselves enough say, *"Oh man! That's a bear!"*

Normally, when "Mom" had her full-size pack on, her camera was conveniently located in a pocket on the hip-belt. When we used our daypacks she had to ask me to reach inside her pack and give her the camera every time she wanted to take a photograph. Without her even asking, I unzipped the rear pocket of her pack, grabbed the camera, and thrust it in her hand.

"What are you doing?" "Mom" asked in a low, yet forceful whisper.

"Oh wow! This is great. Let's get closer so you can get a picture," I jubilantly instructed.

"Ah, excuse me, but we haven't seen the cub's mother," she retorted with a look that could have melted paint off of an iron fence.

"I guess you are right," I reluctantly agreed, now scanning the brush nearby for any sign of the matronly, hairy behemoth that could be the agent of our demise.

Following the advice of virtually every book we ever read regarding what to do if confronted with a bear, we loudly clicked our trekking poles together. Like a flash, the cub scrambled headfirst down the tree as quickly as it had gone up. It hurriedly waddled through the underbrush and was soon out of sight. Feeling somewhat disappointed in not getting a picture of our first bear encounter, but happy we had not become a snack for its yet unseen mother, we put away the camera and started back down the trail. We had not taken four steps when a gargantuan rustle on our left stopped us dead in our tracks—we realized it was the mother bear! She had been watching us, and seeing that her baby was safe, she ran off into the woods after it.

Whew! That was close, but what an adrenaline-filled moment!

Upon reaching New England, we tried the stuffed animal technique with a moose doll. For some strange reason, it never produced the same result. All we ever heard was a moose calling in the distance, a moose crashing through the brush near us and a smelly, partially decomposed moose carcass left alongside the trail by some irresponsible hunters.

When You Least Expect It

We met "V&A" for lunch at Pen-Mar Park, which is on the Pennsylvania/Maryland border. Shortly after lunch, when we crossed the Mason/Dixon Line, we checked off state number six. Wahoo! Crossing that line also held other significance. It is there that the trail is no longer called the *"Appa—latch—un" Trail* but becomes the *"Appa—lay—shun" Trail*. From there north, there would be no more grits, no more sweet tea—no more being called a "Damn Yankee." We were on our home turf now which was exhilarating. From here to Maine we would be counting DOWN the miles left to go instead of recounting the miles we already covered. The highlight of the day came that evening at Antietam Shelter. We arrived at the Old Forge picnic area which has a spigot with clean water year round, and from there it is only a short walk to the shelter. We staggered into the picnic area just in time to fill our water bladders, have dinner, and then get things ready for a welcomed night's sleep. As we sat eating at one of the picnic tables bordering the nearby park, we curiously watched as a large group of people headed from the parking lot toward the shelter area. Each person was laden with food, coolers, chairs, and other items one would have at a picnic. What could all this activity mean? Would we not be able to use the shelter? Would we need to educate these folks on "Leave No Trace" practices and their relation to the confluence of thru-hikers and day hikers who would, undoubtedly, need the shelter? We decided to find out what was going on and sauntered into the shelter area. There we overheard that the gathering was an annual "*Summer Solstice*" party. As we later found out, these long-time friends came to this location every year on the date of the Summer Solstice in order to celebrate its arrival. We thought, *"How cool! Some folks can find any excuse to have a party."*

Even though the size of their group was over the ATC acceptable "legal limit," we did not want to make a scene. We went about our chores of setting up the tent, hanging our food bag, and hanging up some wet clothes to dry. All the while, we noticed they were watching us with as much curiosity as we were experiencing in watching them.

On the A.T. most thru-hikers develop a critical trail skill out of the need for self-preservation. Some perfect it to the level of it being an art form. That skill is called "Yogi-ing"—named after the cartoon bear renowned for creatively separating unsuspecting picnickers from their food. Hikers learn to smell out an opportunity for <u>FREE FOOD</u> early in their thru-hike. Using their disheveled appearance, wilderness aroma, and more than a bit of sorrow-laden theatrics they can wrest a complete meal with all the trimmings from strangers who sympathize with their plight. To watch a polished "Yogier" at work is truly a thing to behold.

Up to this point, we had little need for developing our "Yogi-ing" technique and we had just eaten dinner less than thirty minutes earlier. So even though our neighbors had a picnic table full of food rife for the taking, we saw no real need to beg for food. We simply prepared to slither into the confines of our tent; but as we did, we heard a voice calling out,

"Would you like to join us for some food and beer?"

To a hiker, such a question is akin to asking a homeless person if they would like a check for a million dollars. So what if we had already eaten? That was a half hour ago! We were almost halfway through our hike, so we were willing and able to pack away food at a moment's notice—and we could certainly use the extra calories a bottle of *Rolling Rock* provided. Since we had been *invited* to eat, our track record of not begging for food remained intact. We immediately joined our cordial hosts and enjoyed an evening filled with beer, fresh fruit, vegetables, friendly conversation, and amazing entertainment. A musician played guitar and accompanied himself by making the sounds of trumpets and trombones with his voice. He was remarkably talented and hysterically funny. The account of our hike was of great interest to them, and we were more than happy to oblige their curiosity with anecdotes about our adventure in exchange for all that delicious food. And yes, we were asked, *"So how are you getting along?"*

As the evening wore on and the campfire faded, we thanked our hosts for their hospitality and vowed to see them next year. It was a special evening full of unexpected trail magic and frivolity. It was an experience that turned an otherwise ordinary day on the trail into one carrying a lasting memory.

It's That Way!

Most days hiking the A.T. was serious business for us; hence the chance to lighten things up was rarely overlooked. Unfortunately, none of us could always be where the fun was taking place. We often had to rely on the recounting of those humorous episodes in the shelter registers. One day we reached a shelter in time for lunch, and as was our habit, we grabbed the register to read up on the latest hiker communications, observations, cartoons, and eclectic ramblings.

"Mike & Zan," whom we first met at Garenflo Gap, were two young, somewhat quiet kids. No one would ever imagine them pulling the stunt we read about in the register that day. Perhaps because they were so reserved, made their story even funnier. It seems "Cash" had awoken from a nap, somewhat disoriented, and headed the wrong way on the trail. Knowing "Cash" as we did, that was hysterically funny all on its own. However, there was more to the story. Some time later, "Mike & Zan" ran into him on the trail and advised him that he was going the wrong way. After thanking them for pointing out what, in his own words, *"a "dumb a**"* he was, he turned around and all three of them headed north. It was not long before "Mike & Zan" had walked quite a good distance ahead of him and decided to play a practical joke. They turned around and headed back south until they came upon "Cash" again. As he approached, they told him he was going the wrong way—again. At this point, he was completely confused and, in our mind's eye, we could picture the befuddled expression on his face. Envisioning that scene made us laugh so hard, our stomachs hurt.

Traditions – The Good, the Bad, and the Ugly

With renewed vigor we headed to Pine Grove Furnace Campground in Pennsylvania and to the Iron Master Hostel where we planned to stay. Pine Grove Furnace is very near the geographical halfway point of the trail, so there is always a high level of excitement among the hikers who gather there as they congratulate each other on their accomplishment. When we later learned there were no "semi-private" rooms available for couples—contrary to all the guide books—we decided not to stay at the hostel. We did convince the innkeeper into letting us take showers and do our laundry there. Our chores for the day complete, we made the short walk to "V&A's" campsite to pitch our tent.

When we first arrived we strolled over to the campground's general store where we found "Baro," "Jangles," "Dirt Diva," "Donkey," "Mouse," and "Jellybean" sitting at the tables out front. Of all the customs a thru-hiker can participate in during his/her thru-hike, one of the most notable is the "Half-Gallon Challenge." This competition is a way to celebrate reaching the halfway point on the trail and is a testament to pure gluttony and intestinal fortitude. The rules are simple: a hiker purchases a half-gallon of ice cream and sees how fast he/she can eat it. As we walked up, "Jellybean" was struggling to force down the last few mouthfuls of her entry. It was quite evident by the contorted look on her face that her excitement over attempting this feat had been overshadowed by the physical repercussions of mixing cold ice cream with 90 °F temperatures. A new record recently had been set by "Mystic," who polished off his half-gallon of ice cream in an astounding two minutes and fifteen seconds—shattering the old record by over two minutes. Even as competitive as we are, we chose not to enter this particular contest for fear of falling victim to that sensation you get when you drink an ice-cold *Slurpie* too fast! We also had been warned that more than one participant had later, after attempting to set a new record, left the contents of his/her stomach deposited on the side of the trail not far from Pine Grove Furnace. We remained just spectators and thoroughly enjoyed the entertainment.

There is another long-held tradition on the A.T.—one that requires an even lower level of self-consciousness than inhaling a half-gallon of ice cream. However, it does demand a much higher degree of courage. That is "Hike Naked Day." Since "Mom" and I are not inclined to celebrate holidays that do not include the receiving of some type of gift or start with a parade or end with fireworks, we opted not to participate in this one either. However, there was a very small band of determined hikers who did show their support for this little-appreciated event and hiked a section of the trail in their birthday suits. These very same "extreme hikers" would probably do anything nude if you proclaimed a day for it. This year's "Hike Naked Day" took a rather comical, though embarrassing, twist. According to entries in some of the shelter registers, this group of "au naturel" daredevils came upon a contingent of Mormon girls who were, for some strange reason, quite offended by their display of audacious behavior. Frankly, we were certain we would not have wanted to see those guys naked either—especially after they had hiked 1,000 miles, had eaten nothing but *Ramen noodles, Snickers* bars, and mac n' cheese, and needed shaves and showers. Just pondering the image of that revolting spectacle was hilariously terrifying, and we would have enjoyed seeing the looks on the girls' faces!

Secret Shelter

After only one day of hiking in New Jersey, we were ready to recommend that it change its state bird to the mosquito and we had resolved to apply for blood donor cards from New Jersey. They ate us alive! We went through an entire can of 100 % DEET by 10:00 a.m. We planned to do long miles, but those wretched insects only made the miles, and the day, unbearably long. We did get an occasional break from them such as at the Sunrise Pavilion, where we benefitted from wonderful views and a wind that blew strong enough to keep the mosquitoes at bay. We stopped at High Point State Park, met "V&A," restocked, had some "trail magic," and I made a call to order a pair of boots to be shipped to the post office in Fort Montgomery, New York. My original boots were history, and the ones I currently was wearing most likely would not last the remainder of the hike. As the day wore on, brutalizing us with its unforgiving heat and stifling humidity, we reached a point on the trail where we just happened to glance up. There in the distance, standing above the trees on the summit like a lone concrete sentinel, was a huge monument sporting the identical design of the Washington Monument in Washington, D.C. It was High Point Monument—a remarkable sight mainly because it seemed so out of place. We followed the trail towards it and arrived at "The Observation Platform," which, on a clear day, allows you to see the skyline of New York City. We were rewarded with a strong breeze that not only cooled us off but also renewed our energy. Unfortunately, because of the humidity, a dense blanket of haze enshrouded the skyline, making it invisible. Standing on the platform was a young couple who, upon seeing our packs, asked us where we were hiking. Always happy to oblige anyone who showed an interest in our journey, we talked to both of them for some time. Even though they had just hiked part of the trail, they were not aware that the A.T. went right by the observation platform. This phenomenon was something we noticed more and more as we traveled through the more "metropolitan" areas of the mid-Atlantic; there was less awareness of the trail, less interest in those who were hiking it, and definitely less trail magic along the way.

The day seemed to drag on forever, and we found ourselves incessantly swearing at the mileage inaccuracies in our trail guides. Obviously, our ability to laugh at the things we had no control over had not permanently taken root. Just as we were about to give up all hope of finding the next shelter, we mercifully arrived at Jim Murray's "Secret Shelter." What a fantastic place it was! Sitting on an old farmstead, formerly owned by the Canfield Family, were a number of small outbuildings that included a shelter and a privy—which, by the way, received a rating of "7" and "One Cheek Up". There was also a water pump right in the middle of the grounds with refreshing, cold water. The shelter was an incredible example of designing maximum features into a minimum amount of space! It was not large in size—it would probably sleep six to eight hikers upstairs—but it had everything. It housed a hot shower, a large stainless steel kitchen sink with running water, electricity, heat, a fan (for summer), and a wonderful front porch to sit on. Stretching out in front of the shelter was a large, inviting area that just cried out for tents to be set up on its grassy back. Inviting as it was, we chose to set up our tent in a more romantic spot under a large walnut tree. Later that evening, the wide-open sky blanketed us in the glow of a full moon as millions of stars danced around it like adoring fans. Being a lover of Native American traditions and the spiritual connections Native Americans have to the world in which they live, I could not help but view those stars much as they do—as the lodge fires of those ancestors who have passed over. We knew this was a place—and a moment—that would remain burned into our memories forever because it embodied the atmosphere that is the Appalachian Trail. It reignited in our souls the peaceful wanderlust that we cherished so much—wanderlust, that over the last several days, had been drained from us by the shear brutality of the trail, the weather, and the mosquitoes.

While eating dinner on the front porch with "Sleepy the Arab," a middle-aged woman and three young adults walked up looking like they belonged at the shelter, though they carried no packs. The woman was a descendent of the Canfield family and proceeded to tell us how she lived on the farm that was once there. She blissfully reminisced about her days on the farm and pointed out to us and her entourage where the barn, the house, and all the other outbuildings once stood. It was readily apparent her days here had been fond ones and she seemed happy the land was being put to good use—being left as untouched as possible.

As they walked away down the long road that was once the driveway to the farm, the evening suddenly turned from romantic and sentimental to absurdly funny. Out in a field, separated from us by only a single strand of electric fence, were two donkeys. Their boisterous evening shenanigans were a source of incessant noise but also provided us with some unusual entertainment—made entertaining only by means of my increasingly perverted sense of humor. From all evidence, both donkeys were males and their behavior had me wondering if they had been out in the field together entirely too long. One was apparently suffering from a "Brokeback Mountain" complex, but the other would have nothing to do with it. A strange sense of humor? Probably. Finding humor in the bizarre? Absolutely. Remember, we had been on the trail for a long time and entertainment was at a premium.

Lead Foot

It was an average day, complete with its share of fields, swamps, steep climbs, big rocks, pine forests, and Kamikaze mosquitoes. I swore I saw the silhouettes of humans etched on the sides of more than one of these blood-sucking varmints—in much the same manner as World War II fighter pilots did on their planes for each enemy fighter they shot down. What was not average about this day was that just prior to crossing US 7 in New York "Mom" began complaining that the toes on her left foot hurt more than they had since we started our adventure. That was exceedingly odd because her toes had been continuously numb since the first week of our hike—sometimes to the point where even feeling the rocks beneath her feet had been problematic. At the road crossing, we decided to sit in the grass and take a "boots off" break to give her feet a rest and to have a snack. It was then that "Mom" discovered the source of her foot pain.

The night before, she placed a camera battery in her boot for safekeeping with the intention of taking it out the next morning. However, in our haste to get up and on the trail that morning, she forgot about it and hiked four to five miles with the battery firmly wedged between her boot and her boot insert. Good naturedly she laughed about her faux pas and, as much as I wanted to rub it in, I really could not say too much. You see, it had not been that long ago that I had walked the better part of a day with a cap from a gallon jug of water in my boot. My own *faux pas* notwithstanding, I did not get to razz her too often so I took the opportunity to give her some good-natured ribbing. Before the trail, such an incident would have had us questioning our mental facilities, and we would have chastised ourselves for doing something so dumb. But now, our new-found ability to immediately laugh at something we knew we would probably laugh about later allowed us to enjoy a humorous moment.

Moon Over Massachusetts

After almost a week without seeing a single northbound hiker, one morning we came down the mountain to cross the Massachusetts Turnpike, and just ahead of us we saw four of them. We could not tell who they were, but we surmised they were some of "the kids" because they were moving very fast. Hiking alone for several days had been extremely enjoyable for us, but now we missed the companionship of other hikers. We hurried down the hill to try to catch them. Before we were able to get close enough to identify them, we heard cars on the turnpike endlessly honking their horns.

"That's weird," I said. *"What the heck is going on? There must be an accident or something."*

"It's probably just the people on the highway honking at those hikers as they are going across the bridge. That's not unusual," was "Mom's" logical analysis.

We kept up our rapid pace and before long we reached the bridge ourselves. As we walked across we were puzzled by the fact that, despite our repeated waves to the cars hurtling by below us, not a single one honked their horn in response. As lunchtime approached, we ambled into the October Mountain Shelter and there sat "Identity Crisis," "Rusch Hour," "Indiana," and "Treehouse"—the hikers we had been attempting to catch all morning. It was during lunch that we found out what all the horn honking was about at the footbridge.

"So, did you guys moon the cars on the turnpike?" "Rusch Hour" inquired excitedly.

"Mom" responded, shaking her head, *"No. I guess boys will be boys."*

Apparently, the boys had. Mystery solved.

This Garden Rocks

Over the course of our hike, there were innumerable opportunities to observe the tapestry of natural wonders around us. It was as if we were an integral part of an endless, wilderness IMAX movie. Some days we just sat transfixed by the transcendent beauty in this "sanctuary of solitude" But there were also times that offered us the chance to become a more intimate and active part of what we were experiencing—and, in the process we were able to entertain ourselves.

One morning in Vermont, we started with a leisurely walk around Little Rock Pond. We loved how they called lakes "ponds" in Vermont; but in relation to the enormity of the mountain landscapes, I suppose they were just ponds. We stopped and chatted with the campsite caretaker and remarked about the pristine location she had at which to spend the summer—a gorgeous pond, a musical stream nearby, cool breezes, and abundant wildlife visible at every turn. Abruptly, we came to edge of that pond and found ourselves strolling through a beautiful and stately pine forest. We were overwhelmed by the intense pine aroma that made it seem like Christmas. Purely by accident, I took my eyes off my feet long enough to peer off to the right of the trail where I spotted several large rocks with smaller rocks piled on top of them. Strange, I thought! Just as I noticed these peculiar cairns, I heard "Mom" exclaim,

"Oh wow, you have to see this!"

I came around a large rock pile to where she was standing, and there on the ground, were dozens of various-sized piles of rocks, sculpted by hikers who previously passed through that spot. It was a remarkably whimsical sight. Each pile looked like a small gnome and it was as if we had stumbled into some mythical fairy tale land. We walked another quarter mile, and there the trail went through another area about thirty yards square covered with more of these stone creations. They were all different sizes and configurations, and there even were rocks up in the branches of the trees. Over in one corner, a "peace sign" had been formed on the ground, obviously made by some "child of the sixties" hiker who had passed this way. The massiveness of the surrounding forest became insignificant as our eyes and piquing imaginations became fixed on the community of small stone statuettes scattered as far as the eye could see. We sensed the trees and boulders surrounding this rock garden were there solely to keep watch over and protect their diminutive stone companions. We had been blessed with unending wonders during our hike, but this special place took on a fascination all its own. It was here we felt in true harmony with our surroundings, and each hiker had left a part of who he was as a token of appreciation. The entire sight solicited a myriad of emotions from surprise, to wonder, to amusement, even to envy. For posterity's sake, we added our own sculptures to the mix and then sat down to have a snack. "Mom" and I could see twinkling in each others eyes the wonder of this place and time—a childlike wonder reborn after years of having it swallowed up by the harsh and relentless realities of our hurried lives.

Ever since that chance encounter with the "rock sculpture museum," we often wondered who started that tradition, how long had it been growing, and how, at the very beginning, did other thru-hikers know to add their rock designs to the project? What creative synergy pervaded that area to such a level that, without any formal instruction, hikers simply added their creations, extensions of themselves, to that wilderness museum? In doing so, they created a timeless connection with every hiker who passed that way—past, present or future. I suppose the answers to those questions forever will remain a piece of A.T. mystery and lore. Now, whenever we see a cairn, the memory of that field of playful piles of rocks comes flooding back—and we smile.

Totally Tubular, Man!

When we first came upon this sight in Vermont, we thought we had stumbled into some Twilight Zone episode—some undiscovered alien playground, or some bizarre trap designed to ensnare some unsuspecting animal (or hiker). Meandering through the woods were miles and miles of plastic tubing stretching from tree to tree. Once we recovered from the initial shock and confusion of stumbling upon this bizarre sight, we composed ourselves and came to the realization we were, after all, in Vermont. What we were witnessing was how sap was being harvested from maple trees to make syrup in our "high tech" age.

Gone are the days when farmers would tap the trees with wooden spigots and hang their buckets to catch the sap. Now, each tree is tapped with a short piece of plastic tubing that runs to a larger diameter tube. This large tube runs all through the forest, collecting sap from the entire maple tree stand and then, using only gravity, it flows to the processing barn at the bottom of the hill. This Vermont tradition has changed little over the years and the use of tubing is merely a minor concession to the progress required to bring more syrup and other maple products to market. The essence of how it is processed remains intact as a tribute to the pioneers who put Vermont on the map as the nation's largest provider of maple syrup.

As we pondered this sight, it was difficult for us not to be confounded by the juxtaposition of tradition and progress which somehow coexisted in these woods. We still remembered old photos portraying the harvesting of maple sap and how truly American that appeared to be. We wondered how much maple sugar producers had struggled with this balance of "tradition versus technology," considering that a staunch adherence to tradition and old-time values are both hallmarks of Vermont life. Even though we understand the piping technique is more efficient, there remains something to be said for the love, dedication, hard work, and pioneer spirit that came from doing it the old-fashioned way. We were just glad to see someone was still making *real* maple syrup and things had not deteriorated to the point where Americans were pouring some maple-flavored, chemical concoction onto their pancakes. "Mom" was especially thankful since one of her favorite breakfasts along the trail was blueberry pancakes with syrup.

A Porcupine Named Eyeore

In Vermont at Kid Gore Shelter, which is named after neither Kid Rock nor Al Gore's son, we quickly made our dinner and then sat taking in the magnificent view of the valley spread out before us—all the while talking with a father/daughter team, "Bob" and "Debbie," and also "Sherpa." From the gnawed condition of the front edge of the shelter platform and notes in the shelter register, we knew there were porcupines in the vicinity and we should probably prepare for a late-night visit from one of them. Boots, trekking poles, and anything else with body salt on it were hung to make it impossible for a porcupine to make a midnight snack of them.

Like clockwork, as we all snored away, we were awakened to the sound of gnawing on the front of the shelter. The ancient timbers of the shelter amplified the vibration of the chewing, so it sounded like our intruder was quite possibly larger than any single one of us. Instinctively we all grabbed our headlamps and cameras and pointed them in the direction of the sound. At first we saw nothing; but then, like a submarine periscope breaking the surface of the ocean, the head of a porcupine popped up at the front of the shelter and looked right at us. Wow! We had never seen one in the wild before and we could not decide who was more surprised—the porcupine or us. Spooked by the lights, he waddled off into the long grass and was never heard from or seen again. "Mom," who had developed quite a talent for humorously entertaining our shelter guests, interpreted what had just happened. Taking on the character of the porcupine and mimicking the voice of "Eyeore" from the "Winnie the Pooh" stories, she said:

> *"Well I guess if you're going to shine a light on me, I suppose I won't be gnawing on the shelter anymore tonight."*

Our newfound playful approach to life, and each other, was adding a new and exciting dimension to our relationship. The trail and our lives were fun again.

P.A.T.T.S.D.

We knew our relationship was growing stronger with each passing mile, and we were learning more about ourselves and each other with each passing day. But for some time "Mom" and I had been wondering how many of the idiosyncrasies of the trail—the jargon, the routines, and the mannerisms—would be so ingrained in us that they would pervade our otherwise normal lives once we were off the trail. We soon found we were not alone in wondering about such things. The end-result of our cumulative concerns made for a list of behavioral peculiarities that could be the basis of a research paper suitable for the American Journal of Psychiatry.

August 14th was a hot, muggy day in New Hampshire—not much different from so many of the days we experienced in August. Late in the day we arrived at one of the marvels of the A.T.—the Hexacube Shelter. There we found "Montreal" relaxing and reading a magazine. What made this shelter so unique was its design. Protruding from the heavily wooded and steep hillside was this marvelous, six-sided, gazebo-looking log structure with two of the six sides open to the valley below. A single, large post stood in the center holding up the peak of the roof, and because of the design there was room enough for twelve or more hikers, depending on how everyone arranged himself and his gear. The fact that it was so large was a good thing because, not long after our arrival, "Little Wing," "That Guy" (Little Wing's partner who was hiking The Whites with her), "G-Walk," "Brainfreeze," and "Baldylocks" joined us. "Tecumseh," "Coolhand," and "Bofus" arrived later, but they tented as usual.

As the evening wore on and we corporately wolfed down our evening vittles, "Brainfreeze" told us about a list she and "G-Walk" had been assembling. It was a list of trail peculiarities, which over the many months on the trail, had begun to traumatize them, and they feared these issues would overtly alter their ability to function "normally" in the outside world. They shared their list with all of us so we could be on the lookout for the telltale signs associated with these bizarre behaviors. As "Brainfreeze" read down the list of symptoms of this yet undocumented social ill, we were rolling with laughter on the shelter floor. When she solicited our input, the additional symptoms came fast and furious. The following definition of this malady, along with its list of sinister symptoms, was compiled to educate the public to this dreaded disease and to minimize the stigma associated with it for those who already suffer from it.

Post A.T. Traumatic Stress Disorder (P.A.T.T.S.D.): An inability to readjust to normal society after thru-hiking. Any, or all, of the following symptoms, can characterize this disorder:

- Hanging your food and shoes on the wall or from the ceiling;
- Digging "cat holes" in the backyard and carrying a roll of toilet paper in a *Ziploc* bag everywhere you go;
- Changing your clothes in parking lots *(which "Mom" regularly did)*
- Checking for water sources everywhere you go;
- Asking people how many miles they are planning on going today;
- Swatting at invisible insects or lurching out of the way of invisible spider webs;
- Eating dinner at 4 p.m. and being in bed by 6:30 p.m.;
- Wearing the same clothes for three days and not taking a shower until you change clothes;
- Calling work to take a "zero day" rather than a "sick day;"
- Ripping pages out of books as you read them;

- Asking house guests to "Please pack out their trash" when they leave;
- Asking for a "spork" at restaurants;
- Putting leaves in the toilet;
- Sleeping on your Thermarest or on a 17-inch wide space on the edge of the bed;
- Filtering water from the faucet;
- Gaining 800 pounds because you still think you have your "metrailbolism" *(trail metabolism);*
- Walking around the house with your trekking poles;
- Referring to everyone as "hikers;"
- Asking people if they're going northbound or southbound *(especially on elevators);*
- Referring to floors in buildings by their elevations;
- Using "What's your trail name?" as a pick up line at a bar;
- Eating meals out of the pots they are cooked in;
- Going to the laundromat in your rain suit;
- Looking for "trail magic" under bushes and trees as you walk down the sidewalk;
- Ordering Ramen noodles at a restaurant;
- Not using deodorant.

Here's Mud in Your Eye

The rain that had pummeled the northeast all spring left its indelible mark on the trail. Not a day went by when we did not find ourselves slogging through quagmires that stretched up the trail for hundreds of feet. Hikers traipsing around the edges of the muddy trail in an attempt to save their boots and socks—not to mention themselves—made some of these mud holes up to twenty feet wide. On the way to Gentian Pond Shelter in Maine, we came upon such a mud hole. Right after a relaxing lunch, we came to a section of the trail spanned by a single puncheon that ended at the near edge of one of these "mud puddles." By eye, it appeared to be about eight feet wide and probably sixteen feet long, but there was no visible way of knowing how deep it was. There were numerous sticks and small logs protruding from the sticky ooze, so evidently some hikers threw debris into the mud in order to have footing on which to wade across. Personally, I was dubious about walking on half-submerged logs being a viable option. A closer examination of the site indicated more than a few people took the coward's way out and went around the edge. Sticking our hiking sticks into the mud, it was easy to see why—our poles disappeared right up to the grips. Going around the edge appeared to be the prudent thing to do.

In an unparalleled display of chivalry, I took the lead. Pushing the masses of brush and scrub pines aside, I safely made my way from one end to the other. As I triumphantly reached the far end and started to turn around to direct "Mom," I heard the muffled breaking of wood and, almost simultaneously, heard,

"Oh, my God!"

To my horror, there was my best friend with her left leg in the mud up to her knee and she appeared to be sinking fast. Flashing through my mind were scenes from those old jungle movies where some poor soul wandered into a bed of quicksand and was subsequently sucked into its clutches leaving only a struggling hand protruding up through the slime. I rushed back to help her, not wanting her to fall victim to the same fate.

What had happened was, that while I was feeling my way around the mud hole, she located a rather a good-sized log and laid it across the mud as a bridge. Unfortunately, the log was much more rotten than it appeared and as soon as she placed her full weight on it, it broke. With cat-like reflexes, she quickly sat down on the end of the puncheon to keep from being sucked in any further. As I made my way back, she struggled to free herself and still retain as much dignity as she could while doing so. Once she freed herself and the initial shock of what had happened wore off, we had a good laugh. The next few minutes were spent at a nearby stream washing the mud out of her boots and socks and scrubbing down her legs. On any other day before this monumental journey, our reaction to this situation would have probably been quite appalling. But now, we found ourselves laughing at the pure silliness of it all. How liberating it was and how drawn together we felt because of our new-found outlook.

Pickin' and Grinnin'

We ate dinner at the picnic tables behind The Lakeshore House Pub in Monson, Maine, just days before beginning the final leg of our odyssey— the "100 Mile Wilderness." Sitting on the back lawn of The Lakeshore Inn next to Lake Hebron, with the setting sun leaving a pinkish glow in the sky and its orange reflection illuminating the lake's mirror-like surface, were "Otter," "Cohiba," "Feng Shui," "Burner," "Souleman," "Brownie," and ourselves. It was a wonderful time of just catching up with each other, sharing our tales of the last few days, and voicing our excitement over the days to come. As the sun gave up control of the evening sky to an alabaster moon, we were off to the general store down the street where a group of local musicians was playing bluegrass music inside the front of the store.

This "hootenanny" was a regular Friday night affair in Monson, and the joy of what these simple town folk were doing was infectious. We had a grand time listening to the music, clapping along, and some folks even found a spot of floor large enough on which to dance. For us, simply wandering around the store was like being a child in a toy store. It brought back fond memories of our youth when we spent hours in small, simple stores like this one. Being a part-time live sound engineer, I especially got a kick out of the group's sound system amplifier sitting on a shelf behind the mandolin player—right between the bottles of anti-freeze and 10W/40 motor oil. This was a "real" general store!

In one aisle were snacks, light bulbs, and Styrofoam coolers. In another, just in front of the refrigerators full of beer, was a collection of Monson, Maine, sweatshirts and a rather peculiar selection of local wines. In yet another aisle were rabbit food and dog food in open bags near an old rusty hanging scale. There were also 50-pound boxes of various size nails sitting open that were evidently weighed on the same scale as the pet food. What was out of character for such an establishment was the Chinese food carryout located on one side of the store. As odd as it was, many of the hikers there were topping off the dinners they completed only an hour ago with portions of rice and orange chicken. We caught up with old friends and the latest news from the trail. We also saw many new faces and were finally able to put them with the trail names we had been hearing about for weeks. As the music began to wind down, so did we; it was time for a leisurely stroll back to the hostel, a bit of TV, our evening snack of *Ben & Jerry's,* and then crawling into the decadently wonderful comfort of a real bed. It had been an evening of unadulterated simple pleasures—nothing fancy or structured—just time with friends in surroundings that whispered, *"Welcome, friend. Come sit for a spell, relax, and enjoy life. Worry about tomorrow, tomorrow."*

What our hearts and relationship took away from that evening carried us through the days ahead and remains with us still.

The Humor in Ourselves

Even though pounding our way north on the A.T. was serious business, we could never take ourselves too seriously. To do so took a lot of the joy out of the adventure. There was no room for self-consciousness when thru-hiking the Appalachian Trail; if you were self-conscious, you missed half the fun and you probably would have a hard time taking a pee in the woods. We learned to take a perverted sense of pride in our disheveled appearance, and our musty aroma and the stares of those in town, who had no concept of what we were doing, made us all that more proud of whom we were. In our own minds, we were celebrities; though smelly ones who could clear a room simply by walking into it. To illustrate the lighthearted view thru-hikers take of themselves, Chuckie "Funnybone" Veylupek, in an article he wrote for the *Pacific Crest Communicator Magazine*, quipped, and I paraphrase here, that *"....the only distinguishing difference between a homeless person and a thru-hiker is Gore-Tex."* Should there ever be a collapse of the U.S. economy, throwing us into another era of depression, the homeless and the thru-hikers will be ready—and we will survive.

There was never a time when we deluded ourselves into believing that completing the entire 2,175 miles of the A.T. was going to be easy. In fact, our deepest fear was it could very well strain us, personally and as a couple, to some insurmountable breaking point. But never in our wildest imaginations did we think the months of grueling walking, adverse weather conditions and challenging terrain would present us with so many opportunities to become so at peace with who we were—to be able to view life, and each other, in total wonder and with a more relaxed and playful perspective.

Being on the trail and being able to throw off all the societal and emotional baggage weighing us down for years made us increasingly aware of the lighter side of moments in time and the simple pleasures surrounding us. We came to appreciate them more readily and more fully. We also learned to find the lighter side of ourselves. Most thru-hikers proudly admit that hiking the A.T. was life altering, and we whole-heartedly concur. But was it the trail itself that brought on this paradigm shift? After all, the trail is a relatively inanimate object. What the solitude, beauty, and peace of the trail did provide was an environment where this transformation could take place without interruption or distraction. With the only responsibilities each day being to walk, eat, and sleep, we were free to allow the more important elements of life to permeate every waking minute. Not only did being this free put us in a position to savor the people, places, and things we would have blindly glossed over as unimportant in our "other lives," it also granted us something even more important—the ability to appreciate each other more and find the grace of humor in our relationship.

As we grew closer to the end of our pilgrimage, the lingering question became, *"Would all that we learned about ourselves, each other, and life itself last?"* We found more to laugh about during our six months on the trail than during our fourteen years of marriage. We also found peace in the simplicity of a life devoid of cultural clutter. What would it take to continue experiencing that level of joy in our "man-made world?" What we discovered was that by keeping the memories of our thru-hike alive, we had those experiences to draw upon to keep us on course. In order to maintain a sense of clarity and purpose, every real life experience would now be held up to the mirror of our experiences on the A.T.

How wonderful it was to re-discover the simple pleasures of life and how gratifying it was to know we had the power to keep our life that way— together.

"Mom's" Tips for Couples:

- Laughing is the best medicine for a good marriage. Learn to laugh at disconcerting circumstances because those will pass. If you can say, "You know, some day we will laugh about this," why not laugh about it today?

- You have the choice of laughing together or crying alone. Which is better for you and for your relationship?

- Joy draws you close. If you doubt that, recall the days of laughter during your courtship;

- Turn off the TV, the radio, the iPod, and the internal voice telling you that unproductive time is wasted time. Go on a picnic, take a quiet walk in the woods, say "Hello" to a stranger, and learn to listen to, see, and smell the rhythm of life all around you. Inner peace opens up the door to a stronger relationship.

CHAPTER NINE

SOUL SURVIVORS

"Courage is not the absence of fear, but rather the judgment that something else is more important than fear." Ambrose Redmoon

Mike:

> *"Perhaps one of the hardest parts of the hike was during the floods around Duncannon, Pennsylvania. At no point did we feel we were we actually in danger, but news of the floods made its way back home to Sydney and our parents made us call them daily to confirm that we were safe. It was pretty hard to take them seriously when they were trying to give us advice from the other side of the world, and we had a very hard time convincing our parents that we were in a better position to judge our safety than they were."*

Each day the trail presented new challenges to us, and because of those challenges, we became increasingly aware of our inner-most emotions. Sometimes they appeared only through quiet introspection, creating a window into our souls, but more often those emotions, some buried for years, rose to the surface and were exhibited in visible ways. To face each new day on the A.T. with a childlike sense of adventure required steadfast willpower, ability, resilience and courage. Whether hiking solo or hiking as a couple, these four attributes were conspicuous in virtually every hiker marching his/her way from Georgia to Maine. What was also apparent was that, whether single and having formed relationships with other single hikers or married and caring for the needs of a spouse, a human characteristic of even greater significance came into play: *empathy*. We literately could feel what others were going through—and it mattered to us.

In an American culture that breeds a "me first" mindset—with athletes, actors and politicians all posturing for a self-absorbed, celebrity status—the trail set itself apart as a unique sociological stage. Daily we saw a multi-act drama depicting the most basic of human instincts: an unselfish desire to put another first. The level of compassion and encouragement pervading life on the trail was astounding. It was an unrestrained display of the depth of the human spirit where people put aside their own ambitions and aspirations in order to ensure the safety and well-being of others. It included caring for hiking partners or total strangers and the ramifications, on both the giver and receiver of such acts, became forever etched in the memories of both. The physical and emotional bonding among hikers was evident, for example, in how they came to the aid of "Old Drum" after his nearly disastrous fall. Their empathy and compassion for a fellow traveler manifested itself in seeing that he was able to continue his hike in spite of his injuries. As such, that apparent obstacle turned into a host of opportunities—opportunities for eternal friendships to develop and for a fellow hiker to continue on his journey. With each passing mile we transcended the physical brutality of merely walking together as "solemates" and became emotionally bound together as "soulmates."

For married couples, an additional, underlying dynamic came into play. Unlike the solo hikers, who could afford to be somewhat less emotionally attached to each other because they may never see each other again after the hike, how married couples reacted to each other's needs would have a lasting impact on their relationship long after their hike ended. Common wisdom says the true test of a relationship is how a couple stares into the face of adversity and overcomes it. Successfully living through the good times is rarely a reliable indicator of the depth of a marriage. Like us, the other couples on the A.T. encountered many circumstances unique to our relationships, so surviving, and ultimately thriving, through such circumstances required not only a "meeting of the minds" but a "bonding of their souls"—a bonding expressed in sincere emotional connectivity, heartfelt compassion and empathy, and the pooling of their combined strengths.

The A.T. was a backdrop for displaying the complete spectrum of emotions which constitute the human spirit. Willpower, resilience, love, compassion, empathy, joy, sorrow, and anger all surfaced as powerful weapons against the unceasing travails facing us. Perhaps others were aware of it in themselves, but there was one defining component of our characters "Mom" and I unknowingly overlooked.

Courage

Hiking the A.T. not only required will, ability, resilience, empathy and compassion but equally important was an attribute that never really crossed our minds—courage. Despite any amount of planning, the trail and the weather set the terms for our hike. We must, and inevitably would, meet it on its own terms or we would fail. Mother Nature provided more than her share of harrowing situations and forced of us to continually take stock of our physical conditioning and perseverance. We were also challenged to raise the bar when it came to the amount of risk we felt was reasonable to take. At the same time, we came to accept as normal the associated fear that went with those risks. But as we rock-hopped the field of boulders making up the trail down from the summit of Mt. Washington in New Hampshire, our intricately calculated approach to facing the trials of the wilderness took a sudden and enlightening turn. As we moved to the edge of the trail to give way to an elderly man coming toward us, he stopped and asked if we were thru-hikers. When we answered we were, his comment was,

"That takes a lot of courage."

It never once occurred to us that what we were doing required courage. We had a plan, had prepared ourselves physically and mentally, and now all we were doing was putting all that into action in order to reach our goal. We had been meeting every formidable obstacle with pure willpower and planning—taking every step possible to overcome each as safely as possible. Now we had to view our quest in a totally different light. In retrospect he was right, especially when we considered the difficulty and danger of the last few weeks. Even prior to the White Mountains, we certainly experienced more than our share of circumstances requiring more skill and willpower than we believed we possessed. As he walked away, we realized it must be courage keeping us pressing forward—overpowering the fear that often gripped us.

I remember commenting to "Mom" as we stood at the foot of the first steep, perilous climb of our hike that for me to sanely make it up that section I was adopting the technique used by Jack, the surrogate leader of the plane-wrecked community on the TV show, "Lost." In one of the episodes Jack, a surgeon, told a story of a mistake he made during an operation—a mistake leaving him paralyzed with fear and unable to think of a way to remedy the situation. At that instant, with the patient's life hanging in the balance, he consciously decided to let fear take hold of him for *only* five seconds; then he would shake it off, decide what to do, and move forward thus saving his patient. Feeling this was a logical, though melodramatic, approach to my personal bout with fear, I tried letting the fear have its moment in the sun. I then triumphantly crawled my way up the mountain. "Mom" rarely verbally expressed any fear. However, as I watched her gingerly and deliberately inch her way up and down the vertical obstacles in our path, it was obvious to me that a certain level of fear also had her in its grip. It was also obvious her will to succeed was far greater than her fear, and over time her confidence in dealing with fearful challenges grew. As the miles grew into months, she became increasingly more comfortable in verbalizing her fears, and the intimacy between us was strengthened by mutually sharing those types of feelings. Though we were not always aware of it, the courage we gained from overcoming our fear was as much a solidifier of our relationship as were the moments of serenity, sitting together and lovingly sharing the beauty of a sunset.

Stories of courage and compassion, and the enduring effects they had on relationships, were boundless on the A.T.

It was May 7th in Virginia when in most other places on the east coast spring was in full bloom and temperatures were already moderating considerably. For us, though, it was a less-than-spring day. It was a day fraught with potentially life-threatening circumstances. Were it not for our wilderness first aid training and a "miracle," we would have been in very serious trouble for the first time since we began our odyssey northward. We woke up to rain and a light wind but soon the rain let up. Feeling the break in the rain would probably be short-lived, we quickly packed and started hiking. As expected, before we had traveled too far, the rain began again, and though we were quite wet, we were only mildly uncomfortable. That was until we reached the bald at Buzzard Rock on our way up Whitetop Mountain.

We heard loud voices and hasty footsteps making their way from the bald toward us through the damp leaves. Through the pouring rain ahead we saw several southbound slack-packers, dripping wet, careening toward us as if being chased by a ghost. As they shot past us, through blue, shivering lips they warned us it was nasty up ahead and we should prepare for the worst. As we left the sanctuary of the final grove of trees and started up the bald, the temperature dropped from a balmy 50 °F to 34 °F in a matter of minutes and the wind picked up to 35 mph to 45 mph. We dug our trekking poles into the ground on the downwind side of our bodies just to keep from being blown over. The rain was traveling horizontal to the ground and driving so hard it went right through our clothes and packs. Minutes seemed like hours. By the time we reached the summit, we were soaked, cold, and uncomfortable. Our gloves, which normally kept our hands toasty warm, were now wringing wet—sucking the heat right out of our fingers. Our body temperatures began to fall rapidly, and we knew we could not reach the safety of Thomas Knob Shelter 7.4 miles away—our planned destination for the day.

During our wilderness first aid training we were drilled, repeatedly, on the signs and effects of hypothermia. This killer can so unexpectedly and so elusively sneak up on you that not recognizing its telltale signs of onset can be a matter of life and death. As we stumbled down the trail from the bald toward Elk Garden, we started to lose feeling in our fingers, and we knew it was time to seek shelter. However, we still had 4.5 miles to go before we could reach a suitable spot to set up our tent and get out of the inclement weather. One of the "Catch 22's" of hiking when you are cold and wet is that you need to eat to have the calories to generate body heat. However, as soon as you stop to eat you get colder. We had to keep moving to stay warm and decided to wait to eat until we got into our tent.

This was a bold move on our part, but it was a chance we had to take. It was imperative we constantly talk to each so we could check on each other's condition, and talking also gave us something to keep our minds active so we did not simply concentrate on how cold we were. As we walked down the steep incline, we searched in vain for a level spot for our tent but saw only one small site. "Comfortably Numb" was already setting up his tent there for protection. We would have to move on. By now, our lips were turning blue and our teeth were chattering to the point where it was almost impossible to speak, but we persevered.

"How are your fingers, Babe?" I asked.

"They are pretty numb. How are yours?" was "Mom's" plaintive reply.

"Pretty numb, too, and I can't feel my toes. We need to get to Elk Garden as quickly as possible," I shouted so as to reaffirm the magnitude of our situation.

"I am going as fast as I can! I'm cold and wet and the trail is very slick," "Mom" shouted in response to believing I was scolding her over our pace.

This back and forth went on for what seemed like hours until we reached Elk Garden near VA 600. In spite of our own personal discomfort, our real concern was for each other, and as frightening as this experience was, we never felt closer to each other than we did at that moment. It was as if we could not do enough to help the other person, and vocalizing our concern kept our strength and courage up.

Astonishingly, the rain let up just as we reached our destination, so we quickly set up our tent. While doing so, we noticed "Steech" standing by the road so we went over to see how he was faring. His lips were purple and he was wet and shivering—a black garbage bag covered his pack to ward off the rain. Nevertheless, he stated he was going to continue walking. Knowing what we did about hypothermia, we feared for his safety. With "Steech" now gone and with our tent set up within sight of passing cars, we stood in the freezing cold and stripped off all of our wet clothes. This was extremely uncomfortable and added to the numbness that had taken over our bodies. Putting on every piece of dry clothing from our packs and pulling hats down over our faces to restrict the loss of any more body heat through our heads, we crawled into our sleeping bags to warm up. We huddled together and prepared to ride out the storm. As we lay there, with the shivering yet to show any signs of subsiding, we heard another hiker passing by and peeked out to see who it was. By the side of the road stood "Rapunzel," who was equally as drenched as "Steech" had been. Her slight frame was hunched over, showing the obvious effects of her losing battle with fighting off the cold. Her thumb was out in an attempt to get a ride into town. Before setting up our tent, we made a brief and futile attempt to catch a ride into town so we knew very few cars frequented VA 600. However, "Rapunzel" was one of the lucky ones. As we struggled to stay awake, we heard a car stop and looked out to see her riding away. Later reports from the trail were that when she arrived back in Damascus she was blue, could not move her fingers, and she was in such bad shape, she even needed help getting her pack off.

As the cold in our bodies began to diminish somewhat, we made the heartbreaking decision not to try to continue any further this day. We resigned ourselves to simply counting our blessings for having safely gotten as far as we did. Now we needed a ride to some place where we could finish warming up, dry our clothes, and possibly dry out our tent. Over the last several weeks, it was seldom we had reliable cell service. Our fear was that today would be no different—but we had to give it a try. "Mom" pulled out her phone and anxiously turned it on. Amazingly, for a span of only three minutes, she was able to get two bars of cell service and was able to call "V&A" to come pick us up. Equally fortuitous was the fact that when she called, for the first time all day, "V&A" also had cell service. What a miracle it was and we knew we had nothing to do with it happening. They informed us they were quite some distance away, doing reconnaissance for the next few days' hikes. It would take them at least two hours to come to our rescue. We assured them we were beginning to warm up and could comfortably make it until they arrived. Knowing our rescue was still hours away, we let our 15 °F bags work their magic and took a nap.

Eventually, we awoke to honking from the Elk Garden parking lot and looked out to see "V&A" sitting there. It was a most welcome sight. They took us to a Holiday Inn Express in Abingdon, Virginia, where we spent the night. Along with a long, hot shower to take off the remaining chill, we dried out all our gear and warmed ourselves with a hot meal at the local Huddle House.

This had been a day laden with potential disaster for not only us but also for quite a few other members of our trail family. We later heard that "Team Fourward," including "Boogeyman's" two brothers, who definitely chose the wrong week to hike a section of the trail with their brother, held up at the Thomas Knob Shelter. They thankfully experienced the same type of cell phone miracle we did, but they had been in much more desperate straits than we. With soaking wet clothes and sleeping bags, their options for getting warm were virtually nil. They attempted to call Mt. Rogers Outfitters to pick them up at Elk Garden and take them to Damascus. One of the guys in their group tried to make the call; finding he had no service, he angrily tossed the phone to his buddy at the other end of the shelter—just ten feet away. He tried calling again, found he had two bars and was able to make a call to get them rescued. Unfortunately, they still had to hike the four miles from the shelter back to the road to meet their guardian angels. They later nicknamed that phone their "God Phone."

Needless to say, we were a bit discouraged the elements beat us and we would have to make up the missed miles by doing some extra miles during the upcoming days. But as we lay in our bed at the motel, a sense of contentment overtook us. We survived a dangerous situation by not succumbing to our own fear and discomfort but by staying focused on the needs and safety of our partner. It was a pivotal moment in the growth of our marriage. When we later met up with "Team Forward" and compared notes of our frightening experience on Whitetop Mountain, our relationship with them also grew.

The effect of rain and cold was not restricted to simply a few hikers. At one point or another we were all at its mercy. Thankfully, though there were some narrow escapes, no one succumbed to hypothermia's gruesome results.

Trickster:

> *"One of the most vivid memories we have of our hike occurred in the White Mountains of New Hampshire, just past Mount Washington. "What?!" and I were hiking in miserably cold, windy weather and it was raining and hailing. Even though it is not legal, we made a safety call and set up our tent just below the ridge because the next designated campsite or lodge was more than three miles north. At 1:00 p.m. we set up camp, the earliest time we had ever quit hiking, and proceeded to sit around, endlessly, playing Gin Rummy and snacking on Cliff bars. Around 10:00 p.m. we thought we heard something outside of our tent, but it was hard to tell for sure because of the wind and rain. On our radio we heard a report from Mt. Washington stating the winds were up to 30 mph, so we knew that the*

temperature was going to quickly drop to a dangerous level. Hearing the noise again, and realizing that it was someone yelling in the distance, we jumped into action...thinking that someone must in trouble or lost outside. It was dark and, and because of the fog, there was almost zero visibility. Within a few minutes, both of us were soaked. We were working our way back to the trail where we saw the light from a head lamp further south on the trail in the direction of Mt. Washington. We were frantic and suddenly realized we had lost our own trail back to the ridge. We had to pause and figure out where our tent was, and we were concerned that, if we became disoriented, all three of us could die of hypothermia. Locating our tent, we began yelling to the mysterious person in the distance. Whoever was flashing his light was moving further away from us. Then the light simply stopped moving. Because the fog was becoming increasingly dense, we wanted the person to come toward our light because we were afraid that if we tried to get to them, we would never find our way back to our tent and safety. It was freezing and we were both starting to shiver, which we knew was the first stage of mild hypothermia. After shouting frantically for over five minutes, the person finally began moving toward us. It took another fifteen minutes before we could finally make out the shape of the person coming towards us, and he was precariously balanced on a huge boulder from which he was about to hurl himself in our direction! We screamed for him to stop moving and approached him to help him down safely.

We bombarded him with questions, learned his name, and found out that he was sixteen years old and from California. He was extremely disoriented, and it was clear that he was suffering from advanced hypothermia. He told us that the last time he had seen his aunt and uncle was at 5:00 p.m. It was now 10:30 p.m. It had been raining continuously, but he had taken off his rain jacket and was wearing a sweatshirt, some cotton pants and skateboarding shoes, all of which were soaking wet. We rushed him to our tent and helped remove his clothes before letting him in. Our fear was that if he came in with his wet clothes on, our down sleeping bags would get wet and would lose their warmth—warmth that we all desperately needed. We gave him some of our dry, spare clothes to put on and then zipped our two sleeping bags together. He crawled into the bag with each of us on either side; despite our warm bodies next to his, he continued shivering for almost an hour before we were able to re-warm him. We attempted to recharge his metabolism, but he refused the food we offered him. He simply would not eat. At this point, we were concerned about his family because we did not know if they were also lost. From what he told us, they were dressed similar to him, not having the right clothing or rain gear.

By the next morning, he was feeling much better, and we made our way to the next hut on the trail. It was slow going and we became even more concerned because no one seemed to be looking for him. This made us think that his aunt and uncle had never made it off the mountain to find help. We passed at least twelve hikers who had come from the hut and none of them had heard of a missing boy. We were now extremely alarmed. Late in the morning, we reached the hut only to find that no one working at the hut had heard of a missing boy. It had now been eighteen hours, and no search party was trying to find him! A call from the hut to New Hampshire Fish and Game Department revealed that, yes, his aunt and uncle had made it down off the mountain the night before and had called authorities for help in locating him. They were told to call back in the morning!

Here it was at 11:00 a.m., the day after his disappearance, and Fish and Game was just starting to get a team together to search for him. We believe, very strongly, that he would not have survived the night if we had not happened to camp illegally along the exposed ridgeline.

Our lost boy was reunited with his aunt and uncle, and we had the chance to speak with them. They were very grateful and relieved after the ordeal and told us of the poor organization within Fish and Game. They had tried to get their nephew to turn around and head back when the weather got bad, but he refused because he was determined to reach the peak of Mt. Jefferson, with or without them. The bottom line is that he was simply a teenager whose stubbornness and complete ignorance of the dangers of the White Mountains could have killed him. The fatality list posted at the visitor center on Mt. Washington is not there because it's NOT dangerous. We just felt extremely blessed to have been in the right spot at the right time. That experience definitely worked to strengthen our bond and our sense of being a team. And, God, it gave us one hell of a good trail story!"

July 6th was a cool, clear day with uncharacteristic low humidity and no sign of rain anywhere—a perfect day to rock climb out of Lehigh Gap in Pennsylvania and through the barren wasteland of the EPA Superfund site at the summit. Navigating the long, boot-wide top of "The Knife Edge" several days earlier had been invigorating, but scaling Lehigh Gap's vertical cliffs and loose piles of rust-colored rocks to 1,420 feet looked to be a total "adrenaline rush"—a rush consisting of equal measures of both excitement and fear. Once painlessly through the bottom part of the ascent, we looked up at the challenge that awaited us. It was obvious the remainder of the climb required that both our hands be free to grab onto rocks to keep from falling. We collapsed our trekking poles and put them on our packs. This climb was going to be even more dangerous because of the weight of our full packs. If we were not extremely careful, they could throw us off balance as we negotiated our way across the narrow overhangs skirting the cliff's edge. One small mistake would result in a rapid descent and ghastly consequences.

Picking our way cautiously upward, looking neither up nor down but only far enough ahead to determine our next handhold and foot placement, we inched forward. Then it appeared—a narrow shelf barely wide enough for our feet. Slightly overhanging it was a giant mass of rock just teasing us to attempt to walk along the ledge upright. We stopped to take a deep breath, viewed the rushing traffic and the river below, and with hearts in our throats, made our way across the slender walkway. There was simply no way to make it across this ledge other than to crawl on our hands and knees and hold onto the rocks above us to keep from falling. Even our knees were almost too wide to keep firmly on the ledge. All the while, our packs dragged along the wall of rock at our sides, forcing us toward the edge. It was extremely harrowing, but we eventually arrived at a small open flat spot where we were able to stand upright and we took stock of our accomplishment. The remainder of the ascent was a carefree, boulder-hopping dance which took us past a large American flag painted on the face of one of the larger slabs, and then across the remaining field of rubble to the summit. We looked at our watches and found it took us over an hour to complete the 1,420 feet to the top. But how long it took us was of minor significance when compared to the level of fear we had overcome—and this was not to be the last of such chilling days. As we walked through the zinc-mining-scarred plain of the EPA Superfund site which stretches for hundreds of yards on the mountain's summit, we relived the preceding hour and shared the range of emotions we had just experienced—emotions that, much like "Trickster & What?!'s," brought us closer together as a team.

After re-stocking with "V&A" at Crawford Notch, in New Hampshire, we began the trek to our destination for the day, Mizpah Shelter. In order to get there, though, we had to make the grueling 2,630-foot climb up to the summit of Mt. Webster at 3,910 feet—and to get there we first we had to climb up Webster Cliffs. The fact we had not fully recovered from the 14.5 miles the day before—from the Garfield Ridge Campsite to the Ethan Pond Campsite—would prove making the next ten miles even more difficult than anticipated. The dangerous terrain, the toughest we had yet experienced, would nearly sap our will.

Up until this time, most of the sheer, vertical ascents we conquered were done with the help of wooden ladders or rebar steps provided by the trail maintainers who oversee the trail. These wilderness accoutrements made the most treacherous sections somewhat manageable. But as we completed one of the many switchbacks winding its way up this particular mountain, there, insidiously poised before us and stretching endlessly into the wilderness above, was a shear rock face. This obstacle had no familiar ladders or rebar—only roots and scrub pines lining its edges, which we could use as handholds. We looked everywhere for blazes we hoped would indicate a way around this monster, but there were none. The trail went straight up its face and the trepidation in "Mom's" face was evident. As leader, it was her job to locate the best way up and test the crumbling rock and loosened roots for safety. Adding to the menace of this climb was the fact that this section stood fully exposed to the elements—the gusting wind hit us square in the back and pummeled our packs like a boxer's left jab. This was real danger and the consequences of a false move flashed through our minds. Ahead and straight up stood countless feet of hand-over-hand climbing that would test our strength, will, and courage.

"Mom" started slowly up with moves more deliberate than I saw her ever use in the past. She yanked and tugged on each root and tree limb to test its worthiness before applying her full weight to it. She insisted that I stay further behind her than usual, so if she fell, she would not take me off the mountain with her. As gallant as that decision was for her to make, the thought of her falling and me surviving sent chills up my spine. I simply had to pray nothing like that would happen. Staying further behind her did give me time to dodge the numerous rocks that were kicked loose by her boots and careened down the mountain toward me. Hand-over-hand we climbed, fighting the wind, staring straight at the surface ahead of us, with our noses only inches from the rock in front of us. With each beleaguered step we struggled to find solid purchase for our feet. After what seemed like an eternity, it was over. As we stood at the crest of that precipice, peering down at the sheer magnitude of what we had overcome, we breathed a collective sigh of relief and relished the moment together.

"That was a bit scary!" said "Mom" with more than a bit of understated sarcasm.

"I can't believe we did that with full packs on!" was my astonished reply. *"No one ever suggested we take a rock climbing course before doing the A.T. It sure would have helped."*

We stood there side-by-side; the warmth of the afternoon sun diminishing the coolness of the incessant wind. We were jubilant over conquering not only the mountain, but our fear as well. Simultaneously we raised the same issue that we would not have wanted to climb this section alone. Just the fact we had each other for encouragement through the danger and we shared the same experience brought us closer together. I was proud of "Mom" for what she just led us through—prouder than I probably let her know. I hoped she sensed it anyway.

As we exited the confines of the pines flourishing on this mountaintop, the wind we wrestled with for the last hour hit us square in the face, almost knocking us over. From the windblown flats of Webster Cliff (3,330 feet), we gazed at the outcroppings of granite protruding from the trees on the mountain across the valley far below. Everything was just so BIG from up there, except us. With all the excitement of the past few hours, we forgot to eat lunch or even take a snack. We retired to the solitude of the woods where we located two rocks sticking up like primordial headstones through the blanket of pine needles and grass covering the ground. Happy to be finally out of the wind, we dropped our packs, had lunch, and basked in the sun's warmth.

When it was finally time to move on, the fatigue that plagued us all morning, except when the rush of fear overtook us, made another grand entrance. In the near distance was Mt. Jackson at 4,052 feet; in order to get there, we had to go down sheer near-vertical rocks faces, now fighting winds that had dramatically increased in velocity since lunch. The rock-scrambling confidence we gained only hours before was suddenly ripped from us like trees from the ground in a tornado. We were so exhausted our descent became agonizing. We moved to the edges of these huge slabs of granite, held onto branches and roots for brakes, and slid down on our butts from the top to the bottom. From a technical standpoint, it was not very pretty, but it was extremely effective. How we made it down without tearing holes in the seats of our pants remains a mystery. Our progress was horribly slow, and adding to our aggravation, was the despondency we felt when two teenage boys rushed by us. They walked straight down the same slabs we were sliding down as if they were on flat ground—not even breaking stride. As the afternoon wore on, our speed dropped to 1.0 mph which was an additional frustration to us. We knew we would be slowing down in The Whites, but not quite this much. Our concern now was whether or not we would be able to complete the twelve miles up and over Mt. Washington in one day. (Under a warm, sunny sky and with unusually calm winds, we did make it over Mt. Washington and on to Madison Hut in one day.) We finally reached the AMC Mizpah Hut/Nauman Tentsite at 5:00 p.m., set up our tent, ate, received some valuable information from the caretaker; and with emotions running the gamut from joy and confidence to doubt and exhaustion, we quickly fell asleep.

Compassion & Encouragement

Most days we got up and just knew we could handle anything the trail threw at us. Then there were days when neither of us could get mentally or physically into the "game." The worst type of day was when we both experienced this dilemma. That was the type of day where it became us against the trail, and we felt like the trail was winning. It was on days like that we had to remember the trail, short of rain or snow, was the same that day as it had been the day before and would be the day after today. The only thing that changed was our attitude. And it was on those days that we could not let the trail beat us into changing our plans and hiking short. If we did, each time that type of day challenged us it would only become easier for the trail to win. Then before we would realize it, we'd get up one morning and say, *"That's it, we're done."* No matter what, we had to spur each other on and, if need be, find the humor in how we were feeling. Our ability to comprehend the mosaic of life spread out before us might be clouded by the pain of sore feet, or aching legs or dulled by a bad night's sleep. However, we knew prevailing through days like that would always provide us with a wealth of rewards. If we kept each other's spirits up, the payoff would be soothing views of the valleys below, gardens of trilliums lining the trail, or the added dividend of a sunset painting the sky with colors defying description. It also brought with it a vibrant sense of accomplishment, a renewed sense of self, and a reinforcement of the bond that brought the two of us together in the first place. These rewards alone were motivation enough to keep going and never quit. What motivated others through similar days was as heartfelt and as varied.

Little Wing:

> *"The heaviest thing I carried today was my heart. I learned last night that my sister's husband, Frank, passed away early Tuesday morning. My emotions are pretty raw right now—I've learned that it's possible to hike and cry at the same time.*
> *Here's the thing. If Frankie were out here with me, and essentially he has been for the past two days, in my thoughts anyway, he would tell me to stop sniveling and get moving. Frank loved to work hard, mainly because he nearly always loved what he was working at. That's a little bit like the experience out here. It's hard, sometimes unspeakably hard, but at this moment there is no place I'd rather be. I*

think Frank would understand that and even embrace it. For that
reason, I am dedicating my Appalachian Trail hike to Frank K. Spain.
Each day, even when it rains, I will do my best to bring to this
undertaking the same level of energy, curiosity, and passion that
Frank expressed in his life. I won't stop bitching altogether, though,
as Frank did a little of that during his life, too."

It was May 20th and the weather was breezy, sunny and cool. As soon as we left camp, we heard a coyote off in the woods; we never imagined its plaintive cry might be an omen of what was to come. There was no way of telling. Having completed a four-mile, 1,500-foot climb in record time, we stopped at the Audie Murphy Memorial. This huge, granite edifice had been erected by his friends on this Virginia hillside where the World War II flying ace and movie star died in a plane crash in 1971. The air was thick with the fragrances of spring; daffodils had sprouted up everywhere, and it was simply a glorious day to be alive. We left the memorial and walked on in silence so we were able to hear the sounds of nature awakening from their winter's sleep. In the gap at VA 620 and Trout Creek, we stopped for a long lunch and made what turned out to be a critical mistake that plagued us for the remainder of the day. In fact, so monumental was the oversight, it easily could have resulted in one, or both, of our demises. At the very least it could have brought a sudden end to our hike.

With the temperature so cool and being in a rush to get on the trail as quickly as possible after lunch, I insisted we did not need to refill our water supplies at the nearby creek. We would have plenty to last us the rest of the day. We blithely returned to our "walk through spring," reminiscing about our journey thus far and imagining what the rest of the trail held in store. We soon found out! Our pleasant walk in the woods suddenly transformed itself into a horrendous up and down scramble on the monolith called "Dragon's Tooth." The temperature had suddenly risen to a summer's day intensity, and as we neared the summit, "Mom" ran out of water.

Now, my darling wife's metabolism is such that even as we hiked in the dead of winter, her internal furnace soaked her clothes with sweat and she constantly had to fight off being cold. Whenever temperatures rose to the eighty to ninety-degree mark, this same metabolism required copious amounts of water in order to hold the effects of dehydration at bay. I, on the other hand, was generally oblivious to the onset of dehydration and rarely drank enough water. My propensity for arriving at camp with a half-full bladder constantly concerned "Mom," but this day, it could be our saving grace—we would share my water.

We talked with numerous hikers who hiked the A.T. multiple times, and they were always more than happy to warn us of the difficulties we would encounter. But in none of those warnings did anyone ever tell us about "Dragon's Tooth" and the danger associated with making our way down its precipitous face. The heat, endless climbing, and rationing of our water began to take its toll on us. We were weak and mentally floundering. We found ourselves verbally snapping at each other for no good reason and had to repeatedly remind each other we were in the same predicament. When we finally arrived at the overlook near the summit, we decided getting down off this God-forsaken mountain and finding water was more important than another view, so we bypassed the overlook approach trail and started down.

Much to our horror, on top of the physical and mental anguish of not having enough water to renew ourselves, we looked down to see nothing but a bottomless chasm of unforgiving boulders. Even though the presence of the familiar white blazes gave credence to the existence of a trail, so hidden were most of them we had to arrive at one blaze in order to see the next. Following them required us to scale down numerous headwalls, walk along rock ledges not even as wide as our feet, and then come down the face of large boulders using the metal, ladder-type handles inserted into the rocks for our use. Just the thought of having to go down this section, as tired and as thirsty as we were, brought us to the edge of insanity. Our expectations of a leisurely spring walk had been dashed. In addition to being tired and being firmly entrenched in a dehydration cycle, the weight of our packs often made it difficult to maintain our balance. We were constantly forced away from the surface of the headwalls as we were "free falling," sometimes three to four feet, from one ledge to the next.

It took us almost three hours to complete this one-mile piece of hell. We finally arrived at a flat spot where several "day-hike" trails crossed the A.T. There we took a long rest and attempted to console one another. We shared sips of water from my hydration pack, but, as we did, we heard a sound that struck terror in our souls. It was the wretched and unmistakable gurgling sound of my water bladder getting near empty. My decision not to replenish our water supply at lunch was now coming back to haunt us. A choice had to be made: do we continue on to our planned destination for the day, or do we take one of the "day hiker" trails to the road in search of water? This was a new chapter in the ongoing saga of our hike and our relationship; how we responded to what the day threw at us, as well as how we responded to each other's needs in such a stressful situation, spoke volumes about how much we cared for each other. We somewhat reluctantly chose to keep going and immediately realized, much to our disappointment, we had to go up yet another mountain to Rawie's Rest. Shuffling to the top, we tiptoed across a long knife-edge ridge with what little balance we had left, further sapping our energy.

As the sun began to give up its sovereignty over the sky, we began our merciful trip to the bottom, sharing sips of what little water we had. "Mom" was suffering the most and my consoling words, though meant to be comforting, disguised the fact I was very concerned for her health and safety. According to our *Appalachian Trail Data Book*, there was a water source and campsites at the mountain's base, near VA 624. Knowing this helped to stave off any more doubts we had about making it through the day.

It had been an aggravating day thus far, but when we arrived at VA 624, it only got worse. We could not locate water, anywhere! "Mom" sat down in a rare display of defeat as I went off to explore the area further, thinking we had simply overlooked the stream mentioned in the book. After several frustrating minutes of looking for the elusive water source that would get us out of the funk we were in, I returned to the road and admitted my failure. With this admission, our will all but dissolved. Now we had to make another decision, and based on how poor our decisions had been so far this day, we found ourselves uncharacteristically oscillating back and forth as tempers began to flair. We had the option of hitching into Catawba, where we could go to a store for some supplies and then eat dinner at The Home Place, a favorite of hikers because of its home-cooked delicacies. Or once more, we could trudge on hoping to find a campsite and another stream listed in our *Data Book*. Being obsessively pragmatic, we decided the amount of time and mileage associated with going to Catawba was equal to the time it would take to hike the next 0.9 mile to a stream with a campsite nearby. The choice seemed obvious—the campsite it would be. On top of everything else, it was beginning to get dark.

With a single-mindedness of purpose that we hoped would get us to our destination, we climbed up the hill on the north side of the road and into the vast wilderness awaiting us at the peak. We immediately found ourselves on an old forest service road that gently wound downhill through a stand of stately pines. For the first time in hours, we felt good about how the day would end. Taking the last sips of water we had left and with twilight fast approaching, we made our way down, down, down, confident water and a place to stay was near. As the distant sound of barking coonhounds cascaded through the trees, we arrived at one of the most romantic campsites we could imagine. There, passing under a wooden footbridge was a refreshing stream and next to it was an area shaded by pines that looked so peaceful the cares of the day immediately faded away. "Mom" excitedly waded in the stream and washed the visible memories of our ordeal from her body; I filled our hydration packs and washed my face and arms with my bandana. The cool water was absolute heaven. As the day turned to night, we pitched our tent, filled our stomachs, and collapsed onto our sleeping bags totally wasted.

The day had been agonizing—without a doubt, one of the most physically and emotionally demanding days we could recall. Nevertheless, the end result was that, except for a few brief angry encounters which were more the result of stress and fatigue than anything else, we cared for each other deeply all day. We shared our doubts and disappointments, consoled each other when it was necessary, apologized to each other when imperative, encouraged each other, and looked after each other with a level of concern and compassion that allowed us to persevere. The events of the day could have easily torn us apart but instead they drew us closer together. It was comforting to know the trials we faced were bringing us closer because we faced them *together*. Knowing we did not have to simply rely on the excitement and wonder of our hike to strengthen our relationship made a world of difference. We were learning to somehow embrace adversity and even looked forward to it. In less than eleven days, another encounter with the fickle weather of the A.T. would again put our relationship to a critical test.

It was now Memorial Day. Even on a cool day, conquering a 3,000-foot change in elevation over nine miles was a laborious grind. But today was an unusual day weather-wise in Virginia. Heat, humidity and the ceaseless intermediate ascents and descents comprising our pilgrimage to the top of Bald Knob wore us down very quickly. Had it not been for the trail magic we received along the way from "Expo" and "Recess," who were "back-slacking," and from trail angel/shuttle driver, Ken, at US 60, it would have been an even longer day. At Brown Mountain Shelter we stopped for a morning break. As we were refilling our hydration packs and water bottles, along came our newlywed fellow hikers, "Trickster & "What?!." This was their second attempt at thru-hiking the A.T., and this time they were better prepared, better financed, and, most importantly, married. Just by the way they looked at each other and talked about their adventure, we knew they would make it this time. The morning quietly slipped by with a leisurely excursion along a meandering stream whose gentle waters cooled the surrounding air. But, as the sound and coolness of the stream drifted off into the distance, leaving us once again to battle the oppressive humidity, we were faced with the final long journey up to the top of Bald Knob. The only blessing of our relentless walk toward the sky was that the higher we got, the cooler it became. A gentle breeze vanquished the humidity that had been suffocating us like a wet towel.

At the top of Bald Knob, we ate a relaxing lunch on the edge of the trail. A break in the trees allowed the breeze not only to cool us but also kept the flies away from our sandwiches. We wanted to stay there as long as possible to regain some of the energy we lost from the morning's climb;

however, ominous, blue/black clouds were rapidly drifting our way. The few minor sprinkles of rain that ensued made us believe we were in for nothing more than a brief spring shower, but we covered our packs just to be safe. No sooner had we completed that task than the sky turned completely black and let lose its fury. It was as if some celestial faucet had been turned on full blast. This day turned out to be just one of a total of thirty-nine days of rain we would deal with before the end of our trip.

Since it was still relatively warm and we had not had a shower in several days, we decided we could kill two birds with one stone. We chose not to put on our rain gear and simply let the rain clean our clothes and wash the sweat and other accumulated funk from our bodies. This seemed like a practical idea until a colossal clap of thunder that pounded our eardrums like the percussion of a Civil War cannon broke over our heads. Still reeling from the sound, a bolt of lightning pierced the canopy of oaks nearby and lit up the sky like a huge fluorescent light. Still on the ridgeline, we knew this was no place to be in a storm of this magnitude. The only worse place we could be was just ahead of us on the open ridgeline of Cold Mountain. Had we not lingered so long at lunch, we would have certainly been there by now. The intensity of the thunder and frequency of the lightning forced us to make an urgent decision. We had to start running and get off the mountain and to the safety of a shelter in the valley—FAST!

Attempting to run with 35-lb packs on our backs down a slick and muddy trail was likely to be a recipe for disaster, but it was our only option. Our nearest refuge, Cow Camp Gap Shelter, was still some distance away; then once we located its blue-blazed trail, we still had to travel 0.6 mile off the trail to reach it. Because the shelter was so far off the trail, this would never have been our planned destination, but now it was our nearest safe haven.

As we left the main trail and headed down the blue-blazed trail to the shelter, the intensity of the rain turned the path into a torrent of muddy water. It soaked through our boots and made every step excruciatingly slippery—and our trekking poles virtually useless. More than once, we slid precariously off logs strewn across the trail, and the rain cascading down our faces and into our eyes made it impossible to see where we were going. All the while, the lightning was getting closer, striking the ground within a stone's throw of where we were. We feared that at any moment we would feel the static charge of an impending bolt and then, subsequently, find ourselves glued to the ground by its high voltage blast. We envisioned that in its wake we would be left quivering on the ground, our feet and hair smoking. There was no time for us to discuss our dilemma or verbalize the fear overtaking us. We simply had to keep running—and fast. As the lightning and thunder closed in on us, the shelter appeared; short of having a bolt of lightning strike it as we looked on in dismay, we were home free. We sloshed through what was normally a babbling brook, now turned into a raging river by the storm, and anxiously dove into the security of the shelter.

We were alone, shaking from the cold, and then realized just how close we came to possibly being severely injured or, worse, killed. We stripped off our wet clothes and got into something dryer and warmer. We hung our wet gear on clotheslines we strung up in every conceivable location in the shelter. With no more busywork to occupy our minds, we had the chance to reflect on what we just went through. We held each other and counted our good fortune in making it there unscathed, at least physically. The remnants of the emotional turmoil of this ordeal would stay with us for quite some time. Eventually, that turmoil transformed itself into excitement. We were safe, carried here by our will to survive and our desire to see that our partner was not seriously injured.

Shortly after situating ourselves in the shelter, we decided we would stay there for the night, despite the family of mice residing there. We were certain they would bring us nothing but grief during our stay. Off in the distance, through the driving rain, came two southbound section hikers; it was another married couple named "Pooh Bear" and "Tortoise" and their two dogs, "Cinnamon" and "Gracie." Their story of riding out the storm was not as fortuitous as was ours. They told us of being caught in the fury of the storm just before getting to the exposed bald on Cold Mountain. As the lightning grew closer, they prayed for a place to take cover. Within minutes their prayers were answered and they were provided with a large rock overhang where they and their dogs would be safe and dry. The safety of their spot was short-lived as a bolt of lightning struck nearby. "Tortoise" watched the spark literally jump from her leg to "Pooh Bear's," and one of the dogs started trembling so uncontrollably, it took them some time to calm him down. As the storm subsided, they rushed over Cold Mountain and to the shelter where we all now found safety and companionship.

On the morning of July 24, we arose from a cool, but restful night's sleep, and set out to take on what would turn out to be the most onerous ten miles of trail since our days back in Georgia or the Smokies. We began the day in Connecticut by hiking along the beautiful Sawmill Brook in Sage's Ravine. Then we began the ascent and descent of a series of three very steep mountains with equally steep and rocky paths down. The first was Race Mountain (2,430 feet), and when we arrived at the summit, our climb was rewarded with views that were breathtaking, to put it mildly. In the valleys below were miles and miles of clouds, with only the very tops of the surrounding mountains pushing their way through them toward the morning sun. It was as if we were flying but our feet were still on the ground. The emotional impact of the beauty we gazed upon was quickly overshadowed by the reality of the trail down—an excursion so steep and boulder-strewn, that without the blazes painted on the rocks, we would not have had any idea which way to go—but down. We slid down, twisted between, and hung onto rock ledges with nothing more than one hand, while we searched for the next place for a hand or foot. We no sooner completed traversing this "down" than we were on our way up again—to 2,602 feet and the peak of Mt. Everett. By now the clouds had burned away, allowing us unending views of the majestic valleys and lakes below. The torment of repeatedly struggling up to mountain peaks on rock and root-strewn passageways and being continuously rewarded with mind-numbing views that defied adequate description became an emotional rollercoaster. We arrived at the tops of these mountains, physically and psychologically drained, but immediately had the fatigue washed away and forgotten by the scenic beauty below. The awe we experienced provided us with the impetus or, better yet, the burning desire to scale the next mountain as quickly as possible for our next sensory and emotional fix. We were hopelessly addicted, but what a wondrous and uplifting addiction it was!

At the summit we met Kimberly who was there evaluating the difficulty of a trip up this mountain for a group of teenage girls she and her boyfriend were considering bringing up. Her feeling was that the mountain was more than these girls could handle. Having said our goodbyes and having received our emotional fix from the panorama laid at our feet, we began another slow, grueling, and treacherous descent to the Guilder Pond picnic area. There we had lunch and took advantage of some trail magic left there. We wondered where we currently stood in the sequence of hikers still making their way north, so we stopped at both the Hemlock and the Glen Brook Lean-To. There we signed in and scoured the register pages to see who had passed through and when. We discovered that many of our friends were only days, and some only hours, ahead of us, so we headed up Mt. Bushnell (1,835 feet) and then up Jug End (1,750 feet), hoping we might catch up to them. Neither Jug End nor Mt. Bushnell are exceedingly high, but both have long, rocky, and near vertical descents that reminded us of Dragon's Tooth in Virginia.

As the shadows from the trees grew increasingly longer, our strength waned under the grueling heat and humidity. These descents became more and more dangerous, and our speed got progressively slower. We began to wonder if they would ever end. As we began the final mile down, we reflected on how glad we were we had done Bear Mountain the day before and had not included it with all of today's mountains. As it turned out, our good fortune at doing Bear Mountain the day before became even more evident as we reached what we thought was the final apex before the descent down Jug End. We began our way down cautiously, carefully picking our handholds and footholds amongst the sparse choices the mountain offered. Most of the way was nearly vertical and "Mom" chose to proceed down facing the mountain. I, on the other hand, wanted to be able to see where I might be impaled should I slip and fall, so I went down with my back against the rocks. Finally arriving at what we believed to be the last stretch of trail to Jug End Road and our meeting with "V&A," we enthusiastically envisioned the completion of another memorable day.

Horrors upon horrors! What we first thought was our way out of the woods took us to the brink of yet another vertical climb upwards—one that proved even more difficult because of our rapidly fading energy and will. Believing we were headed to Jug End Road, only to arrive at the top of another crag from which we had to scrape, crawl, and free-fall our way to the bottom, was a scenario which repeated itself for hours. After each disappointment in not reaching our destination, it became harder and harder to call up the motivation to keep going—and the obstacles in front of us seemed insurmountable. We began alternating encouragement to each other and made sure the other was physically and emotionally okay. As hot and as tired as we both were, it would have been easy for either one of us to mentally falter for a brief moment—a moment that could have disastrous results. In the back of our minds, we knew there was a silver lining to the ruthlessness of our descent. Embracing the positive outcome of the drudgery we found ourselves in would just have to wait until we physically and emotionally recovered.

In the late afternoon, after endless hours of picking our way down Jug End Mountain, we mercifully arrived at Jug End Road and met "V&A." They had opened up our hiker boxes to three A.T. south bounders, "Pyro," "B," and "Colby." As we rode back to the campground with extremely sore ankles and knees, we resigned ourselves to the fact that once we got to Vermont, New Hampshire, and Maine every day would be like today. Today had been a test of our mettle and, if nothing else, we agreed that neither one of us would want to be doing this alone. Doing it together and sharing each day, be it good or bad, was the lesson to be learned, and it left an indelible mark on our relationship. We also thanked each other for being a source of encouragement and for furnishing emotional comfort through what was a very trying day.

It was hard to believe it was already September 9th and we had less than two-hundred miles to go! Even though we never doubted we would make it, the fact we were this close to realizing our dream still seemed surreal. What a thought-provoking, eye-opening, soul-searching and undeniably fun and amazing journey it had been so far. Not unlike most other days on the A.T., we began with a steep climb—this one to the Spaulding Mountain Lean-To. Along the way, we passed a plaque affixed to a large boulder commemorating the point where the last section of the trail to be completed began. In the 1930's this final two hundred-mile section had been built, as had many other sections, by the Civilian Conservation Corps. It was our good fortune to spend most of the day hiking with "Model T" and "Ranger Dawg," and we also had the pleasure of running into "Baltimore Bill" for the first time. He was a very nice gentleman who was doing his second, and final, thru-hike of the A.T.

Standing tall against the cloudless blue sky ahead of us was Sugarloaf Mountain, atop which stands the summit house at Sugarloaf Ski Resort at 3,650 feet. Other hikers with a more flexible schedule, speedier pace, and boundless energy took the half-mile side trail to the Summit House. From there they were afforded a view hard to match anywhere else—or so we were told. Since we had a different set of priorities for the day, we passed up the trip to the summit and continued around the back side of Sugarloaf Mountain heading toward the Crocker Mountain.

At first it seemed our trek up and down Sugarloaf was going to be a wondrously uneventful trip. For quite some time, the well-groomed trail wound through the forest which was beginning to show the colorful, telltale signs of the approaching fall months. A steady breeze cooled our sweating bodies, and we found ourselves being lulled into a sense of relaxation by the genteel nature of our walk. Suddenly we were spit out into the blinding sun! There we stood, on a plunging ocean of loose, rock-strewn mayhem which had slid down from the mountain above and now stretched down into the abyss below us.

Fortunately the trail had been rerouted around the most dangerous part of this section. Periodically we left this quasi-avalanche area and wandered back into the forest only to emerge from it shortly thereafter to be faced with still more piles of rubble. Despite the detours, it remained a very steep and narrow rock walkway down to the Carrabassett River. It took us over one and a half hours to make it from the top of the mountain to the bottom, and our feet let us know they were not happy. This was the mountain where the young, male member of "The Wanderers" had fallen and broken his arm—it was easy to see how.

When we arrived at the south branch of the Carrabassett River, we walked across and above the churning water on a 2-inch by 12-inch plank which sat teetering on the tops of boulders at either end. "Mom" has never been a fan of bridges, in her car or on foot. Whenever we approached a suspension bridge on the trail, I was forbidden to take a single step onto it until she was all the way across. Therefore, the narrow gangplank that awaited us was a bit unnerving for her. For me, it was a matter of not being too cocky and falling in the river out of carelessness. We made it across without incident, though there appeared to be a few more gray hairs on both our heads when we got to the other side. As we rested and completed our afternoon snack of "Anita's A.T. Power Cookies," along came "Model T" and "Ranger Dawg" also displaying signs of the beating their legs had taken making it down to the river. They queried us as to how far we were planning to go before nightfall and then they were off, heading up the mountain to their next stop.

Every day on the trail was filled with situations requiring some type of critical decision. Today was no different. We now had to decide: should we go the short distance up the trail from the river to the Crocker Cirque Campsite or press on further to the top of South Crocker Mountain? If we chose the latter, we had only North Crocker Mountain to do the following day should it rain. However, it would make today a very long one! I promised myself I would never push "Mom" past what she could safely and comfortably do in a day's time. With her in the lead, we had stayed on schedule and kept our average daily mileage at a level that would get us to Katahdin in plenty of time. There was no need to change our routine now. I learned early on that when I mentally drifted into "The Zone," I could blindly walk until my body simply gave out and I collapsed. Because of this tendency, I would almost without exception, defer to whatever she wanted to do, and I was fine with that. So, when she said, *"Come on, we can make it to the top of South Crocker Mountain for the night,"* I agreed. By this time in our marriage and our hike, it was doubtful she was second-guessing me and suggesting we hike to South Crocker simply because she thought it was what I wanted to do. We had grown to understand each other far too well than to play head games with each other. Making it to South Crocker was how far she felt <u>she</u> could go before it got dark, so that is what we would do.

We passed "Model T" and "Ranger Dawg" at the entrance to the campsite area near Crocker Cirque, told them of our intention to press on, and expressed our hope we would see them again soon. It was now very late in the day, the sun was starting to set, and the sky was taking on the gray coat of an on-rushing storm—a storm soon confirmed by the rumble of distant thunder.

The hike to South Crocker Mountain was not a hike at all but a portentous climb. Some of it we had to do hand-over-hand, clutching at roots and small trees as a way to pull ourselves up while dragging our trekking poles behind us. We were both extremely beat up, both physically and mentally, so it was important we not withdraw into our own worlds of pain but that we share how we were feeling as a source of encouragement for each other. We had learned the best way to put your own discomfort aside was to focus on minimizing the distress of our partner. At one point I wanted to view the cirque below, so I stopped on a narrow rock shelf to take a look. I was feeling rather confident in my purchase, and foolishly discounting the fatigue I was feeling, I pulled up my poles, turned to face the valley, and stood erect—only to lose my balance. I began to fall forward! Forcing my weight backward toward the face of the mountain, I avoided a horrendous fall. Thankfully, my bride was concentrating on her own climb and did not see my chilling misstep—one that would have put her heart into her throat, as it did mine. When we were not rock climbing, our fingers now bloodied by the constant battle with sharp rocks and equally sharp roots, we were tip-toeing across the piles of boulders blanketing the face of the mountain. At the same time, we gazed at the glacial remains that formed Crocker Cirque, a mile below us. When we thought we had no strength left with which to continue, we reached the final, undemanding and soft, quarter- mile stretch of trail to the top. We were incredibly tired and the only thing that got us to the top was the desire for a shorter day tomorrow— and the fast-approaching storm.

We had been told about a single tent site that existed just off the trail at the top of South Crocker Mountain. As promised, there it was in all its pine needle-covered glory and softness. There was little time to savor our good fortune as the thunder continued to rumble and drops of rain started to fall. We quickly set up our tent and dug a trench around it to deflect the rush of water we were certain would inundate us from the hill above. We then dove inside. *(Following "Leave No Trace" principles, we did fill in the trench the next morning and left the site looking as if we had not been there.)* No sooner were we safely inside than the heavens let lose and tumultuous claps of thunder rocked the mountaintop. Unable to venture outside to cook a much-needed dinner, we huddled in the refuge of our tent and dined on an outlandish mix of pepperoni, cheese, *Nutty Buddy Bars*, GORP and slabs of dark chocolate.

As we sat in our tent and took in the wonderful fragrance of wet pine needles and damp earth, we were more content than we had been for some time. Sharing adversity and pain had created a bridge of compassion between us that never gave way to either pity or criticism. It was a miraculous day—one filled with joy, pain, anticipation, disappointment, and an undeniable sense of accomplishment. That now-familiar synthesis of conflicting feelings manifested itself in a bonding of our spirits and with it came a desire to embrace each other as if to physically share that connection. As usual, we performed our nightly foot rubs and by 6:15 p.m. were ready to fall asleep. We both wondered how we would deal with these early bedtimes once we returned home.

At some point during the night, the storm blew out and a full moon came out as if to put an exclamation point on an extraordinary day. Even the fact the temperature plummeted to 40 °F overnight did not undermine the joy of the day; comfortably enclosed in our down bags, we had one of the best night's sleeps we had in quite awhile.

It was not always triumphs over natural adversities that provoked an increased level of compassion within a couple on the trail. For "Brownie" and "Souleman," it began on their first thru-hike attempt and carried well into their successful completion the following year.

Brownie:

> "In 2005 after three and one half months of unequivocal bliss, I was forced to acknowledge an important detail I had been consciously ignoring. My feet hurt– and not in the typical thru-hiker "my feet have been trudging up and down mountains with extra weight on them" type ache. There were no blisters, no hot spots, and no sprains. I had no bruises, no bumps, and no cuts–none of the "normal" thru-hiker complaints. My feet looked fine. Nevertheless, they hurt. A visit to a doctor confirmed what I had dreaded hearing. I would have to end my hike and give my feet a chance to heal. Dejectedly I paid my bill and headed for a hotel armed with extra strength ibuprofen.
>
> "Souleman" tried to comfort me and discussed options, but, in a manner most unlike me, I stubbornly refused to deal with it. Instead, I took painkillers, settled into the bed at the hotel, and watched mindless TV shows. I talked with "Souleman" about what to eat for dinner, what to watch on TV, who to call with updates, and where our next mail drop was scheduled. <u>I talked about everything except my feet</u>. Heedless of the advice of the doctor, I was determined to press on. I had handled pain for two months. Surely, I could handle it for three and a half more. I rested for two days and then headed back out unwavering in my decision to push on toward Maine.
>
> My stubbornness took me 80 miles further up the trail; painstakingly trudging through Maryland and then through part of Pennsylvania. These were easy miles compared to the relentless PUDS (pointless ups and downs) of the earlier trail. My feet, however, took no notice of the milder terrain and hurt as much as ever. I often was reduced to limping the first few miles each day and was forced to take numerous breaks where I would massage the tender and painful ligaments in my arches and heels. I had to carefully choose each step so as not to step on a pointy rock or an errant stick. One day, during a lunch break "Souleman" asked, "Are you enjoying yourself?""

When I hesitated, he reminded me that this trip was about having fun and I shouldn't be here if I wasn't enjoying myself.

We arrived at Pine Grove Furnace State Park, a place we had been dreaming of since Springer, and settled in to wait for the ice-cream truck. This park, which is near the official halfway point of the A.T., is the location of the infamous "ice-cream challenge" in which a hiker attempts to eat a half-gallon of ice cream in half an hour or less. We had been strategizing our high-speed ice cream eating technique for months. What flavor should we choose? Do we eat it hard or let it melt? Do we wash it down with a drink?

The time of decision had arrived. "Souleman" chose Fudge Swirl and I, quite foolishly, chose Chocolate Peanut Butter Swirl. We attacked that ice cream with a vengeance—our titanium sporks shoveling scoop after scoop into our rapidly freezing mouths. I don't even remember chewing—just an unending pattern of scoop, swallow, scoop, swallow. He finished his in a daunting twenty-two minutes and waved his empty box in the air. With eight minutes still remaining, I was doubtful my stomach could hold any more lactose-infused goodness. Already I was hearing unprecedented gurgling and rumblings from within. I continued scooping the now soupy mess into my mouth and forcing it down while "Souleman," holding his "ice cream challenge" trophy, was turning green beside me. I started decorating my face with the ice cream in the hopes of diminishing the amount I had to swallow and put a dollop on my nose, streaks on my cheeks and a glob on my chin. Finally, realizing the thirty minutes had elapsed, I stopped trying to distract myself from the inevitable. I strode purposefully to the trashcan and threw away my box of ice cream with one-eighth of the ice cream still inside.

I could feel the tears threatening from behind my eyelids. Logically I knew this was only ice cream and, despite that failing at my conquest of the half-gallon was no big deal, I could not stop the burning tears from making their appearance. "Souleman" tried to console me, telling me that proportionally I had eaten at least as much as he had, but I would have none of it. I walked my ice cream-smeared-self across the street, lay down in the grass, and cried all the tears I had held back for the last 1,100 miles. I cried for all the times my feet hurt all night, for the times I couldn't stand up alone, for the times I crawled to the bathroom. I was a sticky, tearful mess, and ants crawled all over me enjoying the sweat and ice cream painted on my skin. Even blades of grass stuck to my face and arms.

"Souleman" crossed the street and sat next to me. He pulled the grass off my face and kissed my nose, which was coated with a generous portion of dried ice cream.

"I can't do it" I lamented, between sobs (you know, the kind that break your words up like inconveniently timed hiccups).

"We can try again another day," he suggested.

However, we both knew this was about more than ice cream. I thought I could be brave. I thought I could push on. I thought I would not become one of those A.T. dropout statistics. My body and my brain were at a stalemate with each one taunting the other to make the final move. "Souleman" reminded me that sometimes being brave meant making a decision you did not like.

At that instant, I knew I was done. I could make it to Maine but I would not be having fun. Moreover, as an intelligent hiker once told me, having fun is what it is all about. I suggested he continue on without me, and started to tell him how I'd send him packages and meet him along the trail. He stopped me quickly, first with the word, "No" and then by emphatically shaking his head while I sputtered through sob-studded sentences about how much fun he would have.

"No," he repeated quietly. "This is our hike. We started this and someday we will finish it—together. Maine will still be there."

Of course, I teared up again and reminded him earnestly that Maine had been there long before me and he could not give up on a dream because of some "girl." He finally put a finger to my quivering lip, silencing my protests, and said:

"You're not some girl. You're the girl I'm going to marry."

And somehow, that fact, never specifically spoken before, explained it all.

We walked away from the park, hand-in-hand, without saying goodbye to anyone. Admitting defeat to all the other hikers who were pushing on toward Mt. Katahdin would hurt too much. In addition, admitting defeat would make it all too real and then we could not change our minds. We walked away from the trail shouldering the weight of disappointment and broken dreams. Our packs had never

*felt heavier. Squeezing each other's hands, we stood by the side of the
road with tears rolling down our cheeks and stuck out our thumbs."*

Regardless of their scenic beauty and the breathtaking magnificence of
their alpine ridgelines, the White Mountains of New Hampshire are
notorious—not only for a level of difficulty that can leave even a veteran
hiker gasping for breath, but also for their unpredictable and violent
weather. On any given day, a hiker can stand at the base of the Presidential
Range, languishing in the bliss of 60 °F temperatures, but upon reaching the
apex of the first mountaintop be pounded with freezing rain that peppers his
face, hands and legs like a blast of buckshot. Knowing full well what to
expect, we were still amazed at how brutal those mountains turned out to be.

After taking two days off in North Woodstock, New Hampshire, to
wait out the rain, the folks on The Weather Channel now assured us that
today, August 21st, was going to be beautiful. We looked forward to the
rigorous climbs because we knew the sunshine would offer us the
spectacular views from the ridgelines we heard so much about. As we
entered the woods at Franconia Notch, the sun was peeking through the
overcast sky and our hope was it would burn away any clouds that would
hinder our views. The 4,250-foot climb to Franconia Ridge was tough; just
the thought of walking above tree line at its summit, and being mesmerized
with the views stretching for miles in every direction, made the time pass
quickly. What passed equally as quick was the nice weather. As we reached
the mountain's apex and saw the undulating, cairn-marked path that lay
before us across endless miles of mountaintops, the sunshine suddenly
evaporated! In its place, fog began to pass over the mountain in endless
waves. As the fog grew thicker, the horizon completely disappeared and our
ability to see what lay ahead was now limited to mere yards. With the sun
no longer anywhere in sight, and the wind gaining intensity with each
passing minute, the temperature began to plummet. Over the next hour it
nose-dived over ten degrees. Our beautiful day evaporated, and memories of
Buzzard Rock in Virginia and our close encounter with hypothermia came
rushing back. We had a long way to go—over fully exposed, treeless
ridgelines—in order to reach the safety of the Garfield Ridge Campsite. If
the weather got any worse, it would be a long and dangerous day.

The fog began to change to a menacing, heavy mist so we donned our
rain gear. We knew we would need fuel to stave off the cold that would
surely rack our bodies, so we huddled behind several large boulders and ate
a calorie-laden, though abbreviated, lunch. On went our winter hats and
gloves. We were determined to use the experience and confidence we had
gained from similar situations to guide us forward. The fog and mist were
now so heavy that at times we were unable to see the next summit until we

were already on our way up it. We had 2.3 miles to go in this meteorological soup—over Little Haystack Mountain (4,760 feet), Mt. Lincoln (5,089 feet), and Mt. Lafayette (5,249 feet), none of which we ever really saw until we were twenty to twenty-five feet away from them. Sometimes our visibility was reduced to just a few feet. The wind now increased to upwards of 30 mph, leaving us no choice but to lean our bodies at a 45-degree angle into it. We extended our trekking poles in front of us to balance ourselves on the slippery, lichen-covered boulders that paved our path. The rain, now significant, was horizontal to the ground, blown by a wind which seemed to change direction with each step. It stung our faces, so keeping our eyes open became very difficult. Our bodies were already soaked, and there was no way to tell if it was from the rain being driven through our gear or if it was simply the sweat from all the energy we were expending. Either way, we were getting very cold.

Suddenly from somewhere in the grey-green ooze enveloping Mt. Garfield, we heard a lot of noise and loud voices. As we drew closer, we saw hazy silhouettes at the top of mountain. As we began our way up, we were surprised to find a group of twenty to thirty teenage boys, a dog, and an adult leader making their way down. We stepped aside as they passed and were absolutely astonished by what we saw! They were all dressed in nothing more than cotton shorts and polo shirts, and most were wearing just sneakers. Only a few appeared to have jackets, and even fewer had backpacks. What immediately went through our minds was, *"Who in his right mind would bring a group of kids out onto this mountain dressed like that? Everyone knows the weather up here can turn lethal in a heartbeat?"* These kids still had to cover the miles we had already completed, and they had yet to see the worst of the weather. In our minds, this was a lawsuit just waiting to happen, and if they were able to make it down without one of the boys succumbing to hypothermia, we would be very surprised. We could not even imagine the fear and concern that must have been running through the minds of their parents.

Under these conditions, all we wanted to do was get off the alpine area as quickly as possible. The amazing views would have to wait for another day. But the fact we now had to make our way down a field of slick, refrigerator-sized boulders, strewn every which way, made moving quickly impossible. Our energy was quickly being diminished by our bodies' use of the calories needed to stay warm. The mental fatigue brought about by the level of concentration required to gingerly walk through this morass of slippery rock was firmly taking hold. Only the inertia of will propelled us forward.

"Are you okay?" I shouted to "Mom" over the din of the gale-force wind.

She did not reply, at first. I was not sure if it was the concentration she needed to exert in order to not fall or the loudness of the wind that kept her from hearing me.

"Hey, Babe! Are you all right?" I screamed even louder.

"Yeah, I'm okay, but let's keep moving. I am soaked and cold and just want to get to camp. How are you?"

"I've been better, but I'll make it. You let me know right away if you start having any trouble, okay?" I forcefully, though lovingly, requested.

"You do the same. We can do this. We have done it before and we have each other to count on," was her reassuring reply.

"Just be careful! This is no place to get hurt."

The fact neither of us was alone minimized the feeling of foreboding that threatened to overtake us.

Because of the rain, fog, and cloud cover, darkness was setting in earlier than usual; on top of that, we still had a steep and tortuous descent into the Garfield Campground. There was a strong possibility we would have to finish our day with headlamps on—something we had never done before. There was only one redeeming virtue of sliding down Mt. Garfield to the access trail that would take us to our home for the night—the further we got from the ridge, the less rain and fog we encountered! It felt good, even if we were still cold and exhausted. We arrived at the campground, thankfully sans headlamps, and found darn near everyone we had been hiking with over the last few weeks huddled on the shelter's platform eating dinner. What a welcome sight they all were! There sat "Rusch Hour," Treehouse," "Identity Crisis," "Yellow Belly," "Brownie & Souleman," and two hikers we had not yet met, "Route Foot" and "Ryan." The shelter was almost full to capacity; but in the first turn of good fortune we experienced all day, there were still two spots left for us. It was crowded, but having so many friends close-at-hand was heartwarming. We said hello to Shawn, the caretaker of the campsite, and then set up our gear in the shelter. Over dinner, we all shared our varied experiences of coming over the ridges and then slithered into our sleeping bags for a well-deserved rest.

As if to mock us, as soon as we were safe and sound in the shelter, the light mist that had continued to fall during dinner gave way to a clear, though still cold, evening sky filled with millions of glimmering stars. Nonetheless, the beauty of the luminescent, pitch-black sky seemed like a fitting conclusion to a very tumultuous day. "Mom" and I cuddled with our arms across each other's chest, and waves of gratitude for having each other to share the day's adventure enveloped us. The peril we escaped by relying on, looking out for, and encouraging one another was another in a long list of defining moments in the life of our hike and the reinforcement of our marriage.

This type of weather-related peril—the type that put our wills to the test, put our emotions on high alert, and brought our caring for each other to a new level—was not uncommon. Others experienced similar situations and their feelings and reactions to them were quite similar to ours.

Tag-N-Along:

"There was one potentially dangerous incident that could have had a disastrous result. We were heading up Sugarloaf Mountain on our way to the summit house because we heard it was open and the views were so spectacular. About 3:00 p.m. "Head-N-Out" stopped at a spring on the blue-blazed trail to get us water. I went on ahead to get settled in and to start preparing dinner. It had just started to rain and when I cleared the trees, I stepped out into the open and into very dense fog and very high winds. I kept my head down and looked up periodically for the blue blazes that would lead me to the summit house. This turned out to be a BIG mistake. The fog was so thick I could barely see fifty feet in front of me and I thought the wind was going to blow me over. Not knowing which way to go, I just went straight hoping to find a blue blaze that would assure me I was going the right way. I arrived at a building, which was out of the wind, but knew I could not stay there. At this point, I had no idea where to go so I began to pray for help.

I started back out and quickly found a blaze on a huge rock which reassured me I was going the right way. A bit further, I came to a fence and, looking around it, I saw another building—it was the summit house. Fighting my way through the ever-increasing fog and wind, I pulled open the heavy door and went inside. I was safe! But now the fear I once felt for myself was directed toward my husband. I had to find out if he was coming. I opened the door and hollered and, of course, he could not hear me over the ear-splitting sound of the wind. What should I do? I did not dare leave and possibly put both of our lives in danger as we staggered around, lost, in the fog. It was now raining harder and it was still very windy. My concern for Tim grew every minute. Thankfully, after about a half hour and a lot prayer, I saw him coming through the fog. My heart skipped a beat or two knowing that he was safe. He was soaked and shivering cold, so as soon as he walked in the door, I gave him some hot soup and hot chocolate to warm him up. Then he got into some dry clothes and into his sleeping bag to finish the job of shaking off the cold that was racking his body. This was the only time on the trail that we had ever been separated for any length of time, and we agreed it would be the last. I have never been as fearful for my husband's safety as I was that day."

Brownie:

"One day early on in the White Mountains, we grossly over-estimated our abilities. We ended up hiking almost seventeen miles, which is practically unheard of in the Whites. We went over Mt. Moosilauke, down the steep descent into Kinsman Notch, and then back up Mt. Wolf. Wearing our headlamps and with our hands clasped, we finally stood in front of the sign at Eliza Brook Shelter. Success! It was a fifteen plus-hour hiking day and by the end of it we could barely stand. We were so tired we did not even eat dinner. Although the day was ridiculously challenging, being together lessened the pain. We bantered back and forth about our stupidity, the awful terrain, and our hunger.

For us a horrific lightning and hailstorm, two trips to the hospital, a weeklong stomach virus, and fighting extreme heat had been among the battles we waged during our hike. I cannot think of one specific day or event that bonded us most, but I can tell you that having my husband there to support me was probably the single thing that allowed me to finish the trail. Whenever I needed encouragement or inspiration, he was there. He reminded me why I was out there and told me I could do it. The ability to share that experience was a true blessing. No one else in this world can understand the experience of our hike. Every profound moment we experienced together."

Trickster:

"It was not a good day to be hiking! And, it was definitely not a good day to be hiking in shorts with no other warm clothes on. "What?!?" and I were attempting a twenty-three-mile slack-pack but *were unprepared for the day's weather. It was, by far, the coldest day on the trail up to this point with 34 °F temperatures, rain, and a very strong wind that brought the temperature down even further. My darling husband was smart enough to bring his rain pants so he was slightly better off, but was still cold! It was not long before my bare legs were scarlet red, stinging, and numb. To keep my hands warm, I stuck them in my jacket and dragged my hiking poles behind me. We kept on hiking because generating body heat was the only way to keep warm. The cold quickly worked its magic on my bladder but, because it was so cold, I did not want to stop to go. Gritting my teeth and walking even faster, I was able to make it to mile five when I couldn't possibly hold it in anymore! After relieving myself, I discovered I was having a very hard time pulling up my shorts. My God, I couldn't feel my fingers!! I had lost all my dexterity and my fingers had become frozen, useless twigs hanging from my hands. I did manage to pull my shorts up but not without my husband's help and we were very lucky no one wandered up the trail to see the wild dance I was performing during this process. Another mile passed and we arrived at a road where there was an abandoned house sitting next to the trail. We climbed onto the covered porch to get out of the rain and had a snack. It was then that I became aware of the horrifying fact that I could not even open up a Ziploc® bag, unwrap a candy bar, or snap the clips on my backpack. "What?!" had to help me with even the smallest of tasks. After it took me a solid five minutes merely to snap my straps, we decided to ask the people in the car across the road if they would give us a ride to Damascus. The cold and rain had forced us to abandon the day's hike! I was so thankful that "What?!" was there with me to alleviate some of my fear, keep me calm, and help me when I desperately needed it."*

Once again the local weather forecasters were a mile off in their predictions for nice weather. Layers of *Gore-Tex*, with our daypacks tucked underneath, quickly covered the shorts and sleeveless shirts we put on for a supposed sunny and warm September day. Light rain and heavy fog bathed the entire mountain; by the time we exited from the trees, we were already soaked by the rain dripping from the branches overhanging the trail. With no sun visible anywhere and the wind furiously sweeping across the open plain ahead of us, the temperature was beginning to drop. Fully aware that with the descending fog there would be no views to greet us, we quickly made our way up the West Peak of Maine's Baldpate Mountain and down the pine-encased path on the other side. Only a few minutes ahead lay its sister peak, the 3,812-foot high East Peak of Baldpate. Having already successfully scaled its brother, we were confident that making our way up the east peak would pose no problems.

As we stood in the escalating mire of rain and fog, ahead were several "southbounders," appearing first as ghostly shadows, wildly sliding down the face of the mountain toward us. They were yelling and screaming, and we could not tell if they were having fun or were scared to death over their uncontrolled slide toward us. Upon reaching us, they warned of the wet conditions ahead and the ice that was beginning to develop at the higher elevations. "Mom" and I looked at each other and shared a brief moment of mutual concern. We then proceeded through the massive, tilted field of stone slabs that made up the entire surface of the trail. There was no way to go other than straight up their lichen-covered faces. Each step required two—the first, to test the footing to see if it would handle our weight without sending us hurtling down into the mist, and the second was the actual step itself. It was slow going and the tediousness of ascending the peak with our muscles constantly stretched taut in various states of balance and unbalance started to wear us down. Once up the slab field, we faced a more foreboding obstacle. From right to left and extending up into the cloud cover above us was a never-ending series of semi-horizontal slabs of rock, tilted upward at assorted angles. Each slab was approximately three to four feet thick and sat precariously, but firmly, on top of the slab below it. The ravages of time and geological changes had shifted each layer, creating narrow ledges along the joints between them. And now with the rain coming down even harder, these ledges created waterfalls that cascaded over the thin layer of ice already accumulating on them. This was going to be an extremely dangerous section to negotiate. "Mom" turned to me, gave me a reserved grin that reflected the concern she was already feeling, and we started up. The wind, now gusting upwards of 30 mph, was already chilling us to the bone.

On such a hard, slippery surface, our poles were useless, but because we were wearing our small daypacks, there was nowhere to put them. We had to hold them in one hand or the other. We had to make our way across the frozen ledges, no wider than our feet, without the use of two free hands with which to grip the rocks above. It was a constant battle to keep our footing and balance. When we boosted ourselves from the end of a ledge to the one above, more than once we nearly slipped and fell. "Mom" had the worst of it because she was the "trailblazer" and was first to test each potential route. All I had to do was follow—but not too closely because doing so generally made her pretty nervous.

Since the beginning, we made it a practice to periodically check on each other's emotional and physical condition with a simple, *"You okay?"* or *"How are you doing?"* It was a way of not only making sure our partner was not in any type of distress but also opened a line of communication should there be something that needed to be addressed. More importantly, it verbally communicated the feeling of love and caring existing between us. To ensure each other's safety, we also turned around after going over, under, or through a problematic obstacle to make sure our partner was going the safest way—and made it through successfully. Climbing East Baldpate put these practices repeatedly into play.

It seemed like I was constantly shouting, *"Are you all right?"* or *"Please be careful!"*

These questions, no matter who posed them, were never perceived as nagging or unwarranted. They were accepted with the spirit of concern with which they were asked. "Mom" had the dubious responsibility of locating safe passage for us and oftentimes had to backtrack because she was unable to find solid footing or a place to get an adequate handhold. In those circumstances she always turned to let me know what was going on.

"This spot's really slippery," "The rock I put my left foot on is loose," or *"The handhold is just off to your right."*

It was reassuring to have her in the lead and being so concerned about my safety and well-being. I think she knew I would do the same for her.

The time dragged on, and sometimes we thought we would never reach the top. But with our hearts still in our throats, we crested the final slab onto a flat area where the wind almost knocked us over. We were relieved our wet and slippery ordeal was finally over. We turned around and caught one last fleeting glimpse of where we had been before it disappeared into the fog forever. We then fell into each other's warm embrace.

Trickster:

"We set ourselves up for success by waking up bright and early this morning at 5:45 a.m.! By 6:50 a.m., we were already marching north, feeling optimistic about the day before us. We hiked the first three miles without water despite passing three "streams." The water in those streams was the color of a putrid shade of rust, dyed by all the tannic acid released by the decaying leaves that completely covered the ground. We eventually found a creek with water that was only a pale yellow, which, to our way of thinking, was a great improvement. We finally stopped to get our water. From that point on, the trail became much more challenging with a lot of climbing

and even more boulders. Our fingers were continually grasping every root in sight and our muscles strained to pull our bodies up and over the massive boulders. The boulders were really slowing us down and we didn't appreciate it one bit. Then the rain came. At first it wasn't too bad, refreshing even, but then it started to pour, making the rocks slippery and treacherous—causing us to hike even slower. Despite taking every precaution possible and even with our snail-like pace, we both still managed to have our fair share of slips and tumbles. It took us five, toilsome hours to hike the first nine miles. We were happy when there was finally a brief break from the rain. It had been a long and dangerous, albeit satisfying, morning."

Tag-N-Along:

"I remember one time I slipped on some huge boulders we were climbing down, and I landed on my back in a huge crevice. I looked like a turtle flipped over on its shell and I was unable to right myself. I yelled out to Tim to come help me because I was afraid a snake might take exception to me invading its hideout and let me know it was not happy about it. The fact that I hate snakes made the situation more terrifying. Had Tim not been there for me, I am not sure what I would have done."

"Puncheons," more commonly known as "bog bridges," span the many marshy areas on the trail. They also traverse the alpine areas above the tree line and protect the sensitive plant life from the damage created by hiking boots. These remarkably innocuous-looking specimens of engineering became a torturous and perilous hurdle for "Mom." She approached puncheons—some of which sat at bizarre angles like some W.C. Escher cartoon come to life—with more than a bit of apprehension. It did not matter if they were wet from a recent shower, covered with layers of thick, damp moss, or were simply lying there dry as a bone, like a zigzag sidewalk of fallen trees. Each posed a potentially lethal threat. Many of the puncheons, especially in the wilderness areas where minimal trail maintenance was performed (which heightened the "wilderness experience"), showed the ill effects of years of purposeful neglect. In more than one instance their presence presented more of a detriment to "Mom's" staying upright than a help. The ones half-floating in marshes and teetering like a child's seesaw presented a special challenge.

"Mom" had been on the losing end of numerous run-ins with these bastions of the trail experience and had found herself face-first and twisted in the dirt off their ends. Because of these episodes, she insisted we develop an effective method of walking these bridges to provide the best chance for her remaining upright and uninjured. The crux of this puncheon-crossing method was that I would never take a step onto a puncheon until she stepped off. This eliminated me inadvertently causing it to rock and unceremoniously throwing her to the ground. This technique was an absolute necessity, since before we honed our new method, I more than once stepped on the back of the log and launched her off the front like a human catapult. Slowing my pace and waiting for her to cross was a simple way for me to show how much I cared for her and her safety.

Despite "Mom's" best efforts to avoid the painful consequences of falling off her archenemy, it was to no avail. Having already had her share of mishaps crossing them, starting in Pennsylvania when a moss-covered and rain slick puncheon left her in a cockeyed heap with her ankle twisted and trapped between its two 2 inch x 10 foot planks, the mere sight of one slowed her to a cautious crawl. However, the "coup de grâce" came in Vermont.

With thunder approaching in the distance, we high-tailed it to Stratton Pond Shelter hoping to beat the rain that would accompany it. As we drew close to our destination, stretching before us like some huge, wooden, slithering snake was the bane of her existence. Even though it was wide and dry and she stabbed her trekking poles into the soft dirt to balance her every step, as she approached the end her foot slipped off one side and down she went.

"Oh, my God!" I cried out as I rushed to help her up. *"Are you all right?"*

My heart was in my throat because, even though I had seen her fall before, this time it looked worse than the previous times.

"I don't think so," she replied, fighting back both the pain and embarrassment of having fallen yet again. *"I think I really did it this time."*

I immediately looked down and realized why she had made such a frightening statement. Her left forearm slightly above the wrist had already begun to swell and, at first glance, it looked as if it could be broken. The first thing that went through both our minds was that this could be the end of our odyssey—foiled not by a rattlesnake bite, a dramatic fall from some cliff, or even from Lyme Disease. Our hike would be terminated by a stinking piece of lumber! However, that demoralizing thought quickly passed and my attention became focused on the pain she must be feeling and how best I could care for her. I took off her extra bandana and tied it around her swelling arm as tightly as she could endure. Then we made our way the remaining short distance to the shelter, all the while thinking her arm may be broken.

The allure of Stratton Pond Shelter is the magnificently serene lake covering acres of the mountain's summit. In the distance we heard the love songs of star-crossed frogs, and a concert of loons provided a touch of natural romance to the air. With "Mom" in a great deal of pain, we set up our camp and then headed down to the lake for a swim. The water was fresh and cool and the medicinal effect of the water on "Mom's" arm miraculously brought down the swelling. Perhaps her injury was not as bad as it first appeared, though it remained to be seen if there was any real damage.

The next morning the swelling returned, though thankfully, not to the extent of the day before. Out of empathy and a desire to ease the doubt in her mind over the extent of her injury, I posed the inevitable question:

"Do you want to go to a doctor in the next town and see if it is broken?"

With absolutely no hesitation in her voice she replied,

"What for? Even if it is broken, I am not going to stop hiking. I may as well keep on going with it just the way it is."

It was difficult for me to determine how much of her moxie was related to her inherent toughness or because she did not want to disappoint me by having to end our hike. Either way, the sense of pride I felt over her courage and determination was indescribable. My respect for her was now even greater than before. Over the next few days, the swelling, but not the periodic pain, subsided. At that moment, I had to question whether my reaction would have been the same had it happened to me. (Only much later would I find out) Off we went and over the next few days the swelling, but not the periodic pain, subsided.

Hers was not the only story of remarkable courage on the A.T. "Postcard," who thru-hiked the A.T. in 2004 and authored a book documenting his journey, was repeating the feat in 2006. In the Whites he fell and broke his arm. As soon as the doctors would allow, he had a special splint made and was back on the trail to complete his second thru-hike. Even more astonishing were the "The Wanderers." This delightful family consisted of a father, his nineteen-year-old daughter, who desired to hike the whole A.T. so she could put it in her yearbook, and her twelve-year-old brother. The son fell on Sugarloaf Mountain and broke his right arm in two places. Even so, he hiked another ten miles to the nearest road where they hitchhiked into town. They then borrowed a car and drove to a bigger town that had a hospital and qualified doctors. Because he would not quit, the boy insisted that his cast be fashioned so he could continue his hike. The insane drive to finish what they start and get to *"The Sign"* is the hallmark of A.T. thru-hikers.

With less than 200 miles to go, the inevitable finally happened. After 1,980.6 miles of flawless hiking, I finally fell. In my mind, I established a personal goal for myself—one that would set my hike apart from everyone else's. It was to complete the A.T. without ever once falling. Now my goal, as well as my ego, was shattered and my perfect hike was marred. The actual fall was nothing major compared to the distress it caused me. I just tried to climb up the face of a medium-size rock with a muddy boot and I slipped, giving my knee quite a shot. Though personally aggravated by my loss of balance, "Mom" was glad I finally took a tumble. Since I had not yet fallen, like virtually everyone else on the trail, she had become increasingly concerned that when I did fall, it would be a fall of monumental proportions. Now she felt she could rest a bit easier. However, with my streak broken, the wheels were set in motion for still more episodes of clumsiness.

Not long after my rock mishap, I found myself sitting in the waters of Long Pond Stream, pack and all, floundering like a beached whale as I tried to get up. I had attempted to rock-hop across, took a wrong step, and slipped on a rock hidden beneath some gentle rapids. Down I went, spewing out a list of demonstrably un-Christian expletives that would have made a sailor blush. Luckily, my pride took more of a beating than either my body or my gear. I looked upstream to where my bride had successfully forded—and had her camera in hand—to see a rather large grin spread across her face. To mitigate the embarrassment of my less-than-graceful dive into the water, I forced a smile onto my own face.

Believing my run of bad luck had ended, I was once again snatched back to the reality of the trail as we left the site of trail magic near Nahmakanta Lake in Maine. Somehow as we waltzed through a rather placid section of trail, I managed to locate the only branch on the trail, got it caught between both of my feet, and did a swan dive into the pine needles that covered the trail. By now, my ego could take no more and I was beside myself. "Mom," on the other hand, giggled again, though only after she was sure I was all right.

We had now made it 2,156 miles and had a measly 18.6 miles left to go! We were almost there and the excitement of being so close to Mt. Katahdin put a lilt in our step that we had not had for some time. Only one more day, and we would stand at the foot of the holy grail of thru-hiking, "The Greatest Mountain." It was an incredible day in every way, except for one potentially disastrous event.

It was the first day of fall, and in retrospect, that turned out to be ironic. Late in the afternoon we neared the Hurd Brook Lean-To where we would undoubtedly rendezvous, possibly for the last time, with a large contingent of our trail family. We approached a bend in the trail blocked by a large oak tree lying across it. Trail maintainers had yet to remove it from the path, and because it was so large, there was no visible way for us to go around it. It was suspended several feet in the air. "Mom" boosted herself up onto the top of it, swung her legs over the opposite side, and then dropped to the pile of rocks below. She accomplished this series of moves with such ease I did not give this barricade the respect it deserved. Taking "Mom's" route, I used the exact same approach to get over the tree. There was one big difference, though. When I swung my legs over and dropped down, I attempted to come down on just my right foot. Because I had severely miscalculated the distance to the rocks below, I found myself free falling, completely missing the resting place for my right foot. I came crashing down on the rocks on my right thigh with the full force of both my falling body and pack. "Burner's" prophetic statement about getting hurt so close to the end of the hike immediately flashed through my mind.

"Oh, my God!" I heard "Mom" scream, before the pain even started to settle in.

She had turned around to make sure I made it over successfully and viewed the entire, gut-wrenching event. As she raced back toward me, the pain began to run through my body like a high-voltage shock. It was the type of pain that instantaneously drained the blood from my head and turned my face as white as the clouds overhead. It caused my stomach to convulse as if I were going to vomit. As I writhed on the ground, clutching my thigh in the most intense pain I had felt since I broke my foot in a wildly flipping go-kart many years earlier, "Mom" stripped my pack from my back. Sensing I was beginning to hyperventilate to counteract the pain, she placed her calming hand on my forehead. In a motherly tone of voice, while resting my head in her lap, she urged me to relax and take slow, deep breaths. It was at that moment that I treasured her being my wife more than life itself. The fact she was there, no matter what the outcome, made everything all right.

I lay on the ground for a long time; as the initial pain subsided, "Mom" suggested I pull down my pants so she could view the damage. Our fear was I had broken my leg, and a break so high up on my femur would surely put an end to our journey. If it was broken, it had not pierced the skin. That was a good sign—but the pain was intense enough to indicate a possible internal break. I was not sure if it was the lingering pain or the thought of having to end our hike that caused my eyes to tear up.

Then thinking back to the courage she exhibited after her fall just before Stratton Pond, my own sense of determination took hold. There was no way that after all we had been through I was going to let my partner down—broken leg or no broken leg. This was not going to be an impediment to us moving forward and finishing what we started. Placing my hand on her shoulder for support, I stood up and put weight on my throbbing leg. It hurt like hell, but it did not give way. Thank God! I hobbled around for a few minutes, giving it a thorough test, and then turned to my best friend, whose face still had grave concern written all over it.

"Let's go! I need to walk this off!" I insisted through clenched teeth.

Since my pace would now be measurably slower than usual, "Mom" insisted I lead the rest of the day so we could walk at a speed comfortable for me. Shortly, the endorphins kicked in, and I was back up to a pace that had "Mom" racing to keep up. As we entered the campground at Hurd Brook Lean-To, I was feeling much better but was well aware of the fact I was going to have an extremely sore leg the rest of the hike. What was truly amazing was that despite the effects of the fall, we did one of our biggest mileage days in only eleven hours. I guess this was an example of what "Old Drum" called the *"crazy drive of the thru-hikers."* That night, as we snuggled in our tent, me with an inordinately large dose of *Advil* coursing through my veins, and "Mom" still showing visible signs of concern, it was all I could do not to break down. The gratefulness I felt for having my best friend there for me surpassed any words I could come up with to define it.

"I love you. Thanks for helping me today. I am not sure how I would have gotten through it without you there."

"You're welcome. I know you would have done the same for me. In fact, you already have, several times. Now, let's get some sleep. You need to give that leg some rest."

Vitamin "I" would be my staple food for the next several days, and I eventually ended up with a leg that was every conceivable color of yellow, blue, and purple one could imagine—from my ankle to my thigh.

Brownie:

> *"I remember that in Mahoosuc Notch I was very nervous. At one trickier than usual spot, I had to make it up a steeply inclined rock ledge underneath a huge overhang. The soles of my boots were wearing thin so, as I leaped up the incline, my shoes lost their grip. Being short, I could not reach high enough to grab onto the rock above me so I slid downward with the weight of my pack flipping me backward. I came to rest upside down in a hole on top of a bunch of pointed rocks. I missed impaling my head on a jagged rock by a mere three inches. Needless to say, I was pretty shaken and was afraid to jump in the notch after that. There were also several spots where my legs were just not long enough to span a chasm and, in "The Notch" that can be disastrous. Now, on top of everything else, I was getting worried about the darkness that was setting in and I was extremely tired. As I approached the next chasm, the fear became overwhelming and tears began to fill my eyes. "Souleman," in his special way, calmed me down with his reassuring words and then just picked me up and deposited me on the other side. His ability to literally pick me up, pack and all, saved me from more than one tear-filled situation."*

After months of overcoming so many potentially devastating events, "Mom" and I were forced to contemplate what it was that kept us going. Were we just stubborn, stupid, or just determined? Possibly it was a combination of all three! Whatever it was, short of death, there was no way we were <u>NOT</u> going to finish what we started—together. It became a moral imperative to complete the entire trail both for ourselves, individually, and for us as a couple. We simply could not, and would not, let our partner down. The respect and admiration we had for each other—plus our commitment to each other—played as compelling a role in our drive to succeed as did any other reason. *"Quitting was not an option!"*

Couples challenged and survived the Appalachian Trail and their success was dependent on courage, will, ability, resilience, compassion, and encouragement. And, as much as none of us would not want to admit, there was a considerable amount of luck involved as well. But what the couples also possessed that the solo hikers did not was a deep and abiding love for their hiking partner. Above all else, this one thing made their adventure unique and served to keep them moving toward Maine when will, ability, resilience, compassion, and encouragement simply were not enough.

Though to the outside world the physical completion of the trail was the most evident manifestation of all these traits, what was equally important, if not more so, was what conquering the trail did to our souls. For some, either married or single, there was personal growth. For others, it was a complete change in perspective on what is important in life. For a few, it was nothing more than an adventure that filled a need to simply do something different from everyone else.

For us, the effect of being on the A.T. and sharing every experience together was immeasurable—and quite frankly, sometimes emotionally overwhelming. Gone was the critical spirit that looked at everything from a perspective of black and white or right and wrong. In its place grew a desire to take things less seriously and to simplify our lives in order to make more room for our real passions—and each other. Most significantly, we developed a clearer understanding of what our marriage really meant and how important we were to each other's peace, security, and happiness. We found the strongest feelings we had for each other were not necessarily borne from how we *physically* *took care* *of each other's physical and emotional needs*. The strongest feelings took root because of how we *internally* *reacted to our spouse's response to our caring for them*. Sometimes it was in the sharing of a romantic location on a mountain where the quiet and lush surroundings inspired longing gazes into each other's eyes and the sharing of intimate feelings. And sometimes, it was in coming to the aid of our spouse in a time of physical and emotional need after an accident. Further still, it came when we joined together to survive a dangerous situation or to aid another hiker. The melding of feelings resulting from those moments profoundly affected how we felt about each other and our reactions to each other only helped our marriage grow deeper and stronger. The end result of all this was we progressed from being *"solemates"*—two people hiking together to achieve another life goal—to becoming *"soulmates."* We became a couple who were now "one," more than ever before, with a new sense of what our relationship had to offer. We became not only *"trail survivors"* but also, and most importantly, *"soul survivors."*

Through the rigors of the trail we had become "soul survivors" because we now better understood how interwoven and interdependent our lives had become. The challenge would be in allowing these changes to continue in our lives off the trail.

"Mom's" Tips for Couples:

- It takes courage for a couple to succeed at a long distance hike or anything else for that matter. Be sure your relationship is strong enough to take the challenge on before you attempt it; though it will grow even stronger on the trail;

- For a couple, the greatest fear on the trail is being afraid to express feelings of fear to your partner. Being able to communicate how you are feeling is the first step to overcoming the fear. Your partner's acceptance of that feeling is the equally important second step. Fear shared is fear overcome;

- Always work as a team to successfully meet the challenges of each day. Put your partner's health, safety, happiness, comfort, and well-being ahead of your own. At the same time, do what is best for BOTH of you;

- The trail is dangerous enough on its own. If you have to take a risk, make it a calculated one. Think first about your partner and then go with your gut;

- Fatigue increases fear and the risk of injury. Take rest breaks during the day and set realistic and achievable mileage goals;

- Trust each other explicitly;

- Constantly encourage each other. It may be the only way you can reach the next summit or walk the final mile to a shelter. It is also amazing how encouragement strengthens a relationship and bolsters your partner's self-esteem;

- Above all, display compassion. Sincerely expressing that you understand how your partner feels helps to lesson their pain or discomfort and draws you closer to each other.

CHAPTER TEN

THE GREATEST MOUNTAIN

"The bravest are surely those who have the clearest vision of what is before them, glory and danger alike, and yet notwithstanding, go out and meet it."
Pericles

When we first saw Mt. Katahdin from the shores of Rainbow Lake twenty-eight miles away, we knew the end of our quest was near, and nervous energy began to surge through our veins. A picturesque seven-mile climb brought us to Rainbow Ledges. There, through a break in the massive pines covering the mountaintop, we again viewed our mystical destination, and the legendary power of this mountain began to invade our beings. There it stood—titanic in stature, grand in scale—against a brilliant blue sky. So mammoth was its presence against the horizon we sensed it was commanding the sun, the wind, and the clouds to bow to its dominion over the surrounding landscape. At 5,280 feet, it was certainly not the tallest mountain we climbed, but the massiveness of Katahdin's brown, barren slopes dwarfed every other mountain we had been on. In our minds Mt. Katahdin relegated them to a realm of insignificance. It truly was, as Thoreau wrote, a *"permanent shadow, a massive and immovable butte on the landscape."*

Honed by glaciers over 400 million years ago, Mt. Katahdin had on its granite sides four glacial cirques: bowl-shaped, steep-sided hollows. Behind these cirques are moraines—areas of glacially accumulated debris—as well as eskers—long narrow, winding ridges of stratified sand and gravel. The raw power of this mountain initially struck us as overwhelming and foreboding; at the same time, however, the thought of walking, climbing, and crawling our way to its windblown summit became overpowering.

Over the ages, the raw power and beauty of this mountain captured the imagination of all who gazed upon it. The Penobscot Indians, a tribe indigenous to maritime Canada and the northeast, especially Maine, consider Katahdin a sacred place. Legend suggests that three great spirits inhabit the stormy mountain, including the Spirit of Katahdin, his wife, and his children. It is also said that the Spirit of Katahdin decreed that *"no Indian shall ever climb this mountain beyond where the trees and bushes grow."* Therefore, travel to the top of the mountain was considered taboo. Many Indians traveled to Katahdin to become closer to the spirits, but rarely climbed to the peak.

They also believe that an angry god, Pamola, known as the *"Storm Bird"* or the *"god of Thunder and protector of the mountain"* inhabits Pamola Peak. Because of his trickster-like behavior, he was banished for eternity to Katahdin by the highest god, Gluskab. The Indians describe Pamola as having the head of a moose, the body of a man, and the wings of an eagle. He has also been described as having *"a head and face as large as four horses, and shaped like that of a man. His body, form and feet are those of an eagle and his strength is such that he can take up a moose with one of his arrow-like claws...a hideously destructive creature."* He is both feared and respected by the Penobscots, and his presence is one of the main reasons climbing Katahdin is considered taboo. Pamola resents mortals intruding from down below.

Henry David Thoreau climbed Mt. Katahdin on a dreary day in 1846, only the eighth or ninth white person to have done so, but he did not make it to the summit. Thoreau Spring, located on The Tableland area just below the summit, bears his name. The harshness of the mountain was not lost on him; as he later wrote, he was overwhelmed by the *"primeval, untamed and forever untamable nature"* he found there. In his book, *"The Maine Woods,"* he wrote, *"The tops of mountains are among the unfinished parts of the globe, whither is a slight to the gods and pry into their secrets...Only daring and insolent men, perchance, go there. Simple races, such as savages, do not climb mountains, their tops are sacred and mysterious tracks never visited by them. Pamola is always angry with those who climb to the summit of Katahdin."*

We heard all these stories miles before we ever reached Katahdin Stream campground at Katahdin's base. Having already come this far, no myth or legend was going to undermine our determination to travel the final 5.2 miles to the top and finally conquer this trail.

At this point in our journey, we knew full well we were operating on pure adrenaline. Should it wane even the slightest bit as we scaled this sacred mountain, our beleaguered bodies would have to function purely on their own. Should that happen, we were not certain they were up to the task. To give ourselves some rest, we decided to take a zero day in Millinocket prior to attempting our summit on September 25th. As luck would have it, September 24th turned out to be a cold, rainy, and miserable day, so our decision to wait a day kept us from having to endure the additional perils of wind, ice and snow that engulfed the mountain that day. Many of our fellow hikers were not as fortunate. Either out of the need to stay to a strict schedule or because they saw challenging the mountain's unpredictable weather as a fitting way to cap off their amazing achievement of having endured so much for so long, they chose to brave the inclement weather that day. Couples like "Enuff & Too Much" and "Feng Shui & Burner" battled the rain, fog, and dropping temperatures as we sat in the warmth of our motel room. Three days later, on an equally cold and wet day, "Brownie & Souleman" completed their adventure.

On our last zero day before taking on "The Greatest Mountain," it was a strange and disconcerting feeling to be putting away our packs and gear and not to be preparing meals for the next day. No longer having to do many of the other usual things we had done on our zero days over the last six months prompted strangely uncomfortable feelings. While I caught up on our trail journal, "Mom" did laundry and prepared all our belongings so they were ready to be boxed and shipped home from the Weights and Measures office in Augusta, Maine. Our decision to summit on the 25th was important because the number twenty-five is significant in our lives, even though it is not one of "Mom's" favorite prime numbers. You see, "Mom's" birthday is on April 25th, and mine is on March 25th, which was the day we started the hike. We were engaged to be married on December 25th and our anniversary is on June 25th. It only seemed fitting we end our great adventure on September 25th—exactly six months after we began.

Equal amounts of excitement and apprehension filled both of us. We could not wait for our adventure to be over; then again, we did not want it to end. Thoughts of having to go home and face the same societal challenges we left behind began to creep uneasily into our minds. We wondered how long it would take to acclimate ourselves to our jobs and daily routines—if we ever would. We wondered if we would ever look at anything quite the same again. Being in the wilderness changed everything, and whether or not it was for better or worse still remained to be seen. For now, though, we had to concentrate on the task at hand—safely getting to the top of Mt. Katahdin and then the more dangerous job of getting down. Our growing excitement made attempting to fall sleep difficult, but six months' worth of fatigue eventually won out and we drifted off.

"Mom" was reflecting on "lasts" again. Before the hike she chronicled her feelings regarding her last week at work, her last day at work, and the last time she would drive her Jeep before parking it for six months. Now we were to the final page in our data book—all the others having been ripped out and tossed aside. Now she reflected on the many things which uniquely symbolized our time on the trail. She pondered the mixed emotions of excitement, agony, and regret that characterized the final 200 miles. She reminisced about our last night on the trail at Hurd Brook Lean-To with fellow hikers we had grown so close to and whom may never see again. She even, whimsically, lamented using a privy for the last time, and our last roll of TP in its protective *Ziploc* bag. And, even now, as we prepared for our final climb, she was already reflecting on what our last day would be like and how it would feel when we reached the summit.

She was not the only one reflecting on the end of this great adventure.

Trickster:

> *"Today we enjoyed our last zero-mileage day on the trail. Today we also enjoyed our last dinner on the trail. Today we anxiously awaited tomorrow: the day we would reach the end of our journey on the Appalachian Trail. Today also marked a very special day for "What?!" and me—our six-month anniversary as husband and wife. Six months ago we vowed in front of our family and friends to love and support each other through life's darkest valleys and highest peaks. How quickly this half year flowed past us. It seems each day came and went in just brief moments. The memories we made here on the trail, the hardships, as well as the joys, and the strength we found in one another will last far beyond Katahdin's grand peak!*
>
> *We were hesitant before our climb of Mt. Katahdin. It was as if the months that seemed so long while we were hiking to this grand end had gone by in a blur. We used up all of our savings and had just enough left to take the bus back to Trickster's family in Boston. After that we would have to return to Asheville and carve out a new life for ourselves. Our comfort was in knowing that, together, all of our questions were going to be answered.*
>
> *The summit of Mt. Katahdin would mark the end of one exciting chapter of our lives and the beginning of a new one. The coming chapter would be filled with unknowns—blank pages waiting to be filled with fresh adventures. Of course, for the next few months those adventures would be finding jobs and a place to live, rather than climbing mountains and setting up our tent beneath the night sky! It will be exciting and scary at the same time. We know that tomorrow when we touch the sign on Mt. Katahdin together tears will probably flow. We will be so happy to make it to our goal and, at the same time, so sad that we made it to our goal."*

The day we had been working toward for six months had finally come! We arrived at the foot of the mountain at 6:45 a.m. just before Baxter State Park officially opened and began our day by signing in at the ranger's office. For the record, we were listed as the 321st and 322nd hikers to take on the mighty Mt. Katahdin that year. As we donned our daypacks in the parking lot, an old hiking companion, "Catskill Eagle," greeted us. We had not seen him since Virginia because he left the trail due to an injury. He had now caught up with us and with him was his friend, "Joe Crow." Also going along to share in "Catskill Eagle's" triumph were members of his family. We traded news from the trail and then wished them luck and safety on their ascent. Our hope was they would meet us at the summit to celebrate.

This mountain, which we had seen only in our mind's eye for so many months and that we finally saw "up close and personal" over the last three days, now lay at our feet. The weather for this time of year was an uncustomary 45 °F, and the sky, crisp and cloudless, was as blue as any we had ever seen. Despite this reassuringly pleasant weather, the rangers still labeled the day as "Class II." The rains the preceding day had turned to ice on several of the other trails to the summit, closing them down. Because of these conditions, a Class I rating was out of the question. Still, it was a perfect day for a race to the top. However, we knew full well all of that could change in a matter of minutes if Pamola took exception to our being there—as it had for our friends the day before.

We said our farewells to "V&A," took a deep breath, turned to each other and shouted yet another affirmative, *"Let's Git 'er Done!"*—a phrase that had become the rallying cry of most of our trail family for the last six months. We started up the trail, still trying to grasp the fact we would climb 4,000 feet in 5.2 miles. As we had done so many times in the past when entering a section of trail that looked so ominous we wondered if we had the mettle to take it on, we simply put one foot in front of the other, verbally encouraged each other, and simply kept going. The bottom line was there was nothing else we could do and there were absolutely no legitimate excuses we could make not to finish our quest. God, we were almost to the top—to the end. It would be sacrilegious and infinitely demoralizing to give up now. There could be no consolation in saying we *almost* made it.

The beginning of the mountain was not much different from many of the other sections of trail we had already trod. It took us past the beautiful Katahdin Stream Falls. Being a lover of waterfalls, I had "Mom" take pictures of most every one we passed. However, we knew the last 10.4-mile round trip could take us up to ten hours to complete and, with the amount of available sunlight at a premium this time of year, we chose to hold off taking photos until we were safely on our way back down. Part way up the first *easy* section, our old hiking companions, "Slick-B" (still carrying two mandolins on his back), "Mule," "Lebowski," "Bofus," "Identity Crisis," and "Treehouse" all went flying by us, the adrenaline pumping. The childish grins on their faces lay bare their excitement about getting to the top.

As she had since March, "Mom" loyally led the way. We danced on the exposed rocks filling the eroded sections of the trail and sometimes had to pull ourselves up by grabbing nearby branches and roots. As the morning wore on, we began to wonder what all the fuss was about. Though steep, the trail was not as formidable as we feared it would be. We did begin to notice that the rocks were exponentially growing in size until they were comparable to that of a mini-van. We were on the Hunt Trail, the same trail taken by Charles Turner, Jr., in 1804, when he was recorded as the first person to summit Katahdin. We planned to reach the summit by the same rocks-and-roots route he took, which is now the A.T. We were as excited as we had ever been and knew we could never describe that level of excitement to anyone in a way that would capture it adequately.

Carbomb:

>   *"On the climb up Katahdin we were mostly focused on the physical aspects of the task, especially once we started using our hands. I paused from time to time to take pictures of the rapidly expanding view."*

Suddenly "Mom" and I exited from the tree-lined section of the trail onto the stark, barren, and untamed "alpine area" covering two-thirds of the mountain's peak. Immediately we were buffeted back and forth by astonishingly powerful winds that had us walking bent over so as not to be blown off the mountain. Our trekking poles, which had been useless appendages just minutes ago, were now pulled out to use as leverage against the strong gusts. We inched our way over, under, and around huge boulders adorned with white blazes—but with no definitive trail indicated. Having short legs, "Mom" located ways up other hikers did not typically take but that allowed us to use somewhat smaller strides. All the while, on either side of that narrow trail, buffered only by random alpine vegetation, was a precipitous drop with no visible bottom.

>   *"It was the worst kind of traveling,"* Thoreau wrote. *"Having slumped, scrambled, rolled, bounced, and walked, by turns, over this scraggy country,...."*

Miraculously, we were able to clamber up what at first glance appeared to be an unclimbable series of boulders. At the top, we finally were able to stand fully erect and view what we hoped would be the final run to the top. However, what we saw standing in our way was indicative of the difficulty and danger we would face in climbing the remainder of this area. The view struck fear and confusion in us right down to the soles of our feet. There, like a mammoth, granite sentry, stood a huge boulder towering six feet or more above our heads. It completely blocked the trail and any attempt to circumvent it would be impossible. On its slick face—taunting us to give up and turn back—was a solitary white blaze. There was no way to go but up its face; using the section of rebar sticking out of the front of it about twelve inches above our heads. Just to the right and leaning against the base of the boulder was one solitary rock that was a step for our right foot. However, where were we to put our left foot? The trick was for us to stand on the rock step with our right foot, grab the rebar with our left hand, and reach up until we could find a handhold for our right hand at the rear of the boulder. Then we had to boost ourselves up until we could let go of the rebar with our left hand, allowing our left foot to dangle in space, and then place our left foot on the rebar where our left hand had been. Added to that acrobatic feat was the fact that just above this boulder was a second one that overhung the first like an awning—leaving only a short space in which to place our bodies once we did pull ourselves up. Having negotiated our way to top of the first boulder, we immediately lay on our bellies and crawled to our left for several feet until we were clear of the overhang. It was a nerve-wracking and invigorating ascent. One thing tempered our excitement over making it up, however. It was the knowledge we had to come back down this boulder on our bellies feet-first. We would not be able to see the rebar and would have to blindly feel for it with our feet.

Bama:

> *"All of my feelings and emotions of joy, exhaustion, fear, awe by the beauty, the cold, the sadness at it being over, the gladness of it being over, and the terror over how I was going to climb down the mountain without killing myself were running full throttle. They sort of merged into a state of numbed shock."*

We were aware how tough this climb would be but had no idea just *how difficult and treacherous* it actually was until that moment. Second only to skydiving, it was the most frightening, yet exciting, thing I had ever undertaken. "Mom" was at a loss for words in her description of how she felt, and for "Mom," that is saying something. Both of us displayed triumphant grins, but there was no denying the trepidation lurking behind them. We vowed to keep our frazzled emotions in check for the rest of the climb and stay focused on safely reaching the summit. Our usual practice of silently walking and clairvoyantly communicating with each other gave way to constant verbal encouragement and reassuring words—words intended to quell each other's concern for our safety. However, we did repeatedly remind each other of the inevitability of our return trip with a disconcerting cry of, "*Oh, God, we have to come down this, too. This is insane.*"

At the top of this first major obstacle, we finally were able to stand fully erect, and we celebrated with "high fives. However, our jubilation was short-lived as we turned and came face-to-face with a new nemesis that made what we just climbed look like a child's *Playskool* jungle gym. Looming on the horizon was "The Gateway." This formidable pile of huge scattered boulders went almost straight up, had no recognizable trail visible on it, and seemed to go on until it disappeared into the sky above. Looking up at its summit, you got the feeling that when you arrived, there would be absolutely nothing on the other side—it was the edge of the world. Molded by millennia of ecological transformation, it had taken on the appearance of the narrow spine of some colossal, prehistoric monster. The once familiar white blazes were now intermittent, communicating only a vague idea of where the trail actually led. Each hiker was now left to his or her own devices as how best to navigate this sinister stretch of trail. The ascending ridgeline was incredibly narrow and the mountain fell off on both sides for thousands of feet. The slightest miscue would result in a rather lengthy and painful fall onto the talus in the gorges below. Again, we turned to each other and communicated with more than a touch of apprehension,

"*We have to come back down this too, you know?*"

We actually had to laugh at the absurdity of the situation—what else could we do, scream or cry?

We each took a deep breath and reassured one another we would make it, and most importantly, we would make it together. Before moving forward and having this boulder-strewn colossus fall victim to our relentless pursuit of Appalachian Trail immortality, we huddled out of the ever-present wind behind a cluster of boulders to have a snack. As we did, a lone hiker appeared over the horizon bounding toward us as if he was coming up a set of steps we somehow overlooked. He stopped only briefly, as most speed hikers do, and we chatted about the immensity of the mountain.

"*It is beautiful, isn't it? I have climbed up here at least seven times.*"

We looked at each other in disheartened disbelief as our sense of accomplishment in getting this far evaporated.

"Are you two thru-hikers?" he asked.

"We are," "Mom" said—her reply now tainted with an obvious lack of enthusiasm.
"That is amazing. I do not know how you thru-hikers do it. Congratulations, you are nearly to the top." (Oddly, he did not ask us how we were getting along.)

As he strode away, up the spine of "The Gateway," his acknowledgement of our impending achievement overshadowed our melancholy over his upstaging us with his prolific travels on this mountain. We felt good about ourselves once more and another set of "high fives" was in order. Our destiny lay only a few miles—and a few thousand boulders—ahead of us, and the overwhelming feeling of success over our impending summit caused us to embrace each other in a prolonged hug.

With our snack completed and our spirits reinvigorated, we turned north and stared down that endless heap of boulders ahead of us for a few seconds. We shouted another, *"Let's Git 'er Done!"* and began to make our way up its narrow ridgeline. Each step was an exercise in utmost concentration as we picked our way over that gargantuan pile of rubble covered with pale, lime-green lichen and rime ice. As we walked, the temptation to gaze in awe at the magnitude of the wilderness around and below us was uncontrollable, but doing so was a recipe for disaster. So, we repeatedly stopped, being sure we had firm footing and leaning on our trekking poles for balance soaked in the breathtaking views. "Mom," as she did the entire trip, documented the views with endless photographs. Everywhere we looked were lush green forests interspersed with the reds, yellows, and oranges of the fast-approaching months of fall. The crystal-clear lakes, seemingly hundreds of them, were a deep blue, reflecting the sky overhead. The only sound was the persistent wind that increasingly chilled the air the higher we climbed. We experienced an illusion of time and distance; everything below appeared so close we felt we could reach out and touch it, and at the very same time, we longed to reach up and grab a handful of sky. As we put the distant landscape into perspective with the mountain on which we stood, we felt so physically small and irrelevant that we were emotionally taken aback. Climbing this vertical obstacle course was a hauntingly exciting experience. We became thoroughly enraptured by what John Muir called the *"Majesty of the Inanimate."*

Pressing on, "Mom" gingerly led the way through areas that tested what remaining physical strength we had. Each time we arrived at a spot where there was apparently nowhere to go, a small trail would amazingly materialize. Sometimes that meant we squeezed through the crack of a huge boulder or side-stepped our way across a narrow ledge with nothing below us but air; but we finally made it to the top. With our spirits soaring, we crested the summit of "The Gateway," and there, stretching before us for what appeared to be miles in every direction, was the most unforgettable site we had ever seen. We had arrived at "The Tableland."

At 5,000 feet this vast field of rocky slabs and rugged, alpine flora looked like a science-fiction depiction of the surface of the moon—it seemed so out of place at this elevation. It caused us to wonder if this is what the world looked like before man ever stepped foot upon it. In the distance was our final ascent with the Katahdin sign appearing as a small, black speck at its vertex. In every direction we saw limitless open sky unencumbered by another imposing mountain. A calming but eerie, sense of utter isolation overtook us. It was as if we had stumbled upon some dusty mountaintop pasture, where rocks came to graze on the surrounding plants and dirt before retreating at day's end to their rightful places on the mountain's slopes. It was a bit spooky, but as Thoreau wrote, it was one of the *"unfinished parts of the globe."* Winding through that windblown field of rubble was a narrow, sandy path clearly defined by ropes that cordoned off the delicate flora lining its edges. We found ourselves totally mesmerized by this incredibly bizarre sight. It was a grandiose example of the handiwork of the Creator.

Thankfully the weather remained perfect for our ascent, though the temperature had dropped to a balmy 34 °F, and a semblance of clouds began to appear in the near distance. Our good fortune over the weather, in all of its crisp and clear splendor, was a source of great relief. It provided the additional impetus we needed to continue. We only imagined how treacherous this section would be on a day when Pamola played his cruel joke of unceasing, split-second weather changes. We could not even imagine how our fellow hikers, who summited the day before in rain, fog, and ice, had accomplished such a feat. We were dutifully impressed even if we thought they were a bit crazy in attempting it in such life-threatening conditions.

This mountain and its erratic weather are nothing to take lightly; both have earned the due respect of everyone who has ever challenged them. Having encountered the raw power of nature more than once on our journey, it was easy to understand how so many who attempted this mountain unprepared either lost their lives or had to be rescued. Thankfully, we had developed a healthy appreciation of the power of nature and developed a responsibility for being prepared for whatever might happen.

Our route still hosted the effects of the previous day's bad weather, so blanketing the sparse assemblage of alpine growth adorning the edges of our path was a thin film of rime ice. This wondrous peculiarity, native to mountain top alpine areas, glistened in the late-morning sun reflecting the sunlight like some vast array of microscopic mirrors.

Old Drum: (BJ, old Drum's wife, joined him on his summit hike)

"I think I was distracted by "BJ" being there. I wanted to be at the top with trail friends, but she could not keep up with me—and I was slow. She was so patient and I hiked right beside her the whole way up. I was worried about how she was doing. Would she make it? She was doing Katahdin in tennis shoes, with no sticks and no training. For her there was no sense of "this is the final climb." We also had a storm come in just as we were about to reach the plateau. The wind was blowing hard, rain started to come down, and we were inside a cloud so we could not see more than fifty feet in front of us. It was then that I started to think "safety." On the plateau, I became frustrated because all my hiking friends were hurrying down off the top. I would not be at the top with "Lone Star," who I camped with my first night on the trail, or "Bumblebee," who did almost all of Maine with me. "Iron Wolf" and I did the Notch together and he asked me if I would partner with him the rest of the way, to which I excitedly agreed. "Trickster and What?!" delayed their summit so they could be up there with me. "BJ," who is a minister, was going to do a wedding vow reaffirmation ceremony with them at the top. They were married on April 2, 2006, and began hiking the trail on April 4, 2006. Sadly, someone told them that we had turned back and quit the summit, so they too were coming down as we were going up."

When we first saw the rocky portal to our final and triumphant ascent from the south edge of "The Tableland," it appeared to be only a few minutes walk from where we stood. Thoroughly exhilarated by the thought of almost being "home," we stepped up our pace. The sign marking the trail's terminus was still just a microscopic silhouette on the ridgeline; but as they passed us on their way back down to the bottom, "Slick-B," "Mule," "Lebowski," "Bofus," "Identity Crisis," and "Treehouse" reassured us it was not much further. We congratulated them on completing their thru-hike and their exuberance over having done so was contagious.

On and on, for what seemed like hours, we marched across "The Tableland," constantly looking up at the approaching ridgeline for a sense of how much further we had to go. It never seemed to get closer, no matter how far or how fast we walked. It was as if every time we took a step, the summit retreated that much further away. After an interminable amount of time, there we stood at the base of our final climb—but the sign had suddenly disappeared over the horizon and out of our line of sight. "Mom" turned, gave me a jubilant smile and I, in turn, let out a *"Let's do it!"* The last two-hundred-plus feet was nothing more than a giant pile of rocks—the kind that, unless we were extremely careful, could break our ankles like twigs frozen by a bitter winter wind. Nonetheless, we threw caution to the wind, at least as much as we were comfortable in doing and quickly made our way up. At exactly 11:02 a.m. we crested the last boulder in our way. There it stood, as if out of a dream—the Katahdin sign! How could this brown, weather-beaten piece of lumber, with its white lettering barely legible after years of brutal winters, and with two small American flags waving from the top corners, elicit such a multitude of conflicted emotions?

There it was, the battered trophy of our amazing odyssey for us to embrace and treasure for the rest of our lives: *"KATAHDIN, Northern Terminus of the Appalachian Trail."* The emotion depicted in that poster on our bedroom wall, the one we had gazed at for so many years, was now coming to rest in our own souls. That sign represented the climax of six months of walking, climbing, sweating, freezing, fighting off mosquitoes, growing, reflecting, and developing relationships with some of the most incredible human beings we ever could have imagined. More importantly, "Mom" and I had done it together; that fact carried as much, if not more, significance than the completion of the trail itself. Our marriage had taken on the ultimate challenge, and aside from a few, comparatively minor lapses of understanding and compassion, it had developed into a love for each other that would epitomize our legacy. What a wonderfully intimate and enthralling feeling that was—and still is. We stood there, with our arms around each other on what felt like the roof of the world. We alternately read and re-read that sign and peered at the vistas below until both views were so etched in our memories, "Mom's" photographic journal of them became unnecessary. And, as if the magic of that moment in time was not enough, the clouds, which had grown thicker and more prevalent over the last few hours and threatened to put a damper on our enthusiasm, astonishingly split and blew to either side of us as they approached that lofty peak on which we now stood.

The excitement expanded as "Catskill Eagle," "Joe Crow," and their entourage made their way to the sign. Our joy spilled over to join with theirs, and we spent the next thirty minutes cheering, congratulating each other, reminiscing and taking photos. Always the planners, the night before in our hotel room in Millinocket, we had prepared two signs, which we held during our photo shoot. In bold black letters, one said *"Thank You"* and the other, *"Merry Christmas."* These digital remembrances were to be used on thank you cards for those who assisted us on our journey and for Christmas cards for our families and friends. After "Catskill Eagle" had taken pictures of us proudly holding these signs displayed against the background of a cobalt blue sky, he asked if he could also use the "Thank You" sign for his photos. That was a "no-brainer," and we proceeded to take an endless array of photos of his group in every conceivable combination.

Old Drum:

> *"At the summit, I teared up only a little. I was relieved. I had done the entire trail and "BJ" had done Katahdin in her tennis shoes. "BJ," "BP," and I shared "high fives" and endless photos were taken with me and the sign, me, "BJ" and the sign, "BP" and the sign, me, "BP" and the sign, and so on and so on."*

Brownie:

> *"The weather was overcast when we began at the bottom of the trail that led to Katahdin. By the time we got to the top, we were completely surrounded by fog. The wind was powerful and a cold rain made it even worse. We spent precious little time on the summit due to the miserable weather and, unfortunately, we weren't able to see a single view from the summit. We did touch the sign, however, which made the completion of our hike official. We huddled with our fellow thru-hikers behind a rock and took a moment to celebrate. The extreme wind and cold precipitation were miserable and, even though we were wearing every piece of clothing we had, we were still cold. Despite the conditions, I remember feeling complete on top of that mountain and standing on top of Katahdin together was powerful. We had been on Springer over a year before and had just met. Here we stood 18 months and 13 days later—married, on top of Katahdin. We had achieved two dreams together—marriage and our 2,000-miler status."*

Tag-N-Along:

> *"Six long months of surviving rocks, mountains, rain, and roots were finally behind us. It was a somewhat surreal moment filled with relief and an overarching feeling of great accomplishment."*

"Mom" and I decided, after our obligatory victory photos behind *"The Sign,"* with trekking poles outstretched into the wild blue yonder, that despite the euphoria of completing our adventure and our desire to make this triumphant moment last as long as possible, we needed to keep our emotions in check if we were to get back down safely. Any pent up emotions would just have to wait to spill forth until we were safely in the parking lot at the bottom of the mountain. We did not bring champagne with us to the summit with which to celebrate though the idea had crossed my mind. Our fear was the alcohol would further degenerate our haggard bodies. The libations would have to wait until later.

Trickster:

> *"We did it! Our six-month honeymoon had come to an end atop the summit of Mt. Katahdin, one day shy of six months from when we started hiking in Georgia. We cannot describe, adequately, how it feels to have completed our hike of the Appalachian Trail. We can say that there are parts of us that never wanted this experience to end, as well as parts of us that were overwhelmed by relief upon the sight of the summit sign. In some ways, it was very depressing. It was a gloomy day to begin with and the summit was completely clouded in. We were clamoring to get our pictures in but had to wait in a line of our fellow thru-hikers to do it. That was kind of stressful...trying to get that "perfect" finish photo while there were so many other people trying to do the same thing. That faded sign was in high demand! Plus...that was it for us...kind of anticlimactic, you know. We wanted to keep going and going but our journey on the Appalachian Trail had ended whether we liked it or not. We popped our champagne bottle and lit our sparklers...then we hugged and cried."*

Bama:

> *"I was very disappointed because it was too cold and windy to sit down and reflect on the past six months. Also, it was too cold and windy to pull out my food and drink. I am sure I was dehydrated, at this point. I took off my gloves to find my rock and my gloves blew*

away. I did manage to run after them before they blew off the mountain."

Robin:

> *"At the summit I felt absolute, pure joy. "Mapman" experienced a myriad of emotions and was happy, exhilarated, relieved, and a little sad to be ending such a great adventure. We both enjoyed welcoming other hikers to the summit and stayed there for two hours enjoying the excitement of seeing so many others make it."*

After spending thirty minutes on the summit and becoming a bit chilled, we started our descent which we estimated would take us about five hours to complete. On our way back across "The Tableland," we passed "Carbomb" and "Lichen," "Sumo," "Lush," "Dirt Diva," "Compass Rose," "Jukebox," and "#2" on their way up. We congratulated each other, briefly talked about how tough and scary the trip up had been, and then continued on. The pull of the summit was unimaginable, and as we made our way down we found ourselves constantly looking over our shoulders for "one last look" until it disappeared over the horizon.

Carbomb:

> *"I first felt the gravity of the situation when we reached "The Tablelands." There we met "Windtalker & Mom," who were on their way down, and they pointed to the summit. For the first time I could see the end. I knew that it was coming—but suddenly, there it was. We both wept a little as we walked.*
>
> *As we approached the summit, we could see "Catskill Eagle" and "Joe Crow" celebrating with their families. I got the camera out and filmed our final moments on the trail. I laid my hand on the sign, followed by "Lichen's" finger, "doink," and that was it. I don't remember any real gush of emotion. We got "Catskill Eagle" to take our pictures. In one picture we held up our hands triumphantly and yelled out loud. We were pretty hungry, so we sat down and ate. We brought celebratory beverages; "Lichen" had French Champagne, and I had brought my Irish Carbomb ingredients. We ended up not partaking of any of it because we were more than a little concerned about the climb down considering the difficulty we faced on the way up."*

Lichen:

> *"We stayed at the summit for about an hour, and I remember just trying to focus on savoring the feeling of being up there and enjoying our six-month accomplishment. I was awestruck by the view and we were so grateful for the beautiful weather. To me, the perfect word for how I felt about summiting was "bittersweet." It was so exciting to have accomplished our goal, but at the same time, I did not want the hike to ever end."*

Our trip down was gut-wrenchingly slow and treacherous. We spent much of our time sliding down boulders on our butts, sometimes freefalling for two to three feet before our feet hit anything solid. We did end up, inadvertently, following some faded blazes on an old part of the trail and for a brief time thought we might be lost because nothing looked familiar. Oddly enough, "Catskill Eagle" and friends were right behind us and did the same thing—an overt demonstration of "the blind leading the blind." Knowing full well that the dreaded rebar boulder still stood in our way, we all stuck together. Exemplifying the relationship that thru-hikers develop on the trail, we assisted each other in safely skidding over its blind edge until we were all safely down. After several hours, we finally found ourselves threading our way through the tree-lined section of the trail. As we passed the falls this time, we stopped to take pictures. With knees and ankles aching to the point where no amount of adrenaline could overcome the pain, we reached the sign-out sheet near the parking lot. My hands were shaking from the ecstasy of the moment, so "Mom" wrote down our historic exit time of 4:30 p.m.—what a moment of unbridled emotion that was!

Old Drum:

> *"BP" headed down the treacherous Knife Edge Trail, but we headed down the less dangerous Hunt Trail. Suddenly from out of the fog, I heard my name being called, and as we walked toward the voices, we found "Trickster & What?!" They had decided to wait for us to make sure we made it down safely; trail angels were always looking out for me. "What?!" decided that the Abol Campground Trail would be out of the wind and it was shorter than the Hunt Trail. Unfortunately, it was also steeper, and steep descents really slowed me down. Now "BJ" and I were both moving very slowly. "What?!" took our car keys and he and "Trickster" hurried quickly down the mountain out of our sight. It was just turning dark when a very tired "BJ" and I walked into Abol Campground.*

"Mom" is a rather emotionally stoic person, so for her our signing out was merely a formality documenting our achievement. If she was feeling any pent up emotions about the successful completion of our journey, she held them in check. That is not to say that, internally, she was not as elated and as overwhelmed by our accomplishment as I was. Her feelings merely manifested themselves in the broad grin and the look of total satisfaction written on her face. For me, though, the multitude of emotions associated with all those months together, sharing the good and the bad, growing, learning and cementing the bond of our marriage even more strongly than before, poured out. We fell into each other's arms and I lost it in a flood of happy and grateful tears.

I have always admired my wife for her toughness and sense of purpose and they are just two of the reasons I married her. But as we embraced at the sign-out sheet at the base of the mountain, that admiration reached an unprecedented level. All those months of watching her heroically lead us up steep precipices, climbing up rickety wooden ladders, and rushing to my aid with comfort and compassion, renewed in me a resolve to be a better husband. For her, it was a moment of quiet introspection; but the way she held my hand as we walked the final few yards of the trail, let me know that the adoration I felt for her, she also felt for me. Our marriage had reached an unforgettable milestone.

Brownie:

"Even though September 28th was the final day in our two-year journey, for me it was really just one more day in this magical adventure. As with most things in life, this trip was about the journey and not about the destination. While I was excited about reaching the top of Mt. Katahdin and the end of the trail, this was not the climax of the trip. "Souleman" and I spent only a few minutes celebrating on top of Katahdin because we knew that the real meaning of this adventure would become apparent as we reflected on all the experiences we had over the last two years. The Appalachian Trail gave me a lot over the 2,000 miles. As I practically ran back down the mountain, I reflected on all the people and experiences we shared over: the faces, the stories, the laughter, the tears, the pain, the towns, the mountains, the weather, the emotions. What an accomplishment! When we neared the bottom and had only a mile to go, we slowed our pace. "Souleman" pulled me onto a rock on the side of the trail and held my hands. "We did it, babe!" he exclaimed. We kissed and hugged and talked about the entire experience. We

discussed how proud we were of each other for finishing and supporting each other through this endeavor. We each took a few minutes to reflect and revel in the moment because we knew that when we reached the campground it was officially over. Before we got up, we talked about future dreams. Finally, knowing we had to go, we hiked the last half-mile holding hands.

Bama:

"Reaching the summit to complete this journey was like having a baby. You spend all those months getting ready and then the day comes. I guess you would call it Postpartum Depression. I enjoyed trail magic in the campground, but I was ready to go to a Bed & Breakfast. I wanted to be clean and warm, and I wanted to EAT. I felt like I was in another country and was totally alone after being with so many people for six months. It was WEIRD! I was excited about going home to my husband and house. Everything felt like a dream. So many questions filled my head. Had I really been gone for six months? Did I really hike through fourteen states? Would I ever see any of the people I met on the trail again? I had lots of questions. It was hard to put my feelings into words."

We exited the trail, hand in hand, under a canopy of leaves now fully transformed into their fall brilliance. As we emerged into the parking lot, I held my trekking poles triumphantly over my head as the warm applause and loud cheers of "V&A" and the parents of "Dirt Diva" and "Compass Rose" greeted us.

"We did it! We went six months without watching "Boston Legal," I jokingly proclaimed.

Once everyone stopped laughing, we grabbed the sandwiches and sodas "Dirt Diva's" and "Compass Rose's" parents offered us. We sat for awhile, which felt great on our knees and ankles, and briefly relived the extraordinary highlights of our day for them. We informed our hosts we had passed the girls on the way up and let them know approximately what time that had been. We bid our trip's final set of "trail angels" goodbye, profusely thanked them for the food, and then headed for the car where our own "very special trail angels" presented us with a cake. Inscribed on the top was *"Congratulations Windtalker and Mom!"* Never before had a cake brought so much emotion rushing to the surface. We thanked them and congratulated them on also completing the trail.

Old Drum:

"We arrived at Katahdin Stream Campground and I thought to myself, "Is it REALLY over?" I didn't think about it being over because, in fact, it was not over. For me, my A.T. hike was not complete yet. I felt that I still needed to go to Trail Days in Damascus, Virginia, next year and see all my hiking family to really make it complete."

Robin:

"Back at the campground, I was so excited to see my parents, who had driven all the way from St. Louis to pick us up. We could not stop sharing the fun experiences of our hike with them and, at times, had them laughing till they were crying! We also shared the wonder of the beauty of nature that had been all around us. "Mapman," as usual, was hungry and was glad to see his in-laws. I wondered if that happiness had anything to do with the fact that they had brought homemade cookies and were also going to take us out for dinner."

Tag-N-Along:

"For 2,175 miles, I had led the way, but today was special. I took hold of Tim's hand and we took the final ten steps together, side-by-side. What a feeling!! We had set a goal and had met it together. This was a day that would live forever; not only in our memories, but in our hearts as well. However, now it was back to reality and a sweet reunion with our three kids and eight grandchildren. We missed them."

Carbomb:

"We slowly made our way down. There was quite a crowd forming at the bottom because so many hikers had waited to summit on the 25th hoping that the weather would break, which it did. I still did not feel any great emotions. For me the hike ended slowly, over several months after we were "done.""

Lichen:

> *"The trail had become such a way of life for me that it didn't really feel like it was over at either the top of Mt. Katahdin or at the campground after we had made our way back down. It was definitely emotional and meaningful, though, but just not a huge welling up of emotion all at once."*

In the introduction to his book, *"The Wilderness Reader,"* Frank Bergon writes about leading students from the Adirondack Institute at Skidmore College on a ten-day backpacking trip into the wilderness area of the San Juan Mountains in Colorado. Although this trip was far from the A.T. and occurred many years ago, the reactions of the students to what they experienced were very similar to those we thru-hikers felt when climbing the mountain ranges making up the Appalachian Trail. Mt. Katahdin epitomized the character of all the mountains which went before.

> *"One person said that he had learned something about the mountains—that people who make a successful climb and are standing on a peak must simply be more happy at that moment than at other times in their lives."*

> *Another commented, 'It wasn't the mountain's hostility he felt, but its unwelcome[ness], letting him feel he didn't belong where it was unnatural for humans to be.'*

> *Still another commented, 'He hadn't felt any of those things; he just saw the climb as a challenge and he never doubted that he would succeed. But now he was scared, because he knew that what he had kept himself from feeling was the fact that he didn't belong on the mountain, rocks did, and that thought scared him because, for a moment, he did not know where he belonged.'*

> *Finally, one said, 'What affected him the most was the view of the country itself, empty of people. It made him sad to know that his grandchildren, and maybe even his children, would never have the chance to see what he had seen."*

Thankfully, because of the dedication and hard work of all the people associated with preserving the A.T. for future generations, its extinction should never become a reality.

How can we sum up our experience of climbing Mt. Katahdin? Thinking back, we would have to say:

"You always fear it and you never really conquer it. The mountain is always in charge. On a clear day, it may allow you, with its majestic benevolence, to revel in the magnificent, seemingly limitless views from its summit. Nevertheless, if it has a mind to, and it oftentimes does, it can emasculate your will with biting winds, pummel your desire with blowing snow, and cripple your body with razor-sharp ice. But, oh, how glorious it all is! You despise it, yet love what it does to your soul."

The remainder of our evening was spent at our celebratory dinner at a country-style restaurant in Millinocket. Sadly, it was the last one at which we could eat anything we wanted and as much of it as we wanted, so we made sure to savor every morsel before returning to the hotel for our last night "on the trail." We were now fully aware of the level of pain we were in, and it was more than even ibuprofen could extinguish, so we lounged in the hotel's hot tub and soaked our trail-worn bodies. It was the perfect ending to a perfect day and a perfect six months. Tomorrow we would begin our slow and relaxing train ride home where once again we would have to stare the mayhem of reality straight in the eye.

The wonder and sense of accomplishment of completing our thru-hike of the Appalachian Trail now pervaded every fiber of our beings. We loved the trail; we loved the many people who shared the adventure with us; most of all, we loved each other. Could life be any richer or sweeter?

"Mom's" Tips for Couples:

- Rely on each other in order to overcome the obstacles that lay ahead of you;

- Learn to recognize that every obstacle is a step toward obtaining your goal and relish what each obstacle teaches you;

- The very act of sharing the adventure and reaching your goal is as significant as attaining the goal itself.

CHAPTER ELEVEN

CONCLUSION or a New Beginning?

"As I look back on my life, I want to see a host of dreams fulfilled—not a list of regrets I allowed to take their place." Windtalker

Over the ages, humankind has constantly worked at developing an endless list of words to describe the people, places, feelings, and things impacting our lives. But having walked the A.T., with the wonder and grandeur of all the landscapes at our feet, and having cultivated relationships with so many people, we defy any hiker to honestly admit any of those words appropriately describe what we all saw and felt. In our minds there was only one logical way to sum it all up, and it was to say: "It was, and still is, all a God-thing."

In many ways, it was an escape for us—an escape from all but the most basic of responsibilities. With the crush of reality miles behind us, we were free to discover, or re-discover, feelings and facets of our lives long ago pushed deep into the recesses of our very beings. It was also a time to re-evaluate long-held beliefs and habits; our faith, as well, became bathed in a new perspective. We heeded the advice of Warren Doyle who suggested that we *"feel free to laugh, and to cry, and to feel lonely, and to feel afraid, and to feel socially irresponsible, and to feel foolish and (most importantly) to feel free."* We had done all of that and had hiked with passion and determination.

> *"From the summits of these mountains, some days you have beautiful views of the world around you or the clouds and fog hides them all. But every day, as you look out, you always have a new view of yourself—who you are and what you have accomplished." ("B.P." –* A.T. thru-hiker 2006)

What was inescapable was the release of emotions permeating every hour, of every day, on every mile of the trail. Being in the wilderness for so long was a type of "rehab" where all the ill effects of lives prone to adhering to the *status quo* were washed away. Birthed in their place were new understandings and feelings that would forever alter who we were and how we viewed life and each other. We not only survived, but also grew—grew in ways we never anticipated and in ways we never knew existed. Next to the birth of our children, our wedding, and the deaths of people close to us, completing this six-month adventure had a more enduring impact on us than anything we ever experienced. Each twist and turn of the trail became a turning point in our lives. Each mile on the trail translated into a moment in time when a new awareness regarding the strength of our characters, our wills, our bodies and our minds became abundantly clear. We also gained insight into what made us tick and how we would live our lives differently once we returned home.

"Old Drum" summed up many of those personal realizations in his list of *"Lessons Learned on the Trail."* They are lessons that, without a doubt, we all now embrace:

- Courage is shown in continuing, not just starting;
- I can live with less;
- I can live with pain;
- I tried being extra polite and it worked;
- I can overcome my fears;
- I can see minor changes in other people's behavior if I work at it;
- I can cope with unpleasantness;
- I need to help others;
- Procrastination is rarely helpful;
- I learned not to feel sorry for myself;
- We all need more peace;
- I learned to listen and take good advice;
- Surround myself with quality people;
- Love God;
- Love God's people;
- All people are God's people;
- Love God's world;
- Leave no trace in nature;
- Leave a positive trace in God's people;
- Don't quit;
- Take one step at a time;
- Each step is important;
- I am not alone;
- God loves me;
- I have no success by myself;

- I am special, but I am not God;
- Worry only about that which I can change;
- Worry only about today;
- Trust God—don't worry about anything;
- Keep your goal simple;
- It is O.K. to cry;
- Listen to my wife—she is wise;
- Sabbath is a really good idea;
- Rest some each day;
- Drink plenty of water;
- Work my hardest to love and understand those who irritate me the most;
- When things seem bad, be patient; something good is about to happen;
- God gives me what I need;
- The world is filled with angels;
- I daily see trail magic; do I daily see life magic?;
- Pain is a friend;
- I need to pray;
- I need to pray for others;
- Don't judge others; I am usually wrong. Just love;
- I love my wife;
- Great views come with a price;
- Life is mainly plodding;
- I will not waste life putting junk in my head;
- Patience sometimes solves problems;
- Life is best with help from others;
- There are no accidents. Everything has a purpose;
- Accept the things I cannot change;
- It is good to be immersed in recreation;
- Singing lifts my spirits;
- Being grumpy at your job is sad;
- When you get lost, go back to where you were when you were on the right path;
- Going downhill is harder than going up;
- Every need of mine has been met, is being met, and will be met;
- It is O.K. to show anger in frustration when it has no negative effect on others;
- I must always have a dream;
- I must always be working to achieve my dream.

For many, any new understanding they gained about themselves on the trail was oftentimes overshadowed by the more practical reality of having their six-month hike come to an end. The single hikers, in general, dealt with those issues more than the couples.

It was two days before reaching the base of Mt. Katahdin. "Jukebox," "Lush," "Eggshells," and "Sumo" were the last arrivals at the shelter, and as was his tradition since he started on the trail, "Lush" built a campfire where the kids all congregated, laughed, and swapped stories. As we all sat and ate, it was evident from the tone in everyone's voice that each person was excited about reaching Katahdin—and at the same time sad about reaching Katahdin. Many of them had no jobs or homes to go back to, and the only sure things they had in their lives they carried on their backs. Out here there were few decisions that had to be made each day. There was simply, *"How far would I hike," "What would I eat," "When would I eat,"* and *"When did I need to get to town to get a shower, wash clothes and get more food?"* For some returning to the real world was going to be quite overwhelming. They knew they would have to make more critical and far-reaching decisions like, *"What should I do for a living?" "Where am I going to live?" "How am I going to pay for all these things?"* And so on and so on. For those who just graduated from college, reality was now going to set in, and they did not seem sure they wanted to deal with that quite yet. The A.T. experience was a way for them to fend off the inevitable—to have time to think through all those things and plan their next "life moves." It was obvious that many were not prepared, nor were they anxious, to get on with their lives. The trail was a pretty safe place—tough and smelly, but safe."

The methods by which everyone processed the people, events, and emotions that made up their thru-hikes were as varied as the people themselves. The effect of the trail on both solo hikers and hiking couples was rife with similarities when it came to the "overall" effect it had on them. After his or her thru-hike, everyone's life would be looked at, compared to, and evaluated against the backdrop of what he or she experienced on the trail. What we saw, heard, touched, smelled, felt, and accomplished would become the yardstick by which every future experience in our lives would be measured.

Jellybean:

> *"My thru-hike was the most exhilarating time of my life. It was like being set free from jail and the freedom I felt was indescribable. I was on my own and I had to figure out my own way of doing things. I had to accept the consequences of those decisions as well. I met so many*

really neat people, and everyday there was something interesting to write about. There were really hard days, and really bad weather, bugs, and heat, but I surprised myself and hung in there. Thankfully, the good days were far more numerous. I remember singing and skipping down the trail, high on endorphins, I'm sure. I remember the anticipation of town days, with hot showers, good food, and soft beds, and the simplicity of those pleasures!

Now that I am home, it is like night and day! My life is now measured in "BK" (before Katahdin) and "AK" (after Katahdin). I'm more determined to live each day to the fullest and to not waste one single moment. Life is so precious. I think I am more selfish now, and I don't tolerate other people's negativity as well as I use to.

I had a hard time going back to work, and it took me two months to do so. Once I did, everyday I had to tell myself, "It's just till I pay off the credit card. Then I can go do it again." It took those first two months back home just to absorb all that happened in the previous five months on the trail. And I'm still absorbing it as I re-walk the trail, remembering the sights and sounds. I will always treasure the time spent there as well as the friends I made along the way. It's as if we went to war together or something!"

Bama:

"My thru-hike was the single greatest thing I have ever done. Aside from raising my children, it was also the hardest thing I have ever done. To thru-hike the A.T., you need to be self-motivated, have willpower, endurance, balance, and strength. Quitting the trail should not be an option unless you hurt yourself.

I will never forget the friendships I made on my thru–hike, and I think of all those people often. The entire trail was an emotional and physical roller coaster. Every day I felt proud, sometimes afraid, happy, sad, and thankful to be healthy enough to hike every day. My life now is very busy with spending time with my husband, family, and friends. I work in my garden every day and share flowers with neighbors. What is comforting is that I don't have to worry everyday about finding water, falling, or being afraid of storms. I also don't have to shop at Wal-Mart or Dollar General Stores for pasta and rice dinners. Despite enjoying the comforts of home and family, I do miss the trail camaraderie and the daily sense of accomplishment."

And what about some of the other couples on the trail? Were their experiences, revelations and memories similar to ours?

Mapman:

"We both learned a great deal about not needing as many material items as one believes he needs to survive in society. Over the course of the hike, the appreciation that we had for each other's contribution to our success grew and grew. We learned to pick ourselves up when we fell and just keep on hiking. Most importantly, we came to understand that if you stay calm, everything would work out eventually!"

Enuff:

"For me, personally, the hike was an exercise in patience and determination. There were great days and then there were some really bad days. It was physically demanding and the urge to stop, when things were bad, like being eaten alive by the mosquitoes in New Jersey or the days of rain and flooding in Pennsylvania, were always lingering in the back of my mind. I knew I could be out of all of that in a just few hours if I wanted to, but I learned that if you stay focused through the pain and enjoyed the good times, it was ultimately worth it. It all depended on the person, though.

What I liked the most about completing the A.T., other than putting another notch of accomplishment on the handle of my gun, so to speak, was the simplicity of life on the trail. It was all worth it for me because it was so different from our normal lives. There were some similarities in as much as we were still dealing with food, water, heat, and cold, but not the complexities of traffic, airline schedules, or money for continuing education. The simplicity was what I enjoyed and will remember the most."

Too Much:

"When I think about the A.T. class of 2006, I often think about the song, "The Long and Winding Road," which was my graduation song from nursing college. There were so many struggles, but ultimately we were all heading in the same direction. We all had different stories to tell and had different perceptions of the experience, but we all ended up at the same place. There was a bit of sadness to the journey because we knew that it was going to eventually end and we would probably never see most of our fellow-hikers again. We encountered so many wonderful people over that six months, and for me, the thought of not seeing them again brought forth a feeling of *melancholy. But, as I think about our time on the trail, a feeling of happiness returns and I find myself smiling when I remember those people and all those shared experiences. Of course, now that I am off the trail and have recovered from the physical pain that sometimes tainted my perspective, I am able to smile when I think of all the other wonderful moments."*

Not every couple came away from the trail with revelations about who they were or what state their relationship was in.

Lichen:

"Our hike did not significantly change our relationship. Rather, it simply confirmed what we already knew and felt about each other.

If one is not careful, the very excitement of completing the Appalachian Trail and the pure joy of accomplishing such a monumental feat can color your recollections of the experience. The irrefutable hardships of hunger, extreme heat and humidity, bugs, dirt, rain, pain and stinking sweat were a daily reality; allowing the excitement of the journey to put a positive spin on them made them seem more glamorous. Through all of the good days and through all of the "glamorous" bad days, there was one unshakeable truth. That truth was that, as a couple, we had the good fortune to experience the trail, and each other, in ways the single hikers were unable to do. Ways that, sometimes only in hindsight, gave our time on the A.T. such a special meaning.

Trickster:

"On April 2nd, Daniel and I were married at Amicalola State Park in Georgia and, since then, we have walked every mile together. We hiked up and down mountains, across streams, and through swamps. Together we continued walking through rain, sleet, and snow....oh, wait a minute! I guess there was never any snow on our trip!!! It sounded good though. Never the less, these last months have been the best of our lives. We encouraged each other when motivation lacked, we picked each other up, we learned from each new day. We grew closer through our shared experience and we were sure that our growth would continue long after we completed the trail in Maine.
Our six-month honeymoon had come to an end as well. Our marriage had grown so much during our time on the

trail...experiencing five years of growth in a fraction of the time. We wanted to keep going until we reached Canada!"

What?!:

"It was amazingly tough and incredibly rewarding. "Trickster" and I formed a bond not unlike that of soldiers in war. Our battle had been the elements, the mountains, the rocks, and the roots. It was a war of attrition and we survived!"

There are certain events in everyone's life that are so dramatic and so engrained in one's memory that even the slightest mention of anything remotely associated with them opens a floodgate of emotions and images. Those emotions and images allow such moments to come rushing back as if it were yesterday. Such were the moments, emotions, and memories from our thru-hike of the Appalachian Trail. It is impossible to describe the scope of what we experienced to someone who has never thru-hiked the Appalachian Trail. It is even more impossible to communicate the range and depth of emotions that accompanied those experiences. For "Mom" and me, there was simply nothing like having a partner to share every minute and every mile of the adventure. As we look back on those six incredible months, we never have to describe what we saw, what we heard, what we smelled, and how we felt. Our souls are living scrapbooks, and all we need do is just mention one of the moments on the trail and we can experience every bit of it, all over again, without saying a word.

Now the mere sight of a mountain, no matter how large or small, harkens us back to the days scaling Clingman's Dome, Max Patch Bald, and Mt. Katahdin. The heat of a summer day and the presence of tormenting mosquitoes remind us of the time we walked the perimeter of the Walkill River Wildlife Refuge wetlands. So abundant and relentless were the mosquitoes there, we nicknamed it the "Walkill Mosquito Refuge." Even sunrises and sunsets painting the sky in brilliant shades of orange, pink, and red revive our recollections of mornings in The Smokies or a quiet, romantic evening sitting on a mountaintop high above Culver Gap in New Jersey. The sight of a wide, pristine river flowing through stands of fir and dogwood trees has us musing over a similar scene on the trail and the remarkable moment that took place there comes rushing back. As we visualize those places, we recall the unexpected human interactions interwoven into the fabric of those memories.

It was September 13th, only weeks before the end of our thru-hike. On this day, two lives would intersect in an emotional and memorable way. We finished our mountain of pancakes at Harrison's Pierce Pond Cabins and bid our host, Tim Harrison, a fond farewell. It was now only three miles to one of the "milestones" of the trail—the Kennebec River. Here we would cross the river in a canoe piloted by Steve Longley who has been ferrying hikers from one side of the river to the other for many years. Some "purists" insist this river be forded—a very dangerous option. The river is extremely wide, although when we arrived, it did not appear to be very deep. The danger of walking across is that, upstream, well out of sight of where we were to paddle across, there is a hydroelectric plant with a dam. Periodically and without much advanced notice, the spillway in the dam is opened to relieve the pressure upstream. This rush of water quickly and dramatically raises the level of the water downstream to where, in the past, a hiker was caught in the rising water and drowned. To avert any similar calamities in the future, Steve's canoe became the ATC-approved method of crossing. There is even a white blaze painted on the bottom of the canoe.

Before piling into the canoe with our gear, we filled out and signed a liability waiver, holding Steve harmless should something unexpected happen on the trip across. After looking at "Mom's" trail name on her release, Steve emotionally commented on how ironic it was that he was ferrying "Mom" across the Kennebec River on this particular day. You see, on this very day, one year before, Steve's own mom had passed away and seeing "Mom's" trail name brought thoughts of his mother rushing back. What were the chances we would be at this place, on this day, and be able to share such a momentous event with someone we had just met? Looking at a river would never be the same.

Since "Mom" and I have each other with whom to daily share our remembrances of the trail, we are continually reminding each other of all the things we miss about our life there. You would think reliving those experiences would be comforting and would make living in the "real world" easier—just the opposite is true. Sometimes the emotions brought on by those recollections can be overwhelming, especially when we find ourselves being sucked into the societal chaos in which we live. Reality and our love of the trail cannot seem to peacefully coexist, and we sometimes become despondent. So, what are some of the things we miss?

- Peace and quiet and fresh air;
- A good night's sleep;
- Feeling healthy;
- Having no deadlines;
- Having no stress;
- Being able to see a sky full of stars;

- The friendliness, trust and compassion of people;
- Not having to take a shower or put on deodorant every day;
- Not being involved in what is going on in our town or the world;
- Being together 24/7;
- Not having cell phones ringing all around us or being forced to listen to other peoples' cell phone calls;
- Not having to deal with traffic and bad drivers;

And then there are the innocuous little things that pop up in our everyday life which immediately transport us back to our six months of unbridled freedom.

- There is the sound of a zipper and we remember all the nights we shared shelters with other hikers and, as we all got in our sleeping bags for the night, there was a symphony of zippers being zipped up;

- Listening to rain falling on the skylights in our bedroom takes us back to rainy nights in shelters and how the rain on the tin roofs lulled us to sleep;

- We cannot eat peanut butter and jelly on bagels without remembering all the times we sat atop a mountain or in a shaded valley and ate the very same thing for lunch; the same goes for tuna on tortillas;

- We cannot see a can of *Sunkist* soda or *A&W Root Beer* and not reminisce about all the times "V&A" provided them to us on hot summer days;

- Each time we hear the dulcet tone of the announcer for The Weather Channel as he gives the local weather report, we remember all the hours we spent in motel rooms, listening to that very same voice giving us the weather conditions that would determine whether we hiked or took a zero;

- In a motel room somewhere in New England, we saw the television advertisement for *"Head-On"* for the first time. We doubled over in laughter at how corny the sales pitch was. Now each time we hear, *"Head-On. Apply directly to the forehead,"* we are suddenly back in the trail town where we first heard it.

- And there are the other endless reminders of our grand adventure such as blueberry pancakes, the sound of trekking poles on rocks, visiting quaint country towns, mashed potatoes and gravy, *Hershey* dark chocolate bars, the sound of Native American flute and *Ziploc* bags that bring the memories rushing back.

- Every time we hear Glenn Frey's hit song, "Sunset Grille" on the radio, we remember the hot summer day in New Jersey when we hiked the beautiful, grassy ridgeline overlooking Kittatinny and Culver Lakes, eating blueberries as we went. We stopped for dinner and a beer along U.S. 206, before heading up to the Culver Gap Fire Tower where we gazed at an inspiring sunset and spent the night. The place where we stopped for dinner was The Sunset Grill.

There is virtually nothing we see, hear, taste, smell, and touch that does not have us longing for those tranquil and life-changing days on the trail.

On the A.T. we often pondered the question of how long it would take us to acclimate ourselves to our jobs and society and if we would ever look at anything quite the same again. Being on the trail had changed everything, and it remained to be seen if it was for better or worse. In a purely practical sense, we wondered if we would be able to get a good night's sleep in a bed again when we returned home. It seemed we slept much better in our sleeping bags and tent than we had in the beds at motels or B&B's. I suggested we pitch our tent in our bedroom for a few weeks and make a slow transition.

Unfortunately the day after we arrived back home, "Mom" found out about the trail's effect on her ability to work. She was immediately thrown back into the same old routine. Despite her passion for what she does, there were the relentless demands on her time and a need to constantly multi-task while making unending decisions critical to the success of her program. Her talent in single-mindedly focusing on the task at hand was noticeably compromised. In addition, her ability to handle noise in her office was apparent on her first day back when a colleague walked by her office and said, *"Welcome back."* She nearly jumped out of her skin as he laughed about adapting to noise.

I arrived home to find my leave of absence was now permanent. For the first time in my life, I was unemployed. "Mom" reassured me that financially we were fine and my income was, at least for now, not critical to our survival. Upon her insistence, I fought off my genetic disposition to always having a paycheck. I devoted all my new-found, free time to completing a Native American flute CD I had been composing and recording for the previous two years. I also found more time to devote to doing live sound for concerts. As a small concession to my need to have a "real job" and to capitalize on my backpacking experience, I got a part-time job at a local outfitter. The rest of the time, I worked on this book and took care of many household responsibilities so we would have time together when "Mom" got home from work. This new arrangement, though unusual and one "Mom" still goes back and forth about being happy with, has worked rather well. There was one additional benefit of my coming home and finding I was unexpectedly unemployed; now I often travel with her on her work assignments so we can share other great adventures together.

Zan:

> *"Life after the trail has taken a bit of adjusting. It has been difficult slotting back into study, work, friends, and family. Every day we think about the experiences we had on the trail, the people we met, and the people we have become. We remain close friends and are lucky enough to have each other with which to share these memories. At times it is difficult to explain to non-thru-hikers about the characters we met, how generous and selfless people were, and that two weeks without a shower is indeed possible."*

When we began our journey, we knew there would be situations that would physically test us. We were also aware those very same situations would undoubtedly conjure up emotional responses we may be more than timid about exposing. This was a risk we were willing to take; ultimately, the results of such a gamble were extremely rewarding.

So what did we learn about ourselves and each other on the trail? For me, who unceasingly suffers from bouts of low self-esteem, conquering the trials of each day provided me with the constant positive reinforcement I needed. By the time the hike was over, I had gained a level of self-worth I had not had for many years. How liberating it was. I discovered my physical and mental ability to overcome obstacles was more than I ever imagined, and my will to succeed found renewed strength. My hope was these realizations would not be fleeting and I could sustain them in "the real world."

I also found I was now more in touch with what my body was doing and how it was feeling. I gained a better awareness of the interaction of muscles and tendons, especially in my legs and feet. Proper diet and nutrition became my new mantra because I had seen their positive effects on my physical and mental health. Weighing heavily on both of us was the reality that, when we got home, we could no longer eat as we had on the trail. This would be the most difficult thing to deal with, especially when half of a big *Hershey's Dark Chocolate Bar* every night for dessert had been a treat we looked forward to having.

I came to enjoy peace and quiet, and I relished every moment of it I could find. After so many years of living within the din of rock music, race car exhaust, and anything else keeping me from having to listen to myself, being able to have moments of peaceful introspection was invigorating—though at first, strange. Now my intolerance for noise, and equally as much for crowds, immediately raises my stress to very uncomfortable levels.

As for our relationship, the hike brought with it moments for marital growth and understanding that could never be found in our "normal" lives. Those moments brought with them development that was both obvious and subtle. All of them would have a lasting effect on how we related to each other for years to come.

For example, though, "Mom" initially spoke of her doubt regarding whether or not her physical condition would hinder her ability to complete our dream. However, it was rare that I saw such doubt manifested in her behavior on the trail. Sure, there were days when she let me know her feet and legs hurt, but her will to endure was always the victor. What I discovered for the first time, and it endeared me to her in a way I had never experienced before, were her moments of fear. I had never seen this in her before. Her fear or, more correctly, her concern over slipping, falling, and being severely injured was ever-present. Because she was so self-assured, this minor chink in her emotional armor gave me an opportunity to connect with her in a deep way. She needed me as a compassionate buffer against those concerns which resulted in a new and powerful emotional facet in our relationship.

Her level of compassion for me—for what I was feeling and for what I was thinking—really blossomed. Not a day went by when she did not ask me how I was doing. The regard she constantly carried with her about my well-being was as much "motherly" as it was "wifely." When we began this journey, we had already been married for fourteen years. We care deeply for each other and look at our relationship, in many respects, as if we are friends—best friends. Without question, we are, but now we believe, above all else, that what our relationship experienced by thru-hiking the A.T. was that our marriage came to the forefront and our friendship more subtly blended in.

"Mom's" job requires she spend an inordinate amount of time traveling. Over the last seventeen years she has visited every state in the United States—many of them multiple times. Initially, her being away was simply a disruption of our life together that we accepted. But now, having been together every hour, every day, for six months, those days away from home have become increasingly traumatic for both of us. Adjusting to her being away now means that when she is home, we spend as many moments together as is humanly possible. We may do something as mundane as making a bowl of popcorn and watching a video on a Friday evening. Or we might simply go out to our favorite restaurant and wile away the hours talking, reminiscing, or planning our next big adventure. Whatever we choose, each moment reinforces the new bond we developed on the trail. The bottom line is we now hate being apart. It is as if we are not "complete" unless we are sharing every moment together.

Aside from the obvious, what else did hiking the A.T. together teach "Mom" and me? What little scraps of wisdom did we accumulate that would guide us, both personally and as a couple, from this day forward?

From a hiking perspective, we learned one cannot <u>totally</u> prepare for hiking the A.T. You can only prepare yourself to be able to adapt to and handle what the trail throws at you each day. Life and marriage is no different and applying the precepts we learned on the trail make living life as husband and wife a refreshingly wonderful journey of discovery and triumph. We experienced daily lessons in perseverance. When we thought we could not take another step, we took one anyway, and then one more, and one more. Before we knew it, we were where we were <u>supposed to be</u>, though not always where we <u>wanted to be</u>. Understanding and accepting the difference became important and liberating.

Every mountain we conquered prepared us for the next one. We reached a point where we looked forward to the next challenge because we knew that with each successful summit we would gain the experience and confidence to make it to the top of the next mountain. Whether or not the mountain allowed us to succeed was another question, but we would not fail for lack of trying. Our relationship could not help but benefit from such a new mindset.

As we drew closer to Mt. Katahdin, we discovered a distinct difference between confidence and egotism. Confidence was built each day in meeting what the trail presented to us. It built upon the success of the previous day and in knowing we had the ability to make it to the next shelter or town. Egotism on the trail, as it is in life, was a recipe for disaster. It put excessive belief in one's own talents or achievements before the fact that the trail and weather were in control; conceit and self-importance were a twisted ankle or broken leg just waiting to happen. We came to understand that wisdom does not mean you have all the answers, but you know when to ask the right questions.

We would slow down our lives. Walking everywhere with thirty-five pounds on your back can do that to you. The trail forced us to measure the length and importance of each day, in miles, feet, and steps. Success was measured by the journey itself and where we ended each day was of little consequence. No longer would we measure our days in hours, minutes, and seconds. Our focus would no longer be on reaching a predetermined goal before time ran out. The focus would be on the wonder along the way.

The more time we spent on the trail and were able to view the negative effects of "progress" on the wilderness, the more it became apparent that our environment and, therefore, our very existence, are under attack. There was unmistakable evidence of encroaching development, pollution, acid rain, and invasive species. Man's belief that exploiting the resources of mother earth is not a "zero-sum" game will eventually culminate in our extinction. Unless we take drastic measures to ensure the longevity of the planet we live on and cultivate a philosophy of peaceful coexistence with nature, man will ultimately become nothing more than a blip in the cycle of the universe.

Pastor Delbert Young of Lifegate Ministries in Lafayette, Georgia, once stated, *"We buy things we do not need, with money we do not have, to impress people we do not like."* As did "Mapman & Robin," we discovered life was pretty complete and satisfyingly simple with just what we had on our backs. When we arrived home, we began getting rid of "stuff" that no longer held any lasting significance but simply collected dust and took up space. People tend to accumulate "stuff" in direct proportion to how much room they have in which to store it. Backpacks are small and efficient, so what we "accumulated" in them was honed down to the basic necessities. Perhaps we would even look at moving into a smaller house with less room to keep "stuff."

On our way to the base of MT. Katahdin, we passed the many bogs and ponds in Baxter State Park—our last chance to succeed at our quest for a "Bullwinkle Experience." Unfortunately, we failed. However, we saw "Cohiba" walking southbound with his wife so he could finish the last piece of his thru-hike. We stopped and chatted for a while. His wife asked us the proverbial question that had been asked of us more times than we could count by folks along the trail:

"So, how are you getting along? Are you still talking to each other?"

Our reply was, as it had been since our first day on the trail,

"Our marriage is stronger now than it has ever been. We have had to rely heavily on each other for moral and physical support, encouragement and, sometimes, even sympathy. That has made all the difference in the world for us."

That was the profound truth. Sure, we sometimes went hours without saying a word to each other; but when it became necessary, one of us always said what needed to be said. We admit to our share of less-than-loving moments, but there were far fewer of them than when we were at home, and on the trail they were short-lived. When it was 90 °F and the mosquitoes were eating us alive, when we were thirsty, tired, and our feet hurt, yes, we got a bit testy and said some things that did not come out quite right—like any normal person. The difference out there was that the other person was experiencing the same things, so a level of understanding and empathy developed that is not often achieved the real world. So exhilarating was that feeling, we vowed to carry it back home with us to our "other life."

There is a significant difference between thru-hiking the A.T. as a solo hiker and as a married couple. As a solo hiker, the outcome of your hike is purely a personal one. If you succeed, though you can communicate to others your sense of accomplishment, how you felt inside and the lasting emotional effects the hike had on you are purely your own—and if you fail, you have only your own sense of failure to deal with. For couples, the results are very different. Success is a shared event that affects how you relate to each other. Failure affects not only yourself, but your partner, and that failure can easily create a relational chasm which influences how you interact for years to come.

So what was the bottom line to this remarkable journey? Would our lives and the life of our marriage be as strong had we never backpacked together? Possibly—but highly unlikely. What happened to our souls cannot be created by some other deliberate, structured, and safe attempt to do so. It cannot be found in a week-long vacation at some romantic hideaway, sipping drinks with umbrellas in them. Nor, can it be purchased at the local shopping mall or online store, or discovered through a weekend marriage retreat. It cannot even be recreated on the couch of a well-meaning, if overly paid, marriage counselor. We know this, because we have done them all.

Our adventure was truly unique, powerful, and unquestionably eternal in its repercussions. It was different, it was dangerous, it was awe-inspiring, and it was way outside our comfort level. It challenged everything we believed about ourselves, our relationship, and the state of our marriage. It offered no place to hide, either physically or emotionally, and therefore required that every moment be faced head-on at that moment and be dealt with. What a frightening, liberating trip it was! To be able to end each day knowing everything that needed to be said, had been said, was wonderful. To purposefully resolve every dispute or miscommunication brought us closer together, because not doing so put our existence in the wilderness, if not our very lives, in peril. To willingly lay every card on the table and have them graciously accepted by your spouse, opened up avenues of communication and understanding that can seldom be found elsewhere. Ours was an adventure we have never regretted taking because it put us on a new "trail" of life—full of peace, wonder, and anticipation. David Roberts, in commenting on his summit of Alaska's Mount Huntington, summed up the real mystic of hiking the A.T. He said,

> *"We found no answers to life but perhaps only the room in which to look for them."*

It was more than just a dream-fulfilling odyssey. It was classroom of sorts where we learned more in six months about life, love and human interactions than we ever imagined possible. From it came a renewed passion to pursue everything life has to offer and to daily dedicate ourselves to the growth of ourselves and our marriage.

What other activity can a couple share that delivers such life-altering and marriage-strengthening results? What activity can bring two people closer together than they ever imagined possible because they have only each other to depend on and support? For us it was many years of living and growing as a couple compressed into six months' worth of being together 24/7. Yes, backpacking as a couple is fraught with risks, but the greater the risks, the greater the rewards. We are now not only older but infinitely wiser, more experienced, and more confident we can overcome life's challenges—*together*. Successfully thru-hiking the Appalachian Trail, or any other long-distance trail together can prepare a couple for the challenges that wait in the years ahead. The strength of their relationship will better prepare them to:

- Overcome the pain and loss of a loved one;

- Support one another through a battle with breast or prostate cancer;

- Build a house together;

- Raise a family together.

All of this strength comes from the simple fact they spent six months of their lives backpacking. And imagine not having to pay for a gym membership to stay in shape! How cool is that?

From the very beginning, before one boot ever hit the Appalachian Trail, we knew we could, and would, succeed at making it from Georgia to Maine. That being said, we are still totally and absolutely amazed we did. Each time we revisit the A.T. for a day hike, we gaze at the short stretch of trail just ahead of us and cannot believe that what we are seeing was repeated thousands of times on our 2,175-mile journey—and we had walked it all. It still takes our breath away and brings a smile to our faces! Would we ever do it again? Maybe—though probably not. There are simply too many other trails we want to hike. However, we are thinking about taking an extended vacation in 2016 and revisit some of the most memorable places along the trail as part of our own *"A.T. Thru-Hike 10-Year Anniversary Celebration."*

In July 2007 we traveled back to Vermont and spent a week backpacking The Long Trail from Killington to Waitsfield in our continuing quest to also complete this 275-mile long trail in sections. It was in Waitsfield that we decided it would be more enjoyable to provide trail support to other Long Trail "end-to-enders," like "Quoddy," so we shortened our trip and did just that. The 1st Annual Long Trail Festival was being held in Rutland, so we attended, heard some great speakers and music, and even gave a talk of our own entitled *"Eating Well on the Trail."* When the itch to get back on the trail gnawed at us, we did some day hikes, such as along the ridgeline of Mt. Mansfield. We even drove north to Troy, Vermont, hiked to the northern terminus of The Long Trail, in Canada, and stayed the night with "Low Impact" and "Backtrack" at Journey's End Camp #2. We ended up giving both of them a ride to Burlington, Vermont, so they could head home. The real highlight of the week was that, on a road near Canaan, Vermont, home of the annual Vermont Moose Festival, we saw our first MOOSE—walking right down the middle of the road toward us! Our "moose conspiracy" theory had finally been dispelled!

We have spent time hiking in the El Yunque rain forest in Puerto Rico and up to Fern Lake on the Fern Lake Trail in Rocky Mountain National Park. Our old A.T. hiking buddy, "Eel" and his wife, Cathy, took us on a magnificent day hike past Bridal Veil Falls and up to Lake Serene in Washington State. Up until 2007, Hawaii was the only state "Mom" had not visited on business, so when the chance came to go there, we jumped at it. We did some kayaking, hiked along Waimea Canyon, the "Grand Canyon of the Pacific," and up to Pihea Peak, the rainiest place on the planet with over 431 inches of annual rainfall. Hiking the A.T. in the rain in Pennsylvania had nothing on this place. One of our favorite places in the world is Arizona, so in 2007, while there spending Christmas with family, we took the opportunity to hike to the top of Bear Mountain in the Red Rock/Secret Wilderness Area just outside Sedona. And closer to home, we finally hiked to the top of Old Rag near Shenandoah National Park. "Mom" also spent several weeks on a business trip to South Africa and the U.K. but, unfortunately I was unable to travel with her. She had the unique opportunity of going on a safari in the Pilanesberg National Park north of Johannesburg. She did not see any moose, but there were plenty of lions, elephants, giraffes, zebras, hippos, and wildebeest.

If you are wondering, we do stay at home sometimes and do things other than hike and camp. With our daughter's wedding is coming up, we went ahead with one of the other things on our "life list" in order to prepare for it; we took ballroom dancing lessons. One of the benefits of having to dance across the endless rocks on the A.T. in Pennsylvania was that it got us ready for the foxtrot, the waltz, and swing dancing.

What is life now like for the others chronicled in this book? By in large, all of them continue to hike as often as possible and, though most of them have returned to somewhat "normal" lives, the impact of their adventure on their lives is inescapable. We stay in touch with most of them and get together at Trail Days in Damascus, Virginia, each year to reminisce.

In 2007 "Bama" was back section-hiking the A.T. in Georgia and North Carolina and she and Bill, her husband, also hiked a few miles on the Pinhoti Trail in Alabama. Bill frequently travels for his job, so she goes with him every chance she can. Her travels have taken her to Nebraska three times in one year where she visited with her daughter and granddaughters and to Florida where she spent time with her son and his wife. She is thoroughly enjoying being a grandmother. She is considering hiking the Pacific Crest Trail in 2009, after she talks with "Old Drum" and "Mapman & Robin" about their 2008 P.C.T. adventure.

"I am either hiking or traveling. When I am home I am gardening and walking on the walking track near my home."

"Mapman & Robin" have been busy caring for their "new," one-year-old grandchild and giving numerous presentations on their A.T. trip to school groups, senior citizens dinner groups, and to interested friends. They continue to hike, backpack, and travel. When they are at home, they are very involved in their church and substitute teach at a local private school. In 2007 and early 2008 they spent a great deal of time preparing for their 2008 Pacific Crest Trail thru-hike. When we spoke with them last, they had just returned from a four-day P.C.T. shakedown hike with "Old Drum & BJ."

By all accounts, "Jellybean" spends as much, if not more, time in the outdoors than the rest of us combined. Her job as a long-haul truck driver is merely a way to finance her adventures, which is not a bad way to live. Over the last several years, in between trucking runs, she has gone canyoneering in Zion National Park, hiked the Wild Olympic Coast, visited the hot springs in Oregon, and did a bit of gold mining. She also spent nine days in the desert area of the Superstition Mountains, went fishing in Colorado, elk hunting in Washington, and did cattle ranching in Oregon and rock climbing—mostly in Arizona. Itching for another long-distance hike, in 2008 she took on the Pacific Crest Trail.

"It's a rough life, but someone has to do it! What's next for me? I still have a dream of living on a sailboat and sailing the seven seas. I don't have a clue how to get there but that doesn't stop the yearning!"

"Brainfreeze" completely immersed herself in the reality of life off the trail. Since completing the A.T., she got married and had a beautiful baby girl. As if that were not a full enough life, she plans on starting graduate school in genetics at the University of North Carolina at the ripe old age of thirty-nine.

"Better late than never, I guess!" Another dream pursued.

When they got off the trail on October 3, 2006, "Trickster & What?!" were nearly broke and had only $150.00 in the bank. "Trail Magic" followed them home to North Carolina where they ran into the owner of Phoenix Outdoors who invited them to stay for free at a house she was renovating. "What?!" went back to Phoenix, Arizona to work and "Trickster" found a job working for a dog grooming business in Asheville, North Carolina. When they saved enough money, they moved into a tiny bungalow in town and "Trickster" returned to college to complete her education degree—she plans on becoming a middle school teacher.

They still hike as often as possible and have done over 100 miles of the Pinhoti Trail in Alabama with their dog, Gaia. During the summer of 2007 they lived in Strafford, Vermont, and worked in Hanover, New Hampshire, which is right on the A.T. "Trickster" got a job at Hanover Outdoors, a fantastic outdoor and fly fishing shop right on the trail and "What?!" worked as a landscaper. He was able to apply his degree in art to designing beautiful flowerbeds. Toward the end of the summer, they headed out onto the Long Trail and finished the 170 miles of trail that begins in Killington and ends at the Canadian border. We were a few days behind them and they left us messages in the shelter registers urging us to catch up to them. (It never happened because we are "gerbils" and they are "gazelles"). They were sad when they ran out of trail near the Canadian border, because that meant they had to return home to North Carolina.

"We both love hiking through the coniferous forests of the north; there's something magical about trekking through a sub-alpine zone!"

Earlier in this book, "Enuff & Too Much" eluded to the fact that they had more than just hike preparations to deal with prior to their thru-hike. They were also preparing to make a life and career change of equal significance. They quit their jobs, sold most of their belongings, and put the rest in storage because once their A.T. hike was over, they did not return to Philadelphia; they went directly from Maine to South Dakota where they were to be on staff in the hospital on the Rosebud Indian Reservation. They worked in the emergency room there for a year which was tough work, both emotionally and physically. According to them it was more difficult than the A.T. in many ways. The people were wonderful, but the conditions were impossible.

After a year in South Dakota, they moved to Evergreen, Colorado, thirty miles west of Denver, where they live in the foothills of the Rockies. Both are still working in the medical field and get out for short hikes weekly. They love the fact that nature is so close and every day they see deer and elk from their windows. They like the fact that the people in the area where they live are so into the outdoors and "Enuff" has started learning to fly fish.

They haven't done any serious hiking since the A.T., but inspired by an article in Backpacker magazine, they went to France to hike in the Chamonix area around Mont Blanc for ten days. They would love to thru-hike the Pacific Crest Trail but putting aside the time to do it is seemingly impossible. Hopefully they will do it some day.

> *"Pat and I truly reminisce about the A.T. every day. Time did not allow us to make Damascus in 2008, but we will definitely be there in 2009. If anyone wants to know, we have the 2006 banner from the hiker parade and will bring it to next year's Trail Days."*

Unfortunately, not all the stories about our hiking family are happy ones. Not long after completing their thru-hike, "Brownie & Souleman" separated and later divorced. We lost all contact with "Souleman" but still hear from Brownie" on a regular basis. After spending so much time outside on the A.T., she realized she could not pursue a career that would have her sitting behind a desk all day. So, she decided to delve into a career in outdoor education and took a job working as an Outdoor Education Coordinator at a year-round camp facility.

> *"My knowledge in the outdoor and environmental education fields has increased dramatically and I am looking forward to continuing to grow in this field."*

She has also found time to cultivate old hobbies like reading and has been learning new skills like playing guitar, knitting, and surfing. As for long-term plans—maybe graduate school, teaching, or possibly more outdoor education pursuits.

"Little Wing" returned to her home in Gainesville, Florida, after leaving the A.T. at the base of Mt. Washington on August 23rd. Because she loves her job and the people she works with, she immediately went back to work even though she was still nursing a stress fracture in her right hip that kept her on crutches for three months. As the director of the Distance Education Program at the University of Florida, she gets to work with wonderful students ranging in age from 18 to 60, brilliant professors, and dedicated student services professionals both at University of Florida and Florida's community colleges.

> *"Scott and I hope to return 'to the scene of the fracture' this summer, and start knocking out week-long hikes—slowly making our way to Katahdin over several years. The slower, and saner, pace will allow us to take time off from work to hike together and hopefully be a little kinder and gentler to my scrawny frame. We completed 'Paddle Florida'—123 miles on the Suwannee River over a week. We*

had a blast and learned that stuffing your gear into the cargo holds of a kayak is a whole lot easier than lugging it around on your back!

For Mike and Zan, post-A.T. life was full of study for both of them. Mike finished his Masters of Media Practice in 2007 and is looking for a journalism job. Zan will finish her Masters of Environmental Education in June 2008. With all of their studying they have not been able to spend much time hiking since they got home.

"We did find time to travel down to Tasmania for a month to hike a few trails. We did the South Coast Track, Freycinet, Tasman Peninsula, and Frenchman's Cap. We also have plans to do the Oxfam Trailwalker charity walk. The aim of the walk is to walk 100 kilometers in 48 hours. That is not very far for a veteran A.T. thru-hiker, but we will need to do some serious training to get ready."

When we last heard from "Head-N-Out & Tag-N-Along," they were already 100 miles into their quest to thru-hike the Pacific Crest Trail from Mexico to Canada. After completing the A.T., their lives reverted back to what they were before their thru-hike. "Tag-N-Along" continued working part time and "Head-N-Out" spent his time planning and prepping things for their P.C.T. hike. They did some winter backpacking, which was fun, and gave them a sense of what hiking in the high elevations of the P.C.T. may be like.

After completing the A.T., "Carbomb & Lichen" settled back into their lives in Austin, Texas. They stayed with some friends for a while and then moved back to the same neighborhood where they lived prior to the hike. They are both still working in the environmental consulting field, "Lichen" with the company she worked for before the hike, and "Carbomb" with a new company. However, there were some major life changes. They are now committed to not working late or on the weekends. They also moved to a smaller place, though they admit they have yet to rid themselves of the storage unit which holds the furnishings and extra stuff that used to fit into their larger place.

"Surprisingly, we have not backpacked much since our A.T. hike. In 2007 we both went backpacking for one long weekend, and "Lichen" went on a 10-day hike at the Philmont Boy Scout Ranch in New Mexico as an adult advisor for a venture crew. We miss backpacking, but we just are not that enthusiastic about the backpacking possibilities in our area. However, we are still physically active.

Hoping to capitalize on our post-trail fitness, we both trained for and ran the Austin Marathon in February 2007. We also continue to run and cycle. We do have a trip to the Tetons in the works for late summer 2008, and our list of other places we want to hike is very long."

Backpacking is in our blood and having to be stuck indoors is frustrating. On nearly every warm and sunny day, one of us says to the other, *"What a great day this would be to be out hiking."* Many a time, we look at the calendar and think about where we were and what we were experiencing on that same day in 2006. The feelings are bittersweet. When we were hiking the A.T., at best, we could only see a mile or so ahead of us; the magnitude of what laid ahead was hidden over the horizon or behind the wall of forest in the distance. But now, as we drive alongside the mountains that the Appalachian Trail traverses in Virginia, Maryland, and Pennsylvania, we often turn to each other and reminiscently remark, *"We hiked all of that. Can you believe it?"* Seeing the full scope of what we accomplished is emotionally overwhelming.

What is most exciting about completing those 2,175 arduous miles is that we did it together; and that is something tremendously rewarding that can never be taken away from us. The memories of those six months are shared ones, deeply engrained in both our souls and for that we are forever grateful. The rewards of completing our journey are too numerous to count and how those rewards positively affect our marriage continue to reveal themselves. From thru-hiking the Appalachian Trail, we discovered that many of life's greatest rewards come not from reaching a goal but are found in simply taking on the challenge. The next challenge was putting together this story about our A.T. adventure; and it was an unbelievably difficult task. But the reward was that during the writing we were again able to revisit places and events and fondly remember the people, who left such indelible marks on our lives. It also allowed us to evaluate the impact of those experiences and put them into a real world perspective and practice.

Since completing our thru-hike, we have been blessed with numerous opportunities to share our adventure through speaking engagements at state and national parks, at churches, for scout troops, professional/civic organizations, and for hiking organizations. As we recount the details of our odyssey and display the photographs of the many places we called home for six months, waves of emotions of that time continue to wash over us.

If you would like us to share the magic of our Appalachian Trail adventure through a presentation, please contact us at *Qualtech.Resource@verizon.net.*

We have four unique presentations tailored to specific audiences and with distinct focuses.

"Dream It!...Plan It!...Live It!"

Using our six-month adventure as a foundation, the *"Dream It!...Plan It!...Live It!"* presentation challenges everyone to pursue their dreams, no matter what their age or however incredible the dream may seem. This presentation is suitable for luncheon or dinner talks and provides an overview about the Appalachian Trail, but also provides insight on identifying dreams, rekindling passions, taking steps in "life planning," and fulfilling life dreams. This is our favorite presentation as we both enjoy helping other people live out their life dreams.

"Spiritual Reflections from the Appalachian Trail"

"Spiritual Reflections from the Appalachian Trail" is tailored for faith-based organizations and, drawing upon the physical, mental, and emotional challenges of this six-month odyssey, the audience is presented with the parallels of this adventure and those of one's walk of faith. It is an inspiring reflection of our life on the trail and looks at following the right path—prayer, perseverance, relationships with people, praise (worship), possessions (simplicity), humility, and service. This presentation is suitable for churches, spiritual leadership conferences, and youth ministries.

"The Care and Feeding of the Long-Distance Hiker"

"The Care and Feeding of the Long-Distance Hiker" is for those planning a moderate or long-distance hike or those associated with hiking/camping/wilderness organizations. It examines the important subject of nutrition on the trail and offers creative alternatives to standard "off-the-shelf" dehydrated meals. Based on our own experience, we also offer nutritional secrets that allow you to remain strong and healthy on a long-distance adventure. Information on various backpacking stoves and water filtration is also provided as are techniques to help keep yourself healthy and fit while on the trail.

"The Joys of Backpacking as a Couple"

Do you wonder if backpacking with your spouse or significant other will be a rewarding experience or just a recipe for disaster? *"The Joys of Backpacking as a Couple"* recounts the trials and rewards of our A.T. thru-hike and describes how completing this journey together has benefitted our relationship in ways we never could have imagined. Practical tips for hiking as a couple are presented as well as the logistical benefits of hiking together.

Each presentation is complete with facts and reflections about life on the trail, answers to "Frequently Asked Questions", and wonderful anecdotes about the people and places that make up the legendary Appalachian Trail.

We are also available to make presentations on other important issues of backpacking, such as:

- *"Your Most Important Piece of Equipment"* - Foot care for pain-free backpacking
- *"Comfort-Light Hiking"* – Using lightweight equipment and clothing without sacrificing comfort
- *"Treat Your Water and it Will Treat You Right"* - Water treatment choices

If you are interested in attending one of our presentations, we have a complete speaking engagement schedule online at *www.QualtechResourceGroup.com*. Simply click on *"Speaking Engagement Calendar"* and then contact us for more details.

For those who wish to see the breathtaking wonders of the Appalachian Trail from the comfort of their home, *"Appalachian Trail Reflections"* is just the ticket. This 50-minute DVD of one-hundred-fifty of "Mom's" beautiful nature photographs captures all the beauty of the trail from Georgia to Maine. These visual wonders are displayed against a backdrop of nature sounds and Native American flute music composed and played by "Windtalker." Prints of many of the photos on the DVD are also available.

And, if you enjoy meditative, relaxing, and hauntingly beautiful music, we have a CD available comprised of songs inspired by the sights and sounds that embraced us on the A.T. *"Windtalker – Native SoundScapes"* is a majestic blend of Native American flute, piano, violin, orchestra and rock instrumentation. All the songs were composed and played by "Windtalker."

"V&A" have put together a wonderful guide book for those who would rather travel the A.T. by RV. It describes their journey on the highways and back roads from Georgia to Maine, as they provided trail support to us. *"Exploring the Appalachian Trail by RV, Sort of..."* is not simply the story of their journey as "trail angels;" it is an atlas for those who desire to wander the byways along the A.T. and partake of the wonder and beauty that can be found there. This book will not only inspire you to pursue your own adventure along the Appalachian Trail but also provides the tools necessary to make your journey a memorable one.

All these items are available at *www.QualtechResourceGroup.com*

Trail Terms

In this book you will come across terminology that may not be familiar to you. This is the language of the Appalachian Trail hiker. Many of these terms are also used by the hikers on the numerous other long-distance trails in the United States. Sometimes unique, sometimes humorous, but always aptly descriptive, it is a language that virtually everyone who has spent any time on the trail uses on a daily basis. This list of terms, words, phrases, abbreviations, and slang have been gleaned from numerous sources familiar to the trail community.

2000 Miler: A person who has hiked the entire distance between termini of the official (white-blazed) A.T., either by thru-hiking or section hiking.

A.L.D.H.A.: The Appalachian Long Distance Hikers Association began in 1983 as an off-trail family of fellow hikers who have all shared similar experiences, hopes and dreams on the Appalachian Trail and other long trails. ALDHA sponsors "The Gathering" each October, and member volunteers compile the "The Thru-hikers' Companion" for the ATC. Membership in this nonprofit group is open to all.

Alpine Zone: The area consisting of all the land above tree line, generally in New England. The alpine zone is best defined by its plant life. Conifers such as spruce and balsam grow as Krumholz near the tree line, giving way to tundra-type lichens, moss, and shrubs above.

A.M.C.: The Appalachian Mountain Club. This group maintains the A.T. in the White Mountains of New Hampshire to Grafton Notch in Maine.

AMC Huts: In New Hampshire's White Mountains, in heavy use areas and above tree line, the AMC provides buildings called Huts for backpackers to stay overnight.

A.T.C.: The Appalachian Trail Conservancy is a volunteer-based, private, nonprofit organization dedicated to the preservation, management, and promotion of the Appalachian Trail as a primitive setting for outdoor recreation (on foot) and for learning. The ATC is both a confederation of trail-maintaining clubs and an individual-membership organization.

Avery, Myron: (1931-1952) The first 2000-miler, and the man credited with building the Appalachian Trail. Chair of the ATC from 1931 until his death in 1952.

AYCE: "All You Can Eat" restaurants that offer all you can eat buffets are very popular with hungry hikers.

Bald: A southern term describing a low elevation mountain surrounded by forest yet devoid of trees on the crown. Typically covered with meadows, balds can offer great views and are a good place to find wild berries. They also attract much wildlife.

Baseball Bat Shelter: An old style of shelter construction in Maine where the floor is constructed out of parallel logs each with diameters not much greater than that of a baseball bat.

Baxter: Baxter State Park, where Mt. Katahdin, the A.T.'s northern terminus, is located.

Bear Bag: The bag used by hikers to hang their food out of reach of bears and other critters (see 'Food Bag').

Bear Cable: A permanent cable rigged high between two trees, specifically for hanging bear bags.

Blackflies: There are about forty species of these tiny, biting insects that breed in running water and flourish in late May and June in Maine. They are the cause for most people to hike the A.T. south to north; they are so aggressive they have been known to drive hikers off the trail.

Bivouac: To sleep outdoors, without a tent or proper gear, usually done only in emergency situations. Alpine climbers may do planned bivouacs on long and difficult routes, carrying gear known as a bivy sacks.

Bivy Sack: A lightweight and waterproof bag that covers a sleeping bag. Simple, sometimes cramped, shelter.

Blazes: Painted, 2-inch by 6-inch, vertical white rectangles placed at eye height on trees and other objects, in both directions, to mark the official route of the Trail. Side trails are marked with blue blazes.

Blaze Orange: A very bright hue of orange visible in low light. The color to wear during hunting season.

Blow Down: (see "Dead Fall) A tree or shrub that has fallen across the trail. Trail maintainers have dozens of words to describe each kind of fallen tree.

Blue Blazes: Blazes that indicate spur trails off the A.T. These spur trails are used as alternate routes in bad weather. They direct you to views, shelters, water sources, etc. On the A.T., these blazes are painted blue.

Blue-Blazer: A long-distance hiker, who substitutes a section of blue-blazed trail for a white-blazed section between two points on the trail.

Bog Bridge: A narrow wooden walkway, often made of spilt logs, placed to protect sensitive wetlands.

Bounce Box: A mail-drop type box containing seldom-used necessities that is 'bounced' ahead to a town where you think you might need the contents.

Bushwhack: To hike where there is no marked trail.

Cache (pronounced cash): A supply of food and/or supplies hidden for later retrieval.

Cairn: A manmade pile of rocks erected as a trail marker. Chiefly used above timberline and should be close enough to see the next one in heavy fog, and high enough to see above fallen snow.

Canister Stove: The type of small backpacking stove that uses metal cans of compressed gas fuel.

Caretaker: The person who maintains and collects fees at certain shelters and campsites.

Cat Hole: A small hole, typically 8 inches deep, dug by hikers for the deposit of human waste.

Col and **Sag:** Dips in the ridge without a road. "Col" is typically a northern term while "Sag" is typically a southern term.

Companion: The ALDHA Thru-Hikers' Companion is an A.T. guidebook compiled by AHLDA volunteers for the ATC.

Cove: A southern Appalachian word meaning a high, flat, valley surrounded by mountains. Cades Cove in the Smokies is the most well-known one.

Corridor: The Appalachian Trail is a long and narrow park, sometimes less than 100 feet wide. The area set aside for the A.T. to pass within is called the Trail Corridor.

Cowboy Camping: Camping without a shelter. The hiker simply spreads his/her pad and bag out under the stars and puts one's faith in his opinion about the weather staying dry.

Croo: The group of caretakers who staff the Appalachian Mountain Club Huts. For the most part, the summer Croos are college students.

Data Book: Published for over 25 years by the ATC, the Data Book is a consolidation of the most basic guidebook information into a lightweight table of distances between major Appalachian Trail shelters, road-crossings, and features—divided according to the guidebook volumes and updated each December to account for Trail relocations, new (or removed) shelters, and other changes. It is keyed to both guidebook sections *and* maps.

Dead Fall: A maintainer's term for a fallen dead tree across the trail. Also sometimes referred to as a "blow down."

DEET: A powerful insect repellant. Don't leave home without it.

Double Blaze: Two blazes, one above the other as an indication of an imminent turn or intersection in the trail. Offset double blazes, called "Garveys," indicate the direction of the turn by the offset of the top blaze.

Dodgeways: V-shaped stiles through fences, used where the trail passes through livestock enclosures.

Duct Tape: A wide, heavy duty, multi purpose tape used by hikers for everything from covering blisters to repairing gear.

End-to-Ender: An alternative term for a 2,000-Miler.

Fall Line: The fall line is the most direct route downhill from any particular point. The Appalachian Trail runs the fall line in much of New England.

Flip-Flop: A term used to signify a hiker that starts hiking in one direction then at some point decides to jump ahead and hike back in the opposite direction. Some hikers on the A.T. will start hiking northbound from Springer Mountain, and at Harpers Ferry they may decide to go to Katahdin and hike back south to Harpers Ferry, thus completing their thru-hike. This is a good way to complete the hike if they are behind schedule and their time is limited due to the onset of winter.

Food Bag: A bag a hiker carries in his pack specifically for keeping all his food. Typically, it is suspended from a tree at night so bears and varmints do not get into it. Also called a "Bear Bag."

FSO "From Skin Out." When considering the weight of gear, it is important to remember that your total gear weight, "from the skin out," is as important a total as what your pack weighs.

GAME or GAMER: A hike or hiker going from Georgia to Maine.

Gap and Notch: Typically larger dips that have a road going through. "Gap" is typically a southern term while "Notch" is typically a northern term. Water Gap, is of course, a "Gap" with a river.

Garvey, Ed: (1914-1999) Celebrated friend of the A.T., conservationist, thru-hiker, author of the 1971 book, *"Appalachian Hiker,"* an adventure story that offers practical advice for A.T. hikers and is widely credited with popularizing backpacking and the Appalachian Trail. A "Garvey" is a double blaze where the top blaze is offset to indicate the direction of a turn in the trail.

Gear Head: A hiker whose primary focus is backpacking and outdoor gear.

Giardia: More properly known as "giardiasis," it is an infection of the lower intestines cause by the amoebic cyst, Giardia Lamblia. Giardia resides in water, so it is wise to always chemically treat or filter your water before drinking. Symptoms include stomach cramps, diarrhea, bloating, loss of appetite, and vomiting. Also know as, a backpacker's worst nightmare.

GORP: "Good ole raisins & peanuts," or some other variation thereof. Also known as "trail mix."

Gray Water: Dirty dishwater. Some campsites have designated spots to dump gray water. Such designated spots may be provided with a strainer so that you can remove your food particles from the gray water and pack those out.

Ground Control: Hiker support that handles the "real world" concerns, like bills and pets, and mails a hiker packages. Also known as Trail Support.

Handbook: The Thru-hiker's Handbook is an A.T. guidebook originally compiled by Dan "Wingfoot" Bruce and now updated by Bob "501" McCaw.

Harpers Ferry: The A.T.C.'s National Headquarters and Information Center is located in Harper's Ferry, West Virginia, about 1000 A.T. miles north of Springer Mountain. A short blue blazed trail leads to the headquarters where A.T. hikers traditionally sign the register and have their photos taken. This is the psychological halfway point on the A.T.

Headlamp: A small flashlight attached to a band or strap and worn on the head.

Hicker: A person who is still trying to figure out the whole hiker/gear thing while on the trail.

Hiker Box: A cabinet or box at hostels where hikers donate unwanted food for the hikers coming behind them.

Hammock: A sleeping system that combines a tent and sleeping bag hung between two trees.

Hostel: An establishment along the trail that has bunks, showers, and sometimes cooking and mail drops for A.T. hikers.

Hydration System: An improvement on drinking out of a bottle. It consists of a plastic bladder, hose, and mouth piece/valve that allows hands-free drinking.

HYOH: "Hike your own hike." Setting your own criteria and pace for your hike and not trying to imitate someone else's.

Hypothermia: Potentially fatal condition caused by insufficient heat and a drop in the body's core temperature. Classic symptoms are called the "umbles," as the victim tumbles, grumbles, mumbles, and fumbles with confused thoughts.

Iceberg: Icebergs are large rocks planted in the ground at an overused campsite to discourage any more tenting.

Katahdin: Mt. Katahdin. The A.T.'s northern terminus is at Baxter State Park in Maine. Katahdin is a Penobscot Indian word meaning "greatest mountain."

Knob: A prominent rounded hill or mountain. A southern term.

Lean-To: Another word for a three sided open shelter used primarily in New England.

Long-Distance Hiker: A somewhat indeterminate term applied to anyone who is hiking more than a few weeks, and who usually has to re-supply at least once during his or her hike; often used interchangeably with the term thru-hiker. At Baxter State Park, an LDH is someone who has hiked in from 100 or more miles south.

LNT: "Leave No Trace" is a philosophy and skill used to pass as lightly as possible when backpacking. It also means that you pack-out all your trash and leave no visible signs that you were there.

Long Trail: Vermont's Long Trail runs from the Massachusetts to Canadian border, the southern third in conjunction with the A.T.

MacGyver: Based on an old TV show where the hero would construct useful devices out of common materials. To hikers it means to build or repair gear with imagination.

MacKaye, Benton: (MacKaye rhymes with "high," not "hay.") The man, who in 1921, proposed the Appalachian Trail as the connecting thread of a "project in regional planning." MacKaye envisioned a trail along the ridge crests of the Appalachian Mountain chain from New England to the Deep South, connecting farms, work camps, and study camps that would be populated by eastern urbanites needing a break from the tensions of industrialization.

Mail Drop: Mail drops are a method of re-supply while hiking. A mail drop is usually made ahead of time, before the hike starts, and a person not hiking (usually a spouse or relative, but it can be a friend) mails the package according to a pre-arranged schedule so it arrives on time for the hiker to receive it at the post office.

Maintainer: A volunteer who participates in the organized trail maintenance programs of the ATC and its member clubs.

MEGA or ME-GA: A hike or hiker going from Maine to Georgia.

Mountain Money: Toilet paper.

Mouse Hanger: A 12 inch to 18 inch length of cord run through a tin can with a small stick tied to the end. Hung from a beam in the shelter, a hiker will hang his/her pack on the stick. Mice, attempting to climb down the rope to get into the pack, are deterred by the tin can.

Nero: Almost a "Zero" ...in other words, a very short mileage day.

Northbounder (NoBo): A thru-hiker hiking from Georgia to Maine (also **GAMER)**

NPS: National Park Service.

Pot Cozy: A foam or cloth wrap to keep a cooking pot warm while it finishes cooking.

Power Hiker: A hiker who habitually chooses to cover very long distances each day, often hiking late into the evening.

Privy: A trailside outhouse for solid waste.

PUDS: Thru-hiker shorthand for "pointless ups and downs," referring to the less interesting sections of mountains thru-hikers encounter from time to time; several PUDS in a row are MUDS, which is shorthand for "mindless ups and downs."

Puncheon: A wooden walkway built to provide a stable, hardened tread-way across bogs, mud flats, and marshy areas. Also called a "bog bridge."

Purist: A hiker who wants to pass every white blaze or a hiker who wants others to pass every white blaze.

Register: A logbook normally found at a trail shelter or a trailhead. The original intent was for hikers to sign in so a searcher needing to find a lost hiker could tell where they last were. Registers are now used for hikers to write information regarding their hike which other hikers may find useful.

Relo: A section of trail recently relocated.

Ridge Runner: A person, paid by a trail-maintaining club or governmental organization, to hike back and forth along a certain section of trail to educate hikers, enforce regulations, monitor trail and campsite use, and sometimes performs trail maintenance or construction duties. Such persons are most often found in high-use areas of the trail.

Section Hiker: A person who is attempting to become a 2,000-miler by doing a series of section hikes over an extended period of time.

Shaffer, Earl: (1918-2002) "The Crazy One," the first person to thru-hike the Appalachian Trail. Poet, WWII veteran, author of "Walking with Spring," and "The Appalachian Trail, Calling Me Back To The Hills," and three-time thru-hiker, northbound in 1948, southbound in 1965, and northbound again at age 79 50 years after his first hike. http//www.earlshaffer.com

Shelter: Three-sided wooden or stone buildings generally spaced about a half-day's hike apart and are near water sources and a privy. The A.T. has many kinds of shelters, from barns to cabins.

Shuttle: A ride from town to a trailhead, usually for a fee.

Skunked: Failing to get a car to stop when hitch hiking.

Slabbing: A hiking term that refers to going around a mountain on a moderately graded footpath, as opposed to going straight up and over the mountain.

Slackpacking: A hiking term coined in 1980 to describe an unhurried and non-goal-oriented manner of long-distance hiking (i.e., slack: "not taut or tense, loose"), but in recent years has been used to refer simply to thru-hiking without a backpack or with nothing more than a daypack; recently called, "Freedom Packing."

Southbounder (SoBo): A hiker who is hiking the A.T. from Maine to Georgia. Only a small minority of hikers actually hike this direction, primarily because of black flies.

Spork: A piece of silverware that incorporates the design and function of both a spoon and a fork into one utensil; Made of metal, often titanium, or plastic.

Spruce Trap: When snow is deep enough that it covers the top of a spruce tree, beware. Since there will be voids in the snow pack, you can fall into those voids and get caught. When you appear to be above timberline, but you know the trees are eight feet high at this place in summer, beware. Since you cannot see where the trail is, you cannot stay on it, and you cannot avoid the spruce traps.

Springer Mountain: The summit is the southern terminus of the Appalachian Trail.

Springer Fever: The almost uncontrollable urge to be back on the trail that hits thru-hikers of past years each spring.

Stealth: A manner of camping where there is no indication that you are there, and no trace of your being there remains after you have left; sometimes used as a term for camping illegally on public or private land.

Stile: Steps constructed over a fence to allow people, but not livestock, to pass.

Swag: In the South, it is the lowest connecting point between two ridges.

Switchback: A method of building a trail that forms a zig-zag across the face of a mountain. The strategy is to prevent erosion and to make the climb easier. Switchbacks are not made to be short-cutted, although some people do, which damages the trail. Switchbacks are often appreciated by hikers.

Tarp: A simple tent with no floor or door.

"Ten Essentials": Short list of 10 or 12 items thought necessary to be carried by backpackers. An example of one list: map, compass, water and a way to purify it, extra food, rain gear/extra clothing, fire starter and matches, first aid kit, army knife/multi- purpose tool, flashlight with extra batteries/bulbs, sun screen/sun glasses.

Tent Pad/Platform: At some camping sites, tenting is restricted to built-up earthen "pads" or wooden "platforms" in order to ease impact on the area.

Thru-Hiker: Traditionally, a person who is attempting to become a 2,000-Miler in a single, continuous journey, leaving from one terminus of the trail and backpacking to the other terminus.

TP: Toilet paper; also known as "mountain money."

Trail Angel: Someone who provides unexpected help or food to a hiker.

Trailhead: Where the trail leaves a road crossing or parking lot.

Trail Magic: Unexpected, but welcome, help or food.

Trail Name: A nickname adopted by, or given to, a hiker. This name is used almost exclusively when communicating with others on the trail and in trail register entries.

Trail Runner: A person who runs the A.T., as opposed to walking it.

Tree Line: The point of elevation on a mountain, above which, the climate will no longer support tree growth; sometimes also referred to as the "alpine" area.

Thru-Hiking: The act of attempting to become a 2,000-Miler in a single, continuous journey.

Tour Hiker: A person who pretends to be hiking the entire A.T., as a thru-hiker, but instead skips sections and usually looks for ways to spend more time lounging in towns, and less time hiking the A.T.; usually scoffs at the traditions of thru-hiking and thinks the phrase "hike your own hike" is an excuse for just about anything.

Ultra Light: A style of gear or hiking that focuses on using the lightest gear possible.

Vitamin I: The nickname given to Ibuprofin, by thru-hikers. Virtually every hiker, especially thru-hikers, use it extensively.

Waterbar: A log or rock barrier that diverts water off the trail in order to prevent erosion.

Webface: What happens to the first person on the trail each morning – they clear away all the spider webs across the trail with their face.

Web Master: The first person on the trail each morning – result (see Webface).

The Whites: The White Mountains of New Hampshire.

Whiteblazer: A term from the Appalachian Trail to describe a person hiking "pure" (see purist); that is, hiking past every white blaze, which are the standard trail markers on the A.T. Also, what members of the website, www.whiteblaze.net, are called.

Widowmaker: Limbs or whole trees themselves, that have partially fallen but remain hung up overhead and so pose a danger to a person below.

Wilderness Area: An official designation for public lands set aside to protect them from humans.

Work for Stay: Some hostels, the AMC Huts in The Whites, and a few other places along the A.T. allow hikers to perform work, rather than pay the fee, for lodging.

Yogi-ing: The good-natured art of "letting" food be offered cheerfully by strangers without actually asking them directly. (If you ask, it is begging!)

YMMV: "Your Mileage May Vary," hiker jargon for "this worked for me, but your results/opinions might not be the same for you."

Yo-Yo-ing: The act of completing one A.T. thru-hike, then immediately turning around to begin another in the opposite direction.

Z Rest: A closed cell sleeping pad that folds into a rectangular block, rather than rolling up.

Zero Day: A day in which no miles are hiked, usually because the hiker is stopping in a town to re-supply and/or rest.

Gear List

ITEMS	MANUFACTURER	MODEL	W oz	M oz
PACKS				
Pack	ULA	P1/P2	43.03	43.03
Pack Rain Cover	Gregory		8.50	8.50
SHELTER				
Tent & Fly	REI	Quarter Dome		44.59
Ground cloth	REI	Quarter Dome	7.27	
Poles	REI	Quarter Dome	16.05	
Stakes (8)	Varga	Titanium (Small)	0.32	
Rope	REI	Quarter Dome	1.62	
SLEEPING				
Sleeping Pad	Therm-a-Rest	ProLite 3	19.68	19.68
Sleeping Bag (winter)	Marmot	Helium EQ w/SS (down)	43.67	43.67
Sleeping Bag (summer)	Mont-bell	ULSS Down Hugger #7	17.35	17.35
Silk Bag Liner	Mont-bell		5.52	5.52
WATER				
Hydration Pack	Camelback	3 Liter	7.41	7.41
Water Filter	First Need		18.62	
COOKING				
Stove	Snow Peak	Giga Power (standard)	3.14	
Fuel (Canister)	MSR	8 oz.	12.63	
Wind Screen	Snow Peak	GP-008	1.932	
Pot (No handle) – 1.5 L	EverNew	Titanium/Non-stick	6.14	
Pot (No handle) – 1 L	EverNew	Titanium/Non-stick	4.23	
Large Lid (w/handle)	EverNew	Titanium/Non-stick	3.92	
Small Lid (No handle)	EverNew	Titanium/Non-stick	3.67	
Pot Carrying Bag	EverNew	Net	0.56	
Clamp Handle	MSR		1.06	
Dish Soap (full bottle)	Sierra Dawn	Campsuds	3.88	
Bowl (Plastic w/lid)	Glad		3.03	3.03
Spoon	MSR	Titanium	0.81	0.81
Cup	MSR	Titanium		2.40
Cup	Snow Peak	Titanium 600	2.01	
Water Bottle	Nalgene	1 Liter, Large Mouth		7.37

ITEM	MANUFACTURER	MODEL	W oz	M oz
			Weight	
COOKING (Continued)				
Water Bottle	Nalgene	14 oz.	3.10	
FOOTWEAR				
Boots	Tecnica	High-Tops		46.70
Boots	Vasque	Vasque Caldera GTX		39.86
Boots	Salomon	Mid (2 pairs by end of hike)		14.75
Boots	Salomon	Trek GTX	48.18	
Camp Shoes	"Crocs"			9.74
Camp Shoes	"Waddies"		8.61	
PERSONAL HYGIENE/ & FIRST AID				
First Aid Kit		(incl. 2 emergency blankets)		25.32
Ditty Kit	McNett	(incl. hygiene items)	17.04	11.43
Shovel	Coghlans	Plastic "Back Pack"	1.94	
Insect Repellent	Deet – 100%	(small spray can)	1.09	1.09
Duct Tape			1.90	
Toilet Paper	Angel Soft	Small Roll (in Zip-Lock bag)	2.65	
Wipes	Wet-Ones			0.18
STUFF SACKS				
Air Space Zipper Sack (M)	Granite Gear	(food)	1.66	1.66
Air Space Zipper Sack (M)	Granite Gear	(clothes)		1.66
Air Space Zipper Sack (S)	Granite Gear	(first aid)		1.31
Air Space Zipper Sack (M)	Granite Gear	(for summer sleeping bag)	1.66	
Air Compressor Sack (S)	Granite Gear	(clothes)	3.17	
Waterproof Comp. Sack	Event	Medium (tent & fly)		4.90
Waterproof Comp. Sack	Event	Small (sleeping bag)	4.27	
Hydro Seal #5	Outdoor Research	Bear Bag	3.77	
Hydro Seal Comp. Sack #1	Outdoor Research	(sleeping bag)		6.46
CLOTHING				
Gaiters	Black Diamond	Sportee		6.91
Gaiters	Green Mountain	Equinox	4.80	
Rain Jacket	Marmot	Precip		13.12
Rain Pants	Galyan's			11.75
Rain Jacket	Intregral Designs	Event Thru-Hiker Jacket	8.78	
Rain Pants	Marmot		7.16	

ITEM	MANUFACTURER	MODEL	W oz	M oz
			Weight	
CLOTHING (continued)				
Winter Jacket	Beyond Fleece	Custom Made		19.88
Winter Jacket	Moonstone	Synthetic	22.54	
Wind Jacket	Integral Designs	Pertex		5.2
Vest	Polartec	Fleece	9.31	
Hat (Winter)	Mountain Hardware	Gore Wind Stopper		2.47
Hat (Winter)	High Point	Windstopper	2.12	
Balaclava	Outdoor Research			1.98
Balaclava	Outlast		0.95	
Bandana (2)			1.84	1.84
Gloves	Mountain Hardware			1.41
Gloves	Black Diamond	Solstice	2.40	
Pants (Winter)	Patagonia	R-1	6.98	6.98
Pants (Winter)	REI	Schoeller Dynamic	15.52	18.38
Pants (Winter)	REI	Schoeller Dynamic		15.52
Shirt (Fall/Winter) (2)	Arcteryx	Pull-Over	7.58	8.32
Shirt (Pullover) (2)	Patagonia	Flash R-1		11.18
Belt (lightweight)	Patagonia		2.54	
Shirt (short sleeved)	UnderArmour			4.02
Shirt (sleeveless)	UnderArmour			3.03
Shirt (short sleeved)	Mountain Hardware		4.06	
Shirt (sleeveless)	North Face		3.53	
Pants	Ex-Officio	Convertibles	8.96	
Pants	Montbell			9.42
Shirt (long-sleeve)	Patagonia	Lightweight	5.29	
Shirt (long-sleeve)	UnderArmour			6.98
Shorts	Columbia		8.50	
Shorts	LL Bean		8.04	
Shorts	Nike	Men's running w/liner cut out		4.90
Socks	SmartWool	Medium	2.54	2.54
Socks	SmartWool		3.21	3.21
Sock Liners	Bridgedale		1.27	1.27
Sock Liners	Thorneburgh	Cool-Max	1.23	1.23
Long Underwear	Mont-bell	Zeo-Line	9.03	9.45

			W	M
			Weight	
ITEM	**MANUFACTURER**	**MODEL**	**oz**	**oz**
CLOTHING (continued)				
Underwear	Ex Officio	Boxer	2.72	
Underwear	Ex Officio	Black Boy Cut		1.88
Spare Boot Inserts	Superfeet	Green	3.00	
Spare Boot Inserts	Sole			4.13
Sock Liners	Thorneburgh	Cool-Max	1.23	1.23
TECHNICAL GEAR & MISCELLANEOUS				
Hiking Poles	Leki	Makalu Air Ergo	17.99	
Hiking Poles	Leki	Super Makalu		21.73
Crampons	Yaktrax		3.32	3.32
Head Lamp	Petzl	Tikka Plus	1.48	1.48
Cell Phone	Palm	Treo 650		8.5
Spare Battery	Palm	Treo 650		2.56
Cell Phone	Samsung	A-630	3.95	
Watch	High Gear	CR-2032 (wtemp/compass)		2.69
Watch	Suunto	(w/temp/alt./compass)	2.65	
Camera	Canon	PowerShot SD-500		12.06
Camera Battery (extra)	Canon	PowerShot SD-500		1.56
Wallet	Eagle Creek	Slim Line	1.23	1.23
Glasses	CVS	Fold-Up	1.41	
Knife	Schrade	Cooking		1.34
Knife		Pocket		1.52
Knife	Barlow	Swiss Army	2.79	
Miscellaneous Bag	Zip-Loc Bag	Batteries, journal, pen	5.22	
Flute	Colin Peterson	Wood	2.65	
Lighter			0.35	
Rope (for bear bag)	Kelty	Triptease Lightline	4.55	
Maps/Guides/Data Book	ATC			
AT Thru-Hikers Companion	ALDHA			

- Some of the duplicate types of clothing and the additional pairs of boots listed were not carried all at once. They are shown in order to provide the full breadth of items we used at some point during the hike. Mom" used a total of eleven pairs of boots during the hike—all different brands and styles. "Windtalker" used three pair, all the same brand and style.

- No food items are shown because our choices and their associated weights varied from day to day. Typically we carried 3-4 pounds of food per day.

- There are also many items that were never used but were carried by our "trail support" should we ever need them.

- We also did not carry the complete "Thru-Hikers Companion" book or the entire "Trail Data" book. We pulled out only the pages we needed for each section we were going to hike before meeting up with our trail support to re-stock.

Food for Thought

It was seldom that we ate the dehydrated meals available at outfitters. Over the years we did considerable testing of prepackaged meals and found them to be less-than-desirable in both flavor and variety. If we were going to eat them every day for six months, we wanted to be sure they tasted good and that we weren't going to be relegated to eating the same thing four or five times a week. This is not to say some of them were not tasty, but ones we liked were few and far between. The main advantage to the prepackaged meals is that you can cook them right in their foil pouches, thus eliminating the cleaning of pots.

We chose to dehydrate our own meals which offered us a wider variety of meals—though it was much more expensive than purchasing the prepackaged types. After many weeks on the trail, we also decided that the addition of protein to our meals was critical. We ate snack bars high in protein (18 to 30 grams) and added protein powder to puddings, instant breakfasts and cereals.

Here are some of our favorite foods. You can use these in their entirety, or simply use them to augment the prepackaged meals that you may buy.

- Mashed potatoes (purchased in foil packs and in different flavors)
- Chicken breasts (in vacuum-sealed pouch)
- Gravy (powdered)
- Corn or peas (dehydrated – these we did purchase at an outfitters)
- Salmon steaks (in vacuum-sealed pouch)
- Tuna steaks (in vacuum-sealed pouch)
- Tuna chunks (in vacuum-sealed pouch)
- Soy Chili (made from dehydrated soy crumbles and tomato sauce with chili seasoning)
- Spaghetti Sauce (made from dehydrated soy crumbles, tomato sauce and seasoning)

- Ramen (used as spaghetti or to pour chili over)
- Dehydrated brown rice with brown and red beans (see note)
- Couscous
- Whole wheat, square, bagels (used with peanut butter & jelly/honey for lunches, toasted in a frying pan for breakfast or, toasted with garlic powder and oil, to make garlic toast, for dinner)
- Whole wheat pita bread or tortillas with tuna
- Dehydrated pineapple slices
- Dehydrated apple slices
- Pepperoni slices
- Summer sausage
- Cheese (low fat cheddar holds up the best in warm weather)
- Kashi Go-Lean and Kashi Go-Lean Crunch cereal mix, Craisins, NIDO powdered whole milk and protein powder
- Carnation Instant Breakfast with NIDO powdered whole milk and protein powder.
- Scramblettes powdered whole eggs (not egg whites)
- South Beach breakfast bars
- Lipton Cup of Soup with Ramen added
- Luna Bars, Pria Bars, and other high protein bars (many available with 18 to 30 grams of protein)
- Powdered ice tea mix
- Kool-Aid
- Tang
- Gatorade (often mixed with Tang)
- Hot cocoa
- Emergen-C (powdered vitamin and mineral supplement added to drinks every day)
- Hershey dark chocolate bars
- GORP (mixed nuts, Craisins, and M&Ms)

NOTE: We found we had the most success with re-hydrating the rice and beans if we poured water into a *Ziploc* bag with the rice and beans at lunchtime or during our afternoon snack, so that it could soak while we hiked in the afternoon.

Anita's A.T. Power Cookies

Here's the recipe for the nutrient dense cookies that kept us going over the course of our entire Appalachian Trail thru-hike. The original recipe for the *"Baker's Breakfast Cookie"* was slightly altered by "A" but, if you want to use the original version, it can be found at,

http://www.cdkitchen.com/recipes/recs/32/Bakers_Breakfast_Cookie41962.shtml.

If you decide to freeze them, package them individually, because they do not separate well.

Servings per recipe: 30

INGREDIENTS:
2 cups brown sugar
2 1/2 cups rolled oats
4 cups all-purpose flour
1 tablespoon baking soda
1 teaspoon baking powder
1 teaspoon salt
2 teaspoons ground cinnamon
1/3 cup canola oil
3/4 cup prune plum pastry filling (1/2 can)
2 tablespoons water
3/4 cup egg whites (refrigerated section @ grocery)
2 teaspoons vanilla extract
3/4 cup raisins
1/2 cup chopped walnuts or pecans (or ¼ cup of each)
1/2 cup chopped dried apricots
1/2 cup sunflower seeds

DIRECTIONS:
Preheat oven to 350 °F.
Spray cool cookie sheets with canola cooking oil spray.
In a large bowl, mix the flour, sugar, baking soda, baking powder, salt, and cinnamon.
Blend in oats.
Make a well in the center and pour in the canola oil, prune puree, water, egg whites, and vanilla.

Mix until well blended. (Mixture will be extremely stiff.)

Stir in the raisins, walnuts, sunflower seeds, and apricots.

Scoop the cookies with large spoon, into golf-ball sizes.

Place cookies 2" apart onto the prepared cookie sheets and, with wet fingers, flatten to ½" thick

Bake 8 minutes for chewy cookies or 10 minutes for dry cookies.

Do not over-bake; cookies will not get crisp.

Remove from cookie sheets to cool.

Leave No Trace & Hiking in Harmony

There is a set of guidelines, a code of ethics if you will, for wandering the trails and parks of America. These *"Leave No Trace"* guidelines are designed to preserve not only the pristine majesty of the wilderness but also the richly rewarding experience of communing with nature. By following them, the impact on our natural resources can be minimized and the blight of civilization can be kept from invading the solitude of the wilderness.

This copyrighted information has been reprinted with permission from the Leave No Trace Center for Outdoor Ethics: www.LNT.org

"Leave No Trace" Principles

Plan Ahead and Prepare

- Know the regulations and special concerns for the area you'll visit.

- Prepare for extreme weather, hazards, and emergencies.

- Schedule your trip to avoid times of high use.

- Visit in small groups when possible. Consider splitting larger groups into smaller groups.

- Repackage food to minimize waste.

- Use a map and compass to eliminate the use of marking paint, rock cairns or flagging.

Travel and Camp on Durable Surfaces

- Durable surfaces include established trails and campsites, rock, gravel, dry grasses or snow.

- Protect riparian areas by camping at least 200 feet from lakes and streams.
- Good campsites are found, not made. Altering a site is not necessary.

In popular areas:

- Concentrate use on existing trails and campsites.
- Walk single file in the middle of the trail, even when wet or muddy.
- Keep campsites small. Focus activity in areas where vegetation is absent.

In pristine areas:

- Disperse use to prevent the creation of campsites and trails.
- Avoid places where impacts are just beginning.

Dispose of Waste Properly

- Pack it in, pack it out. Inspect your campsite and rest areas for trash or spilled foods.
- Pack out all trash, leftover food, and litter.
- Deposit solid human waste in catholes, dug 6 to 8 inches deep, at least 200 feet from water, camp, and trails. Cover and disguise the cathole when finished.
- Pack out toilet paper and hygiene products.
- To wash yourself or your dishes, carry water 200 feet away from streams or lakes and use small amounts of biodegradable soap. Scatter strained dishwater.

Leave What You Find

- Preserve the past: examine, but do not touch, cultural or historic structures and artifacts.
- Leave rocks, plants and other natural objects as you find them.
- Avoid introducing or transporting non-native species.
- Do not build structures, furniture, or dig trenches.

Minimize Campfire Impacts

- Campfires can cause lasting impacts to the backcountry. Use a lightweight stove for cooking and enjoy a candle lantern for light.

- Where fires are permitted, use established fire rings, fire pans, or mound fires.
- Keep fires small. Only use sticks from the ground that can be broken by hand.
- Burn all wood and coals to ash, put out campfires completely, and then scatter cool ashes.

Respect Wildlife

- Observe wildlife from a distance. Do not follow or approach them.
- Never feed animals. Feeding wildlife damages their health, alters natural behaviors, and exposes them to predators and other dangers.
- Protect wildlife and your food by storing rations and trash securely.
- Control pets at all times, or leave them at home.
- Avoid wildlife during sensitive times: mating, nesting, raising young, or winter.

Be Considerate of Other Visitors

- Respect other visitors and protect the quality of their experience.
- Be courteous. Yield to other users on the trail.
- Step to the downhill side of the trail when encountering pack stock.
- Take breaks and camp away from trails and other visitors.
- Let nature's sounds prevail. Avoid loud voices and noises

For more detailed information on "Leave No Trace" guidelines, visit http://www.lnt.org

"Hiking in Harmony"

There are also other undocumented rules that every thru-hiker should subscribe to. Unfortunately, there are a small minority who feel that the very nature of *"hiking your own hike"* and living outside the confines of society allows them some special dispensation. Their behavior jeopardizes the availability of services in the towns along the trail. For years the Appalachian Long Distance Hiking Association has been promoting *"Hiking in Harmony Principles"* as part of its *"Endangered Services Campaign."* This campaign serves to educate hikers to act responsibly when they are in trail towns as well as when they are on the trail. Following these principles will assure that all future A.T. hikers will have the services they need in the towns along the trail that serve thousands of other hikers.

What "hiking your own hike" is not, or should not be, is
- Using your rugged individualist, trail persona as an excuse to justify rude and unruly behavior in trail towns;
- An opportunity to participate in illegal activity—on or off the trail.

The overarching "code" of hiking your own hike, unequivocally is:
- To hike responsibly;
- To hike "in harmony" with both the wilderness and the towns through which each hiker passes. Every hiker is an ambassador for every other hiker that is to follow them.

What made our thru-hike so rewarding was that we hiked in harmony with each other and with the communities that welcomed us.

The copyrighted material below has been reprinted with permission from the Appalachian Long Distance Trail Association. For more information on both "Hiking in Harmony" and ALDHA, go to www.ALDHA.org.

HIKE IN HARMONY

**Leave no trace in trail towns, not just in camp.
Follow the rules as you would the white blazes.
Help keep the Appalachian Trail a good neighbor.**

The Endangered Services Campaign
Appalachian Long Distance Hikers Association

Just because you live in the woods doesn't mean you can act like an
ANIMAL

Be a social animal.
Hike your own hike, but don't make other people hike yours.

* If it says no smoking, it means no smoking
* If it says no alcohol, it means no alcohol
* If it says no pets, it means no pets

* Obey the "Leave No Trace" ethic while in town, too
* Respect the rights of others on and off the trail
* Act so that townsfolk will welcome hikers

The Endangered Services Campaign

Appalachian Long Distance Hikers Association

REFERENCE/BIBLIOGRAPHY

GENERAL REFERENCES

Appalachian Trail Data Book - 2006. Daniel D. Chazin, Editor
© 2005 Appalachian Trail Conservancy
Appalachian Trail Conservancy
P.O. Box 807
Harpers Ferry, WV 25425
www.appalachiantrail.org

Appalachian Trail Thru-Hikers Companion – 2006. Coeditors Cynthia Taylor Miller &
Carol Barnes
© 2006 Appalachian Long Distance Hikers Association
Appalachian Long Distance Hikers Association
10 Benning Street
PMB 224
West Lebanon, NH 03784
www.aldha.org

Trail Journals®: www.trailjournals.com

INTRODUCTION:

"Walking the Entire Appalachian Trail – Fulfilling a Dream by Accomplishing a Task" - © Warren Doyle, 26th Edition, May 2007 (used by permission of Warren Doyle)

CHAPTER 3: *HIKE YOUR OWN HIKE*

"Walking the Entire Appalachian Trail – Fulfilling a Dream by Accomplishing a Task" - © Warren Doyle, 26th Edition, May 2007 (used by permission of Warren Doyle)

Dahlonega, GA:
http://en.wikipedia.org/wiki/Dahlonega,_Georgia#History

The Len Foote Hike Inn:
http://hike-inn.com (Len Foote Hike Inn) - Used by permission

CHAPTER 4: *WALKING IN STEP*

"Walking the Entire Appalachian Trail – Fulfilling a Dream by Accomplishing a Task" - © Warren Doyle, 26th Edition, May 2007 (used by permission of Warren Doyle)

"….structure and equality, balance and beauty," from *"Rocking the Roles,"* by Robert Lewis and William Hendricks. Navpress Publishing Group; Rev Updated edition (January 1999)

CHAPTER 5: *IN SICKNESS AND IN HEALTH*

"Giardiasis": www.cdc.gov

CHAPTER 6: *FAMILY*

"Old Dumb": www.kewpie.net/davecurtis.html
(used by permission of David Curtis)

CHAPTER 8: *LAUGHING TOGETHER AND OTHER SIMPLE PLEASURES*

Maple Syrup Harvesting: wwww.superiorbroadcast.org/MapleSyrup.htm

Maple Sugar Harvesting:
www.dnr.state.wi.us/org/caer/ce/eek/veg/trees/maplesyrup.htm

Maple Sugar Harvesting:
www.gsfc.nasa.gov/scienceques2001/20020315.htm

Brainfreeze's 2006 Appalachian Trail Journal:
www.trailjournals.com/entry.cfm?trailname=4328
(used by permission of September Mihaly)

CHAPTER 10: *THE GREATEST MOUNTAIN*

Mt. Katahdin:
www.destinationmaine.com/thoreau/mountain.htm

Mt. Katahdin:
www.fossweb.com/resources/pictures/605609717.html

Mt. Katahdin:
http://en.wikipedia.org/wiki/Penobscot

Pamola:
http://en.wikipedia.org/wiki/Pamola

Penobscot Indians:
www.geocities.com/bigorrin/penobscot_kids.htm

Mt. Katadin/Pamola:
www.geocities.com/schlaikjer/carpe_diem.html

Mt. Katahdin: "The Wilderness Reader," Frank Bergon, © 1980, First
Mentor Printing

Introduction: "The Wilderness Reader," Frank Bergon, © 1980, First
Mentor Printing

Mt. Katahdin: "Ktaadn" from "In the Maine Woods," Henry David Thoreau,
Tickner & Fields, © 1864

CHAPTER 11: *CONCLUSION (or a new beginning?)*

Introduction: "The Wilderness Reader," Frank Bergon, © 1980, First
Mentor Printing

APPENDIX #1: *TRAIL TERMS*

"The Thru_Hiker's Handbook," Dan "Wingfoot" Bruce, © 2006, Dan Bruce
for The Center for Appalachian Trail Studies
(used by permission)

VARIOUS CHAPTERS

All hiker stories and quotes are from email interviews, and/or from internet journals, and are used with each hiker's permission.

Trickster and What?!'s 2006 Appalachian Trail Journal:
www.trailjournals.com/entry.cfm?trailname=4387

Little Wing's 2006 Appalachian Trail Journal:
www.trailjournals.com/entry.cfm?trailname=3967

"Kewpie of the Month" for May/June 2006 - Dave Curtis - Class of 1963:
www.kewpie.net/davecurtis.html
Enuff & Too Much's 2006 Appalachian Trail Journal:
www.trailjournals.com/entry.cfm?trailname=4069

Brownie and Souleman's 2006 Appalachian Trail Journal:
www.trailjournals.com/entry.cfm?trailname=4395

Jellybean's 2006 Appalachian Trail Journal
www.trailjournals.com/entry.cfm?trailname=3677

Bama's 2006 Appalachian Trail Journal
www.trailjournals.com/entry.cfm?trailname=4231

Carbomb & Lichen's 2006 Appalachian Trail Journal
www.trailjournals.com/entry.cfm?trailname=4130

Mike & Zan's "Out of the Jungle & Into the Woods"
http://eggswithlegs.blogspot.com

Jim & Karen Hertlein *("Mapman & Robin")*

Tim & Nancy VanNest *("Head-N-Out & Tag-N-Along")*

FOOTNOTES

[1]Phoenix Outdoor - www.phoenixoutdoor.com

ABOUT THE AUTHORS

Georgia L. Harris, a.k.a. "Mom," has a Masters Degree in Technical Management and is a physical scientist with the National Institute of Standards and Technology in Gaithersburg, Maryland. In her role in the Division of Weights and Measures, she is responsible for overseeing the metrology laboratories located in the United States and trains the metrologists in these state laboratories as well as those in private industry and in the Department of Defense. Her job of assuring the measurement standardization of mass, length, volume and temperature has taken her to every state in the United States, as well as Puerto Rico, South Africa, and the United Kingdom; but these travels were always by plane or car, never with a 30 lb pack on her back. She is an avid photographer, and a small portion of the 5,300 photos she took along the Appalachian Trail are available online and on the DVD, *"Appalachian Trail Reflections."*

Randy A. Motz, a.k.a. "Windtalker," has been an ASTM-certified heli-arc welder, a solar sunspace designer, carpenter and general manager, and part owner of one of the largest weighing equipment distributors in the United States. Just prior to hiking the Appalachian Trail, he was a producer and marketing director for Gospel and Contemporary Christian Artists at the largest recording studio in Washington, D.C. He has several production credits to his name and in 2007 he released his own CD of Native American flute music entitled, *"Windtalker – Native SoundScapes."* He is president of The Qualtech Resource Group, Inc., a multi-media creation company, as well as, the driving force behind Windtalker Music, a music production company. Currently he performs live sound production work for concerts, corporate and civic events, is Supervisor of Activities for the Potomac Appalachian Trail Club and continues to compose, record and perform music.

Backpacking information, daily A.T. thru-hike journals, and stories about many of their other hikes can be found at *www.rmghadventures.com* or at *www.trailjournals.com*

"Windtalker & Mom" are proud members of The Appalachian Trail Conservancy, Appalachian Mountain Club, Pacific Crest Trail Association, Appalachian Long Distance Hikers Association, Rails to Trail Conservancy and the Potomac Appalachian Trail Club for which they are "trail talkers," informing the general public about the A.T. and answering questions about backpacking. They also make numerous presentations about their Appalachian Trail thru-hike and give motivational talks that urge people to pursue their dreams. "Dream It! Plan It! Live It," "The Joys of Backpacking as a Couple," "Spiritual Reflections from the Appalachian Trail," and "The Care and Feeding of the Long-Distance Hiker" are just a few of the presentations made at state and national parks, churches, scout troops and professional and civic organizations.